AF361543

# SPONTANEOUS COMBUSTION

SUNY series, Praxis: Theory in Action

Nancy A. Naples, editor

# SPONTANEOUS COMBUSTION

## The Eros Effect and Global Revolution

Edited by

JASON DEL GANDIO and AK THOMPSON

Foreword by

PETER MARCUSE

Published by State University of New York Press, Albany



For information, contact State University of New York Press, Albany, NY
www.sunypress.edu

Production, Diane Ganeles
Marketing, Fran Keneston

**Library of Congress Cataloging-in-Publication Data**

Names: Del Gandio, Jason, editor.
Title: Spontaneous combustion : the eros effect and global revolution /
  edited by Jason Del Gandio and AK Thompson.
Description: Albany, NY : State University of New York Press, [2017] |
  Series: SUNY series, praxis: Theory in action | Includes bibliographical
  references and index.
Identifiers: LCCN 2016056707 (print) | LCCN 2017023220 (ebook) | ISBN
  9781438467290 (ebook) | ISBN 9781438467276 (hardcover : alk. paper)
Subjects: LCSH: Love. | Insurgency. | Revolutions. | Counterculture. | Social
  change. | Social movements.
Classification: LCC BF575.L8 (ebook) | LCC BF575.L8 S643 2017 (print) | DDC
  306.7—dc23
LC record available at https://lccn.loc.gov/2016056707

10  9  8  7  6  5  4  3  2  1

# Contents

# Foreword

PETER MARCUSE

This is a brave book, and it tackles one of the most daunting political questions of our time: What induces people to act together in large numbers to influence the basic conditions of their life in society? And how should we understand the fact that sometimes these eruptions seem to happen spontaneously while at other times they only take place after long periods of organizing? Such eruptions are sometimes realistic and sometimes utopian. Sometimes, people act rationally in their own self-interest, and sometimes they proceed in apparently ignorant or stupid ways. Questions pertaining to the motivation underlying or impetus behind mass uprisings are not pursued by the editors and contributors to this volume out of sheer intellectual curiosity or in pursuit of a titillating topic—though it surely amounts to one: as I write, mass media in the United States express bewilderment as Donald Trump provokes massive enthusiasm for a program that shows little regard for the objective interests of constituents who seem destined to vote in a way they will surely regret.

It is in this context that *Spontaneous Combustion* asks a series of opposite but symmetrical questions: What produces massive support for social and political change, and how does that support explode at given moments, unpredicted by conventional explanations? How does this support become the foundation for historic revolutions, and why does it sometimes end as a flash in the pan?

Such questions remain difficult to answer. However, there seems to be general agreement that one historical fact—prominently elucidated by Herbert Marcuse—opens the door to such events in the present: the development of society's productive and technical forces makes want, pain, and lack of basic necessities unnecessary. Consequently, the fact that these persist becomes intolerable. Today, it is not solely desperate poverty or forcible oppression that provokes protest and kicks off revolts suggesting the possibility of revolution. It is also the vision of other possibilities, the vision of a better society that is clearly feasible but not in the works, which drives the mass actions examined in this book.

To make sense of such events, the authors draw on George Katsiaficas' conception of the "eros effect," which picks up and takes off from concepts developed by Herbert Marcuse. This effect describes moments in which the instinctual human need for justice and freedom undergoes a massive spontaneous awakening. Drawing on Marcuse, the concept foregrounds the instinctual foundation of the desire for freedom, in which a biologically based pleasure drive—eros—is given free play. With *Spontaneous Combustion*, this seductive and provocative concept is explored through a sweeping historical overview of its elaboration followed by contributions to its theoretical development, case studies exploring its applications, and comments on some of the difficulties it may engender.

Refreshingly, the authors included in this volume make regular admissions that further work needs to be done. According to the central thesis, in which spontaneous social combustions denominated as eros effects arise from the realization that the world could be different, utopias are no longer utopian—and the logical unfolding of history is not yet complete. Accepting this premise, we must ask: Why do these spontaneous eruptions occur in some times and places and not others? Is it the nature of the material circumstances, the extent of deprivation and oppression? Is it leadership? Is it an accumulation of causes? The book does not pretend to provide all the answers; it is very welcome in its lack of dogmatism.

One hopes its provocations will lead to further research, and perhaps to action as well. The book promises to be productive for a long time to come.

July 15, 2016

# Introduction

JASON DEL GANDIO AND AK THOMPSON

## MAKING SENSE OF MASS REVOLT

Since at least the time of the First International, questions concerning the precise character of political spontaneity and the role of spontaneous action in revolutionary transformation have provoked heated debate. From the split between anarchist and communist factions in the First International to debates between Rosa Luxemburg and Vladimir Lenin during the lead-up to the first World War, the problem has returned with a frequency that has only underscored its importance. Although Luxemburg was convinced of the need for disciplined socialist organization, her analysis of the dynamics of mass strikes alerted her to the undeniable importance of spontaneity. Recalling the "general rising of the proletariat" that took place in Russia in January of 1905, Luxemburg summarized its outward manifestation as nothing short of a "declaration of war." Still, it was the internal or psychological transformations that seemed most compelling to her, since the actions "for the first time awoke class feeling and class consciousness in millions upon millions as if by an electric shock."

> And this awakening of class feeling expressed itself forthwith in the circumstances that the proletarian mass, counted by millions, quite suddenly and sharply came to realize how intolerable was the social and economic existence which they had patiently endured for decades in the chains of capitalism. Thereupon there began a spontaneous general shaking of and tugging at these chains. All the innumerable sufferings of the modern proletariat reminded them of the old bleeding wounds.[1]

Along with consciousness and organization, then, spontaneity seemed to play a key role in pushing struggle to new heights. Frantz Fanon noted a similar dynamic in the colonial context. By his account, although the nationalist parties that arose in the towns of the colonized countries were objectively better prepared to navigate the political terrain on which they found themselves, it was the peasantry that "spontaneously gives form to the general insecurity." Objectively reactionary but with far less contact with or investment in the conqueror's reality, Fanon felt that it was this force that gave the anticolonial struggle its vitality and élan.[2]

The spontaneous shaking of chains that Luxemburg recounted more than a century ago continues today. In July 2013, George Zimmerman was acquitted of the murder of Trayvon Martin. In response, Alicia Garza, Patrisse Cullors, and Opal Tometi created the hashtag BlackLivesMatter. The following summer, the police murders of Black people including Eric Garner, Michael Brown, and John Crawford III captured national headlines. Similar incidents occurred over the next year—Tamir Rice, Akai Gurley, Walter Scott, Sandra Bland, and many others. Following the November 2014 exoneration of Darren Wilson, the officer who shot and killed Michael Brown, Ferguson became ground zero for a new Black freedom movement. In April 2015, Baltimore erupted in rebellion in response to the police killing of Freddie Gray. Beginning with actions at the University of Missouri, student protests swept across the country's college campuses the following fall. After periods of demobilization, waves of protests can often seem to flare up out of nowhere. Given the speed and frequency of their emergence and the similarity of the events, one might say that Black Lives Matter has inaugurated a period of spontaneous mass revolt.

In late 2010, twenty-six-year old Tunisian street vendor Mohamed Bouazizi immolated himself in response to ongoing police harassment. After local officials refused to hear his case, he attained a canister of gasoline, stood in the middle of traffic, and cried out, "How do you expect me to make a living?" He then lit a match. After surviving in the hospital for three weeks, Bouazizi passed away on January 4, 2011. Massive protests broke out after his death. By January 14, Tunisian dictator Ben Ali was ousted from power and forced to flee the country.[3] Mass revolts soon spread throughout the region, affecting Egypt, Libya, Syria, Yemen, Kuwait, Sudan, Omar, Morocco, and numerous other countries.

These uprisings were powerful, but their dynamics were not necessarily unique. Similar patterns of intense and rapid revolt occurred during Spain's September 15 movement (spring 2011), Chile's student protests (summer 2011), the Occupy movement (fall 2011), and the Quebec student strike (spring and summer 2012). Other examples of spontaneous mass rebellion include Iran's 2009 Green Revolution; the Greek riots of 2008; the anti–Iraq War demonstrations of February 15, 2003 (in which an estimated thirty million people participated worldwide); the global justice movement and the flurry of Latin American anti-neoliberal movements throughout the late 1990s and early 2000s; the international fervor surrounding the Zapatistas in the mid-1990s; the 1989 Tiananmen Square uprising; the mid-1980s People Power Revolution that ousted Ferdinand Marcos as president of the Philippines; the rebellions of Gwangju, South Korea, in 1980; Italy's confluence of student, worker, feminist, and countercultural revolts of the 1970s; the US-based anti–Vietnam War movement of the late 1960s and early 1970s; the 1969 Stonewall riots in Greenwich Village, New York; and the events of May 1968 in France. Considering such history, it is easy to conclude that rebellion is a natural response to oppressive conditions and that acts of revolt inspire others to follow suit.

Such revolts also spark reflection. Why, at given historical moments, does resistance develop spontaneously at multiple geographical points? How can that resistance be understood, and how can it be furthered? *Spontaneous Combustion: The Eros Effect and Global Revolution* addresses the dynamics of such revolts to understand them and help to push them further. To do so, the contributors to this volume have endeavored to clarify, apply, and critically extend George Katsiaficas' notion of the "eros effect." First elaborated in the context of doctoral work carried out under the supervision of Herbert Marcuse and concerned with the dynamics of global insurrection in 1968, Katsiaficas' eros effect is an analytical tool for explaining mass political awakenings and spontaneous rebellions. This "effect" involves an eroticization of politics—and of everyday life—that motivates people to create an alternative world of solidarity, self-determination, and bottom-up social relations. Following Marcuse, Katsiaficas argues that the human species is hardwired for freedom and justice and that human nature is an aid to the revolutionary process. However, sociopolitical repression often inhibits people from enacting such life-affirming qualities. The contradiction between the impulse toward freedom and the conditions of oppression often leads to social rebellions.

In these moments, thousands and even millions of people sweep into the streets to demand an end to oppression and to advance visions of collective liberation. The basic impulse in each case is the same: the people themselves should rule. Putting this political ethos into practice is a life-affirming and erotic experience, which helps explain why millions of people become attracted to (and subsequently participate in) mass political rebellions. As their impulses toward freedom and justice become activated, participants begin to see what form their realization might take. Paradoxically, it is only by way of immersion in the ecstatic experience of struggle that the universal *rationality* of rebellion is discovered.

Skeptics may argue that such a description is more hopeful than actual, that it succumbs to the Romanticism that found its way into political philosophy through figures like Hegel, who proclaimed that it was "solely by risking life that freedom is obtained."[4] Two responses are in order. First, hope and the vision it inspires are part of human experience and necessary for social change. As Marx made clear in chapter 7 of *Capital*, the human labor process begins with imagination.[5] Without the ability to envision the desired goal prior to embarking on our labors, humans remain indistinguishable from other creatures. In that field of human labor known as "politics," the imagination is directed toward questions with universal implications: How, for instance, can our reality be brought into accord with our desires? Second, skepticism concerning the power of the imagination to lead us toward more realized versions of ourselves through struggle ignores the historical and empirical fact that rebellions happen every day. Such rebellions often remain small and contained. Nevertheless, even seemingly ineffective rebellions—like the self-immolation of Bouazizi—can spark much broader insurgencies. Indeed, small revolts sometimes ignite national and even international uprisings.

Rebellions, however, do not inevitably lead to revolutions. Some are violently crushed while others disintegrate under the weight of their own contradictions. Some fade away while others carry on for years before achieving concrete change. Such events should not solely be conceived as "failed revolts." Instead, they are flash points through which people's political consciousness can be and often is transformed. Brief but intense moments of radical democratic practice challenge the self-evidence of power's constituted form. Participants develop a deep desire for freedom and autonomy. When this happens, an important question arises: What would it mean to stand before an open horizon of infinite possibility?

Such dynamics highlight the nature of "spontaneous combustion" as simultaneously absolute and conditional. The *hope* is that revolt becomes absolute, that it becomes global and fundamentally alters human sociality. Mass rebellions sweep across nations and entire regions, so why not across the entire planet? Over seven hundred Black Lives Matter protests occurred in its first two years, and the movement has garnered support in Canada, France, Germany, Britain, Brazil, Palestine, Ghana, India, Japan, and Australia; Occupy involved more than eight hundred encampments worldwide; the Arab Spring inspired movements across oceans; the global justice movement that emerged from the depths of the Laconda jungle reached numerous countries around the world; and the radicalism of the 1960s involved everything from young hippie kids smoking dope to anti-colonial struggles and Third World revolutions.

But examples such as these also highlight revolt's conditional dimension. Each locale is unique, and people must respond to the specific conditions of their own oppression. This involves challenging and overturning everything from white supremacy and heteropatriarchy to theocratic dictatorships, military regimes, corrupt two-party systems, top-down "socialist" governments, and the exploitative relations and institutions of capitalism. Meanwhile, capitalism's capacity to channel rebellious desires into commodified "resolutions" presents another series of unique challenges. Obstructions to rebellious aspirations include an obscene variety of banalities and brutalities, including: mass-marketed Che Guevara tee shirts and "punk fashion" in shopping malls; legal loopholes used to squash unionized labor; corporate propaganda that transforms nonviolent animal rights activists into "terrorists"; and the incorporation of flex time and "work from home" policies, which seem worker-friendly on the surface but in reality erase the boundaries between work and leisure. What is needed, then, is total liberation—a perpetual vigilance against *all* oppression, and a perpetual exploration of newer and deeper forms of freedom and justice. As Marcuse put it, "The individual liberation (refusal) must incorporate the *universal* in the particular protest . . ."[6]

This sensibility helps to build forms of solidarity that can overcome national borders and regional differences. People begin recognizing their own struggles in the struggles of others. As this happens, oppression—in whatever form it takes—becomes a catalyst for resistance. Complicated and contentious though it may be, a *universal* solidarity begins to emerge. On the surface, the struggles of Occupy and the Arab Spring have little in common. Indeed, economic inequality in the United States is both qualitatively and quantitatively different from the political repression that characterized Egypt prior to Tahrir Square. But in October of 2011, protestors in Cairo marched in solidarity with Occupy Oakland and in opposition to police repression and the brutalization of activist Scott Olsen. The signs of the Cairo protestors read, "From Egypt to Wall Street, Don't [Be] Afraid, Go Ahead, #OccupyOakland, #OWS" and "From #Tahrir to #OccupyOakland and #USA One Case, One Goal #SocialJusticeforAll, Fuck Police."[7] A similar example occurred when Palestinian activists took to Twitter expressing support for Black Lives Matter, posting, among others things,

"The Palestinian people know what [it] mean[s] to be shot while unarmed because of your ethnicity. #Ferguson. #Justice."[8] Over eleven-hundred Black activists, scholars, students, artists, and organizations followed suit, issuing a "Black Solidarity Statement with Palestine."[9] According to Katsiaficas, such transnational solidarity owes to the eros effect—the flourishing of a politicized sensuality capable of transcending immediate conditions and enabling disparate struggles to forge common bonds.

But how does this actually happen? What are the internal operations of this "effect"? Are particular social conditions necessary for it to emerge? Why, at certain moments, does the eros effect take hold while, at other times, it appears to be absent? What theoretical models might help us to understand, and thus to intensify, this revolutionary process?

Given these questions, it is not surprising that recent political upheavals have sparked wide-ranging conversations addressing numerous aspects of mass revolts: historical factors, sociopolitical conditions, use of social media and the role of more traditional forms, the psychology of mass revolt, the epistemology of resistance, and so on. These conversations emerge from a variety of sources, including popular and academic presses, special issues of scholarly journals, first- and secondhand narratives, journalistic accounts, and political manifestos.[10]

*Spontaneous Combustion* contributes to this conversation by combining social movement scholarship and critical theory to devise a kind of critical social movement theory. Like social movement scholarship more generally, this approach is interdisciplinary by its very nature and inter-sects with such fields as sociology; political science; communication; anthropology; media studies; legal studies; ethnic, gender, and sexuality studies; and critical pedagogy. Our approach to critical theory is similarly broad and incorporates elements from traditions including the Frankfurt School, French poststructuralism, feminism, and cultural studies. While traditional theory provides models of understanding, critical theory provides models for altering both understanding and action. For these reasons, critical social movement theory is an apt framework for *Spontaneous Combustion*.


## THE EROS EFFECT


Katsiaficas first developed the concept of the eros effect as a way to "explain the rapid spread of revolutionary aspirations and actions during the strikes of May 1968 in France and May 1970 in the United States . . ."[11]

In assembling his empirical studies, he was "stunned by the spontaneous spread of revolutionary aspirations in a chain reaction of uprisings and the massive occupation of public space—the sudden entry into history of millions of ordinary people who acted in a unified fashion, intuitively believing that they could change the direction of their society."[12] From those case studies, Katsiaficas began "to understand how in moments of the eros effect, universal interests become generalized at the same time as the dominant values of society are negated (such as national chauvinism, hierarchy, and individualism)."[13]

Throughout his work, Katsiaficas emphasizes the similarity of mass rebellions. For example, rebellions in both industrial and preindustrial nations exhibit shared interests in antiauthoritarian self-governance, international solidarity, the transformation of everyday life, and the creation and promotion of alternative values and ethics. Such rebellions also involve high degrees of spontaneity, with thousands and even millions of people seeming to join movements overnight. The US-based student movement of the 1960s and '70s exemplifies this phenomenon. According to Katsiaficas, by mid-May of 1970, "more than 500 colleges and universities were on strike, and by the end of the month, at least one-third of the nation's 2,827 institutions of higher education were on strike. More than 80 percent of all universities and colleges in the United States experienced protests, and about half of the country's eight million students and 350,000 faculty actively participated in the strike."[14]

When accounting for such phenomena, Katsiaficas acknowledges that global communications networks (of radio, television, newspaper, and—nowadays—social media) are contributing factors. Nevertheless, he contends that the diffusion of information concerning localized insurgencies cannot fully explain the unmistakable *allure* of spontaneous rebellions. Consequently, Katsiaficas argues that a deeper, innate human quality must tie such mobilizations to one another.

> Such spontaneous leaps may be, in part, a product of long-term social processes in which organized groups and conscious individuals prepare the groundwork, but when political struggle comes to involve millions of people, it is possible to glimpse a rare historical occurrence: the emergence of the *eros* effect, the massive awakening of the instinctual human need for justice and freedom. When the *eros* effect occurs, it becomes clear that the fabric of the *status quo* has been torn, and the forms of social control have been ruptured.[15]

To understand the origins of this conceptualization, it is useful to recall that Katsiaficas was active in the New Left and experienced the radicalism of the 1960s firsthand. These experiences led him to emphasize the important role played by spontaneous rebellions when he turned to the scholarly study of social movements. Finally, Katsiaficas was a student of Herbert Marcuse's and was deeply influenced by his work.[16] Through *Eros and Civilization*, *One-Dimensional Man*, and other works, Marcuse helped to shape the practices and sensibilities of the New Left.[17] Indeed, the central themes of free love, anticapitalism, communal living, existential fulfillment, and self-expression were all at least partly influenced by Marcuse's writings.[18]

To get a sense of Marcuse's influence on the conceptual development of the eros effect, it's useful to quickly review his contributions to contemporary radical sensibilities. In brief, Marcuse argued both with and against Freudian psychoanalysis and Marxist criticism to formulate a critique of society and a philosophy of liberation. According to Freud, innate human drives were incompatible with modern civilization. Indeed, "[t]he liberty of the individual is no gift of civilization. . . . The development of civilization imposes restrictions on it, and justice demands that no one shall escape those restrictions."[19] Consequently, Freud believed that it was necessary to repress some of our individual wants, needs, and desires in order to live in relative peace. Marcuse agreed that psychological repression is part of the human condition. Such repression mediates between the pleasure principle ("I want to experience this, now!") and the more restrictive reality principle ("I must do this to avoid harm or death!").[20] However, according to Marcuse, while such repression may have been necessary at given stages of human development, the productive capacities of contemporary societies increasingly make it superfluous. That it should persevere, he argued, owed more to the demands of a system founded on profit maximization than on human needs per se.[21] In opposition to the prevailing conditions of "surplus repression," Marcuse encouraged his readers to begin envisioning human societies founded on the premise of an ongoing liberation that would enable people to reach greater depths of happiness, joy, and wonder. Human drives are not necessarily dark and evil, he maintained. Instead, they point to reservoirs of untapped potential and ingenuity.[22]

Along with his critical reevaluation of Freud, Marcuse also sought to unsettle the economic determinism that had come to define Marxist orthodoxy during the early part of the twentieth century. Repression was not simply an economic issue, he argued, but also a social, cultural, political, and existential one. Revolution must therefore involve more than a worker uprising against bosses or a "regime change" that replaces one hierarchy with another; revolution must cut to the core of one's being and involve, for instance, the development of different languages, gestures, and impulses to safeguard against "cruelty, brutality, and ugliness."[23] As this occurs, the individual rejects the entire system and begins to develop a more life-affirming existence. For Marcuse, this liberation is rooted in eros, which is the innate human drive toward pleasure, joy, and happiness. Eros motivates us to live fully satisfying lives in conjunction with other people; however, under contemporary social conditions, eros is so severely distorted that we become accustomed to (and even come to desire) aggression, repression, and control. As Marcuse states, "the societal authority is absorbed into the 'conscience' and into the unconscious of the individual and works as his own desire, morality, and fulfillment. In the 'normal' development, the individual lives his repression 'freely' as his own life: he desires what he is supposed to desire; his gratifications are profitable to him and to others; he is reasonably and often even exuberantly happy."[24] This internalized repression is so encompassing that, for Marcuse, only a complete revolution will do.[25]

Such a revolution must begin with a "new sensibility" that fosters alternative ways of seeing, hearing, feeling, and understanding. In *An Essay on Liberation*, Marcuse finds evidence of such a sensibility in the occurrences of his time—the hippie subculture, the Black Power movement, the French uprising of May 1968—as well as in art movements like blues, jazz, surrealism, and stream-of-consciousness poetry. By his account, these movements provoke new sensoria—new modes of experiencing that constitute alternative environments capable of facilitating revolutionary action. The basic insight is this: experiencing the world through a new sensorium enables one to think and act differently, which in turn enables one to move beyond the current regime of repression and to manifest a world of sensuous connection, to act on erotic impulses that are common to the human organism.[26] Those erotic impulses are different for each individual and do not, in and of themselves, posit preestablished blueprints for a new society. Indeed, for Marcuse, the forthcoming institutions and relationships "cannot be determined *a priori*; they will develop, in trial and error, as the new society develops. If we could form a concrete concept of the alternative today, it would not be that of an alternative," but that of the society we are rebelling against.[27]

Katsiaficas extended Marcuse's philosophy of political eros by transposing it into the operational realm of social movement action. Using the concept of the "eros effect" to understand the connections among movements, he approaches the study of political uprisings by focusing on the intuitive ties that are forged between participants. From this vantage, "episodes of the eros effect are regarded as the collective sublimation of the instinctual need for freedom."

> The eros effect reflects an understanding that inner nature is a source of rational action—of freedom—an insight which leads to the postulation of a liberatory dimension to certain types of popular outburst. In moments of the eros effect, there is simultaneously a negating of the systematic institutionalization of the 'survival of the fittest' as the organizing principles of society and a spontaneous cathexis [emotional attachment] between human beings at fundamental levels of social solidarity. Mobilization for action occurs through participants' intuition as much as through their rational beliefs, and this intuitive species identity forms a basis for collective activity.[28]

Although they emerge spontaneously, such moments are not accidental; they derive from inherent desires for freedom. Such desire is a general human quality that transcends space and time. We are hardwired for freedom and thus respond in similar fashion when that freedom is threatened. In this way, the conditions for global solidarity come into being: recognizing the common dimension of our collective plight enables us to sympathize with—and motivates us to participate in—one another's struggles. Katsiaficas thus argues:

> thousands of people acting in social movements embody the concrete realization of freedom: outside established norms and institutions, thousands of people consciously act spontaneously in concert. In such moments . . . genuine individuality emerges as human beings situate themselves in collective contexts that negate their individualism. Vibrant democratic movements enhance the autonomy of the individual and simultaneously build groups that break free of the centralizing uniformity of the corporate-state behemoth.[29]

For Katsiaficas, genuine human liberation becomes possible only when we begin to think and act at the level of the species. Following Marcuse, he advocates a mode of being-in-the-world that stands in fundamental opposition to repression. This mode of being challenges alienating social systems (like capitalism, state-administered socialism, and theocratic dictatorships) and creates the conditions for life-affirming and collectively empowering ones instead. Katsiaficas argues that the desire for this form of collectively coordinated existence is a driving force behind mass rebellions. However brief these might be, such moments provide glimpses of a future in which we are self-organized in accordance with our impulse toward freedom. From there, we can begin changing our current world of repression into an alternative world of liberation.

## RELATED TRADITIONS

To be sure, neither Katsiaficas nor the other contributors to this volume are alone in grappling with the nature of spontaneous mass rebellion. Three of the more well-known efforts to address such dynamics include the collaborative works of poststructuralists Gilles Deleuze and Félix Guattari, Italian Autonomism, and the sociological study of diffusion within social movements.

Inspired by the French uprisings of 1968, Deleuze and Guattari approached spontaneous mass rebellion as an explosion of desire.[30] For them, desire is really *desiring*—a general, impersonal process that is ontological rather than psychological. Individual desires (for fame, fortune, sex, or romance) obviously exist; however, for Deleuze and Guattari, such individual wants and needs are secondary. Although we have desires, we are, first and foremost, *of* desire. In other words, human beings are an *effect of* the desiring process.[31] This desiring process is a constant, *prepersonal* assembling-disassembling-and-reassembling of connections and associations. Anything can link up and connect with anything else in the prepersonal realm of desire: this-and-that, blank-and-blank.[32] At the same time, however, this fluid process is copresent with stoppages, blockages, and mechanisms of control. Social institutions like the government, the nation-state, capitalism, and the family capture the flow of desire and route it toward particular ends—patriotism, consumerism, patriarchy, and so on. When this happens, desire begins desiring its own repression.[33] During spontaneous mass rebellion, however, desire breaks free from such constraints. Consequently, the "local and singular manifestation of the desire of small groups" begins to "resound with a multiplicity of repressed desires which had been isolated and crushed by the dominant forms of expression and of representation. In such a situation there is . . . a *univocal multiplicity* of desires whose process secretes its own systems of tracking and regulation."[34] Conceived in this way, mass revolt is a release of desire from its capture—an enabling of desire to reroute itself without preestablished patterns or endpoints.

Although they share definite points of contact, Deleuze and Guattari's poststructuralist framework is very different from Katsiaficas' Marcusian-inspired philosophy, which attributes the desire for freedom to a universal quality inherent in human existence. Following Marcuse, Katsiaficas argues that the human species is characterized by a personal-yet-universal longing for freedom and self-determination. Whereas Deleuze and Guattari see the world as an ever-changing composite of impersonal forces void of either a stable origin or direction, Katsiaficas sees it as a dialectical relationship between subjects and objects, with the human being standing in but also against the objective world. The former system understands liberation as an act of accessing, intensifying, and holding points of resistance.[35] The latter understands it as an act of negating the objectification of one's own subjectivity to allow for the development of fully realized human beings.[36]

The relationship between Katsiaficas' work and the tradition of Autonomous Marxism is similarly complex. Throughout *The Subversion of Politics*, Katsiaficas makes his intellectual and political indebtedness to the *Autonomen* clear; at the same time, however, he also sets out to distinguish himself from some of the tradition's antihumanist and antidialectical sensibilities. These sensibilities are more prevalent in the Italian current of Autonomism, which has been more influenced by the insights of Deleuze and Guattari than has its German counterpart.[37] In both cases, Autonomous Marxism begins with the observation that resistance is primary to human experience. It is commonly assumed, for instance, that rebellion is a response to oppression (this is true in Katsiaficas' work, where the eros effect is an innate response to repressive conditions); however, Autonomism foregrounds the degree to which it is in fact *repression* that responds to humanity's unruly nature. For this reason, repressive dynamics are constantly rearranging themselves to overcome and subjugate resistance. This thesis can be traced to an essay entitled "The Strategy of Refusal," in which Mario Tronti argues that working-class subjectivity precedes and exceeds capitalism's capture and control.[38] In this view, working-class subjectivity is inherently subversive and resistant to capitalism. Although oppression and exploitation occur, they never become total. Working-class subjectivity is thus *ontologically autonomous*. Within this framework, spontaneous mass rebellions express humanity's inclination toward free and open-ended creation. Although his thought aligns with the insights of Italian Autonomism in many important respects, Katsiaficas nevertheless distinguishes himself through his ongoing emphasis on the importance of dialectics (which leads not so much to an emphasis on working-class auto-valorization as to the cultivation of new sensoria) and his identification with humanistic rather than machinic metaphors.[39]

Touching upon similar themes to those addressed by Deleuze and Guattari and Autonomism, the sociological analysis of diffusion investigates the dispersion of ideas, values, practices, and rebellions across social landscapes. Theories of diffusion start from the presumption that changes within a milieu often occur as a result of factors that are introduced from outside of it. In the context of social movement dynamics, the analysis of diffusion can help to explain why certain tactics and sensibilities that were previously absent are adopted at particular moments. Social movement scholar and diffusion theorist Lesley Wood argues that "the successful diffusion of an innovation is dependent upon the transmitting context, the channels of communication, the context of the innovation's reception, and the character of the innovation itself."[40] By analyzing social movement dynamics in this way, scholars aim to understand how events in Tunisia, for instance, could spark similar uprisings throughout the region before finding reverberations in points as far away as Wisconsin and Wall Street. In contrast to Katsiaficas' account of the eros effect, which emphasizes the role played by the innate desire for human freedom to explain the often-simultaneous eruptions of insurgent struggles, social movement theories of diffusion tend to emphasize the "structural conditions" that allow the diffusion of tactical innovations and movement sensibilities to occur.[41]

Along with Katsiaficas' work on the eros effect, contributors to *Spontaneous Combustion* engage with and draw upon aspects of these (and other) important theoretical traditions. Until now, however, there has been no systematic attempt to clarify and extend the unique contribution that Katsiaficas' concept might make to our understanding of the dynamics of global revolution. It is this gap that *Spontaneous Combustion* aims to fill.

Katsiaficas' understanding of the eros effect is intellectually rich and politically provocative. Nevertheless, it deserves—and even needs—more rigorous attention and analysis. At present, Katsiaficas' work is underscrutinized. Unlike the attention provided to the work of Deleuze and Guattari or to the related traditions of Italian Autonomism and the sociology of diffusion, literature concerning the eros effect remains rare. Meanwhile, despite his obvious indebtedness to Marcuse, it is clear that other thinkers, theories, and traditions might help to extend Katsiaficas' concept.

In a similar fashion, Katsiaficas has thus far tended to focus his analysis of the eros effect on a particular type of case study (e.g., masses of people self-assembling into political forces over a relatively brief period). To gain new insights into the dynamics of the eros effect, it is necessary to consider how the concept might be used to explain other related but different phenomena (e.g., collective efforts that arise in response to natural disasters or the unspoken micro-coordination of black bloc participants).

Finally, since the goal is not merely to interpret the world but to change it as well, the strategic implications of the eros effect must be explored more fully. For instance, can the eros effect be consciously deployed or does it arise independent of conscious control? If it can be deployed, then how might this aim be accomplished? If it cannot, then how should movements orient to it when it arises? Since Katsiaficas' studies have tended to be historical in character, these questions and their strategic implications have thus far remained largely unexplored. By drawing Katsiaficas' work into conversation with related traditions, extending the scope of relevant case studies, and clarifying the eros effect's strategic implications, *Spontaneous Combustion* aims to spark dialogue, debate, and—hopefully—much more.

## STRUCTURE OF THE BOOK

*Spontaneous Combustion* is organized into four main sections. "Section One: The Eros Effect" includes three pieces by Katsiaficas. The section begins with "Remembering May '68: An Interview with George Katsiaficas." The interview was originally conducted in 2008 for the fortieth anniversary of the May 1968 uprisings; it covers a range of topics, including the dynamics of the eros effect, the contributions of Autonomous Marxism and social movement theory, and the strengths and weaknesses of political spontaneity. In "Eros and Revolution," Katsiaficas takes up Marcuse's understanding of Nature—not only external nature but humanity's inner nature—as an "ally" in the rapid spread of revolutionary aspirations. In "From Marcuse's 'Political Eros' to the Eros Effect: A Current Statement," Katsiaficas draws on Marcuse's later writings to reconsider the eros effect as the public embodiment of what Marcuse called "political eros."

"Section Two: Extensions and Elaborations" includes four essays. Arnold L. Farr's "Eros in a One-Dimensional Society: Katsiaficas, Marcuse, and Me" connects Katsiaficas' eros effect to Marcuse's dialectical analysis of the relationship between one-dimentionality and liberation. Farr uses his own struggle with racism, sexism, and homophobia as a concrete example to reveal how eros can negate one-dimensionality. In "Rethinking the Eros Effect: Sentience, Reality, and Emanation," Jason Del Gandio reconceptualizes the eros effect through a tripartite understanding of the body. Combining phenomenology, poststructuralism, and Italian Autonomism, he constructs an alternative ontology for understanding mass revolt. Richard Gilman-Opalsky's "Revolt *as* Reason, Reason *as* Revolt: On the Praxis of Philosophy from Below" moves beyond the intellectual analysis of revolt to an understanding of revolt as a form of intellectual analysis in its own right. He argues that, since revolt is reason-in-action, it provides a unique domain of philosophical inquiry. Jack Hipp closes out the section with "The Eros Effect and the Embodied Mind," which illustrates how the sense of collective reason associated with the eros effect is mirrored in the work of George Lakoff and Mark Johnson, two thinkers who draw on cognitive science to show that reason is an emergent quality of the embodied mind. In particular, Hipp foregrounds how the eros effect might literally restructure the mind.

"Section Three: Case Studies" includes three essays. In "Kindling for the Spark: Eros and Emergent Consciousness in Occupy Oakland," Emily Brissette and Mike King draw on their experiences as participants in Occupy Oakland to provide a temporal rather than merely spatial account of the eros effect's resonance. In "Eros Effect as Emergency Politics: Empathy, Agency, and Network in South Korea's Sewol Ferry Disaster," Gooyong Kim and Anat Schwartz look at moments of tragedy and the relationship between social media and on-the-ground organizing. They focus on the 2014 Sewol tragedy, in which a sunken ferry led to three hundred deaths. The final essay of this section—Sabu Kohso's "Climatology of the Eros Effect: Notes from the Japanese Archipelago"—develops a unique cartographic understanding of the eros effect to explain the intersection of natural disasters, migrations of people, and the formation of the Japanese nation-state.

"Section Four: Rejoinders" includes three essays. In "Feminism and the Eros Effect," Nina Power argues that feminism's concern for everyday care, social reproduction, and modes of relationality extend and enrich our understanding of the eros effect, and that such concerns coexist with, and are perhaps even the cause of, militant spontaniety. Lesley Wood's "Waves of Protest, the Eros Effect, and the Social Relations of Diffusion" examines the 2012–2013 Idle No More protests that spread through online and offline social networks to challenge both the Canadian state and colonialism. Wood both complements and challenges Katsiaficas' heuristic by emphasizing the social and relational microprocesses of theorization, identification, and deliberation that underpin the diffusion of new tactics. The section closes with AK Thompson's "Eros Effect or Biological Hatred?" In contrast to Katsiaficas' framework, Thompson argues that revolutionary impulses arise not from eros but from the universal experience of lack. Eros may lead to the circulation of revolutionary energies, says Thompson, but it should not be mistaken for their cause.

The book concludes with an Afterword by distinguished critical theorist and Marcusian scholar Douglas Kellner.

As readers of this volume will likely know firsthand, forging life-affirming erotic bonds can be difficult in a world of peril and destruction. Capitalist exploitation, imperialism, theocratic dictatorships, indiscriminate drone strikes, mass surveillance, whistleblower persecution, mass incarceration, police brutality, and ingrained racism, sexism, and heteronormativity (not to mention gross economic inequality, human trafficking, environmental degradation, famine, genocide, nuclear meltdowns, and oil spills) are everyday global occurrences. Nevertheless, and as the contributions in this volume make clear, rebellion and liberation are also central aspects of human experience. To be sure, the desire for meaningful connection can taunt us when the pathway to a more just society seems blocked. At the same time, however, this desire can also spur us to action. The myth of disengaged scholarship died long ago, and the present begs for intervention. Without such a spark, there would be no *Spontaneous Combustion*.

## NOTES

1. Rosa Luxemburg, "The Mass Strike, the Political Party, and the Trade Unions," in *The Rosa Luxemburg Reader* (New York: Monthly Review Press, 2004), 168–199 (181).

2. Frantz Fanon, *The Wretched of the Earth* (New York: Grove Press, 1963), 116.

3. For brief overviews of these events, see: Bob Simon, "How a Slap Sparked Tunisia's Revolution," *CBS News*, February 22, 2011, http://www.cbsnews.com/news/how-a-slap-sparked-tunisias-revolution-22-02-2011; and Rania Abouzeid, "Bouazizi: The Man Who Set Himself and Tunisia on Fire," *Time*, January 21, 2011, http://content.time.com/time/magazine/article/0,9171,2044723,00.html.

4. G.W.F. Hegel, *Phenomenology of Mind*, trans. J. B. Baillie (Mineola: Dover, 2003), 107.

5. Karl Marx, *Capital, Volume 1*, trans. Ben Fowkes (New York: Vintage, 1977), chap. 7.

6. Herbert Marcuse, *Counterrevolution and Revolt* (Boston: Beacon Press, 1972), 49.

7. See, Ishaan Tharoor, "Hands Across the World," in *What Is Occupy? Inside the Global Movement*, ed. Time (New York: Time Home Entertainment, 2011), 25–33 (26); and Xeni Jardin, "Egyptians March from Tahrir Square to Support Occupy Oakland Protestors," *Boingboing*, October 28, 2011, n.p., http://boingboing.net/2011/10/28/tahrir.html.

8. Alexis Goldstein, "Palestinians and Ferguson Protesters Link Arms via Social Media," *Yes Magazine*, August 15, 2014, n.p., http://www.yesmagazine.org/peace-justice/palestinians-and-ferguson-protesters-link-arms-via-social-media.

9. See, http://www.blackforpalestine.com.

10. Here is a brief sampling of such sources and topics: Dario Azzellini and Marina Sitrin, *They Can't Represent Us! How the New Global Movements Are Putting Forward a Radical Conception of Democracy* (London: Verso, 2014); Jack Bratich, ed., "Occupy Communication and Culture," Special Issue, *Communication and Critical/Cultural Studies* 11, no. 1 (March 2014): 1–84; Christopher Malone, Meghana Nayak, Matthew Bolton, and Emily Welty, eds., *Occupy Political Science: The Occupy Wall Street Movement from New York to the World* (New York: Palgrave Macmillan, 2013); Anna Feigenbaum, Fabian Frenzel, and Patrick McCurdy, *Protest Camps* (London: Zed Books, 2013); Kate Khatib, Margaret Killjoy, and Mike McGuire, eds., *We Are Many: Reflections on Movement Strategy from Occupation to Liberation* (Oakland: AK Press, 2012); Manuel Castells, *Networks of Outrage and Hope: Social Movements in the Internet Age* (Malden: Polity Press, 2012); Anya Schiffrin and Eamon Kircher-Allen, eds., *From Cairo to Wall Street: Voices from the Global Spring* (New York: New Press, 2012); Graeme Hayes et al., eds., "Occupy!," Special Issue, *Social Movement Studies: Journal of Social, Cultural and Political Protest* 11, nos. 3–4 (August–November 2012): 279–485; The Invisible Committee, *The Coming Insurrection* (Los Angeles: Semiotext(e), 2009); Barbara Ehrenreich, *Dancing in the Streets: A History of Collective Joy* (New York: Holt Paperbacks, 2007); and Ives Fremion, *Orgasms of History: 3,000 Years of Spontaneous Insurrection* (Oakland: AK Press, 2002).

11. George Katsiaficas, *Asia's Unknown Uprisings, Volume 1: South Korean Social Movements in the 20th Century* (Oakland: AK Press, 2012), xxvii n1.

12. Ibid.

13. Ibid.

14. George Katsiaficas, *The Imagination of the New Left: A Global Analysis of 1968* (Boston: South End Press, 1978), 120.

15. Ibid., 10 (all emphases in original).

16. For a sense of their relationship, see George Katsiaficas, "Marcuse's Cognitive Interest," *New Political Science* 18, nos. 2–3 (1996): 159–170.

17. Herbert Marcuse, *Eros and Civilization: A Philosophical Inquiry into Freud* (Boston: Beacon Press, 1992); *One-Dimensional Man: Studies in the Ideology of the Advanced Industrial Society* (Boston: Beacon Press, 1991).

18. For more on this point, see Herbert Marcuse, *The New Left and the 1960s: Collected Papers of Herbert Marcuse, Volume 3*, ed. Douglas Kellner (New York: Routledge, 2005).

19. Sigmund Freud, *Civilization and Its Discontents*, trans. James Strachey (New York: W.W. Norton, 1989), 49.

20. For more on these principles, see Marcuse, *Eros and Civilization*, especially chap. 1.

21. For further clarification on these issues, see Marcuse's treatment of two related concepts, "surplus-repression" and the "performance principle," *Eros and Civilization*, 35–54.

22. For further clarification on these related issues, see Marcuse, *Eros and Civilization*, chap. 11.

23. Herbert Marcuse, *An Essay on Liberation* (Middlesex: Penguin, 1969), 30.

24. Marcuse, *Eros and Civilization*, 46. Also note that we have decided to keep Marcuse's context-bound gender-exclusionary language to make for an easier read.

25. Marcuse, *One-Dimensional Man*, xlv.

26. Marcuse, *An Essay on Liberation*, especially chap. 2.

27. Ibid., 88 (original emphasis).

28. George Katsiaficas, "The Eros Effect," personal website, 1989, http://www.eroseffect.com/articles/eroseffectpaper.PDF, 8.

29. George Katsiaficas, *The Subversion of Politics: European Social Movements and the Decolonization of Everyday Life* (Oakland: AK Press, 2006), 259.

30. Tracking the Deleuzoguattarian philosophy is difficult given the authors' idiosyncratic and ever-changing terminology. In *Anti-Oedipus: Capitalism and Schizophrenia* (New York: Penguin, 2009), their terminology included "desiring-machines," "schizoanalysis," and "deterritorialization" and "reterritorialization." Later, in *A Thousand Plateaus: Capitalism and Schizophrenia* (Minneapolis: University of Minnesota Press, 1980), their terminology shifted to "rhizomes," "assemblages," "micropolitics," and "segmentarity." But their philosophical concerns remained relatively stable across these terminological changes. In brief, they were concerned with how "desire can come to desire its own repression"—particularly in relationship to the capitalist mode of sociality—and how repressive processes can be perpetually resisted and overcome.

31. This is a basic premise articulated throughout *Anti-Oedipus* and *A Thousand Plateaus*.

32. For more on this, see the concept of "desiring-machines" in Deleuze and Guattari, *Anti-Oedipus*, 1–50, and the related concepts of "assemblage" and "rhizome" in Deleuze and Guattari, *A Thousand Plateaus*, 22–23.

33. Deleuze and Guattari, *Anti-Oedipus*, 29 and 32.

34. Félix Guattari, "Everybody Wants to Be a Fascist," in *Chaosophy: Texts and Interviews 1972–1977*, ed. Sylvere Lotringer (Los Angeles: Semiotext(e), 2009), 154–175 (159).

35. For more on this, see Deleuze and Guattari's notion of "micropolitics" in *A Thousand Plateaus*, chap. 9.

36. For more on this, see Katsiaficas' notion of "a rationality of the heart" in *The Subversion of Politics*, 228–233.

37. What we are here referring to as Italian Autonomism has a long and complicated history, involving Workerism, Post-Workerism, Autonomism, Post-Autonomism, Italian Feminism, and other offshoots. For more on this history, see Sylvere Lotringer and Christian Marazzi, eds., *Autonomia: Post-Political Politics* (Los Angeles: Semiotext(e), 2007); Paolo Virno and Michael Hardt, eds., *Radical Thought in Italy: A Potential Politics* (Minneapolis: University of Minnesota Press, 1996); and Franco Berardi, *The Soul at Work: From Alienation to Autonomy* (Los Angeles: Semiotext(e), 2009), chap. 1.

38. Mario Tronti, "The Strategy of Refusal" (1965), available at Libcom.org, http://libcom.org/library/strategy-refusal-mario-tronti. Other thinkers have extended

and adapted Tronti's ideas. See, for instance, Michael Hardt and Antonio Negri, *Commonwealth* (Cambridge: Harvard University Press, 2009), chap. 1.3 and chap. 2.1. Hardt and Negri's interpretation is influenced by Michel Foucault's notion that power and resistance are copresent. See Michel Foucault, "Afterword: The Subject and Power," in *Michel Foucault: Beyond Structuralism and Hermeneutics*, ed. Hubert L. Dreyfus and Paul Rabinow (Chicago: University of Chicago Press, 1982), 208–226.

39. For more on these Autonomist concepts, see select passages in Lotringer and Marazzi, *Autonomia*, and Virno and Hardt, *Radical Thought in Italy*.

40. Lesley Wood, *Direct Action, Deliberation, and Diffusion: Collective Action after the WTO Protests in Seattle* (Cambridge: Cambridge University Press, 2012), 17.

41. Ibid., 3.

Section One

# THE EROS EFFECT

1

# Remembering May '68

## An Interview with George Katsiaficas

AK THOMPSON

*George Katsiaficas has been active in social movements since 1969. A target
of the FBI's COINTELPRO program, he was classified "Priority 1 ADEX,"
meaning that, in the event of a national emergency, he was to be immediately
arrested. For eleven years, he worked in Ocean Beach, California, as part of
a radical countercultural community. For years, he was active in the cause of
Palestinian rights. He is the author of* The Imagination of the New Left: A
Global Analysis of 1968 *(South End Press 1987) and* The Subversion of
Politics: European Autonomous Social Movements and the Decolonization of Everyday Life *(AK Press 2006). With Kathleen Cleaver, he coedited*
Liberation, Imagination and the Black Panther Party *(Routledge 2001). At
the time of this interview, he was based at Chonnam National University in
Gwangju, South Korea, finishing the two-volume book* Asia's Unknown Uprisings *(PM Press 2012, 2013). This interview was conducted by AK Thompson
in February of 2008 and originally published in* Upping the Anti: A Journal
of Theory and Action *6 (April 2008): n.p.,* http://uppingtheanti.org/journal/
article/06-remembering-may-68. *Only minor editorial changes have been made
for the present reprint.*

AKT: This May marks the fortieth anniversary of the 1968 rebellion in
France. For people who have not lived through a period of global uprising,
the events that took place during that time are hard to fathom. Can you
describe some of the key features of that period and why you feel they
continue to be important?

23

GK: The most important thing to remember was the global character of struggle during that period. Television brought major political uprisings taking place around the world to people's attention. But something else was happening, too. There was a connection between the Tet Offensive in Vietnam and the May events in France. The Columbia student strike was connected to the Civil Rights Movement as well as the struggle in Vietnam. The global character of the uprising meant that many of us began to learn about places like Uruguay for the first time through the prism of social movements, political economy, and political culture.

In 1968, there was a kind of worldwide synchronicity. When Martin Luther King Jr. was killed, we began to get a sense of how the whole world was changing. African American communities exploded. Many people living in American cities felt the need to go out and do something. Across the country, the inner cities went up in flames and insurrection. It was the worst crisis since the Civil War. There were machine guns on top of major government buildings. Civil unrest during this period damaged Washington, DC, more than the British managed to do during the War of 1812.

Pentagon reports from the time indicate that they thought they didn't have enough troops to fight the war in Vietnam and to maintain order at home. Between the Tet Offensive in Vietnam and the African American uprising in America, they were facing a crisis of major proportions. But then, on top of that, there was the militant student movement on dozens of campuses, protests against the Democratic National Convention in Chicago, and movements erupting in all these different countries. Around the world, people's actions were beginning to have a huge impact.

In Paris, students declared a soviet at the Sorbonne. When the Sorbonne was occupied, people from all walks of life came to learn about what was going on and to discuss political strategy. It's my understanding that the occupation of the Sorbonne was inspired by older activists from the marginalized antiwar movement against the French war in Algeria. They came up with the idea that the Sorbonne should be occupied and they led the occupation. This soviet, or council, became a transmission belt that spread the movement to the factories and to the outskirts of Paris.

The fact that they thought of their occupation as a "soviet" is also instructive. In moments of global insurrection, people actively grasp their connection to past revolutions. Similarly, activists in the United States instinctively identified with the Tupamaros and the struggle in Uruguay without really knowing a lot about them. Even though there were gaps in our understanding, we intuitively and instinctively identified with them. That year was a moment when there was a kind of global identification through the possibilities of struggle. Hearing about other struggles encouraged us all to continue.

As I mentioned, there were a number of objective reasons for this. Television played its part. And more and more people were reading about the increasing synchronization of world economic factors. But as important as these reasons were, I think the explosion of 1968 arose primarily from a subjective phenomenon. In 1848 and 1905, people didn't have television or well-developed networks of global communication. Nevertheless, those years saw global waves of struggle. What caused them? I think it can be explained by looking to the human capacity to understand the promise of freedom contained in given situations and the corresponding desire to move beyond prior constraints.

AKT: In *The Imagination of the New Left*, you investigate 1968 through the lens of "the eros effect." What do you mean by this concept? How would you situate it in relation to the Marxist and Freudian traditions, and how does it relate to the work of Herbert Marcuse?

GK: Marcuse had a profound influence on me. I met him around January of 1973, soon after Hanoi was bombed by the United States. Within a few months, we planned a series of events about Vietnam in San Diego. We were able to raise some money and do some interesting political education. By the time the United States was expelled from Vietnam in '75, Marcuse and I were working together. It was a very important relationship. He taught me a lot. But we were also friends. We would hang out and relax and talk.

I began to develop the ideas behind the eros effect through these discussions. It was then that I came to see how social movements were a way that people sublimated their basic need to become better human beings. Marcuse emphasized how work and society needed to become forms of artistic expression. It was an idea that was in the air during the late '60s and early '70s. The White Panthers described revolution as a way of life. Similarly, the May '68 slogan "Don't beg for the right to live—take it!" made clear that revolution was a struggle of life against death. The Vietnamese struggle pitted individual human freedom against totalitarianism. It's a struggle that continues today.

Marcuse convinced me to go to Germany to finish my dissertation. When I came back, I was sitting alone for days pulling together hundreds of pages of research notes. I had this moment of realization when I noticed that all these movements shared an important connection. It wasn't just in Europe, where the Tet Offensive led to the Berlin student conference where a couple thousand Berliners and activists from France decided to do actions that led to others in Italy, Spain, and many other countries; there were also students in Mexico, Dakar, Belgrade, and elsewhere who were in open and concurrent revolt. I began to see how all of these pieces fit together. I lived in the same building as a friend of mine, Rick Nadeau, and I walked down the hall and knocked on his door. After I explained my realization to him and called it "political eros," he suggested that I call it the "eros effect."

If we look at the unfolding of life and struggle on this planet, we can uncover a logic of human action analogous to the logic of the historical-philosophical laws uncovered by Hegel in the nineteenth century. By uncovering that logic, we can see how the unfolding of social movements includes the eros effect. Forces of life build upon each other. They have a direct relationship to each other through intuition, identification, and other processes. Along with the economy, the eros effect is a key feature of the historical process and the struggle for freedom. Other dimensions of the grammar of contemporary liberatory movements include autonomy and direct democracy.

AKT: How does an analysis of the May '68 uprising conducted in reference to the eros effect coincide with or differ from other modes of analyzing social movements, like the autonomist Marxist notion of the circulation of struggles or social movement theorizing that emphasizes processes of diffusion? Why, in your view, is the eros effect the best means of analyzing global uprisings?

GK: The Marxist notion of the circulation of struggle and the concept of diffusion are valuable because they show that struggles impact each other. Diffusion—what Samuel Huntington called "snowballing"—can help us to trace how one thing causes another, which causes another in turn. But neither theory allows us to comprehend the simultaneity of struggles that occurs during moments of the eros effect. It's not just causes, not just A plus B equals C. Events erupt simultaneously at multiple points and mutually amplify each other. They produce feedback loops with multiple iterations. To put it in terms of a mathematical analysis, we could say that diffusion and the circulation of struggles describe the process of movement development geometrically. The eros effect describes these same developments in terms of calculus.

In May of 1970, activists from all across the United States began to block highways. There was no central organization and no real news coverage. People didn't block highways because they heard that people elsewhere in the country were doing it. It was just what people thought they should do. They said, "Society is corrupt and people are just going off to do their thing while we're destroying hundreds of lives every day in Vietnam." Activists on the West Coast clogged Route 5 while, at the same time, activists in other parts of the country were doing the same thing. People do learn from each other and tactics do move from point A to point B. But we can't ignore how spontaneous tactical innovations can also happen simultaneously.

AKT: Political activity during the "anti-globalization" cycle of struggle between 1999 and 2003 seemed to share a bond with the dynamics you identify in *The Imagination of the New Left*. Spontaneity, self-management, and forms of social critique that called everyday life itself into question seem to have been as pervasive in 1999 as they were in 1968. How does the anti-globalization period fit into an analysis of the eros effect?

GK: The New Left was a world historical moment. People began to collectively recognize that they did not need vanguard parties. This was true in the United States, in France, and around the world. The New Left had the characteristics you describe—the emphasis on spontaneity, the political struggle for everyday life—because these were part of an overall ethics. They were part of the same grammar of struggle that reappears in world movements during different historical epochs.

The Zapatista uprising shared many of these characteristics. They were not a traditional working-class constituency; they brought questions of everyday life to the center of the movement; they did not try to seize state power directly; they tried to change their lives through counterinstitutions. They even talked about the idea of creating a "new person." These were also features of "New Left" politics in the anti-globalization movement. They were embodied in the forms of decision-making that emerged among many groups. The decentralization of communication made possible by projects like Indymedia allowed for the ethic to spread. All of these developments were extraordinarily important. They helped to highlight and intensify the globally interconnected character of struggle.

Many people say that Seattle was the beginning of the anti-globalization struggle. However, in 1999, Third World opposition to IMF programs had been going on for at least a decade. Hundreds, if not thousands, of people lost their lives in struggles against globalization a decade before Seattle. Nevertheless, Seattle was important for a variety of reasons. N30 was a powerful day of action in dozens of countries. From the grassroots, people mobilized in their own localities with a sense of connection to the broader struggle.

The Zapatistas and their *encuentros* helped to get activists to focus on Seattle. They emphasized the globally connected character of struggle. The Zapatistas called upon the people of Europe, who responded by following their calls for action. It gives an indication of the effect that revolutionary activity in Mexico can have around the globe. People used to think that it took a vanguard party to pull off this kind of coordination. But these movements arose from a call to action that—in a moment marked by the eros effect—resonated internationally. The multitude has its own intelligence. It's the intelligence of the life-force and the intelligence of the heart. It's not an intelligence of Cartesian duality. It's completely different. The eros effect describes those moments when the intelligence of the multitude expresses itself on a global scale.

AKT: The eros effect seems notable for its unpredictable and episodic historical recursions. If this is the case, and if the outcome of the political action it inspires has not always been social revolution, how should people committed to revolution relate to it? What tasks would you identify for revolutionaries living and struggling in periods not marked by the ascendance of the eros effect?

GK: In periods when there aren't globally insurgent movements, one of the things we need to do is work to build the capacity to act in a collective fashion. In the United States, social conditions like racism and sexism work against people's capacities and prevent social movements from reaching their potential. It's necessary to ensure that the values of the system don't creep back into our organizing. One way to prevent an elite from emerging within movements is to have magazines and newspapers that can encourage democratic communication and allow diverse perspectives to be heard even when they stand in opposition to each other.

But how do we create institutions in which new collective forms can develop and in which all people can play a leadership role? In order to develop these capacities, we also need to cultivate eros. For me, eros is not just about sex. It's about all our real and living connections to one another. These connections are forged in struggle and help to build trust. They act as a guiding force and as a life-affirming principle. As people unite in political activism, a level of trust develops that provides a great resource in moments of crisis.

We know from our experience in the United States that police sent agents into the movement. Organizations like the Black Panther Party had dozens—even hundreds—of infiltrators in their organization. At a certain point, the Black Panthers had to stop admitting new members because they felt that many of the people joining were just police of one kind or another. Under conditions like these, building relationships of trust is extraordinarily important. However, I think we need to be clear—and it needs to be understood—that, in the long haul, some individuals show that they are simply not worthy of being trusted.

During the '70s a group of radicals built a dozen counterinstitutions in Ocean Beach, California. In a countercultural community of fifteen thousand people that had everything from Hell's Angels and surfers to radicals and Deadheads, we built a free school, a people's food store with connections to organic farms, a community newspaper, bookstore, and childcare center—as well as activist centers to counter police repression and rape. Several politically active collectives were driving forces within these projects. Some of us gravitated toward the work of James and Grace Boggs. We tried to understand how to build a solid base in the community. Other people gravitated more toward Prairie Fire and the Weather Underground. They were trying to build an immediate impetus for some kind of armed insurgency. Despite these differences, we all wanted to change the system. We all thought of ourselves as revolutionaries.

On February 22, 1974, Ocean Beach was heavily attacked in a shootout involving more than a hundred police. I was arrested along with a couple of others. For years, FBI and police attacks continued, facilitated in part by the work of infiltrators. I don't want to be too specific. But one of the Free School children told a member of the Prairie Fire collective that his parents were working for the FBI and photographing everybody who went into Red House, the communal house where I was living. People from the Prairie Fire collective talked about this information but decided not to tell us because "we weren't working together politically."

This lesson is not something that's comfortable to talk about. It highlights what we might think of as the death forces within the movement. Marcuse described these tendencies as a kind of psychic Thermidor. By this, he meant that there are impulses within every movement that lead people to actively work against their own interests. Psychic Thermidor is the name of the process by which the movement defeats itself before its enemies even have a chance. It is one of the key reasons that elites are able to maintain power through periods of revolutionary upsurge.

The Communist Party of France sold out the movement of '68. The Italian Communist Party used the crisis of '77 as a way to enter mainstream politics. Recently, I've been doing research on East Asian uprisings at the end of the twentieth century and have found that almost all of the political parties sold out popular movements in order to gain a modicum of recognition or legality. In order to explain this dynamic, whereby the movement acts in ways that seem to be deliberately self-defeating, I think it's useful to draw on the tools of psychoanalysis. In order to unlock our true potential, we need to look to our own experiences of struggle. Part of that process has got to be an honest assessment of the real history of betrayal.

AKT: You've noted that the movements of 1968 were not able to follow through on their revolutionary potential and that, despite the tremendous energies unleashed, they were eventually recuperated by the emergency maneuvers of bourgeois actors. Do you take this to mean that the eros effect is a necessary but insufficient ingredient for social revolution? If this is the case, then what else is required? Do you think it's possible to dialectically resolve intoxication and discipline—the two seemingly antithetical habits of insurgency—as Walter Benjamin proposed?

GK: It's not only a possibility; it's a necessity. We need to cultivate our capacities to love and to act in an efficient manner—to combine love with mathematical logic, if you will. The eros effect is about people continuously activating their inner desire for freedom, which is the greatest force for liberation on the planet. However, activating this desire is one thing and coordinating it is another matter entirely. Activating and coordinating this need for freedom is precisely what movements need to be about. Academic theorists of social movements have tended to focus almost exclusively on the question of coordination. This is important, but it leaves out the discussion of inner desire. It asks how we fight without considering why we fight. However, the solution can't just be to switch the focus. Inner desire is not enough. It needs to be channeled. As I mentioned before, the movement is a means of sublimating eros.

AKT: Despite the failures of the movements of 1968, you indicate that they were nevertheless responsible for significant social transformations. Among these, you include the social spaces and countercultural practices that developed throughout the '70s and '80s, where people could experience moments of reprieve from the logic of capital. Some theorists have recently argued that these spaces have been harnessed to the production of new needs and, in this way, have been taken up by the market. Conversely, it seemed that the 1999–2003 cycle of struggle, especially in Europe, actively worked from these spaces as a social base for their insurgent activities. How should we relate to these spaces in the present? Is there a danger that they might as easily become ends in themselves as become the infrastructure for revolutionary action?

GK: These liberated spaces are incredibly significant. Every instance, every bit of fighting for liberation, every millimeter of that space is important. It provides liberation from the state and allows people to envision their lives in terms that are not geared solely to subsistence. We know that the system encroaches upon these spaces and uses them to spread death and make profit. The greatest natural resource on the planet is the human need for freedom. It is tremendously seductive to capital. The East Asian uprisings that took place throughout the 1980s against dictatorship, repression, and, in some cases, even against capitalism, enabled the IMF and World Bank to broaden their markets. They used the new democratic administrations to implement neoliberal programs that permitted foreign investors to penetrate previously closed markets. They were able to discipline workforces of millions of people in order to extract greater profits.

Does this mean that all the democratic revolutionaries in history have contributed to the intensification of international exploitation? Absolutely. Look at the United States of America. In the nineteenth century, it was a great beacon of freedom. It's still a beacon of freedom to many people. But it is clearly also a source of great death in the world. Everything that exists on this planet has more than one tendency. A beautiful flower contains deadly poison. I think it's unfair to critique countercultural spaces on the basis that they're harnessed to the system. Everything is. Name one thing that isn't. The point is that countercultural spaces *also* contain opportunities for women, for minorities, for gays, and for youth. They contain opportunities for music, even though music has been transformed into a massive commodity.

Those spaces are essential to people building experiences. In parts of the world where people have these spaces, their everyday lives are profoundly different than the ones lived in the hierarchical, competitive, and patriotic spaces of the dominant culture. I think that it's in those areas that the movement can begin to fight death. There, they can react to wars and other atrocities and create visionary new programs. Because of this, we can't understand them just as "countercultural spaces" in the way that the term gets used by the mainstream or by sociologists. At their best, they are spaces for the cultivation of the desire to live.

AKT: In the preface to *The Imagination of the New Left*, you describe how the movements of 1968 managed to "change the world without seizing political power." Which is to say: although 1968 marked a radical break from the sensibilities of the past, the movement was not able to marshal the energies it had unleashed to usurp the political power of capital. Were you surprised, then, to find John Holloway turning your description of a partial victory into a political principle in *Change the World Without Taking Power*?

GK: I was surprised and also felt validated. I am pleased that *The Imagination of the New Left* still resonates after the fall of Communism in 1989. I think this is because I was able to highlight those things that were more important than any specific party or political formation coming to power. The New Left essentially challenged modern civilization and rationality. It rejected the idea of armed nation-states with weapons of mass destruction, whether capitalist or communist. It rejected the idea that competition between elite leaders was the best way for human beings to organize themselves. In the end, the movement was not able to smash the system. It was not even able to maintain its own momentum. One of the great disappointments of my life involved learning that movements could reach such great heights only to fall off.

But we have to be nuanced in our analysis of victory and defeat. New Left movements did not seize political power, but they did open up spaces of freedom within capitalist society. They also helped to change the dynamics of global geopolitics and, for a while, it was difficult for the United States to engage in the kind of war that it tried to fight in Vietnam. Arrighi and Wallerstein have argued that the fall of the Soviet Union in 1989 was a continuation of 1968. This contextualizes the New Left's global significance, not only in Europe but also in Asia, where we saw uprisings throughout the 1980s and 1990s.

On the other hand, the Leninist revolution—which was officially successful and which involved the seizure of political power—helped to produce a situation that actively worked against human freedom. But even then, the Russian revolution was probably the reason that workers in the advanced capitalist societies were able to win higher wages and better working conditions. Now, in the absence of this so-called alternative to capitalism, neoliberalism has been very successful in undoing those gains.

The idea of changing the world without seizing power is contradictory. But I think that the lessons of the Leninist revolution call for a sober reassessment of our understanding of political power. I think Holloway's work is less about strategy and more about possibilities. Although the Zapatistas cannot objectively seize power, they are having a profound impact on Mexican politics. Their activity seems to point not toward the seizure but rather the destruction of power. And I think that's what many people are trying to say.

When, in 1970, the US New Left reached its high point at the Panthers' Revolutionary Peoples' Constitutional Convention, more than ten thousand of us spent days rewriting the constitution. We would have loved to dismantle the standing army and police forces of the United States and replace them with popular militias and community groups—and to redistribute the world's wealth. I know that I would like to see the United States broken into many different states, none of which would have an army with nuclear weapons. I think we need to find forms of governance that can work to enhance all forms of life, including the natural environment.

AKT: In *The Subversion of Politics*, you argue that the Marxist left needed to adopt a less hostile position toward identity politics because the recomposition of capital in the post-Fordist era has led people to experience their class position in more immediate, embodied, and autonomous ways. To date, this proposed rapprochement seems not to have been widely adopted by the advocates of either orthodox Marxism or orthodox identity politics. In the present context, where even identity politics have begun to lose their place of prominence, how should radicals go about exploring and explaining the interrelation between class exploitation and lived experience?

GK: The tension between Marxism and identity politics is an important one. In many ways, it highlights the more general tension between the universal and the particular. Marxism is often thought of in terms of universal truths that apply to any situation. Identity politics have arisen in a variety of contexts where people have rightly pointed out that the universal story does not include their experiences. Politically, these two positions are connected to the impulses toward dogmatism, in the case of Marxism, and sectarianism, in the case of identity politics. Contemporary dogmatism and sectarianism are conditioned by the capitalist system. They have to do with the ways in which we are able to construct our understanding of the world and make our lives intelligible. One solution to this dilemma is to understand that particular identities are themselves expressions of universal truths. Hip hop started out as a Black thing in the United States but has now become global music. The feminist movement spoke to women's particular desires for freedom but also changed global culture more generally. The women's movement enabled me to free myself as a male from my own macho life. The things we normally think of as particular are actually universal. At the same time, we can see how the universal truths of Marxism only become meaningful in particular contexts.

It seems as though identity politics were an important corrective to the universal pretenses of the previous phase of struggle, where everything was subsumed under the category "worker." This led people to argue that particular oppressions were problems arising in the "superstructure" that couldn't be dealt with without first addressing capitalism, the "structure." It was an analysis that led people to want to ignore difference in the interest of a kind of mechanical solidarity. At the same time, the way that difference has been understood by identity politics has sometimes been a dead end. Rather than conceiving of identities as situationally constructed, they have often been treated as essential categories of being.

When the impulse toward either the universal or the particular becomes rigid, it works against developing an understanding of truth. I wouldn't want to formulate or frame my investigations in accordance with either principle without also considering the other. Your generation has begun to develop in a noncompetitive, nonhierarchical fashion. Information technology now allows people to build instantaneous connections. All of these innovations allow people to develop new relationships between the universal and the particular. I suspect that, in the future, both your generation and my generation will look at the new radicals and say, "Wow, these kids really understand the importance of identities and the importance of universal truths." It will be an organizational victory and a theoretical one, too.

AKT: Another change in the theoretical landscape highlighted in *The Subversion of Politics* concerns the demotion of dialectics among autonomist Marxists. This tendency, which finds its contemporary roots in the work of Deleuze and Guattari, is made explicit in Negri's *Marx Beyond Marx*. Despite this turn, you've proposed that dialectical thought remains an important resource for revolutionary movements. Why is this the case? Is there anything to be gained from the work of radical thinkers in the Deleuzian tradition who have actively renounced dialectics?

GK: The Deleuzian tradition's focus on micro-dynamics is incredibly important. It grows out of the same impetus as the New Left's desire to change everyday life. Despite this, we can't surrender the notion of dialectics. This is because it enables us to see that what currently exists isn't everything. No matter how good or bad society gets, we've not yet seen its full character. Looking at historical processes and locating the negation of everything that came before is the essence of dialectics. If we lose sight of this dynamic process, if we just focus on what's immediately tangible, then we are left with a theory that basically says, "What you see is what you get." It makes revolutionary social transformation very difficult to imagine.

The Stalinist Third International demoted dialectics in favor of what we can understand as a kind of vulgar materialism. In a way, Negri continues this tradition by flattening out revolutionary theory, by cutting out its radiant heart and arguing that Marx wasn't dialectical, that reality isn't dialectical. Now, Negri's work is very important. His recent works with Michael Hardt played an important role in helping activists get a sense of the new terrain of struggle. Because of his importance, it's necessary to take his attack on dialectics seriously.

When we look at the practical consequences of ignoring dialectics, when we conceive of ourselves as machines of struggle, when we imagine that we are cyborgs, the images go in the opposite direction to the ones required by revolutionary politics. Rather than thinking in terms of machines, we should endeavor to become *more* human. The capacity of human beings to love is what keeps us from death. It's the impulse underlying our will to freedom. Machines don't need to love. Machines don't need freedom. Negri rejects humanism. He rejects Marcuse's idea that eros is an important force, that it is the basis of collective action against the forces of domination. But without these ideas, it's hard to understand why people would struggle.

Dialectics proceeds through the negative. However, in order to create movement and change by negating the world, you have to first of all acknowledge that it's there. Soviet Marxism argued that dialectics was a mode of abstract thought in opposition to the historical and the concrete. And we certainly see dialectics being used in that way by people like Francis Fukuyama and Samuel Huntington. But a dialectical investigation of these thinkers reveals the extent to which the uses they make of the dialectic are extremely undialectical. If dialectics tell us anything, it's that things continually change and that there's no end. Every day, you go halfway. As you travel, your needs change and your understanding of what freedom means changes. You go halfway and halfway again, but you never actually arrive.

AKT: Your recent work focuses on the mass uprisings that shook East Asia during the 1980s, and especially on the 1980 Gwangju Uprising in Korea. Although the uprising was smashed, the event—which you've likened to the Paris Commune—lived on as a beacon in the radical imagination. In your account, the dream of Gwangju was realized during the Minjung revolts of 1987 that called for and won direct presidential elections. What is the place of memory in revolutionary politics? How should revolutionaries respond to the systematic erosion of the capacity to remember in the present? How should we relate to its distorted and conservative forms like nostalgia or myth?

GK: On May 21, 1980, the people of Gwangju expelled the military from their city and put it under people's rule. Although the uprising did not last long, people developed important forms of self-governance. On May 27, the military dictatorship of Chun Doo Hwan took back the city with US encouragement and support. Since then, the government has tried to suppress and destroy the memory of the Gwangju Uprising. For years, the event only appeared in block prints, popular songs, whispered conversations, and hastily performed public theater sketches. The first book about the uprising only appeared five years after the event. It was published in secret and circulated through informal networks.

The June uprising of 1987 in Minjung was primarily motivated by the memory of Gwangju. "Remember Gwangju!" was one of the most popular chants on the street. After nineteen consecutive days of illegal demonstrations, people compelled the military dictatorship to agree to direct presidential elections and expanded civil liberties. The struggle for the memory of Gwangju continued for nearly a decade after 1987. About a dozen people committed suicide, demanding that the truth about Gwangju be told. Finally, after a million people signed a petition—and in the context of ongoing protests—a special act was passed by parliament. Two former presidents were sent to prison because of their role in the suppression of the uprising. Such was the power of memory.

This example might not be applicable to the global North, where memory seems to be in a state of shock. Nostalgia and myth are problems. But we need to remember how the glorification of slavery and of the massacre of native Americans—the stuff of Hollywood westerns in the '50s and '60s—have distorted people's fundamental values to the point that the function of memory is radically different in the United States than it is in Asia. This is not to say that people in Asia have not endured centuries of exploitation. But, even with this history, the fact remains that common, ordinary people have values that make the place seem so civilized and enlightened in comparison.

The other night, I was walking through Chonnam National University after midnight. All but a few lights were out. I was walking alone and there were young people sitting on benches, walking in the street, and hanging out. The society is so safe. It's often hard to imagine that this is how things could be everywhere, that daily life could revolve around basic values like cooperation, politeness, and respect for other people. I think people in the global North have a hard time imagining a life like that because the experience of slavery and genocide—for both oppressed and oppressor—is embedded in our psyche. People don't really want to remember. Despite this, I think people will continue to learn from past experiences of the eros effect, where the desire for freedom triumphs over death.

# 2

# Eros and Revolution

GEORGE KATSIAFICAS

In his last three books—*Counterrevolution and Revolt, Essay on Liberation,* and *The Aesthetic Dimension*—Herbert Marcuse concerned himself as never before with questions raised by contemporaneous social movements. His work on Nature in these three books was central to his notion that there may be a "biological foundation for socialism," that Nature—not only external Nature but our own inner human nature—is an "ally" in the revolutionary process. As Marcuse so clearly formulated it, humans have an instinctual need for freedom—something that we grasp intuitively.[1] Unlike Habermas, who considered the unconscious "inner foreign territory" as part of his overly rationalistic model of humans, Marcuse's understanding embraced the erotic and unconscious dimensions of human nature as central to the project of liberation.

Following Marcuse's formulation of political eros, I developed the concept of the eros effect in my book on the global imagination of 1968 to explain the rapid spread of revolutionary aspirations and actions.[2] The eros effect is crystalized in the sudden and synchronous international emergence of hundreds of thousands of people who occupy public space and call for a completely different political reality. Other dimensions of this phenomenon include: the simultaneous appearance of revolts in many places; the intuitive identification of hundreds of thousands of people with each other across national and ethnic dividing lines; their common belief in new values; and suspension of normal daily routines like competitive business practices,

This chapter was previously published in *Radical Philosophy Review* 16, no. 2 (2013): 491–505, doi: 10.5840/radphilrev201316238. The essay is reproduced here with minimal editorial changes.

criminal behavior, and acquisitiveness. In my view, it is the instinctual need for freedom that is sublimated into a collective phenomenon during moments of the eros effect.[3] After 1968, other such moments are evident in the Arab Spring and the Occupy Wall Street protests that spread to more than one thousand cities globally as well as in the less well-known wave of Asian uprisings in the 1980s and 1990s.

The eros effect first appeared to me as I completed a decade of research on social movements in 1968. As I sat overlooking the Pacific in Ocean Beach, California, I had a eureka moment as I uncovered the specific synchronic relations to each other of spontaneous uprisings, strikes, and massive occupations of public space. During this world-historical period, millions of ordinary people suddenly entered into history in solidarity with each other. Their activation was based more upon feeling connected with others and love for freedom than with specific national economic or political conditions. No central organization called for these actions. People intuitively believed that they could change the direction of the world from war to peace, from racism to solidarity, from external domination to self-determination, and from patriotism to humanism. Universal interests became generalized at the same time as dominant values of society (national chauvinism, hierarchy, and domination) were negated.

When the eros effect is activated, humans' love for and solidarity with each other suddenly replace previously dominant values and norms. Competition gives way to cooperation, hierarchy to equality, power to truth. During the Vietnam War, for example, many Americans' patriotism was superseded by solidarity with the people of Vietnam, and in place of racism, many white Americans insisted a Vietnamese life was worth the same as an American life (defying the continual media barrage to the contrary). According to many opinion polls at that time, Vietnamese leader Ho Chi Minh was more popular on American college campuses than US President Nixon. Moments of the eros effect reveal movements' aspirations and visions as embodied in actions of millions of people, a far more significant dimension than statements of leaders, organizations, or parties.

European philosophers of the seventeenth and eighteenth centuries sought to understand the structure of individual thought and to classify it according to its various dimensions and historical unfolding. Using a similar analytical method, we can today comprehend social movements as the logical progress in history that unfolds within the praxis of thousands—and sometimes millions—of people as they rise up to change their lives. The inner logic in seemingly spontaneous actions during moments of crisis—particularly in events like general strikes, uprisings, insurrections, and revolutions—constitutes the concrete realization of liberty in history. People's collective actions define the specific character of freedom at any given moment. By reconstructing the actions of hundreds of thousands of people in insurgencies and uncovering concrete dynamics of the unconscious, we can contribute to a philosophical history not simply from my own mind but from the actions of thousands of people. As Susan Buck-Morss put it, what is needed is to "construct not a philosophy *of* history, but a philosophy *out* of history, or (this amounts to the same thing) to reconstruct historical material as philosophy."[4]

One after another, insurgencies at the end of the twentieth century illustrate that ordinary people's collective wisdom is far greater than that of entrenched elites, whether democratically elected or self-appointed. Whether we look at France in May 1968, the Prague Spring, or Occupy Wall Street, people's common sense is greater than the "rational" knowledge of elites. Throughout the world, throngs of ordinary citizens who go into the streets and face violence and arrest, endangering their own lives and their families' futures, have visions of freedom writ large. Empirical analysis of the actions of hundreds of thousands of ordinary people—millions if we total the number of participants—reveals that ordinary people want peace, greater democratic rights, equality, and simple forms of progress, while elites are more concerned with cutting taxes on the rich, extending national sovereignty, and protecting corporate profits. In the transformed reality constructed by people power, mobilized throngs have newfound capacities to enact change. Inspired by previous movements of common people to overturn elites at the apex of power, popular movements continue to enlarge the scope of human liberty. Without highly paid trainers, insurgent activists adapt new technologies (such as the fax machine in China in 1989, the cell phone video in Burma, and social media in Egypt) and bring them into use far faster than the corporate or political elite.

Forms of direct democracy and collective action developed by the New Left continue to define movement aspirations and structures. This is precisely why the New Left was a world-historical movement. In Gwangju, South Korea, in 1980, people refused to accept a new military dictator and stayed in the streets for democracy. When the army brutally attacked the city, outraged citizens beat back a vicious military assault and held their liberated city for a week, using general assemblies and direct democracy to run their commune. Abetted by the United States, the South Korean military crushed the commune with tanks and helicopters, killing hundreds of people (at the time, Human Rights Watch estimated the carnage in the thousands). Within the Zapatistas, in the protests in Seattle in 1999, and in the more recent wave from Tahrir Square to Wall Street, general assemblies and direct democracy remain movements' modus operandi.

Alongside participatory currents, the history of social movements is also the history of popular insurgencies being placated, accommodated, and sold out by reform-minded parties and organizations of all kinds—whether French and Italian Communists, Czech or Bangladeshi democrats, and Korean or US trade unions. Ritualized protests organized by top-down groups with "progressive" leaders no longer suffice to bring the "masses" into the streets. Apparently, after 1968, centrally controlled elites, like Leninist-style parties, are no longer needed to transcend the reformism of spontaneously formed movements since these movements are themselves capable of developing a universal critique and autonomous capacities for self-government. Since World War II, humanity's increasing awareness of our own power and strategic capacities has continually manifested itself in sudden and simultaneous contestation of power by hundreds of thousands of people.

A significant new tactic in the arsenal of popular movements, the eros effect is not simply an act of mind, nor can it simply be willed by a "conscious element" (or revolutionary party). Rather, it involves popular movements emerging as forces on their own as ordinary people take history into their own hands. The concept of the eros effect is a means of rescuing the revolutionary value of spontaneity, a way to stimulate a reevaluation of the unconscious and strengthen the will of popular movements to remain steadfast in their revulsion with war, inequality, and domination. Rather than portraying emotions as linked to reaction, the notion of the eros effect seeks to bring them into the realm of positive revolutionary resources whose mobilization can result in significant social transformation.

## LIMITS OF THE EROS EFFECT

Uprisings may be powerful vehicles for overthrowing entrenched dictatorships, but they are also useful to global elites whose interests transcend nations. Massive occupation of public space was clearly effective in overthrowing existing regimes (such as Marcos in 1986, Korea's military dictatorship in 1987, and Mubarak in 2011), but the system has become adept at riding the wave of uprisings to stabilize its operations. The wave of Asian people-power uprisings from 1980 to 1992 helped to incorporate more of the world into the orbit of Japanese and US banks.[5] The South Korean working class' heroic struggles for union rights became useful to neoliberal economic penetration of the country.[6] In democratic South Korea and Taiwan, as in the Philippines after Marcos (and elsewhere), newly elected administrations accelerated neoliberal programs that permitted foreign investors to penetrate previously closed markets and to discipline workforces of millions of people in order to extract greater profits.

Although Egypt's future has yet to be written, the military's control after Mubarak's imprisonment is another example of how dictatorships in danger of being toppled—and possibly taken out of the orbit of the United States—can be salvaged by deposing a few men at the top while retaining the core of the system. Egypt's military leaders enforce Mubarakism without Mubarak, a more stable system ruled by an elite friendly to the United States. As we saw in the Philippines without Marcos, Korea without the military dictatorship, and Taiwan without the White Terror, unstable countries were turned into fertile grounds for US and Japanese banks and corporations. An end to "crony" capitalism meant the expansion of transnational corporate markets and profits.

Humanity's unending need for freedom constitutes the planet's most powerful natural resource. In the struggle to create free human beings, political movements play paramount roles. Uprisings accelerate social transformation, change governments, and revolutionize individual consciousness and social relationships. Most popular insurgencies result in expanded liberties for millions of people; when they are brutally repressed, the regime's days are numbered. Uprisings' enormous energies transform people's everyday existence and continue to energize long past their decline. Uprisings activate civil society and mobilize subaltern groups, such as the working class, students, minorities, and women. After uprisings, autonomous media and grassroots organizations mushroom, feminism strengthens, and workers strike. Even among nonparticipants, bonds are created through powerful erotic energies unleashed in these exhilarating moments. These instances of what Marcuse called "political eros" are profoundly important in rekindling imaginations and nurturing hope.


## REVISITING THE EROS EFFECT

Although contemporary rational choice theorists (who emphasize indi-vidual gain as the key motivation for people's actions) cannot comprehend instinctual motivations, even George Kennan, who famously started the Cold War with an essay written under the pseudonym Mr. X, found the antinuclear wave of protests in the early 1980s to be an "expression of a deep instinctual insistence, if you don't mind, on sheer survival. . . . This movement is too powerful, too elementary, too deeply embedded in the natural human instinct for self-preservation to be brushed aside."[7]

A similar basis for action was also gleaned by social scientist Choi Jungwoon in reference to the Gwangju Uprising. As an established scholar unfamiliar with what had transpired in 1980, Choi was subsequently approached by his professional academic association to investigate the uprising. After extensive research, he concluded that Gwangju citizens had crystallized an "absolute community" in which all were equal and united by love.[8]

So impressed was Choi with the solidarity he uncovered in Gwangju, he believed "[t]he most basic human values travel beyond history and culture; they began with the birth of humankind and will continue into the unknown future. . . . The term to refer to this primeval instinct has not been found in South Korea's narrow arena for political discourse and ideology." The empirical history of crowd behavior in the late twentieth century—most clearly in Gwangju—demands a reevaluation of the frozen categories of crowds, through which they are viewed as emotionally degraded, when Gwangju's people were passionately intelligent and loving.[9]

For Choi,

> It was not "mobs" of cowardly people hoping to rely on the power of numbers. The absolute community provided encounters among dignified warriors. The absolute community was formed only from love. . . . In Western Philosophy, reason is derived from solitary individuals. However the Gwangju uprising demonstrates that human beings who were conscious of being members of a community achieved reason. Reason was the capability of the community, not that of individuals.[10]

The connective threads running through grassroots movements around the world are often intuitively woven together in innumerable strands of what might seem like very different struggles. In the 1970s, Italy's Metropolitan Indians, the most spectacular of dozens of autonomous groups that constituted Italian *Autonomia*, adopted very similar notions to the US Yippies and Black Panthers, Dutch Provos, and Christiania's communards.[11] No organizational means of communication tied together these communities of struggle; rather, intuition and common sense made the same conclusions flow naturally from people's hearts.[12]

Diffusion—what Samuel Huntington called "snowballing"—can help us to trace how one movement causes another.[13] Snowballing is a postmodern version of the "Domino Theory" that guided American anticommunism in the 1950s. Based upon the assumption that there is a single point of origin for insurgencies, this concept expresses the paranoid fears of a center for social control that perceives itself to be surrounded by enemies, not the wondrous joy at the simultaneous emergence of freedom struggles. Tied as Huntington was to Washington policymakers, his ideological presuppositions blinded him to the emergence of polycentric grassroots movements. The distance between his theory and law enforcement officials is not great. As the US Civil Rights Movement accelerated in the 1960s, sheriffs and police continually blamed Martin Luther King or Malcolm X for their own city's problems, and campus administrators often insisted that "outside agitators" caused university protests.

What Huntington called snowballing has been described by others—even by progressive academics in what Barbara Epstein dubbed the "social movement industry"—through terms like demonstration effect, diffusion, emulation, domino effect, and contagion. The sheer number of labels is one indication of this phenomenon's recent emergence as a significant variable. The concept of diffusion and Marxist notion of the circulation of struggle are valuable because they show that struggles impact each other. Leaving aside the difference in values embedded in disease-laden labels like "contagion" and less pejorative terms like "diffusion" and "demonstration effect," they all assume a single, external point of origin. None of these concepts comprehends the *simultaneous* appearance of insurgencies among different peoples, even across cultures. It's not simply a chain reaction, not just that A causes B, which causes C. Events erupt simultaneously at multiple points and mutually amplify each other. They produce feedback loops with multiple iterations. To put it in terms of a mathematical analysis, we could say that diffusion and the circulation of struggles describe the process of movement development geometrically, while the eros effect describes these same developments in terms of calculus.[14]

While the influence of one event upon another is no doubt substantial, to comprehend movements as externally induced—much as a collision of bowling balls—is to miss something essential about their inner logic and meaning. Simultaneous emergence and mutual amplification of insurgencies are alternative understandings, ones embedded in the notion of the "eros effect." Rather than a simple monocausal process of protest, the eros effect provides a way to comprehend the polycentric—indeed decentered—source of movements' energies. For Huntington, simultaneity was "impossible," and he excluded it in advance.[15]

Out of a series of struggles in France, activists developed a very similar notion to the eros effect: "Revolutionary movements do not spread by contamination but by *resonance*. . . . An insurrection is not like a plague or a forest fire—a linear process which spreads from place to place after an initial spark. It rather takes the shape of music, whose focal points, though dispersed in time and space, succeed in imposing the rhythms of their own vibrations, always taking on more density."[16] In many places, grassroots activism made possible "discoveries" of this same phenomenon with a simultaneity and autonomy that defied "scientific" understanding.

Long before the social media, simultaneous tactical innovations occurred in different places. To name just one example, in May of 1970, after the United States invaded Cambodia and killed college students on its own campuses, activists from across the country simultaneously blocked high-ways. There was no central organization directing people to do so. People didn't obstruct highways simply because they heard that people elsewhere in the country were doing it but because people thought they should do something effective to stop a society destroying hundreds of lives every day in Vietnam. Without direct lines of communication, activists on the West Coast clogged Route 5 while, at the same time, activists in other parts of the country stopped traffic on nearby roads. Tactics may move in a line from point A to point B through a process of diffusion, but we can't ignore how tactical innovations can also happen simultaneously.

## CARL JUNG AND SYNCHRONICITY

How can we understand simultaneous emergence of freedom struggles in many places? One avenue was explored by Carl Jung, for whom synchron-icity was so abstract and "irrepresentable" that he insisted we abandon completely the notion that the psyche is connected to the brain.[17] Instead, through archetypes, he understood that unconscious impulses could influ-ence consciousness. Such instinctual impulses originate in the deep layers of the unconscious, in what Jung called the "phylogenetic substratum."[18] They function to return our unknown lives from a distant past to conscious-ness—from the world of communalism at the dawn of human existence. For Jung, "[i]n addition to memories from a long-distant conscious past, completely new thoughts and creative ideas can also present themselves from the unconscious—thoughts and ideas that have never been conscious before. They grow up from the dark depths of the mind like a lotus and form a most important part of the subliminal psyche."[19]

The unconscious may not be rational, but it can certainly be more reasonable than "rational" thought. Consider the intuitive revulsion everyone feels for the wanton destruction of Nature caused by "rational" industrialization.[20] When the unconscious is aroused, it flows toward consciousness—a psychic process very similar to what I understand as the eros effect.[21] Jung refers us to something that "indwells in the soul" and has the power to transform things, especially in moments of "great excess of love or hate."[22] We should note that by love, he meant eros in all its forms, not simply sex. According to Jung, Freud attempted to understand the inner erotic necessities emanating from our instincts according to that one dimension. Freud sought to "lay hold of unconfinable Eros within the crude terminology of sex."[23] In our age, when reversal of commodification of the life-world is paramount, can we reclaim eros from the throes of its reification as sex?

For Marcuse, political eros was "Beauty in its most sublimated form."[24] The eros effect emanates from the instinctual reservoir, the collective unconscious, and is a form of sublimation of instinctual drives into erotic channels of human solidarity and love of freedom. Despite his conservative political orientation, Carl Jung also recognized ways that instinct makes rebellious actions necessary on our part: "The growth of culture consists, as we know, in a progressive subjugation of the animal in humans.[25] It is a process of domestication which cannot be accomplished without rebellion on the part of the animal nature that thirsts for freedom. From time to time there passes as it were a wave of frenzy through the ranks of humans too long constrained within the limitations of their culture."[26] For Jung, these internally necessary drives for change manifested themselves in the European Renaissance and other forms of cultural expression. Under certain conditions they could produce social eruptions: "Separation from their instinctual nature inevitably plunges civilized humans into the conflict between the conscious and unconscious, spirit and nature, knowledge and faith, a split that becomes pathological the moment their consciousness is no longer able to neglect or suppress their instinctual side. The accumulation of individuals who have got into this critical state starts off a mass movement."[27]

The eros effect rests on intuition, an unquantifiable quality that may make its simultaneity impenetrable to the social control center (the police)—as well as impossible to verify "scientifically." For Jung, synchronistic phenomena are akin to magic and are not statistically verifiable.[28] "Meaningful coincidences" cannot be explained by rational cognition, but to recall them is to prepare the ground for their future recurrences. Just as keeping a dream journal enhances remembering dreams, so recalling instances of the eros effect prepares the ground for further episodes. Revolutionary spirit for Jung would arise outside the realm of sense perception: "The hallmarks of spirit are, firstly, the principle of spontaneous movement and activity;

secondly, the spontaneous capacity to produce images independently of sense perception and thirdly, the autonomous and sovereign manipulation of these images."[29]

When time and space are drastically altered in moments of the eros effect, explanations that assume linear conceptions cannot comprehend what is happening. Thus, the cause of the eros effect may not be capable of being understood within the framework of academic social science. As Jung describes such moments: "There I am utterly one with the world, so much a part of it that I will forget all too easily who I really am. 'Lost in oneself' is a good way of describing this state. But this self is the world, if only a consciousness could see it."[30] In a similar vein of thought, Marcuse understood primary narcissism as "more than autoeroticism; it engulfs the 'environment,' integrating the narcissistic ego with the objective world."[31] He derived his understanding of this "oceanic feeling" from Freud's realization in *Civilization and Its Discontents* that "narcissism survives not only as a constitutive element in the construction of the reality . . ." For Freud, the content of the ego-feeling was "limitless extension and oneness with the universe (oceanic feeling)."[32] In our feeling of merger with all of humanity, time does not exist, which may help us understand why outbursts of insurgencies so often appropriate past movement identities as their own.

Being "one with the world" implies bonding with those around us, a process similar to what Gaetano Mosca conceived as a human "instinct" for "herding together" that underlies "moral and, sometimes, physical conflicts."[33] Such smart group behavior—containing no centralized control yet eliciting appropriate responses to local situations—is present already among caribou, birds, bees, and ants. Swarm theory seems an appropriate means to comprehend protests like those in Seattle in 1999, when cell phones, texting, Internet, and people's common sense created a "smart mob" that came together, dispersed, and reconstituted "like a school of fish."[34]

## EROS' AESTHETIC DIMENSION

Seldom do self-appointed theorists of the working class mention women or minorities, and only in rare cases (as Herbert Marcuse did in his final book) do they even consider the possibility of freedom meaning to live without the compulsion to work.[35] At a time when it is possible for human beings to work twenty hours per week for twenty years and to retire with enough money to live decently, the state-capitalist system demands we work longer hours and for more years in order for governments and corporations to continue to function. The Soviet Union's variety of state socialism was little better. Indeed, that variety of Marxism was rightly perceived as wanting to make the entire world into a factory.

Much like medieval theologians who debated how many angels could dance on the head of a pin, idealistic categorical imperatives define many leftists' means of analyzing the strategic value of sectors of the population and long-term goals. For mainstream democratization theorists, a bias exists in favor of the middle class as the vehicle of democratization, while academic Marxists insist rigidly that the working class is key, even to the point of excluding from conferences and journals those they regard as outside lines they draw in the sand.[36] In our world where humanity is the identity of movements emerging across the world and where Nature's destruction approaches a tipping point, species is key. For many Marxists, however, the "working class" functions as a collective father figure, a thing-in-itself fixed once and for all time in a frozen metaphysic, universally "valid."

The history of recent uprisings provides a rich empirical resource from which to evaluate the political positions of sectors of the population, to gauge the concrete historical meaning of "class-for-itself." Revolutionary subjects reveal themselves in concrete praxis, not in the obscure calculations and charts of "analytical Marxians." As Marcuse formulated it, "The search for specific historical agents of revolutionary change in the advanced capitalist countries is indeed meaningless. Revolutionary forces emerge in the process of change itself."[37] Proletarian dogmatism of the Left leaves it playing in the academic sandbox or searching the refuse bin of history for a nonexistent "master class."

If Marxists reify categories of production and seek to make the whole world into a factory, reducing humanity to the proletariat, feminism is a vital counterforce that organically constitutes human life in domains other than work. As Marcuse so eloquently reminds us: "In a free society . . . existence would no longer be determined by life-long alienated labor."[38] If Soviet Marxism turned art into an instrument of the state, Marcuse offered a different interpretation. At a time when consumerism envelops the continent of Desire and weapons of mass destruction destroy the foundations of the Beautiful, art's own autonomous logic might be its salvation. The resolution of this apparent contradiction is the understanding that within art's formal aesthetics, a truth is contained that transforms society. For Marcuse:

> Art can express its radical potential only *as art*, in its own language and image. . . . The liberating "message" of art . . . is likely to persist until the millennium which will never be, art must remain *alienation*. . . . Art cannot represent the revolution, it can only invoke it in another medium, in an aesthetic form

in which the political content becomes *meta*political, governed by the internal necessity of art.[39]

The call for art to obey the dictates of the political struggle would mean "the imagination has become wholly functional: servant to instrumentalist Reason."[40] Especially in an era when the system delivers the goods so that people live to work in order to buy into consumerism, art's role may even be that of "An Enemy of the People" as it seeks to change the world.[41]

## ACTIVATING THE EROS EFFECT

People's intuition and self-organization—not the dictates of any party—are increasingly keys to the emergence of global protests. While political leadership based upon authoritarian models of organization has withered among freedom-loving movements, the power of example and synchronicity of uprisings are increasingly potent—especially when their promulgators are among the poorest inhabitants of a world capable of providing plenty for all. Actualized in the actions of millions of people in 1968, the eros effect continues to define an essential core of movements, and as such it is a weapon of enormous future potential. Both the disarmament movement of the 1980s and the alterglobalization movement of the 1990s experienced periods of rapid international proliferation. With the rise of the Arab Spring and Occupy Wall Street protests, transnational eruptions of protests have become widely visible.

Instances of the spread of movements across borders, involving a process of mutual amplification and synergy, are significant precursors for future mobilizations. In the period after 1968, as the global movement's capacity for decentralized international coordination developed, five other episodes of the international eros effect can be discerned:

1. The disarmament movement of the early 1980s

2. The wave of East Asian uprisings in the 1980s and 1990s

3. The revolts against Soviet regimes in East Europe from 1989 to 1991

4. The alterglobalization wave and antiwar protests on February 15, 2003

5. The Arab Spring and Occupy Movements of 2011

Continuing global upsurges pick up from the international synchronicity and expanding popular involvement of movements since World War II. The next generations of protests—drawn from the trajectory of Chiapas; Caracas; Gwangju; Berlin; Seattle; February 15, 2003; and the Arab Spring—will surpass these other waves in a cascading global resonance. As the global tendencies of the world system intensify in their impact on millions of peoples' everyday lives, internationally coordinated opposition is more and more a necessity.

For the eros effect to be activated, thousands and then millions of people who comprise civil society need to act—to negate their existing daily routines and break free of ingrained patterns. This process is not simply enacted by the will power of a small group—although small groups may help spark it. Without help from anyone, the global movement is building toward a protracted people's uprising that breaks through regional cultures and confronts the planetary constraints on people's freedom. As the target is fixed, its bull's-eye will be reached: the hundred billionaires who greedily hoard humanity's collective wealth, an even smaller number of gigantic global banks and corporations, and militarized nation-states armed with weapons of mass destruction. People used to think that it took a vanguard party to provide this kind of coordination, but these recent episodes of the eros effect prove otherwise. The multitude has its own intelligence—an intelligence of the life force, of the heart. The eros effect is not an intelligence of Cartesian duality, yet it is a moment of extraordinary reasonability.

The twentieth century will be remembered for its horrific wars, environmental devastation, and mass starvation amid great prosperity. It will also be known as a time when human beings began a struggle to transform the entire world system. Uprisings at the century's end reveal people's attempts to enact global justice. From the grassroots, millions of people around the world in the past three decades have constituted a protracted people's uprising against capitalism and war. Without anyone telling people to do so, millions of us in the alterglobalization movement have confronted elite meetings of the institutions of the world economic system—practical targets whose universal meaning is profoundly indicative of people's yearnings for a new world economic system. No central organization dictated this focus. Rather, millions of people autonomously developed it through their own thoughts and actions. Similarly, without central organization, as many as thirty million people around the world took to the streets on February 15, 2003, to protest the second US war on Iraq. As the global movement becomes increasingly aware of its own power, its strategy and impact are certain to become more focused. By creatively synthesizing direct-democratic forms of decision-making and militant popular resistance, people's movements will continue to develop along the historical lines revealed in 1968 and subsequent Asian uprisings: within a grammar of autonomy, "conscious spontaneity," and the eros effect.

As we move into the twenty-first century, the Arab Spring and Occupy protests provide empirical evidence of the growing consciousness of ordinary people who go into the streets to change history. In 1968, "the whole world was watching." Today, it is increasingly the case that the whole world is awakening. Our ultimate goal should be to forge permanent popular assemblies as forms of governance, to enlarge and solidify the kinds of small general assemblies proliferating from the grassroots. Previous historical examples of such forms of governance can be found in the 1871 Paris Commune and the 1980 absolute community in Gwangju.[42]

No one could have guessed that the suicide of a vegetable vendor in a small Tunisian town would set off the Arab Spring. Not even Mohamed Bouazizi himself had any idea that his solitary act of despair and anger would resonate among so many people. It appears that leaderless conjunctures most often produce the eros effect. Like falling in love, enacting the eros effect is a complex process. Can we make ourselves fall in love? Can we simply will ourselves to remain in love? If the eros effect were continually activated, we would have passed from the realm of prehistory to a world in which human beings for the first time are able to determine for themselves the type of society in which they wish to live.

## NOTES

1. Herbert Marcuse, "A Biological Foundation for Socialism?," in *An Essay on Liberation* (Boston: Beacon Press, 1969), 6–22.

2. George Katsiaficas, *The Imagination of the New Left: A Global Analysis of 1968* (Boston: South End Press, 1987).

3. For Marcuse's formulation, see *An Essay on Liberation* (Boston: Beacon Press, 1969).

4. Susan Buck-Morss, *The Dialectics of Seeing: Walter Benjamin and the Arcades Project* (Cambridge: MIT Press, 1989), 77, 55 (original emphasis).

5. See George Katsiaficas, *Asia's Unknown Uprisings, Volume 2: People Power in the Philippines, Burma, Tibet, China, Taiwan, Bangladesh, Nepal, Thailand, and Indonesia, 1947–2009* (Oakland: PM Press, 2013).

6. See Loren Goldner, "The Korean Working Class: From Mass Strike to Casualization and Retreat, 1987–2007" (lecture, International Studies Conference, University of Padua, January 12, 2008), http://libcom.org/history/korean-working-class-mass-strike-casualization-retreat-1987–2007.

7. George Kennan, "On Nuclear War," *The New York Review of Books*, January 21, 1982, http://www.nybooks.com/articles/archives/1982/jan/21/on-nuclear-war/.

8. Choi Jungwoon, *The Gwangju Uprising: The Pivotal Democratic Movement That Changed the History of Modern Korea* (Paramus: Homa and Sekey Books, 2006), 85, 131. For background on the uprising, see George Katsiaficas, "Remembering the Kwangju Uprising," *Socialism and Democracy* 14, no. 1 (Spring–Summer 2000): 85–107, http://eroseffect.com/articles/rememberingkwangju.pdf.

9. See George Katsiaficas, "Remembering the Gwangju Uprising," in *South Korean Democracy: Legacy of the Gwangju Uprising*, ed. George Katsiaficas and Na Kahn-Chae (London: Routledge, 2006), 1–23.

10. Choi, *The Gwangju Uprising*, 134.

11. See Mary Anne Staniszewski, Dara Greenwald, and Josh MacPhee, eds., *Signs of Change* (Oakland: AK Press, 2010).

12. Compare with Habermas' negative assessment in Jürgen Habermas, *Toward a Rational Society: Student Protest, Science, and Politics*, trans. Jeremy J. Shapiro (Boston: Beacon Press), 35–36.

13. Samuel Huntington, *The Third Wave: Democratization in the Late Twentieth Century* (Norman: University of Oklahoma Press, 1991), 46.

14. I first expressed this idea in: George Katsiaficas, interviewed by AK Thompson, "Remembering May '68: An Interview with George Katsiaficas," *Upping the Anti* 6 (April 2008): n.p., http://uppingtheanti.org/journal/article/06-remembering-may-68/.

15. Huntington, *Third Wave*, 33.

16. The Invisible Committee, *The Coming Insurrection* (Los Angeles: Semiotext(e), 2009), 12–13.

17. Carl G. Jung, *Synchronicity: An Acausal Connecting Principle* (Princeton: Princeton University Press, 1973), 89.

18. Carl G. Jung, *The Archetypes and the Collective Unconscious*, trans. R. F. C. Hull, vol. 9, part 1 of *The Collected Works of C. G. Jung*, 2nd ed. (Princeton: Princeton University Press, 1969), 286.

19. Carl G. Jung, "Approaching the Unconscious," in *Man and His Symbols*, ed. Carl G. Jung (New York: Dell, 1968), 25.

20. Teodros Kiros considers a "rationality of the heart" an antidote to contemporary civilization's misuse of reason. See Kiros, *Zara Yacob: Rationality of the Human Heart* (Trenton: Red Sea Press, 2005).

21. Jung, *Synchronicity*, 30.

22. Ibid., 32. As Jung notes, the concept is originally Avicenna's. Three hundred years later, Ibn Khaldun similarly discussed forms of cognition outside the realm of rational thought. See George Katsiaficas, "A Personal Perspective on Individual and Group: Comparative Cultural Observations with a Focus on Ibn Khaldun," *Journal of Biosciences* (Indian Academy of Social Sciences) 39, no. 1 (March 2014): 1–6.

23. Carl Jung, "The Eros Theory," in *Two Essays on Analytical Psychology*, trans. R. F. C. Hull, vol. 7 of *The Collective Works of C. G. Jung*, 2nd ed. (Princeton: Princeton University Press, 1967), 28.

24. Herbert Marcuse, *The Aesthetic Dimension: A Critique of Marxist Aesthetics* (Boston: Beacon Press, 1978), 64.

25. In this quote and the next, the original text uses "man" and "his"—historically influenced gender-exclusionary forms. I have substituted "humans" for "man" and correspondingly substituted "their" for "his."

26. Jung, "The Eros Theory," 19.

27. Carl G. Jung, *The Undiscovered Self*, trans. R. F. C. Hull (New York: Signet, 2006), 79.

28. See Jung, *Synchronicity*, 95, 103, 106–107.

29. Jung, *Archetypes*, 212.

30. Ibid., 22.

31. Herbert Marcuse, *Eros and Civilization: A Philosophical Inquiry into Freud* (Boston: Beacon Press, 1955), 168.

32. Ibid.

33. Gaetano Mosca, *The Ruling Class*, trans. Hannah D. Kahn (New York: McGraw-Hill, 1939), 163.

34. For more on swarm theory, see Peter Miller, "Swarm Theory: Ants, Bees and Birds Teach Us How to Cope with a Complex World," *National Geographic* (July 2007): 146.

35. Herbert Marcuse, *Aesthetic Dimension*, 28–29.

36. A recent example is American Sociological Association president Erik Olin Wright's refusal in 2011 to approve a panel on autonomous social movements because he considered them not to be "working class."

37. Marcuse, *Essay on Liberation*, 79.

38. Marcuse, *Aesthetic Dimension*, 28–29.

39. Herbert Marcuse, *Counterrevolution and Revolt* (Boston: Beacon Press, 1972), 103–104 (emphases in original).

40. Ibid., 107.

41. Marcuse, *Aesthetic Dimension*, 35.

42. See George Katsiaficas, "Comparing the Paris Commune and the Gwangju Uprising," *New Political Science* 25, no. 2 (June 2003): 261–270, doi:10.1080/07393140307195.

3

# From Marcuse's "Political Eros" to the Eros Effect

## A Current Statement

GEORGE KATSIAFICAS

Some of my earlier work attempted to juxtapose my understanding of the eros effect with such ideas as contagion theory, convergence theory, and emergent norm theory.[1] Those theories, I argued, often relied upon a reductive understanding of group psychology and collective behavior, approaching spontaneous mass uprisings as emotionally irrational or as mechanistic and unreflective. I understand that social movement theory, which is now a cross-disciplinary endeavor spanning such fields as sociology, political science, urban studies, geography, communication, anthropology, and others, has made great strides in its understanding of collective resistance. But my work began as, and is still motivated by, an alternative understanding of spontaneous resistance, one that maintains and even foregrounds the uniquely human attributes that are concomitant with political rebellion. I argue, in brief, that spontaneous rebellion is not pathological, irrational, emotionally immature, or deterministic. Instead, I believed early on in my career, and still believe today, perhaps even more so given the uptick of mass rebellions across the world, that collectively and spontaneously confronting and challenging oppressive conditions is a conscious expression of humanity's innate desire for freedom. By freedom, I mean the dialectical unity of

This chapter has been adapted from a paper presented at the 2013 Conference of the International Herbert Marcuse Society, Lexington, Kentucky.

what are generally regarded as opposites—autonomous individual existence and collective solidarity. And it is this instinctual need for freedom that is activated during moments of the eros effect.

I comprehend mass uprisings as the collective embodiment of what Herbert Marcuse called "political eros."[2] Like autonomy, which Western philosophy generally treats in individualistic terms, our bodies' libidinal drives also exist in communal forms. In moments when millions of people establish erotic-political connections to each other, affirming solidarity and peace in contrast to dominant values such as chauvinism and competition, communal emotions change human beings in profound and long-lasting ways.

As elaborated by Freud in his late theories of the instincts, Marcuse embraced a concept of human nature driven by both eros and thanatos. By synthesizing Freud's individualistic theories with those of Karl Marx, Marcuse provided an understanding of how "material" reality includes not only "objective" economic factors but also contains a dimension of subjective forces including the unconscious. Marcuse's analysis of instinctual drives led him to develop the notion of eros as an ally in the revolutionary process.[3]

Marcuse's Freudian roots often serve to give the impression that eros is simply individual, as when he wrote: "A radical character structure is defined, on a Freudian basis, as a preponderance in the individual of life instincts over the death instinct, a preponderance of erotic energy over destructive drives."[4] For Marcuse, eros remains largely individualized.[5] But I wondered, can eros, like autonomy, be reconceptualized as a collective phenomenon?

Moments of the eros effect point in the direction of free and reasonable collective subjectivity. When the New Left movement reached its high point, Marcuse glimpsed collective eros:

> What the force of Eros is powerful enough to do is the following. It serves to move a non-conformist group, together with other groups of non-silent citizens, to a protest very different from traditional forms of radical protest. The appearance in this protest of new language, new behavior, new goals, testifies to the psychosomatic roots thereof. What we have is a politicization of erotic energy. This, I suggest, is the distinguishing mark of radical movements today [1979]. These movements do not represent class struggle in the traditional sense. They do not constitute a struggle to replace one power structure with another. Rather, these radical movements are existential revolts against an obsolete reality principle. They are a revolt carried out by the mind and

> body of individuals themselves. A revolt which is intellectual
> as well as instinctual. A revolt in which the whole organism,
> the very soul of the human being, becomes political. A revolt
> of the life instincts against organized and socialized destruction.[6]

Like so many people, Marcuse was deeply affected by the 1960s global upsurge, so much so that in a new preface to *Eros and Civilization* he understood that "[t]oday the fight for life, the fight for Eros, is the political fight."[7] By eros, Marcuse meant more than its common understanding as sex:

> In contrast to sexuality, the "localized" manifestation of Eros,
> which is essentially "asocial" and even anti-social, Eros involves
> "socialization," the sublimation and extension of the instinctual
> aim not only to one other but to the others and to the common
> universe . . . the instinct seeks satisfaction in more than sexual
> relationships and objects: in cooperation, love, friendship; in the
> pursuit of knowledge, in the creation of a pleasurable environ-
> ment, in . . . the beautiful and the good—transformation of the
> sensuous into the aesthetic.[8]

Compared with the era of repressed Victorian sexuality, contemporary forms of sexuality, including the emergence of feminism and LGBT activism, may appear to be liberated, but their appropriation within militarized nation-states distorts their full expression. Feminism is interpreted to mean women in combat and corporate boardrooms rather than the abolition of war and hierarchy; and same-sex marriage, while challenging heteronormativity, gestures toward homonormativity. In a society based upon profit and power, eros is repressively desublimated. As Marcuse understood: "what is happening to Eros, to the life instinct, in this new society which has succeeded in opening up the instinctual sphere of humans and administering even their instinctual needs and satisfactions, is a repressive liberation of Eros."[9]

Marcuse noted that the liberation of eros from its reification as sex sets a course of confrontation with society: "Evidently, in the transformation of sexuality into Eros, a change in the original aim and object takes place, a primary non-repressive, liberating sublimation. Far from destroying civilization, it strives to destroy the destructive basis of civilization. Thus it is sooner or later bound to clash with the established 'reality principle.' "[10] Pointing to the future when eros would be freed from the one-dimensional shackles of sex, Marcuse anticipated that "[a]uthentic, non-repressive desublimation would be the liberation of erotic, and not only sexual, energy . . . in the ascendency of truly liberated energy we would notice a de-socialization from a repressive society. An authentic desublimation would mean that the instinctual need for privacy, for quiet, for tenderness, for solidarity, for peace, indeed gain ascendancy over and above destructive and competitive instincts."[11]

Marcuse envisioned a long process of modification of the instincts as a necessary part of creating a free society. He understood the transformation of eros as part of the long-term cultural revolution, a process he believed required conscious direction: "the self-transformation of sexuality into Eros, which would characterize human relationships in a free society is certainly not a 'natural' process."[12] The outcome of this revolutionary transformation "would, for the first time, put the self-determination of man [sic] in all spheres and dimensions of his [sic] life, and not only at work, on the agenda."[13] In contrast to theories of revolution that propose delaying cultural transformation until after seizure of state power, Marcuse spoke clearly that the kind of changes needed were "not merely a question of changing the institutions but rather, and this is more important, of totally changing human beings in their attitudes, their instincts, their goals, and their values."[14]

For centuries, humankind has sought to elevate the species. Buddha and Jesus, for instance, both crystallized peaceful methods to control aggression. While they failed to produce long-lasting eradication of chauvinist behavior from "true" believers, they nonetheless pointed humanity in promising directions. For Marx, labor was the key variable for the historical transformation of the human species into a "species-being." More recently, Habermas includes communication as a dimension of the prolonged process of the self-formation of the human species. In my view, revolution—moments of rapid change when history accomplishes in days what normally takes decades—should be positioned as a central dimension of species transformation.[15]

Revolutionary insurgencies are significant moments for the transformation of instincts through a galvanization of species-consciousness. During episodes of the eros effect, communities emerge that negate everyday norms and values. Within the movement, others are seen not as competitors but as an organic part of the individual's well-being. Lifelong friendships form, and new values emerge that contradict commodity culture and go on to affect future generations. Most significantly, the unconscious is transformed, for as Marcuse understood, the socialization of eros "modifies the instinct and the mode of its satisfaction."[16] On the surface, the "conversation is changed" (as with the concepts of the 1 percent and the 99 percent after

Occupy Wall Street, for instance), but the transformation is much deeper—reaching into people's aspirations for their lives, their need for justice, and their dreams for their future.

Our erotic passions for freedom and justice are sublimated through political movements that unite us. These passions grow from the tender feeling for ourselves and the extension of that kindness to others. The life forces within us bring us together and make us stronger. To the extent that we are fond of others when they grow more and more different, we grow freer.[17] This phenomenon is visceral. As Jason Del Gandio observes, in such moments, "Our bodies can *feel* the collective urge toward social change. . . . All the senses are stimulated; alternative patterns of thinking occur; fears and self-doubts are lessened; and risk and courage are accentuated."[18]

The concept of the eros effect is most indebted to Marcuse's thinking about "political eros" in *The Aesthetic Dimension,* where he celebrated "the quality of Beauty in its perhaps most sublimated form: as political Eros."[19] My work with the eros effect seeks to operationalize political eros by uncovering its emergence in history. Understanding eros as an ally in the prolonged transformation of human needs and instincts provides not only critical insight into the cultural revolution, but it also identifies a new tactic in the strategic quest to transform the world system. Not simply a general strike, an armed insurrection, or a massive mobilization, the eros effect can be all these and more. It is not an act of mind, and it cannot be willed by a "conscious element" (or revolutionary party). Rather, it involves popular movements emerging in their own right as ordinary people take history into their hands. The concept of the eros effect is a means of rescuing the revolutionary value of spontaneity, a way to stimulate a reevaluation of the unconscious as an ally of social transformation.

## DEVELOPING THE EROS EFFECT

As I wrote my conclusions from years of research on global movements of 1968, I uncovered the eros effect after a eureka moment. While I attempted to discern a pattern in the emergence of insurgencies around the world, the synchronicity of international uprisings leapt out of my data. All at once, I grasped how insurgencies around the world were specifically tied to eruptions in distant places. In May 1968, for example, when a student revolt led to a general strike of nine million workers in France, there were significant demonstrations of solidarity in Mexico City, Berlin, Tokyo, Buenos

Aires, Berkeley, and Belgrade. Students and workers in both Spain and Uruguay attempted general strikes of their own. In Beijing, half a million Red Guards marched in solidarity with the French strikers. Massive student strikes in Italy forced Prime Minister Aldo Moro and his cabinet to resign. Germany experienced its worst political crisis since World War II. And a student strike at the University of Dakar, Senegal, led to a general strike of workers.[20] These movements were clearly tied more to each other than to each nation's political or economic conditions (which I will say more about later).

As I sought to understand the global movement of 1968, I could not find a theory to satisfactorily explain the global simultaneity of uprisings and their connections to each other. The heroic resistance of the Vietnamese people was, of course, the primary source of the global movement's inspiration, but a multitude of other focal points of resistance built upon each other in very specific ways—from the American Civil Rights Movement and the emergence of the Black Panther Party, to Uruguay's Tupamaros, Che's selfless dedication, the movements among Native Americans, Chicanos, and Australian aborigines, and the emergence of women's and gay liberation. More than the sum of these separate strands, the global movement synthesized a new form of life—a planetary consciousness-in-action, a global culture of resistance. Our ties to each other were based on love and solidarity, an intuitive sense that we were all in the struggle together and that what is needed is a global change of civilization.

Since World War II, humanity's increasing awareness of our own power and strategic capacities has become manifest in sudden and simultaneous contestation of power by hundreds of thousands of people. During moments of the eros effect, universal interests become generalized at the same time as dominant values of society (national chauvinism, hierarchy, and domination) are negated. As Marcuse so clearly formulated it, humans have an instinctual need for freedom—something that we grasp intuitively, and it is this instinctual need that is sublimated into a collective phenomenon during moments of the eros effect.[21] Dimensions of the eros effect include: the sudden and synchronous emergence of hundreds of thousands of people occupying public space; the simultaneous appearance of revolts in many places; the identification of hundreds of thousands of people with each other; their common belief in new values; and the suspension of normal daily routines like competitive business practices, criminal behavior, and acquisitiveness. People's intuition and self-organization—not the dictates of any party—are key to the emergence of such moments. Actualized in the actions of millions of people in 1968, the eros effect  continues to characterize global insurgencies, and to have enormous future potential.

Transformation of people's intuition, values, and unconscious may well be the most significant reason why the New Left was "world-historical." After the upsurge of 1968, the women's movement was nationally prominent in the campaign for abortion and the Equal Rights Amendment, and the gay movement blossomed globally; apartheid became globally isolated; direct US military intervention in Central America became out of the question; a global disarmament movement emerged; a series of protracted strikes and intense labor struggles occurred; massive movements against nuclear power stopped new plants in the United States and Germany; and hundreds of ongoing worker-controlled collectives and alternative institutions were established.

## CAPITALISM'S COLONIZATION OF THE UNCONSCIOUS

At the same time that global revolutionary aspirations emerged since 1968, the system has made significant adjustments. As early as 1973, John D. Rockefeller, in *The Second American Revolution: Some Personal Observations*, foreshadowed the massive cutbacks in government spending and the enormous profits for financial capital that we know today as neoliberalism.[22]

Neoliberalism penetrates realms of our everyday lives previously closed off to capitalist market relationships at the same moment as it incorporates peripheral capitalist areas into the orbit of global corporations. Whether American, Japanese, Chinese, or European flags are flown, neoliberalism's relentless assault on the integrity of our world simultaneously demands that we work longer weeks for more years with less pay and fewer benefits. For billions of us, compulsion to work means that "life becomes earning a living rather than living, a means which is an end in itself."[23]

Giant global corporations accumulate ever-greater wealth and the whole world is subjected to the irrational demands of a system based upon expanding profit. Even our unconscious is not immune to neoliberalism's contagion. Our free time and privacy is invaded by the neoliberal state, and our everyday lives are increasingly colonized by global capital through imposition of market relationships. As Marcuse understood: "Achievement of modern industrial society is the social conquest of the total existence of man, including his instinctual sphere, including his unconscious. . . . Can we really still speak of an unconscious (in the sense in which Freud used the term) when this unconscious has become so easily subject to social management—through the techniques of publicity, industrial psychology, or the science of human relations?"[24]

Repressive desublimation of libido today is necessary not only as a market enhancement but as political control:

> This society . . . must mobilize our aggressive instincts to an exorbitant degree to counteract the frustration imposed by the daily struggle for existence. The little man who works eight hours a day in the factory, who does inhuman and putrefying work, on the weekend sits behind a machine much more powerful than himself, and there he can utilize all his antisocial aggressiveness. And this is absolutely necessary. If this aggressiveness were not sublimated in the speed and power of the automobile, it might be directed against the dominant power.[25]

Several factors in the twenty-first century indicate the increasing importance of unconscious dynamics in social behavior. The rise of mass society—especially the mass media and, more recently, social media—condition the shrinkage of the individual ego and a concomitant expansion of the social superego in people's personality structure. With reduced control of the individual ego over the instinctual substructure of behavior, deep-seated emotional responses to an increasingly invasive social order are ever-more significant determinations of group dynamics. Facebook's enormous global popularity is an indication of individual privacy's devaluation, of the ego's voluntary subservience to society. People today voluntarily and enthusiastically reveal their private affairs in public space, creating "friends" who are often unknown to each other. As Harry Halpin explains, "With Facebook, users freely surrender their most personal of data to marketers in return for ease of communication with their friends. Yet Facebook is only the most visible point of a phenomenon much larger in scale that encompasses nearly every click on the Web."[26]

The system's continual success in accumulating greater profits destroys even its greatest achievements. The autonomous individual is destroyed by mass consumerism and government surveillance; by "democracy" increasingly becoming oligarchic; and by education—a potential resource for emancipation—being turned into production of a workforce suited to corporate capitalism.

This last point is most troublesome given education's perpetuation of social norms and structures. After World War II, the university-military relationship expanded greatly, placing universities at the center of the global capitalist system. As the numbers of students, faculty, and university employees multiplied many times over, the universities changed from a peripheral place where elite rulers of the system were indoctrinated to a training grounds for the organizational men and women needed to manage the expanded reproduction of capital, a process continually enlarged through new conquests of workers, markets, and resources.

Universities have been tailored to production of a workforce subservient to the needs of global capital, prominently including academics focused on social science and philosophy. Psychologists are recruited to help torture people identified as enemies. A gigantic "social movement industry" has been created, employing tens of thousands of researchers and writers around the world, with a mission to provide the control center with collective intelligence aimed at suppressing insurgencies. The Pentagon's "terrorism studies" includes a new Minerva Research Institute through which it has employed universities (including Cornell, University of Maryland, and University of Washington) to study dissident populations in order to neutralize them. Of particular interest is their attempt to ascertain when "contagions" reach a "critical mass" and pose a threat to power.[27]

The eros effect, arising as it does from the unconscious, cannot be scientifically verified or completely determined in advance. I agree that there is a level of predictability to the unconscious, as indicated by the operations of advertising, mass marketing, and public relations. Advertisers can predict, with some accuracy, for instance, how consumers might respond. However, such an operation is an inexact science because the unconscious can never be fully mapped out. The unconscious is always open to permutation, variation, deviation, and the unexpected. So difficult is it to accurately predict the emergence of the eros effect that in 1984, five years before the outbreak of uprisings in Eastern Europe, conservative political scientist Samuel Huntington incorrectly surmised, "The likelihood of democratic development in Eastern Europe is virtually nil." He then continued, arguing that, "with a few exceptions, the limits of democratic development in the world may well have been reached."[28] He was not alone in his mistaken assessment. In a multivolume study of democratization published in 1989—just before the collapse of Soviet regimes—Juan Linz, Seymour Martin Lipset, and Larry Diamond (leading thinkers of mainstream "democratization theory") did not include a single communist country because "there is little prospect among them of a transition to democracy."[29] These predictive failures point to the capricious nature of the unconscious and help explain why it is a primary aid in spontaneous, liberatory activity—we can never know for sure when an uprising will erupt, making it difficult for institutions of power to predict and control mass awakenings and actions.

## EXPLAINING UPRISINGS: ARE SOCIAL AND ECONOMIC FACTORS ENOUGH?

For decades, social scientists have sought to locate specific variables and relationships that could predict the occurrence of social insurgencies, an elusive goal that continues to plague researchers. As early as 1937, Pitirim Sorokin analyzed thousands of cases of "social disturbances" in the quest for a universal formula. Much to his surprise, Sorokin found "that war, internal disturbances, and economic fluctuations all move fairly independently of one another and that the causes of war and revolutions are not mainly economic."[30]

Following in the footsteps of Sorokin's empirical work, subsequent research correlated declining status and falling economic position with right-wing movements. The classic example is the rise of Nazism from Germany's economic crisis after World War I. Although it is often assumed that progressive movements emerge as a result of economic crises, as exemplified by the rise of US Communism in the 1930s, this is not necessarily the case. Rather, the insight that periods of prolonged economic hardship and falling status produce right-wing social movements seems valid in many different times and places. For example, the US Communist Party is better linked to worldwide reaction in the forms of Stalin, Hitler, and Roosevelt, all of whom embraced statist economic centralization, militarization, and fervent patriotism. Liberatory revolutionary upheavals instead appear to be generated when ascendant prosperity and rising expectations are followed by a sharp drop-off in economic growth. This insight was initially formulated by James Davies, whose "J-curve" was drawn after investigations of the Egyptian revolution of 1952 and Russian revolutions at the beginning of the twentieth century.[31]

Despite these findings, no mid-range theory appears to remain universally valid.[32] For instance, data related to late-twentieth-century progressive Asian uprisings, which I collected for my two-volume set, *Asia's Unknown Uprisings*, does not validate Davies' J-curve hypothesis.[33] Economic development was robust in South Korea before the victorious 1987 June Uprising, when the economy steadily expanded, reaching a healthy 12.4 percent growth in 1986. Likewise, Thailand's economic output increased an average of 10 percent in the two years prior to its victorious uprising in May 1992. However, no similar economic conditions can be discerned in the years before other Asian uprisings. In Indonesia, the Philippines, and China, economic crises—especially inflation—caused great fears among people and contributed to the unrest. In the Philippines and Indonesia, *negative* GDP growth was experienced prior to the uprisings, reaching minus 13.1 percent during the 1997 IMF crisis in Indonesia. Prior to the overthrow of Suharto, more than twenty million citizens saw their standards of living plunge below the poverty line. In the Philippines under Marcos, the economy stagnated for years before the 1986 uprising that sent him into exile.

If economic crises lead to uprisings, we should have seen major mobilizations throughout the region during the IMF crisis of 1997 when global investors led by George Soros pillaged Thailand and Korea. Yet Korea's general strike against neoliberalism began in December 1996, well before the crisis first broke out in Thailand in July 1997. After a decade of robust expansion, Korea's economy lay in ruins in 1998, quieting the working class in the name of national salvation. In Thailand, after more than one million people fell through the poverty line by 1998, the people's response was to save themselves rather than go into the streets to protest.

Table 3.1. Inflation and GDP Growth Rate before Asian Uprisings

| Country (Uprising) | Years | Inflation | GDP Growth Rate | Years |
|---|---|---|---|---|
| Nepal (1990) | 1980–1990 | 9.1% | 7.2%, 4.2% | 1988, 1989 |
| Bangladesh (1990) | 1980–1990 | 9.6% | 2.9%, 2–5% | 1988, 1989 |
| Philippines (1986) | 1980–1986 | 18.2% | –7.3%, –7.3% | 1984, 1985 |
| Indonesia (1998) | 1998, 1999 | 58.5%, 20.5% | 4.7%, –13.1% | 1997, 1998 |
| Thailand (1992) | 1980–1992 | 4.2% | 11.6%, 7.9% | 1990, 1991 |
| South Korea (1987) | 1980–1987 | 5% | 6.9%, 12.4% | 1985, 1986 |
| Taiwan (1990) | 1980–1987 | 1.3% | 4.9%, 11.6% | 1985, 1986 |
| China (1989) | 1988, 1989 | 18.8%, 18.0% | 11.3%, 4.1% | 1988, 1989 |

*Sources*: Junhan Lee, "Primary Causes of Asian Development: Dispelling Conventional Myths," *Asian Survey* 42, no. 2 (November/December 2002): 825; *China Statistical Yearbook*, 2002, as cited in China Institute for Reform and Development, *Thirty Years of China's Reforms: Through Chinese and International Scholars' Eyes* (Beijing: Foreign Languages Press, 2008), 81.

"Democratization theorists" have identified an array of variables posited to be significant indicators of the possibility for lasting democracy. In 1959, Seymour Martin Lipset wrote a seminal article in which he hypothesized that a middle-class threshold for democracy needed to exist before democratization could be long-lasting.[34] Lipset hypothesized a correlation between economic development and democracy, asserting that once societies reach a wealth threshold, their chances of being democratic are significantly higher than those of poorer societies. Various theorists subsequently operationalized Lipset's theory with specific quantitative predictions correlating wealth to the survival rate of democratic systems of governance. Although Lipset's hypothesis was widely accepted, it does not appear to be valid for the Asian uprisings of the late twentieth century. Data reveal a wide variation in levels of economic prosperity, and even in impoverished Nepal, lasting democratization was forged. Uprisings' success does not appear to be a function of the creation of a large middle class or of GNP per capita.

Both of Nepal's successful uprisings occurred despite a low level of economic prosperity. After overthrowing the absolute monarchy in 1990, the country's first act after the 2006 uprising was to abolish the monarchy altogether. While it may still be too early to determine if democracy will continue, this data indicates that the correlation between levels of economic development and uprisings is not significant in Asia at the end of the twentieth century. Uprisings are apparently not primarily moments in the movement of capital, as economic determinists maintain.

Table 3.2. GNP per Capita at the Time of Uprisings

| Country | Year | GNP/capita |
| --- | --- | --- |
| Nepal | 1990 | $170 |
| Bangladesh | 1990 | $210 |
| Nepal | 2006 | $268 |
| China | 1987 | $290 |
| Philippines | 1986 | $560 |
| Indonesia | 1998 | $636 |
| Thailand | 1992 | $1,840 |
| South Korea | 1987 | $2,690 |
| Taiwan | 1987 | $5,325 |

*Sources*: Lee, "Primary Causes of Asian Development," 823; Roger V. Des Forges, Ning Luo, Yen-bo Wu, eds., *Chinese Democracy and the Crisis of 1989: Chinese and American Reflections* (Albany: State University of New York Press, 1992), 224.

Mainstream social science has failed to produce robust correlations that might help the control center to prevent uprisings and revolutions. Samuel Huntington's observation that urbanization is a prerequisite for democratization led him to recommend "forced-draft urbanization," a notorious policy that resulted in free-fire zones and rural saturation bombing of Vietnam as a means of forcing peasants into cities.[35] The United States dropped more bombs on Vietnam to "create the preconditions for democracy" than had been used everywhere during World War II, yet Vietnamese nationalism prevailed.

Some theorists also believe that the West's leadership of the world into the industrial (and "postindustrial") epoch indicates a superior form of social development. The West, it is said, has brought "democracy" back to life, based upon the autonomous individual and open civil society.[36] In Asia, the penetration of such "superior" national cultures has led to the slaughter of millions of people in the Philippines, Korea, Indonesia, Vietnam, and elsewhere. Colonialism's effects on social movements do not appear to be a significant factor in the Asian wave, since former colonies, whether Dutch (Indonesia, Taiwan) or places previously ruled by the United States (the Philippines), Japan (Taiwan, Korea), and Britain (Nepal, Bangladesh, Burma), all experienced strong democratization uprisings—as did Thailand, a nation that escaped colonial domination. The failure of former French colonies (Vietnam, Cambodia, and Laos) to be part of this wave of democratization movements may be more a factor of intensive US bombing during the Indochina War (which decimated their societies and economies) than of their previous colonization by France. Even here, a counterexample can be found in South Korea, where people rose for democracy and overthrew the Syngman Rhee dictatorship only seven years after their country had been devastated by US air power during the Korean War (1950–1953).

This brief review of possible explanations for the occurrence of uprisings reveals no single satisfactory dimension to which we can point. Rather than locating the primary cause of uprisings in domestic economic and political variables, the relationship of one revolt to another seems most significant. The eros effect—people's ties to each other—is the most important variable in the Asian wave from 1986 to 1992, for instance, as was also the case in 1968 and more recent waves. This is further supported by the interviews I conducted with key activists of the Asian uprisings. In just about every case, activists indicated that great inspiration and energy crossed borders and taught lessons.[37] If the Asian movements had erupted within months of each other rather than years apart, as during the 2011 Arab Spring, no doubt more recognition would have been given to their "meaningful coincidence."

## THE FUTURE OF THE EROS EFFECT

Measured in discrete units of time, direct insurgencies may fail. Leaders may either be killed or imprisoned, casualities can occur, and groups that openly express themselves may again become dormant and silent. However, uprisings' open expression of grievances and visions, even when bounded in time, undermine the existing system's stranglehold on defining political reality. After popular insurgencies, existing parties begin to lose the type of approvals they had earlier. Huge political gaps develop that the parties have either to deal with by making genuine changes or risk becoming irrelevant. Sometimes the impact of particular uprisings, however brief their eruption, goes on for decades. The ultimate destruction of previously legitimate political parties and outmoded norms of everyday life may take place slowly, but the impact of insurgencies persists.

Conscious and unconscious forces today are more rapidly shifting than ever before in world history. Noting with care specific social strata that mobilize during crises may be a better means of comprehending the future of political dynamics than one hundred telephone opinion polls conducted in quieter moments. Individuals who seem to be agreeing with the course of politics-as-usual often have other streams of thought in the back of their minds. The tremendous power of the mass media notwithstanding, uncontrolled intuitions and insights remain operative even when they are not overtly expressed.

Uprisings cluster in an eros effect of concatenation and mutual rein-forcement. During the Arab Spring of 2011, this phenomenon was readily visible. Aided by Facebook, YouTube, and text-messaging, people's intuition motivated them to join uprisings. Intuitive reworking of directly democratic forms of governance, increasingly sophisticated in the face-to-face meetings of Occupy Wall Street, demonstrated an advanced level of consciousness in action, of movements building upon the legacy of their precursors. Moments of the eros effect reveal the prominent contours of the global movements' unfolding *collective wisdom*. The system's intelligence may be rational but it is not *reasonable*—unlike our collective wisdom that capitalism is destroying the planet, that the world system systematically produces wars, that patriarchal hierarchy is one of many authoritarian dimensions of culture that must be transformed.

For more than fifty years now, global movements have emerged in largely spontaneous, internationally synchronized eruptions. Since the global eruption of 1968, at least five great waves of globally synchronized uprisings have transformed world economics and politics:

1. The disarmament movement of the early 1980s that helped to end the Cold War and reduce the threat of nuclear holocaust

2. The wave of Asian uprisings from 1986 to 1992 that overthrew eight dictatorships in nine places

3. Revolts against Soviet dictatorships in Eastern Europe (partly catalyzed by the Asian wave) that emerged victorious from 1989

4. The alterglobalization summit confrontations from Seattle, 1999, to the antiwar mobilizations of February 15, 2003, that galvanized synchronous international protests and revealed the global depth of people's rejection of corporate capitalism and militarized nation-states

5. The Arab Spring, Spain's *indignados*, and the Occupy Movement of 2011 that spread anticapitalist ideas and deepened people's democratic impulses and capacities

As Marcuse never tired of saying, the revolutionary subject emerges concretely in history, and I believe that these waves are historical contours of the developing subjective factors in the contemporary world. Wherever we look today, from Taksim to Tahrir Squares, from *indignados* to Occupy, from Ferguson to Baltimore, people seize public space where they can speak freely, challenge their governments' policies, and build forms of organization based upon direct democracy. This global grammar of insurgency includes rejection of control by political parties in favor of autonomous modes of decision-making. These three qualities—autonomy, international solidarity, and direct democracy—globally tie together movements that appear to be vastly different on the surface. This grammar of insurgency reaches beneath and above insurgencies' specific demands, aims, and ideologies.

Although generally regarded as a theorist, Marcuse articulated a dialectical relation of spontaneity and consciousness:

But spontaneity is not enough. It is also necessary to have an organization. But a new, very flexible kind of organization, one that does not impose rigorous principles, one that allows for movement and initiative. An organization without the "bosses" of the old parties or political groups. This point is very important. The leaders of today are the products of publicity. In the actual movement there are no leaders as there were in the Bolshevik Revolution, for example.[38]

Rather than a centralized party, he advocated for locally based planning. At the same time, Huey P. Newton named the Black Panther Party's goal "revolutionary intercommunalism" and Murray Bookchin advocated "municipal libertarianism." Anticipating the system's gradual disintegration, Marcuse believed, "We will see that what we have to envisage is some kind of diffuse and dispersed disintegration of the system, in which interest, emphasis and activity are shifted to local and regional areas."[39] Douglas Kellner reminds us that Marcuse steadfastly remained committed to a break with capitalism and named himself a "socialist" his entire adult life—ever since he was part of the soldiers' councils at the end of World War I. By socialism, Marcuse meant a society that included "the planned utilization of resources for the satisfaction of vital needs with a minimum of toil, the transformation of leisure into free time, the pacification of the struggle for existence."[40] Later, Marcuse clarified: "I still believe the alternative is *socialism*. But socialism neither of the Stalinist brand nor of the post-Stalinist brand, but that *libertarian* socialism which has always been an integral concept of socialism, but is only too easily repressed and suppressed."[41]

Economic, cultural, ethnic, and national differences, while appearing to constitute tremendous differences between various social movements, are obscured by the essential similarities of movements all over the world today. The forging of a global culture of resistance to corporate capitalism since 1968 is nothing less than a world-historical force that is elevating humanity from nationalities and races into a species-being that recognizes all humans as part of Nature. Whatever the culture, religion, or national identity today, people recognize that their ties to each other in insurgent movements are far more important than their ties to the rulers of their societies. More than at any other time in modern history, people reject the world capitalist system and seek to replace it with directly democratic forms of self-government that respect all human life and protect the planet from predatory corporations.

The history of modern revolutions reveals that the world system cannot be transformed unless its strongest links are broken. Previous revolutions have only streamlined and strengthened capitalism, not transformed it. From all previous revolutions, capital has drawn strength and expanded its domain. Even as the system destroys many of its own accomplishments, its collapse is not the same as its transformation. Freedom worthy of the name requires subversion of politics as we know it—and not simply reforms in existing militarized nation-states or the collapse of giant corporations, but rather, an individual-and-collective transformation of human subjectivity itself. In my view, if there were a "grand narrative" of such a revolution, it would be based upon eros. Eros is historically shaped but eternally emergent.

Love binds us together, gives us the courage to make history, to stare down our fears, and to act decisively. Love makes our blood sparkle with courage, makes us willing to take risks and gives us the nerve to be resolute. Love gives us senses more powerful than touching, smelling, tasting, seeing, and hearing. Unlike the cute and flighty eros of ancient times, our erotic impulses are at the center of everything humans have produced, and thus an essential aid in the fight for a better world.

## NOTES

1. George Katsiaficas, "The Eros Effect," personal website, 1989, http://www.eroseffect.com/articles/eroseffectpaper.PDF.

2. Herbert Marcuse, *The Aesthetic Dimension: Toward a Critique of Marxist Aesthetics* (Boston: Beacon Press, 1972), 64.

3. See, for instance: Herbert Marcuse, *Counterrevolution and Revolt* (Boston: Beacon Press, 1972). Marcuse's view is unlike that of his younger colleague Jürgen Habermas, who views the unconscious as inner foreign territory. See Jürgen Habermas, "On Systematically Distorted Communication," *Inquiry: An Interdisciplinary Journal of Philosophy* 13, no. 1–4 (1970): 205–218 (207), doi: 10.1080/00201747008601590.

4. Herbert Marcuse, "Ecology and the Critique of Modern Society," in *Philosophy, Psychoanalysis and Emancipation: Collected Papers of Herbert Marcuse, Vol. 5*, ed. Douglas Kellner and Clayton Pierce (New York: Routledge, 2011), 206–221 (209).

5. For more on this, see: Herbert Marcuse, *Art and Liberation: Collected Papers of Herbert Marcuse, Vol. 4*, ed. Douglas Kellner (New York: Routledge, 2007), 199 and 221.

6. Marcuse, "Ecology and the Critique of Modern Society," in *Philosophy, Psychoanalysis and Emancipation*, 212.

7. Herbert Marcuse, "Political Preface," in *Eros and Civilization: A Philosophical Inquiry into Freud* (Boston: Beacon Press, 1966), xxv.

8. Herbert Marcuse, "Cultural Revolution," in *Towards a Critical Theory of Society: Collected Papers of Herbert Marcuse, Vol. 2*, ed. Douglas Kellner (New York: Routledge, 2001), 121–162 (133). He clarified the distinction: "*Eros*, as distinguished from *Sexuality*: sexuality: a partial drive, libidinal energy confined and concentrated in the erotogenic zones of the body, mainly genital sexuality. Eros: libidinal energy, in the struggle with aggressive energy, striving for the intensification, gratification and unification of life and of the life environment; the Life Instincts versus the Death Instinct (Freud)." Herbert Marcuse, "Marxism and Feminism," in *The New Left and the 1960s: Collected Papers of Herbert Marcuse, Vol. 3*, ed. Douglas Kellner (New York: Routledge, 2005), 165–172 (165) (all emphases in original).

9. Herbert Marcuse, "The Containment of Social Change in Industrial Society," in *Towards a Critical Theory of Society*, 89. In this quote, the original

text uses "man" and "his"—historically influenced gender-exclusionary forms. I have substituted "humans" for "man" and correspondingly substituted "their" for "his."

10. Marcuse, "Cultural Revolution," in *Towards a Critical Theory of Society*, 133.

11. Marcuse, "The Containment of Social Change in Industrial Society," in *Towards a Critical Theory of Society*, 81–94 (90).

12. Marcuse, "Cultural Revolution," in *Towards a Critical Theory of Society*, 148.

13. Marcuse, "The Movement in a New Era of Repression" in *The New Left and the 1960s*, 142–153 (147).

14. Marcuse, "Marcuse Defines His New Left Line," in *The New Left and the 1960s*, 100–117 (101).

15. Merely extending the logic of labor to all realms through such concepts as "social labor" and the "social factory" fails to appreciate the difference between working and making revolution. The self-production of the species through labor does not encompass all dimensions of liberation. Indeed, Soviet Marxism, limited by its own ideology, sought to make the whole world into a factory. A more recent result of the extension of commodity culture and mechanics into all aspects of our lives is to regard humans as cyborgs.

16. Marcuse, "Cultural Revolution," in *Towards a Critical Theory of Society*, 133.

17. For discussion, see A. Bronson Feldman, *The Unconscious in History* (New York: Philosophical Library, 1959), 217.

18. Jason Del Gandio, "Extending the Eros Effect: Sentience, Reality, and Emanation," *New Political Science* 36, no. 2 (2014): 129–148 (139), doi: 10.1080/07393148.2014.883799 (emphasis in the original).

19. Marcuse, *The Aesthetic Dimension*, 64.

20. For more on these events, see: George Katsiaficas, *The Imagination of the New Left: A Global Analysis of 1968* (Boston: South End Press, 1987); and, George Katsiaficas, *The Subversion of Politics: European Autonomous Social Movements and the Decolonization of Everyday Life* (Oakland: AK Press, 2006).

21. For Marcuse's formulation of a "biological basis" for freedom, see: Herbert Marcuse, *An Essay on Liberation* (Boston: Beacon Press, 1969).

22. John D. Rockefeller, *The Second American Revolution: Some Personal Observations* (New York: Harper & Row, 1973).

23. Marcuse, "The Ideology of Death," in *Philosophy, Psychoanalysis and Emancipation*, 122–131 (129).

24. Marcuse, "The Containment of Social Change in Industrial Society," in *Towards a Critical Theory of Society*, 88.

25. Marcuse, "Marcuse Defines His New Left Line," in *The New Left and the 1960s*, 109.

26. Harry Halpin, "The Philosophy of Anonymous: Ontological Politics Without Identity," *Radical Philosophy* 176 (November–December 2012): 19–28 (20). I want to note, too, that my critique of mass media and social media that is presented here is limited. The powerful forces of socialization and control that

emanate from mass media and social media simultaneously produce new openness to synchronous social movements. It's a double-bind, at the very least.

27. Nafeez Ahmed, "Pentagon Preparing for Mass Civil Breakdown," *The Guardian*, June 12, 2014, http://www.theguardian.com/environment/earth-insight/2014/jun/12/pentagon-mass-civil-breakdown.

28. Samuel Huntington, "Will More Countries Become Democratic?," *Political Science Quarterly* 99, no. 2 (Summer 1984): 217–218. Even partisans of revolution like Lenin failed to anticipate coming massive uprisings: In January 1917, Lenin wrote, "We, the old ones, may never see the decisive battles of the coming revolution."

29. Edward Friedman, ed., *The Politics of Democratization: Generalizing East Asian Experiences* (Boulder: Westview Press, 1994), 33.

30. Pitirim Sorokin, *Social and Cultural Dynamics, Vol. III: Fluctuations of Social Relationships, War, and Revolution* (New York: American Book Company, 1937), 238.

31. James C. Davies, "Toward a Theory of Revolution," *American Sociological Review* 27, no. 1 (February 1962): 5–19.

32. By "mid-range," I mean nongrandiose theory, such as Marx's notion of class struggle.

33. George Katsiaficas, *Asia's Unknown Uprisings*, 2 vols. (Oakland: PM Press, 2012 and 2013). For the arguments presented here, see, specifically, vol. 2, chap. 15.

34. Seymour Martin Lipset, "Some Social Requisites of Democracy: Economic Development and Political Legitimacy," *American Political Science Review* 53, no. 1 (March 1959): 69–105.

35. Samuel Huntington, "The Bases of Accommodation," *Foreign Affairs* 46, no. 4 (July 1968): 642–656.

36. Huntington applied Max Weber's notion of a positive correlation between capitalism and the Protestant ethic to Asia through analysis asserting an inverse relationship between Confucian values and democratization. Although East Asia's economic rise has given such theorists pause, communal Confucian values continue to be understood as a "kernel of traditional culture that is unfavorable to democracy." See Liu Jianfei, "Chinese Democracy and Sino-U.S. Relations," Institute of International Strategic Studies, The Central Party School of the Chinese Communist Party, September 2007, 8. For Huntington, Confucian democracy was an oxymoron, a "contradiction in terms." See Samuel Huntington, *The Third Wave: Democratization in the Late Twentieth Century* (Norman: University of Oklahoma Press, 1991), 307. Following his lead, Euro-American theorists have understood a dearth of American-style "civil societies" as a reason for an absence of democracy.

37. See my list of interviews in *Asia's Unknown Uprisings, Vol. 1*, "Appendix," 421–423.

38. Marcuse, "Marcuse Defines His New Left Line," in *The New Left and the 1960s*, 102.

39. Marcuse, "On the New Left," in *The New Left and the 1960s*, 122–127 (124).

40. Douglas Kellner, "Introduction: Radical Politics, Marcuse, and the New Left," in *The New Left and the 1960s*, 1–37 (8); Marcuse, *One-Dimensional Man: Studies in the Ideology of the Advanced Industrial Society* (Boston: Beacon Press, 1991), 252–253.

41. Marcuse, "On the New Left," in *The New Left and the 1960s*, 122.

Section Two

# EXTENSIONS AND ELABORATIONS

4

# Eros in a One-Dimensional Society

## Katsiaficas, Marcuse, and Me

ARNOLD L. FARR

### ONE-DIMENSIONAL SLEEPWALKING AND THE
### EROTIC DRIVE TO WAKE UP

My entire adult life has been defined and motivated by a thirst for a fair, just, and democratic society. I hoped for the Beloved Community that Dr. Martin Luther King Jr. dreamed about. I hoped for a society where "freedom" was more than a meaningless word that anyone could easily drop when it suited one's needs. However, living with such a vision can be frustrating for many reasons. First, there is the problem of other people. Why can't people get over themselves and live in a community based on mutual respect and recognition? And second, there is the problem of my own social/political conditioning, which provides some insight into the first problem. I discovered that while I labored toward "social justice for all," I was to some extent sleepwalking, not fully awake, not cognizant of my own participation in systems of injustice and dehumanization. In other words, I was in the dark regarding my own one-dimensional thinking[1] and my acceptance of values that restrict the rights and freedom of other

---

This essay is dedicated to the memory of my beloved uncle, Mr. Donald E. Chisholm. My uncle passed away on September 30, 2014, as I was beginning my work on this essay. The first section of the essay includes a reflection on a conversation that I had with my uncle and one of my brothers several years ago, after I realized that I was guilty of tacitly supporting a system by which they were oppressed.

people. My particular form of one-dimensional thinking revealed itself as homophobia and heteronormativity.

A few years ago, I suddenly realized that I was benefiting from heterosexual privilege. Although I was personally accepting of people who identified as LGBTQ, I was not in complete solidarity with them. While I could easily take a stand against racism and economic injustice, for instance, standing up against homophobia was not so easy. Over a period of time, I had the opportunity to get to know more and more people of LGBTQ orientations. Even though I grew up with a gay uncle and a gay brother, I was completely blind to their needs as individuals. Locked in my own one-dimensional world, I was desensitized to their daily suffering. Two other brothers (who are heterosexual) and I used to take great pride in bringing new girlfriends home to meet our parents. These occasions were always exciting. I was in my early thirties before it occurred to me what these occasions must have been like for my gay brother. He would never have been allowed to bring home a boyfriend.

Homophobia is not limited to any particular region of the United States, but some regions are more extreme than others. It is also possible that the severity of homophobia may vary along race and class lines (something that this current essay does not allow me to fully explore). In brief, I was raised in a small, loving community in the South that involved not only strict but also oppressive and problematic views about sexuality. My community also revolved around a very conservative form of Christianity that undoubtedly contributed to homophobia. This conservative Christianity is complicated, however. On the one hand, it has been a source of unity and community for African Americans who were victims of racism and segregation. But on the other hand, it has been a source of exclusion and oppression for those of nonheterosexual and non-gender-conforming orientations. People would preach love, equality, and freedom, but only for members of a particular social group or sexual orientation. It was easy to reject race-based inequality. But oppressions related to gender and sexual identity were not only invisible, but often perpetuated and reinforced.

Heteronormativity was so dominant in my community that it was almost impossible to consider what life must have been like for my gay brother and gay uncle. Everyone had their "theories" about why people are gay or why they did not have to listen to gay people. Even those of us who were mature and sensitive enough to not intentionally marginalize gay people were complicit through our silence.

I eventually realized the oppressive nature of my silence and decided to talk with my brother and uncle. I conceptualize my sudden awareness as a form of "democratic attunement" wherein I was sensitized to the unjust treatment of my brother and uncle (and others). These two beautiful and wonderful people with so much to offer the world were being forced to live on the margins, unable to fully express themselves in ways that made them happy and fulfilled. My two heterosexual brothers and I were free to express our sexuality and love with whomever we chose. Our sexuality was to be celebrated while the sexuality of my uncle and gay brother was to be ignored and repressed.

In my uncle's case the repression was multilayered. He explained to me that when my brother and I were children, he knew that my brother was most likely gay. Knowing this, he had a desire to reach out to my brother and mentor him because he knew of the difficulties of being a Black gay man in the South. However, he repressed his desire to help my brother because he feared that he would be blamed for my brother's sexual orientation. Consequently, my uncle was unable to help my brother, and my brother did not receive the support that he needed and deserved.

I conversed with my brother and my uncle separately. Both were emotionally moved, shedding tears as they informed me that I was the only family member—and as I recall, the only member of our community—to come forth in such a way, affirming them and their sexuality. They were also moved when I offered to take my wife on a double date with them and their partners. My brother and I have talked about this conversation many times since then. He is always grateful that I stepped up to become an ally, and he continues to reference how much that conversation meant to him. My uncle passed away in September of 2014. However, in the summer of 2013, he mentioned that talk for the first time since it occurred almost twenty years earlier. It was clear from his comments that he thought about that talk often and was deeply moved by it. Prior to our talks, my brother and uncle both felt completely alone. This was no longer the case as a few other younger family members have also overcome the trappings of homophobia and heteronormativity. I should note, too, that I am also grateful for those initial conversations, and not only because I found the courage to broach the topic, but for their forgiveness and embrace. My life has been deepened and enriched ever since. After seeing how deeply my brother and uncle were affected by our conversation, I was even more convinced that I had taken the right position with respect to fighting against homophobia. My own commitment to social justice was strengthened.

Although the cause for gay rights has gained momentum in recent years, there is still great resistance in many parts of the country. My hometown is one of those places that haven't changed. There are only a few of my family members who share my position on gay rights. Most of them are still strongly homophobic and heteronormative. My parents love my gay brother as much as they love my other two brothers and me. But their religious convictions influence their rejection of his sexuality. My own vocal position on these issues, along with my children's gay rights activism, has helped to loosen my parents' convictions. But it is unlikely that they will make major identity changes this late in life while living in a one-dimensional, homophobic community. My father is also a minister and community leader, making it even more difficult for them to change their long-held traditional beliefs.

Despite my parents' shortcomings, I believe that my own transformation highlights the possibility of social change. How is it that individuals—or, in some cases, massive groups of people—can undergo social and political metamorphosis? How is it that people living within a one-dimensional society suddenly develop two-dimensional thought? How can people from different social groups learn to empathize and act in solidarity with one another? In the following pages, I draw on Herbert Marcuse and George Katsiaficas, as well as on my own concept of democratic attunement, to better understand these transformations and solidarities. While Katsiaficas' notion of the eros effect emphasizes the development of new sensibilities within the context of global movements, my concept of democratic attunement highlights how this happens at the individual level. Toward the end of the chapter, I return to my own narrative of transformation to help demonstrate the validity of these theories.

## MARCUSE, KATSIAFICAS, AND THE POSSIBILITY
## OF EMANCIPATORY SOCIAL CHANGE

The work of Herbert Marcuse seems to entail two themes that are seemingly contradictory. The first is that in advanced industrial societies there is a great tendency toward one-dimensional thinking. In these societies, certain mechanisms are in place that prevent the development of critical consciousness and emancipatory action. However, that same society also creates the possibility for resistance. Following Sigmund Freud, Marcuse believed that eros was a creative impulse and life principle that could never be fully repressed because it is a natural drive that, by its very nature, seeks fulfillment. Even repressed drives find fulfillment through sublimation (i.e., modes of fulfillment that are deemed acceptable by the wider society). Freud himself argued that the repression of a drive is never completed once and for all.[2] The act of repression must therefore be continuously repeated because drives do not simply go away. Eros, as a creative life impulse, seeks to assert itself against this repression and domination. At one level, Marcuse's theory examines the obstacles to social change. At another level, Marcuse seeks to disclose the hidden possibilities for social change. This apparent inconsistency is actually a form of dialectical or *two*-dimensional thinking that reveals the contradictions in our society. Although repressive mechanisms are in place, resistance simmers beneath the surface of whittled down consciousness and may eventually boil over into revolutionary action.

There are many examples of this over the last half-century. Events ranging from the student revolts of the late 1960s and early 1970s to the Arab Spring, Occupy, and Black Lives Matter uprisings testify to the ongoing negating force of eros. The work of George Katsiaficas and his theory of the eros effect has been instrumental in further developing Marcuse's theory of the emancipatory function of eros. Katsiaficas' attempt to reintegrate the emotional and the rational is a further development of Marcuse's call for a rationality of gratification in *Eros and Civilization*.[3] According to Katsiaficas, following Marcuse, the emotional and the erotic are not irrational but rather engender their own form of rationality. As he states, "My theory [of the eros effect] attempts to reintegrate the emotional and the rational at a level on which emotional and irrational are not synonymous in their usages nor derogatory in their characterizations. I seek to affirm the emotional content of social movements as erotic action, action which may be considered collective liberatory sublimation—a rational way of clearing collective psychological blockages."[4] In highlighting how eros operates within liberatory social movements, Katsiaficas is also demonstrating that one-dimensional forces do not go unchallenged. For this reason, even in the midst of what appears to be the victory dance of one-dimensionality, there remains hope for liberation.

Marcuse begins chapter 1 of *One-Dimensional Man* with the following: "A comfortable, smooth, reasonable, democratic unfreedom prevails in advanced industrial civilization, a token of technical progress."[5] This statement captures the precise problem that gave rise to the Frankfurt School for Social Research in the 1920s and 1930s. That is, in a society that alienates its workers and produces great wealth for the few and great poverty for the many, why do those who are dehumanized and exploited not rise up to throw off the chains that bind them to a life of suffering and injustice? Why do people believe that they are free when the details of their daily lives signify a lack of freedom? Marcuse offers many reasons, but one of the main reasons is that people have come to identify with their own oppression. Marcuse writes:

> The result is, not "adjustment" but *mimesis*: an immediate identification of the individual with his society, and, through his part of society, with the society as a whole. . . . In this process, the "inner" dimension of the mind is whittled down: the dimension in which protest and opposition to the status quo can take root, in which the power of negative thinking is at home—Reason as the critical power of negation. The loss of this dimension becomes manifest in the weakening of the non-apologetic, nonconformist elements of the ideology, of those ill-defined values, images, ideas which were once incorporated not only in the key vocabulary of literature and philosophy but also of ordinary language in personal communion.[6]

Society is one-dimensional to the extent that its members have lost the ability to envision a nonrepressive, free, real democratic society that has purged itself of surplus repression and domination. Marcuse defines surplus repression as "the restrictions necessitated by social domination." This is different from basic (psychological) repression, which is "necessary for the perpetuation of the human race in civilization."[7] In brief, it is necessary for humans to repress some of their basic instincts in order to coexist in a somewhat peaceful, functional society. But, according to Marcuse, contemporary forms of society impose additional and unnecessary forms of repression. These additional repressions institute and maintain a society organized around power and domination. In such a society, pleasure, in the form of creative expression, philosophical wonder, and human solidarity, is decreased while pain, in the form of daily toil and organized scarcity, is increased. It would only make sense for people to rise up and overturn such a society. But within a one-dimensional society, the present oppressive social reality is taken to be the only possibility. This is a "comfortable, smooth, democratic unfreedom" insofar as the oppressed and dominated freely accept their oppression; the oppressed groups come to internalize and identify with the values of the dominant group. The one-dimensional society is proof of the claim made by Marx that "the ideas of the ruling class are in every epoch the ruling ideas."[8] According to Marcuse:

> The technological and political conquest of the transcending factors in human existence, so characteristic of advanced industrial

civilization, here asserts itself in the instinctual sphere: satisfaction in a way generates submission and weakens the rationality of protest.

The range of socially permissible and desirable satisfaction is greatly enlarged, but through this satisfaction, the Pleasure Principle is reduced—deprived of the claims which are irreconcilable with the established society. Pleasure, thus adjusted, generates submission.

In contrast to the pleasures of adjusted desublimation, sublimation preserves the consciousness of the renunciations which the repressive society inflicts upon the individual, and thereby preserves the need for liberation. To be sure, all sublimation is enforced by the power of society, but the unhappy consciousness of this power already breaks through alienation. To be sure, all sublimation accepts the social barrier to instinctual gratification, but it also transgresses this barrier.[9]

In brief, Marcuse argues that in advanced industrial societies the impulse for liberation in oppressed groups is contained by the proliferation of forms of pleasure that merely satisfy the false needs produced by that society. But this is not the end of the story. In his writings that follow *One-Dimensional Man*—such as *An Essay on Liberation*, "Beyond One-Dimensional Man," *Counterrevolution and Revolt*, and *The Aesthetic Dimension*[10]—Marcuse returns to his hope for the formation of radical and critical subjectivity by once again exploring the erotic dimension and the instinctual/biological basis for social transformation. In these later works the theoretical insights are redeveloped within the context of the new social movements of the late 1960s.

Katsiaficas continues and expands Marcuse's search for radical and critical subjectivity. Generally speaking, Katsiaficas' work provides historical accountings of various manifestations of what Marcuse called the Great Refusal—grand protests "against that which is."[11] Katsiaficas focuses on group and even global forms of the Great Refusal. He argues that these moments result from the "eros effect." He writes:

The eros effect is crystallized in the sudden and synchronous international emergence of hundreds of thousands of people who occupy public space and call for a completely different political reality. Other dimensions of this phenomenon include the simultaneous appearance of revolts in many places; the intuitive identification of hundreds of thousands of people with each other across national and ethnic dividing lines; their common belief in new values; and the suspension of normal daily routines like competitive business practices, criminal behavior, and acquisitiveness. In my view, it is the instinctual need for freedom that is sublimated into a collective phenomenon during moments of the eros effect.[12]

The eros effect is a global rupture that, according to Katsiaficas, is inexplicable by using conventional social science theories. The social sciences have, historically, been concerned with prediction. Therefore, the methodologies applied by such sciences are based on the model of the natural sciences. "At the beginning of the twentieth century, sociological theories sought to explain revolutions and social movements through analogies to nature."[13] The goal of predictability in the realm of human social action leads to an erasure of a particular form of human subjectivity. That is, social scientists have developed models of objectivity in social research that can blind them to global expressions of *radical* subjectivity. Many of the social sciences seem to be influenced by a residual positivism that takes social facts as something eternal and immutable. Any deviations from what are taken to be the immutable facts are seen as pathological. In this case, then, moments of sudden rupture are understood as abnormal and deviant—strange events happening outside the "normal" functioning of society.

This type of thinking in the social sciences is a reflection of the one-dimensional thinking that permeates capitalist and modern societies. That is, social facts are treated as immediate rather than mediated, they are viewed as eternal rather than historical or temporal, and they are believed to be final rather than transitory. Such a view of social facts leads to a distorted view of human action and it legitimates systems of oppression and repression. Further, it makes it difficult to understand those actions by social actors that go against the established social order. In his reflections on sociological studies of the 1968 student revolts, Katsiaficas writes: "Unfortunately, sociological studies since 1968 have more often than not attempted to fit social movements into preconceived theoretical frameworks rather than constructing investigations of them as attempts to transform an irrational system."[14] In other words, there are certain theoretical frameworks that serve as epistemological lenses through which the theorist interprets particular social movements. What is key here is the tendency of social scientists to see the given society as rational and well organized so that social movements and radical protests are viewed as irrational, carried out by persons who are maladjusted to the rational society. This misinterpretation of social movements is a result of taking society to be a unified whole.

Katsiaficas argues, instead, that society is fragmented along a multiplicity of lines.[15] It is not a unified whole wherein each member has a particular function or place. Human society is the site of various relations, struggles, oppressions, repressions, and systematically and systemically produced inequalities. Hence, human society itself is constituted by the irrational and the pathological. It is permeated by contradictions. Therefore, human society is also the site of struggle *against* the aforementioned social pathologies, and these struggles, as constituted through social movements, may have as their goal a *more* rational society purged of such pathologies.

Too often, research in the social sciences involves an unfortunate form of reductionism and even reification. That is, social action and its causes are often reduced to one aspect of social reality while omitting other important factors. Katsiaficas explains:

> Each of these theories seeks to explain social movements in relation to *partial* aspects of social reality, aspects which the theory defines as significant. Consensus theorists focus on the maintenance of social equilibrium and have little to offer about conflict; social-psychological theorists focus on the changing norms of human actors and have little to say about power and economics; conflict theorists focus on the structures of power but fail to explain the formation of collectivity; organizational theorists offer insight into the mobilization of resources by activists but neglect their "hearts and minds"; status theorists focus on the ways in which social problems are cognitively defined and the interests such definitions actually serve but give little insight into objective structures; mass society theorists deal with the relationship of elites to masses but have little to say about the subjectivity of human actors and the cultural sources of cohesion and conflict.[16]

Another example of the one-sidedness of many of the social sciences comes from economics. Many economists concern themselves with equilibrium in the market. Their view of a smooth, well-organized, and well-running economy does not include a critique of poverty and the means for eliminating poverty. As I was once told by an economist, "the market is not concerned about justice." So, how would an economist understand the motive behind antipoverty movements, mass strikes, or Occupy and the implication of these movements for future economic planning? The science of economics involves a form of reification insofar as what we call the market is often used to explain human economic behavior. However, the market itself is the product of, and is nothing more than, human behavior. But in economics, the market is spoken of as if it is an individual agent. It serves to conceal the type of unjust decision-making processes performed by the capitalists as well as the forms of ideology that must be internalized by the working population to keep capitalism afloat.

However, from time to time, there are uprisings, displays of social unrest by members of society who are being crushed under the weight of an oppressive economic, social, and political system. They know that they are not irrational. Instead, it is the social order of which they protest that is irrational. In several of his works, from *The Imagination of the New Left* to *The Subversion of Politics*, Katsiaficas examines a wide variety of social movements across the world in the context of their development. He demonstrates the rational-and-erotic impulse of these movements as rooted in a universal desire for a free and rational society. As he writes:

> When the eros effect is activated, humans' love for and solidarity with each other suddenly replace previously dominant values and norms. Competition gives way to cooperation, hierarchy to equality, power to truth. During the Vietnam War, for example, many Americans' patriotism was superseded by solidarity with the people of Vietnam, and in place of racism, many white Americans insisted a Vietnamese life was worth the same as an American life. . . . According to many opinion polls of that time, Vietnamese leader Ho Chi Minh was more popular on American college campuses than US President Nixon.[17]

This is a significant observation because it demonstrates the human ability to transcend parochialism and to embrace a certain kind of global solidarity. And it is eros—the life instinct—that sits at the root of that solidarity.

## THE DIALECTICAL TENSION IN EROS

Marcuse, following Freud, described eros as striving to create higher unities.[18] Marcuse then goes on to extend Freud's theory, writing:

> In the light of the idea of non-repressive sublimation, Freud's definition of Eros as striving to "form living substance into ever

greater unities, so that life may be prolonged and brought to higher development" takes on added significance. The biological drive becomes a cultural drive. The pleasure principle reveals its own dialectic. The erotic aim of sustaining the entire body as subject-object of pleasure calls for the continual refinement of the organism, the intensification of its receptivity, the growth of its sensuousness. The aim generates its own projects of realization: the abolition of toil, the amelioration of the environment, the conquest of disease and decay, the creation of luxury.[19]

Every human being has an erotic drive, which, being given its mission by the pleasure principle, seeks fulfillment and satisfaction. However, satisfaction and fulfillment depend on external as well as internal conditions. The individual shares the world and its resources with other individuals who are also equally motivated by the pleasure principle. Hence, there arises in eros a tension that produces its sinister twin drive,[20] thanatos, or the death drive. In the splitting of eros into *eros as life drive* and *eros as death drive*,[21] there emerges a dialectic that is at work in human relations and history.

To make matters clear, it is necessary to examine the work of eros at two distinct levels. At the first level, eros seeks to establish a universal unity because it has been torn from a unity wherein it experienced total satisfaction. That is, while in the mother's womb, the infant has no desire (which is like a prebirth state of Nirvana) because whatever it may possibly need is provided by the body of the mother even before the need occurs. Through the process of postbirth development, the separation between mother and child grows as the infant can no longer have its needs immediately met but must await a response from its mother. This gap between the occurrence of a need and its satisfaction is the beginning of the development of the conscious ego as the infant experiences the reality principle. Hence, there is a loss of the unity once experienced by the infant. The remainder of life is the quest for fulfillment, which is frustrated by other individuals who fail to meet the needs of the individual or interfere with attempts at satisfaction. It is not my current intent to provide further details to justify this view. What is more important is the second level of eros.

The second level of analysis examines eros as striving to overcome the death drive. The death drive does not refer simply to a desire to die but, rather, to achieve a state of oneness or absolute wholeness. It is a desire to be free of the kind of tension produced by finite, human life. The only way to be free of life's tensions and frustrations is through death. Marcuse writes: "The death instinct is destructive not for its own sake, but for the relief of tension. The descent toward death is an unconscious flight from pain and want."[22] The idea of Nirvana in Buddhism is an attempt to escape pain and want through a life of meditation. This is why Marcuse refers to the death drive as the Nirvana principle. The death drive becomes social insofar as it is turned outward toward others who are viewed as the source of our pain. For Freud,

> [t]he element of truth behind all this, which people are so ready to disavow, is that men are not gentle creatures who want to be loved, and who at the most can defend themselves if they are attacked; they are, on the contrary, creatures among whose instinctual endowments is to be reckoned a powerful share of aggressiveness. As a result, their neighbor is for them not only a potential helper or sexual object, but also someone who tempts them to satisfy their aggressiveness on him, to exploit his capacity for work without compensation, to use him sexually without consent, to seize his possessions, to humiliate him, to cause him pain, to torture and to kill.[23]

Eros, as the life drive, seeks to be unified with the other, to enter community, while eros, as the death drive (thanatos), seeks to use or destroy the other. Through the death drive the other is seen as an obstacle that stands in the way of my happiness. For Freud, the two twins birthed by the pleasure principle are at war.

Marcuse advances beyond Freud, showing that there is no compelling reason to believe that the life drive and the death drive are locked in an endless battle beyond human control. Which one gets the upper hand in this battle is influenced by the organization of society, or what Marcuse refers to as the present performance principle. It is the presence of the life drive that prevents the death drive from plunging humanity into total destruction. A major point of *Eros and Civilization* is to demonstrate that eros, as the life drive, does not exclusively serve the performance principle.[24] According to Marcuse, imagination and fantasy play active roles in the erotic drive of resistance.

> The truth value of imagination relates not only to the past but also to the future: the forms of freedom and happiness which it invokes claim to deliver the historical *reality*. In its refusal to accept as final the limitations imposed upon freedom and happiness by the reality principle, in its refusal to forget what *can be*, lies the critical function of phantasy. . . .

This Great Refusal is the protest against unnecessary repression, the struggle for the ultimate form of freedom—"to live without anxiety."[25]

The Great Refusal occurs at both the individual and group levels, the latter of which, as stated earlier, is Katsiaficas' focus and contribution. The eros effect, according to Katsiaficas, creates a bond between individuals all over the world who are tired of the destructiveness of the present performance principle. While the present performance principle attempts to colonize eros for its own purposes, eros never fully accepts the conditions that enable, and that are produced by, surplus repression. This is the main argument of the previous Marcuse quote, and Katsiaficas holds a similar position. For Katsiaficas:

Without a reworking of the psyche and reinvigoration of the spirit, can there even be talk of revolution? On the one side, the system colonizes eros, turning love into sex, and sex into pornography. Labor becomes production, production a job; free time has been turned into leisure, leisure into vacation; desire has been morphed into consumerism, fantasy into mediated spectacle. Autonomous movements respond by rescuing eros from its commodification, expanding its space, moving beyond patriarchal relationships, beyond conceptions of love solely as physical love. The politics of eros infuse everyday life with a content that subverts its would-be colonizers and preserves it as a reservoir of the life-force. The "eros effect" indicates how social movements are an expression of people's loving connectedness with each other. . . . [M]y view of the role of movement participation is that it preserves and expands the domain of the heart—of all that is uniquely human, all that stands opposed to the machine culture.[26]

The present capitalist performance principle seeks to colonize every domain of life. Eros, as the life drive, is distorted for the sake of maintaining the present performance principle. The result is unnecessary violence, poverty, repression, exploitation, alienation, and so on. The very attempt at such colonization produces a form of one-dimensional thinking wherein one sees the present order of things as the way things must be. However, eros continues to assert itself by demanding a new and qualitatively better social reality. Eros pushes us to see the concealed possibilities for liberation already present in our society. The social movements discussed by Katsiaficas are global manifestations of the Great Refusal, that is, moments of collective resistance to the colonization of everyday life.

## THE EROS EFFECT AND DEMOCRATIC ATTUNEMENT: TOWARD A NEW SENSIBILITY

Katsiaficas focuses primarily on the eros effect as it is manifest in global movements. I agree that these movements are motivated by a global erotic drive for a qualitatively better form of life. However, I believe that the eros effect can also be described at the level of individual experience. With regard to social transformation and social movements, I believe that there is transformation at both the social and individual level. The individual— and not just the group—must develop what Marcuse referred to as a "new sensibility," that is, new ways of thinking and experiencing that enable us to move beyond the one-dimensionality of our current society.[27] A new sensibility is one in which eros functions more fully within our thinking and living, allowing us to develop deeper unities and communal relations with others. This transformation requires a dual moment of deconstruction and resensitizing, which I refer to as the process of "democratic attunement."[28]

Democratic attunement occurs within the context of an encounter with the Other, wherein an individual is awakened to a new sensibility. The Other approaches me as one in need of recognition, love, and support. My ethical awareness is then stimulated during this encounter. In Freudian terms, the Other can be approached as the target for my aggressive drives or as the source and object of mutual help. Democratic attunement is a moment when the latter comes to the fore. It is a form of sensual, embodied, eros-driven empathy that attunes us to the real, concrete, material situation of the Other. It is a moment when the needs and desires of the Other are felt, recognized, and understood.

Democratic attunement is made possible by the workings of eros. Eros, as the builder of culture and seeker of higher unities, is capable of bringing people together into newer and more enriched relationships. It is capable of bridging the social gaps between people who belong to different social groups; it is able to affect the process of identity formation, enabling us to transcend the boundaries of our own group identities and to act in solidarity with members of other social groups. Emancipatory social transformation is made possible by our potential to work for the liberation of groups to which we do not belong. Without that potential, personal and social change are unlikely, perhaps even impossible.

This understanding of human relations challenges the view of human subjectivity that we have inherited from the Western intellectual tradition. That tradition has separated logos (the principle of reason or rationality) from eros (the principle of desire, love, and creativity) and has emphasized the former over the latter. This view has led to what Max Horkheimer and Theodor W. Adorno call instrumental rationality and what Marcuse calls the logic of domination.[29] Such developments have restricted, however partially, erotic impulses and have helped subdue the "will to gratification." Hence, the creative, sensuous, and erotic side of the individual has been repressed. Such repression produces in us the inability to empathize with and connect to the Other in ways that create caring communities. But as the work of Katsiaficas makes clear, transformation, connection, and solidarity do occur, often unexpectedly. My own narrative of self-transformation, which opened this chapter, helps to highlight this occurrence, albeit on an individual and interpersonal level.

I cannot fully explain how I suddenly became democratically attuned to the wants and needs of my brother, uncle, and, more generally, the LGBTQ community. It seems likely that it was the result of a long process of thinking about social justice and the human condition. It was as if eros (the builder of community) asserted itself in my life at a moment when I thought that I was safe from the influence of homophobia. Although I was not consciously or intentionally homophobic, I was also not consciously or intentionally attuned to the needs of gay people. This sudden moment of attunement led to an increase in my gay rights activism. At some point, I moved beyond just letting people be to actively participating in the struggle for LGBTQ justice. I attended and spoke at events during Rainbow Week each year when I taught at St. Joseph's University in Philadelphia. In many of my classes I take time to address the issue of gay rights. My kids and I are regulars at the Pride Festival in our city, and we have participated in protests and actually marched to a place of employment where a transgender person had been fired on the basis of sexual/gender discrimination. When I was teaching in Philadelphia, I and several other faculty members walked out on our commencement speaker, Senator Rick Santorum, who had made very disturbing comments about people of non-heterosexual orientation. We stood in solidarity with our gay, lesbian, and transgender students as people insulted us with derogatory names. These are risks that I would not have taken prior to my erotically aroused democratic attunement.

My decision to talk with my brother and uncle came suddenly when I was lying in bed and for no apparent reason began to think about my own efforts in the struggle for social change. I believe that this moment emerged from a longer period of development that traces back to my earliest struggles for social justice while in college. I have previously pointed out the contradictions that were present in the community in which I was raised. It is these contradictions that simultaneously produce systems of oppression as well as spaces and/or moments for resistance. I was raised in a Black conservative Christian family that disavowed homosexuality. My subjectivity, then, was shaped by two different and conflicting sensibilities—racial and economic justice, on one side, and sexual/gender discrimination, on the other. The latter was inconsistent with the more general message of love and inclusion that I grew up with. But neither side of the contradiction was fixed or final. There is also the beauty, dignity, and raw humanity of people who were excluded—particularly my brother and uncle—that opened the door for the development of a new sensibility. It is this encounter with the Other that enabled my own transformation.

This essay began with and returns to my personal experience because it hopefully provides insight into the possibility of social change. My experience highlights the connections between Katsiaficas' notion of the eros effect and Marcuse's view on eros, one-dimensionality, and social transformation. It also highlights the correlation between localized, individual experience and broader, collective movements. My own transformation, for instance, began at a personal level and then connected me to the larger community of those who fight for gay rights and liberation. In this sense, I individually experienced an "erotic effect" that democratically attuned me to the needs and conditions of the Other and then pulled me in to a larger social movement. This experience also made me realize that any demand for justice and fairness must transcend the boundaries of one's own social group. To fight for justice for one's particular social group while ignoring the suffering of others is to fight for *partial* justice. But the demand for justice and fairness implies a *total* transformation of any society that would oppress any social group. As Dr. Martin Luther King Jr. says: "Injustice anywhere is a threat to justice everywhere. We are caught in an inescapable network of mutuality, tied in a single garment of destiny. Whatever affects one directly affects all indirectly."[30]

## INDIVIDUAL AND STRUCTURAL TRANSFORMATION

A theory of one-dimensionality must account for *both* individual *and* structural transformation. The very concept of one-dimensionality as used by Marcuse is designed to disclose social, political, moral, emotional, and psychological mechanisms that whittle down critical consciousness so that the present reality/performance principle goes unchallenged. The development of human consciousness in a one-dimensional society is shaped by forces that work against the free, rational development of the individual. But forces of one-dimensionality are successful only to the degree that they can manipulate all corners of society, including the individual psyche. Hence, liberation must be total insofar as domination is total.

The whittling down of critical consciousness occurs not only in the economic sphere, but also in and through multiple forms of human relations and interactions. One of the main reasons why radical social change does not occur more often is because segments of society are pitted against one another. White, working-class, straight men, for instance, might vote for right-wing political candidates based on their own ingrained sexism, racism, and homophobia rather than advocating for just economic policies and the fair treatment of others. These same people might also disparage calls to (left-wing) political revolution because they cannot imagine themselves being displaced from the center of cultural privilege and power. In a society that is replete with many forms of domination, one-dimensional thinking functions well beyond the economic sphere. This is why Marcuse recognized such varying groups as the hippie counterculture, the student movement, and Black Power as catalysts for wider liberation.[31] Marcuse also argued that the women's liberation movement "is perhaps the most important and potentially radical political movement that we have seen."[32] In brief, he saw these movements as manifesting various forms of the Great Refusal.

The groups that Marcuse attended to as possible revolutionary forces are still engaged in the struggle for liberation today. They are struggling against long-term systems of injustice and fighting for the transformation of an oppressive, one-dimensional society. But the fact that these struggles are often reduced to the rhetoric of cultural wars and multicultural initiatives, and are often seen as mere struggles for inclusion, testifies to the ongoing work of one-dimensional thinking. In this case, one-dimensional thinking preserves the present order by reducing contemporary struggles to a mere desire for inclusion rather than a push for radical change.

The kind of change that Marcuse envisioned demands the transformation of social reality at multiple levels, and that type of transformation requires a new type of human being. As Marcuse writes in "Marxism and Revolution in an Era of Counterrevolution":

> The development of socialist institutions and relationships requires, rather, a new type of man, a different type of human being, with new needs, capable of finding a qualitatively different way of life, and of constructing a qualitatively different environment.

If this often-forgotten idea, this insistence on a new type
of human being as prerequisite to the transition to socialism, is
reexamined, the radical libertarian trend in Marxian theory must
be recognized. This trend is telescoped in the concept of the
"all-around individual." Marx explained this concept by another
difficult, strange, and provocative term. He spoke of "the sensuous
species being of man." "Sensuous species being"—a type of man
who fulfills the potentialities of the human species not only in
and with his mental faculties but also in and with his senses, in
his sensibility and sensitivity. And among these potentialities of
man as species being is precisely the capability of transforming
his environment, his world, into a universe where his sensibility
can freely develop.[33]

Marcuse seems to use the term "man" in the plural, but the preceding
passage also indicates that some form of individual transformation must occur
if we are to eventually enjoy the freedom produced by socialist institutions
and relationships. The critique of one-dimensional society is at once a
critique of social institutions *and* individual psyches. They are inseparable,
mutually informing and conditioning one another; the transformation of
social institutions is not possible without the transformation of individuals.
For Marcuse, individual transformation has an impact on the individual's
entire environment.

My personal narrative outlined in this chapter is *one* example of individual transformation that hopefully contributes to larger structural change.
My transformation occurred within a context that originally conditioned me
to think in a one-dimensional way about sexuality. Heteronormativity, for
instance, is an institutionalization of sexual desire that excludes and represses
nonhetero desires and expressions. The transformation of individuals within
such a context is a Great Refusal of heteronormativity. Admittedly, marching
in the streets, walking out on a Rick Santorum speech, and speaking with
my students is not enough to bring about total liberation. But the ideas
presented in this chapter are intended to complement Katsiaficas' theory of
the eros effect with an account of individual transformation that can also
be understood as "contagious." The work of eros in the individual must, like
Marcuse argues, transform the environment in which the individual lives.

On the structural end of transformation, we have the example of
the 2015 Supreme Court decision to legalize same-sex marriage. Despite
some backlash to the Supreme Court decision, there was an outpouring of
support for gay rights. Again, gay rights are not the same as gay *liberation*.

But such legislation underscores how the awakening of individuals—first on smaller scales, then on larger scales—can influence and transform the overall environment. We might also argue that the eros effect was at play across the country as heterosexually identified people stood in solidarity with those of nonheterosexual orientation. A certain kind of love and affirmation were fanning the flames of the Supreme Court decision.

Transformation is not an issue of the individual *or* the structural. Instead, we must seek to understand how each plays its own unique role in the pursuit of a fair and just society. Eros operates on both levels, and theories of one-dimensionality must account for both. Katsiaficas tends to focus on group-level transformation, but the group is made up of individuals who are already perhaps experiencing some form of transformation in their personal lives. These larger group movements might then be viewed as constellations of individuals who are in the process of becoming what Marcuse calls the "new humanity"—those who pave the way for social revolution.

## NOTES

1. The term "one-dimensional" is based on Marcuse's analysis of advanced industrial society. The opposite of one-dimensional thinking is two-dimensional or dialectical thinking. To think one-dimensionally is to reduce all social reality to the "facts" or to the present order of things. To think dialectically is to see in the present order of things their principle of change or other possibilities. Dialectical thinking discloses other possible ways of being that do not perpetuate oppression, exploitation, violence, and so forth. See: Herbert Marcuse, *One-Dimensional Man: Studies in the Ideology of Advanced Industrial Society* (Boston: Beacon Press, 1966).

2. Sigmund Freud, "Repression," in *Sigmund Freud: Collected Papers, Volume IV*, ed. Ernest Jones, trans. Joan Riviere (London: The Hogarth Press, 1949), 84–97.

3. Herbert Marcuse, *Eros and Civilization: A Philosophical Inquiry into Freud* (Boston: Beacon Press, 1966), 224.

4. George Katsiaficas, "The Eros Effect," 1989, personal website, http://www.eroseffect.com/articles/eroseffectpaper.PDF.

5. Marcuse, *One-Dimensional Man*, 1.

6. Herbert Marcuse, "The Problem of Social Change in the Technological Society," in *Herbert Marcuse: Towards a Critical Theory of Society*, ed. Douglas Kellner (New York: Routledge, 2001), 37–57 (53–54).

7. Marcuse, *Eros and Civilization*, 35.

8. Karl Marx, "The German Ideology," in *Karl Marx: Selected Writings*, ed. David McLellan (Oxford: Oxford University Press, 2000), 175–208 (192).

9. Marcuse, *One-Dimensional Man*, 75–76.

10. Herbert Marcuse, *An Essay on Liberation* (Middlesex: Penguin Books, 1969); Herbert Marcuse, "Beyond One-Dimensional Man," in *Herbert Marcuse: Towards a Critical Theory of Society*, 107–120; Herbert Marcuse, *Counterrevolution and Revolt* (Boston: Beacon Press, 1972); Herbert Marcuse, *The Aesthetic Dimension: Toward a Critique of Marxist Aesthetics* (Boston: Beacon Press, 1978).

11. Marcuse, *One-Dimensional Man*, 63.

12. George Katsiaficas, "Eros and Revolution," *Radical Philosophy Review* 16, no. 2 (2013): 491–505 (491–492).

13. George Katsiaficas, *The Imagination of the New Left: A Global Analysis of 1968* (Boston: South End Press, 1987), 234.

14. Ibid., 239.

15. Ibid., 238–241.

16. Ibid., 240 (original emphasis).

17. Katsiaficas, "Eros and Revolution," 492–493.

18. In his essay "The Libido Theory," Freud writes: "The other set of instincts would be those which are better known to us in analysis, the libidinal, sexual or life instincts, which are best comprised under the name *Eros*, their purpose would be to form living substance into ever greater unities, so that life may be prolonged and brought to higher development." Sigmund Freud, "The Libido Theory," in *Collected Papers, Volume V: Miscellaneous Papers, 1888–1938*, ed. and trans. James Strachey (London: The Hogarth Press, 1950), 131–135 (135).

19. Marcuse, *Eros and Civilization*, 211–212.

20. Although Marcuse often uses the term "instinct," and the English translations of Freud use the term "instinct," I prefer drive. In the German, Freud used the term *Trieb* not *Instink*. *Trieb* has a history in German philosophy and is most often translated as "drive," which is not as deterministic as instinct. The term drive lends itself to the historical and social malleability of the drive that is so important to Marcuse.

21. This distinction between eros as life drive and eros as death drive is my own. I am not sure if Freud or Marcuse would agree with my language. However, I find this distinction necessary to understand and develop Marcuse's argument. This may be a moment when the attempt to think with Freud and Marcuse requires thinking beyond both of them. My point is that both Freud and Marcuse see the death drive and the life drive as having their source in the pleasure principle.

22. Marcuse, *Eros and Civilization*, 29.

23. Sigmund Freud, *Civilization and Its Discontents*, trans. and ed. James Strachey (New York: W.W. Norton, 1961), 68–69.

24. Marcuse, *Eros and Civilization*, 84.

25. Ibid., 148–149 (original emphasis).

26. George Katsiaficas, *The Subversion of Politics: European Autonomous Social Movements and the Decolonization of Everyday Life* (Oakland: AK Press, 2006), 221.

27. See Marcuse, *An Essay on Liberation*, particularly chapter 2.

28. See Arnold L. Farr, *Critical Theory and Democratic Vision: Herbert Marcuse and Recent Liberation Philosophies* (Lanham: Lexington Books, 2009), particularly

pages 176–178. I began developing a theory of democratic attunement a few years ago, after reading Cynthia Willett's *Maternal Ethics and Other Slave Moralities*. One of the key passages that influenced my thinking about democratic attunement is the following: "While Levinas misconceives ethics through the metaphorics of war, he is correct, I believe, to reorient the primary impetus for philosophical thinking away from epistemologies of reason or ontologies of Being to the intersubjective dynamic of the face-to-face encounter. An ethics that could break down what American multiculturalists term the 'us versus them' dichotomy must break out of the logic of identity and difference that supports dichotomy in general. First philosophy should enlist not a logic of identity and difference but an 'attunement' to the face of the Other." Willett, *Maternal Ethics and Other Slave Moralities* (New York: Routledge, 1995), 55.

29. Marcuse, *Eros and Civilization*, 124–125. See also, Max Horkheimer and Theodor W. Adorno, *Dialectic of Enlightenment*, trans. John Cumming (New York: Continuum, 1993), as well as Max Horkheimer, *Critique of Instrumental Reason*, trans. Matthew J. O'Connell (New York: The Seabury Press, 1974). Marcuse, Horkheimer, and Adorno believed that in a capitalist society reason has lost its critical function whereby it was capable of envisioning a better society based on resources already at hand. Instead, reason becomes a tool for the maintenance of the present oppressive social order. Reason no longer posits ends that function to create a better, and liberated, society. Instead, reason becomes a means to a pre-determined end, an end that is determined by the dominate members of society.

30. Martin Luther King, Jr., "Letter from Birmingham City Jail," in *A Testament of Hope: The Essential Writings of Martin Luther King, Jr.*, ed. James M. Washington (San Francisco: Harper & Row, 1986), 289–302 (290).

31. See Marcuse, *An Essay on Liberation* and *Herbert Marcuse: Towards a Critical Theory of Society*.

32. Herbert Marcuse, "Marxism and Feminism," in *Herbert Marcuse: The New Left and the 1960s*, ed. Douglas Kellner (New York: Routledge, 2005), 165.

33. Herbert Marcuse, "Marxism and Revolution in an Era of Counterrevolution," in *Herbert Marcuse: Marxism, Revolution and Utopia*, ed. Douglas Kellner and Clayton Pierce (New York: Routledge, 2014), 343.

5

# Rethinking the Eros Effect

## Sentience, Reality, and Emanation

JASON DEL GANDIO

George Katsiaficas developed his conception of the eros effect from within the Marcusian tradition, which combines Marx's critique of capitalism with Freud's understanding of the human psyche. Katsiaficas thus conceptualizes the eros effect in terms of innate psychological drives, arguing, in brief, that moments of spontaneous mass rebellion are outpourings of humanity's drive toward freedom and pleasure. As he states:

> Such spontaneous leaps may be, in part, a product of long-term social processes in which organized groups and conscious individuals prepare the groundwork, but when political struggle comes to involve millions of people, it is possible to glimpse a rare historical occurrence: the emergence of the *eros* effect, the massive awakening of the instinctual human need for justice and freedom. When the *eros* effect occurs, it becomes clear that the fabric of the *status quo* has been torn, and the forms of social control have been ruptured.[1]

First, this chapter is derived in part from a previously published article; and second, the ideas presented in this chapter are part of a longer, ongoing project. For the original article, see: Jason Del Gandio, "Extending the Eros Effect: Sentience, Reality, and Emanation," *New Political Science* 36, no. 2 (2014): 129–148, doi: 10.1080/07393148.2014.883799.

Although I am sympathetic to this framework, I want to reconceptualize the eros effect from a different theoretical perspective, one that borrows, sometimes liberally, from phenomenology, poststructuralism, and Italian Autonomism. I borrow from phenomenology's emphasis on the coconstitutive relationship between the lived-body and the surrounding environment, from poststructuralism's understanding of power relations and the decentered subject, and from Italian Autonomism's understanding that humanity's capacity for resistance is ontologically primordial to any and all systems of oppression. The syncretic philosophy outlined in this chapter is not intended to trump or even argue against Katsiaficas' Marcusian approach. Rather, it is attempting to create space for alternative theorizing.

The chapter is organized around three theoretical principles. The first principle grounds the eros effect in the sentient body—that is, the body's ability to feel itself and the world in ways that precede and exceed not only perception and language but any and all oppressive conditions. This notion of the sentient body provides a way to understand the nature of radical social change. The second principle argues that the sentient body is a reality-creating organism that is inhibited and/or hindered by various oppressive conditions. This tension between creation and oppression produces the conditions of mass revolt. The third and final principle introduces the phenomenon of bodily emanation—often referred to as "the vibe"—to explain the magnetic allure of mass rebellion: spontaneous mass revolts emanate a tangible and experiential energy that attracts people to radical activity. Overall, this philosophy of sentience, reality, and emanation is an attempt to rethink Katsiaficas' eros effect in the hopes of advancing radical praxis.


## FIRST PRINCIPLE: THE SENTIENT BODY

My approach to the phenomenon of spontaneous mass rebellion begins with the body. My use of "the body" does not refer to specific body types that are codified through socially constructed categories of race, sex, gender, size, ability, or other classifications. I agree that our bodies are *always* socially coded and that we should *continuously* interrogate those codes to reveal and critique discriminations and oppressions of all kinds. But my use of "the body" refers to a most general observation: to be human is to be an embodied organism. If this is true, then the body is the concrete site of both oppression and social change.[2]

To understand this perspective, we must realize that the body is not simply a carrying case for the abstract mind. The Cartesian notion of a mute body void of life and feeling was delegitimized long ago.[3] Instead, the body is an intelligent organism that experiences the world in a sentient fashion—that is, the body feels itself and the world in ways that precede and exceed signs, symbols, language, discourse, and even perception.[4] If that is true, then sentience also functions prior to and beyond control and repression. We may exist in a repressive society, but those repressive conditions are neither the beginning nor ending point of human experience. If the inverse were true, then resistance would be futile and even ontologically impossible. We are sentient beings, first, and all these other things occur only secondarily.

This "philosophy of sentience" is adapted from the phenomenological work of Eugene Gendlin. Gendlin is not a political philosopher. Instead, he is an epistemologist who has spent the last fifty years constructing a theory of knowledge based on embodied sentience. For instance:

> To begin philosophy [or in this case, politics] by [first] considering perception, makes it seem that living things can construct reality only through perception. But plants *are* in contact with reality. They *are* interactions with their environments, and that is not lost just because our bodies also have perception. On the contrary, for us that functions in many additional ways. Animal bodies—including our bodies—sense themselves, and thereby sense the interactional living we are. In sensing themselves, our bodies sense our physical environment and human situations. The perception of colors, smells, and sounds is only a small part of this.
>
> Our bodies sense themselves in living in our situations. Our bodies do our living. Our bodies *are* interaction in the environment; they interact as bodies, not just through what comes with the five senses. Our bodies don't lurk in isolation behind the five peepholes of perception.[5]

Gendlin is not saying that we are ever without perception, or without language, discourse, signs, or symbols. These things are *always* part of human experience. But just because we are never without perception or language does *not* mean that we are reducible to perception or language.

But how does this pre-perceptual body function and operate? Gendlin argues that the body is a *pre-separated multiplicity*.[6] In other words, the body is a multiplicity that is not yet separated. The body is composed of a multiplicity of possible actions, thoughts, emotions, desires, and abilities;

then, depending upon the situational conditions, some of those possibilities are actualized while others are not. But all possibilities are ever present, always and already. Gendlin expresses this pre-separated multiplicity with the following symbol: ".<u>. . . .</u>". The five dots are an extended ellipsis that depicts the body as a continuous process endlessly adapting and adjusting to the best of its ability. The quotation marks and the underline express a *temporary* and *contentious* grounding and stasis to the process. That grounding/stasis allows us to experience the world as a stable and coherent phenomenon; there would be nothing but flux and chaos without that grounding/stasis. These various factors come together to form a processual yet stable form of life: ".<u>. . . .</u>".

This concept of the ".<u>. . . .</u>" enables us to understand the body as an open space of becoming that is constantly interacting with and responding to the surrounding situation. The body and its situation mutually evoke one another into existence.[7] For instance, burying a seed in dirt provokes the formation of a plant. The plant and its environment (of dirt, sun, and water) provoke flowers, fruits, and vegetables. Lungs and oxygen provoke breathing, a mouth-food-and-digestive system provokes eating, and waste-intestines-and-orifices provoke defecation and urination. Likewise, dry deserts, lush forests, and crowded city streets all provoke unique responses from the body, which might include differences in heart rates, perspiration, pupil dilation, and speed and range of one's gait. Psychological and emotional conditions also factor into the body-situation relationship. Abused children might react *defensively* to signs of love and affection, soldiers suffering from posttraumatic stress disorder often respond *erratically* to specific triggers, and grieving mothers might sob *unexpectedly* to seemingly benign comments. But different forms of healing and therapy can help one overcome these issues. In other words, our bodily experience precedes and exceeds abuse, trauma, and grief and enables us to live fully and happily.[8]

This interactive-and-responsive process between the body and its situation operates according to attraction and repulsion: The body is *attracted to* experiences, thoughts, and relations that facilitate its own becoming; and likewise, the body is *repulsed* by experiences, thoughts, and relations that inhibit its own becoming. Just as plants grow toward sunlight and away from darkness, so, too, does the body move toward and away from particular phenomena, stimuli, processes, and conditions. Regardless of the specifics that the body moves toward and away from, it seeks to follow the trajectory of the ".<u>. . . .</u>". This trajectory is nonfoundational, nonlinear, and nonteleological. The body *might* move from A to B to C. But it might *also* move from A to K to R or from J to Z to E or from Q to * to "<u>    </u>".

These nonlinear progressions commonly zigzag back and forth and even jump from one connection to another. In this sense, then, the quotation marks are also "scare quotes," because you can never fully anticipate the direction or trajectory of the ".....".[9]

This nonlinear directionality is often revealed during our dreams, thoughts, emotions, and imaginations in which seemingly incongruent strands and associations link up and attach in previously unthinkable ways. Such connections are then understood as brilliant and ingenious. This points to the ability of the sentient body to sense which moves, actions, and choices will lead to its own furtherance. For example: the poet needs another line, the speaker needs another word, the philosopher needs another argument, the lover needs another position, and the revolutionary needs another tactic. In each case the person feels lost, as if there is no way to bridge the present need with the future answer. But we can attune ourselves to our felt-sensing and enable our bodies to respond to the demands of the situation. The next thought, line, or action then *comes forth*. Numerous possibilities usually come forward together, and we must sift through them, sense the exactness of each, and make a choice. The sentient body thus *moves toward* aspects of the situation that advance its own becoming and *moves away from* aspects of the situation that inhibit its own becoming. This tension between attraction and repulsion is a sentient experience: we can *feel* our bodies responding to their *own* attractions and repulsions; we can *feel* our bodies moving of their *own accord*.[10]

This attraction and repulsion can be observed during mass political actions. For example, I am attending a protest and marching through the streets with thousands of people. The riot police suddenly show up and begin surrounding everyone. They are there to break up the demonstration and if necessary to beat and arrest people. The police make a move and everyone runs, scatters, and screams. Pepper spray and percussion hand grenades fill the air. Everyone is surrounded. What do I do?

Numerous options run through my head, but none of them *feel* right. But amid the chaos I find a way to sink into and listen to my body. This is not the body of my conventional thoughts and ideas that are filled with fears and self-doubts. Instead, I am attuned to the pre-separated multiplicity of my embodied sentience that precedes and exceeds habitualized thinking. My body then senses that something will happen, and I can *feel* myself moving toward a particular direction. A hole in the police line suddenly opens. I grab a couple friends and run toward the opening. I make it out and even save a few of the others. At no point could I consciously determine that this would happen. There were no announcements, and nothing in my immediate perceptual periphery indicated that this hole would open. But somehow my body sensed this unfolding interaction.

This is not to suggest, however, that escaping is the only possible action or only possible felt-sense. Perhaps my body senses that there is no escape and, consequently, I should stand my ground and fight off the police. Either way, the movements toward escape and/or confrontation are not top-down conscious choices. But neither are they completely random and happenstance. Rather, the felt-sensing of the situation exists as a *border zone* between conscious and unconscious thought; it is a form of experience that happens both before and after any discrete, analytical formulation. Such felt-sensing cuts through any preplanned normative frameworks of "right" and "wrong." Thus, in this case, one cannot determine beforehand whether escape or confrontation is the "best" option; they are simply two options among many that may come to the fore as the situation plays out. The trick is to allow the felt-sensing to function more fully in one's thinking and acting; to allow the "_ . . . ._" to sense its own environmental interactions that are, generally speaking, imperceptible to the conscious mind. This type of epistemological orientation posits no guarantees; it does not and cannot absolutely anticipate what is coming next. That is because the sentient body, as a pre-separated multiplicity, is perpetually changing; it is an ongoing, nonlinear, decentered process. As soon as my body senses *that*, the dots of the "_ . . . ._" rearrange themselves, which then changes the particulars of the situation, which again changes my bodily sense, ad infinitum. This is also occurring with every other person at the protest, thus constituting an ongoing, hyperprocessual ontology that can never be fully predicted, grasped, captured, or controlled. But that is the power of the "_ . . . ._". It is never completely controlled or exhausted. It is always open to the implicit possibilities of the surrounding situation.[11]

I argue that this sentient process is the basis of the eros effect. My argument begins with the basic observation that mass political awakenings are responses to oppressive conditions. Those oppressive conditions seek to habitualize the "_ . . . ._" into submission, to have one's "_ . . . ._" submit to particular regimes of power, to have the "_ . . . ._" align with and accept the oppressive conditions. The "_ . . . ._" often *does* submit, but never fully and for only so long. The "_ . . . ._", as a sentient, pre-separated multiplicity that moves toward its own becoming, continuously seeks escape from the oppressive conditions. This tension between submission and rebellion helps explain the mental and emotional anguish of oppression: the "_ . . . ._" seeks escape, but the ego (as the realm of habitualized thinking) fears the consequences and thus submits to control.[12] Feelings of dejection, melancholy, and hopelessness then arise. In many ways, it is much easier to just submit; as the saying goes, ignorance is bliss. But the ". . . . ." always lurks beneath the surface, constantly sensing its own exit.

The tension between the ". . . . ." and one's egoic submission to repression can be sensed on a collective level. People might say things like "you could feel the tension building for years," "a tipping point was bound to be reached," and "it was only a matter of time." That unspoken collective sense is the ". . . . ." speaking back to the ego. But it's not as if this communication between the ". . . . ." and the conscious mind happens all at once. Instead, flashes of the ". . . . ." appear to us all the time, and usually in positive, life-affirming ways: individually, we have moments of revolutionary clarity while watching videos, reading books, or simply staring out the window; and collectively, we have inspiring discussions and share unspoken understandings about the possibility of revolutionary change. These brief moments usually bring a sense of peacefulness and tranquility—that everything will be alright and everything will eventually work out. Such flashes also stimulate and excite the ". . . . .", especially during collective gatherings like protests, demonstrations, conferences, or even while collectively listening to a good speaker. Our bodies become alert, attentive, and titillated. Our bodies can *feel* the collective urge toward social change. Then, one day, seemingly out of nowhere, spontaneous rebellions occur. The moment arrives and an outpouring begins. This is not entirely accurate because there are always precipitating conditions. But what once seemed impossible suddenly erupts. Thousands and even millions of people take to the streets. We rise up against oppression and begin searching for a different world.

This "taking to the streets" is not rhetorical hyperbole. Instead, there is something unique about the copresence of bodies acting together in public space. Mass collective actions set conditions for the possibility of arousing the ". . . . ." to a heightened sense of being-in-the-world. All the senses are stimulated, alternative patterns of thinking occur, fears and self-doubts are lessened, and risk and courage are accentuated. An exponential effect then occurs—bodies beget bodies beget bodies—and our bodies begin to *move themselves* to the streets. It's as if we are liberated from our socialized compliance and our bodies seek their own intersubjective affirmation of their own becoming. Our bodies, together, then form long, complicated chains of ellipses. At that point, it is no longer about the individual body expressing itself like this ". . . . .". Instead, our collective bodies interlink to express themselves like this <!. . . . .!>---<!. . . . .!>---<!. . . . .!>---<!. . . . .!>---<!. . . . .!>.

That is the moment in which our sentient bodies burst through and generate a militant becoming oriented toward postoppressive realities.

## SECOND PRINCIPLE: THE CREATION OF REALITY

The second principle begins with the last word of the previous section: reality. The sentient body is a reality-creating organism, but that reality-creating process is often hindered and/or inhibited by oppressive conditions. This tension between creation and oppression produces the conditions of mass revolt. The "_____" *is* a reality-creating organism that follows its *own* trajectory. It will endure oppression and prohibition, but only for so long. In the end, it will overcome its oppression and reclaim its reality-creating processes. It is like trees growing through fences, flowers blooming in cracked sidewalks, and seeds outsmarting genetic engineering. Where there is a will, there is a way, and the "_____" is a will-to-create. Mass resistance, rebellions, and revolutions therefore occur when large segments of the population begin to recognize and act upon this will-to-create, transforming the "_____" into <!_____!>---<!_____!>---<!_____!>.

My understanding of the reality-creating process is influenced by the phenomenological tradition. For example, in *Analyses Concerning Passive and Active Synthesis*, Edmund Husserl explicates, among other things, the body's responses to and interactions with its surrounding environment. Husserl refers to this process as "affectivity," which is:

> the allure . . . the peculiar pull that an object given to consciousness exercises on the ego; it is a pull that is relaxed when the ego turns toward it attentively, and progresses from here, striving toward self-giving intuition, disclosing more and more of the self of the object, thus, striving toward an acquisition of knowledge, toward a more precise view of the object.[13]

Husserl's *Analyses* is a complicated work outlining various levels of affection within different realms of experience. This is neither the time nor place to review all the complexities. Suffice it to say that, at the most basic level, "affection" is the awakening of attention toward an environment by virtue of the environment's solicitation of my attention.[14] For example, my body, insofar as it is inserted into an environment of definitive objects, is drawn to particular aspects and features that constitute and actually enable a field of experience. That field-of-experience comes into relief—becomes prominent for me—as my attention is drawn toward particular details, data, and stimuli. The environment and my experience are thus coconstituted in that each gives definitive shape to the other—that is, each side *affects* the other. This coconstitutive process is not based solely upon that which is present, but also on that which is absent. Something becomes prominent only insofar as a field of nonprominence supports it. My *attraction to* particular phenomena simultaneously *diverts my attention away from* other phenomena; each is constitutive and operative. To see one thing is to not see something else, and what I am attracted to and notice in this moment may be different from that of past and/or future moments.

The affectivity of the body-and-environment relationship is not simply the constitution of awareness in the most general sense but also, and more dramatically, the very genesis of experience. As Husserl says, "when there is no affection coming from the diverse objects, then these diverse objects have slipped into sheer nightfall, in a special sense, they have slipped into the unconscious."[15] In other words, the affective allure between my body-and-its-environment is the very condition that enables me to experience anything at all. My body and the environment are "coawakened" through the affective allure that each exerts on the other. This insight helps describe what I am referring to as the reality-creating process: The attraction and repulsion between our bodies and the world reveal and conceal different phenomena and experiences and thus evoke a multiplicity of thoughts, understandings, and perspectives—that is, realities. Each human being embodies and evokes a different reality because each human being is uniquely constituted through their situational condition. We are therefore perpetually engaged in the unfolding of diverse realities, with each reality relating to every other reality. Our realities are not necessarily separate from one another but, instead, intertwined in an intricate web of world-becoming.

This type of decentered, bottom-up understanding of world-creation runs through most if not all spontaneous mass political awakenings. This is one of Katsiaficas' major points—most if not all spontaneous uprisings share similar visions of human beings simultaneously pursuing and supporting the free creation of unique realities: the Black Panther's "All Power to the People," Occupy's "We are the 99%," the Arab Spring's "We are all Egyptians now," and the Zapatista's "One no, many yeses." Such slogans highlight issues of self-determination, collective empowerment, solidarity, and/or mutual aid. Unfortunately, the current world is not structured according to these values and practices but, instead, is riddled with hierarchies of control and oppression. This is largely due to particular configurations of power that organize our collective lives. As feminist author/activist Star-hawk explains, there are different types of power: power *over* people, power *with* other people, and power *from within* yourself.[16] The first form of power obviously dominates the world. If that is true, then most human beings are inhibited from creating the realities that they truly desire.

One way to understand this relationship between oppressive power and the creation of reality is through Michael Hardt and Antonio Negri's reformulation of Michel Foucault's analysis of biopolitics and biopower.[17] For Hardt and Negri, biopolitical production is a plane of interaction in which bodies, existing in relation to one another, generate the world from the bottom-up. Biopolitical production is a *creative power*; it is the power *of* life—*of bodies*—to produce, endlessly. This endless production coexists with the ability to *resist* subjugation and to determine *alternative* thoughts, practices, subjectivities, and, in this case, *realities*. To borrow the language of Deleuze and Guattari, biopolitical production exists on a plane of imma-nence in which everyone—and presumably everything—relates to everyone and everything else.[18] This type of radical relationality sets the conditions for the possibility of decentered, nonhierarchical realities. This is the basis of biopolitical production.

Biopower is just the opposite—it is the organization, management, and institutionalization of bodies through top-down relations and structures. Biopower is the power *over* life—*over bodies*—and is therefore a *created power*; it is something that occurs *after* the primordial interaction of biopolitical production. Biopower is something that is enabled by and emerges from the primordiality of biopolitical creation. But biopower then manages the production of the biopolitical—it channels the primordial interaction in particular ways and for particular ends. The "......" is prohibited from following its own free-flowing trajectories and, instead, is corralled toward specific productions that result in specific effects and consequences.

This type of power enables small pockets of people to disproportionately benefit from the collective lot of human creativity. Such a form of power manifests in different ways: capitalism; state-run socialism; mass media that manufacture unreflective consent; racism, sexism, and homophobia; dictato-rial regimes; and even liberal democracies in which a sovereign power (a nation-state) bestows "liberties" upon its citizens. These manifestations are not all the same; each operates according to its own organizing apparatus and engenders a specific form of oppression. But the underlying issue *is* the same: one's capacity to create reality is tethered to and channeled toward the empowerment of another—toward capitalists, racists, dictators, nation-states, and so on. Although we are reality-creating beings, we are not always free to create whatever realities we please. Instead, we often create realities that empower exterior forces—that is, forces that are exterior to the progression and trajectory of the "_ _ _ _ _."

This exteriorization can be understood as a form of estrangement rather than alienation. According to Franco Berardi,[19] alienation is often understood as the loss of an "essential humanity"—that is, some foreign, dominating system captures and controls our natural-born essence, and we will never be whole and free until we reclaim that essence. Berardi believes this to be a mistaken conceptual terrain, since it bounds us to an exterior power that determines who and what we are and delimits the conditions of our freedom. We are one down and one removed, so to speak. Berardi amends this conceptualization by denying the very idea of essence. He posits, instead, that we are processual, adaptive creatures constantly giving rise to, and then ebbing and flowing with, various forms of sociality. Those forms of sociality must then be subjected to critical analysis, from which we can develop tactics of resistance and social change. While alienation designates a loss of essence, estrangement denotes a conscious awareness of the historically situated conditions of oppression and a refusal to identify with those conditions. We may therefore be estranged from living more fulfilling, enjoyable lives but not from our essence, because there is no essential, transhistorical "thing" that we *are*.[20]

Estrangement, thus understood, is positive and productive because it designates the possibility of and desire for resistance: we are free to resist and to alter our historically situated forms of oppression because we are not and can never be identical to the surrounding conditions. We are always and already free to resist and rebel. This is not always easy to do, and in some cases it may be fatal and perhaps discouraged. But resistance is structured into the very fabric of human experience. School children loosen their ties beneath the collar, raise their hemlines just above the knee, and inscribe love poems on the bottom of their soles. Prisoners import illegal contraband, communicate in secret codes, and fashion weapons from bare essentials. Undocumented immigrants cross borders, climb walls, and dig tunnels. Overworked and underpaid temporary workers organize campaigns for guaranteed social income. And plenty of average, everyday people find ways to challenge the corruption and cruelty of present-day systems. Even conformity can be interpreted as a way to resist marginalization and exclusion, which, under particular conditions of survival, could mean the difference between life and death. Such acts of resistance do not always gesture toward revolutionary ends, but they do demonstrate the human will to resist and create. Oppressive systems, understood as human-created realities, emerge from and then capture and control the "_____". But the "_____" always precedes and exceeds the realities that it creates. Estrangement is an experiential recognition of this gap and therefore a contributing factor to the eros effect: estrangement enables us to sense not just our oppression, but also our liberation; not just our dejection, but also our coming celebration; not just our underutilized "_____", but also the militant assertion of <!_____!>.

This dual sensing of the world-that-is and the world-to-be helps move our bodies toward action: our bodies move *away* from this world and *toward* the forthcoming world. This movement toward a decentered world of multiple realities provokes a sense of global solidarity. People of different backgrounds and different locations suddenly identify with one another: young hippie kids identifying with Latin American and Southeast Asian revolutions; global justice activists participating in a "movement of movements"; 2011 Cairo protesters carrying signs that read, "From Egypt to Wall Street, Don't [Be] Afraid, Go Ahead, #OccupyOakland, #OWS" and "From #Tahrir to #OccupyOakland and #USA One Case, One Goal #SocialJusticeforAll, Fuck Police";[21] and Palestinian and Black Lives Matter activists supporting one another's struggles. Such solidarity is not a denial of social and cultural differences; it is just the opposite. People realize that unleashing their reality-creating abilities inherently involves an embrace of radical difference, and that those differences are at the very center of the world-to-come. That is the only way that a decentered, bottom-up world can exist. Such solidarity does not eradicate ingrained prejudice and privilege. But these problems tend to resurface *after* the initial moment of political awakening. In the actual moment of awakening, people are thinking and acting from the militant becomings of the <!_____!>---<!_____!>---<!_____!>. Those militant becomings precede and exceed chauvinism—that is, an excessive attachment to a particular marker of identity. It is usually on the downside of the awakening that patterns of prejudice begin to wear on the solidarity of rebellion. It is at those times that we organize workshops and teach-ins on racism or sexism, argue about different tactics and strategies, and begin to worry about division, disintegration, and cooptation. But the actual moment of awakening generates a different reality—a reality of many realities coexisting as a movement of rebellion and liberation.

## THIRD PRINCIPLE: BODILY EMANATION

The final principle focuses on the magnetic allure of mass political awakenings in which hundreds, thousands, and even millions of people take to the streets seemingly overnight. Katsiaficas argues that these eruptions exert an alluring effect that radiates outward and attracts people to the action. Katsiaficas even describes this affective allure in existential and quasi-spiritual terms: the eros effect "emanates from and reaches the deepest dimensions of the souls of human beings";[22] metaphorically, it resembles the "religious transformation of the individual soul through the sacred baptism in the ocean of universal life and love";[23] and the experience is similar to a "traditional Korean shamanistic ritual, or *shinmyong*—a collective feeling of ecstasy when *han* (sorrow, pent-up grief) is discharged."[24]

I agree with these descriptions. But I want to ground this magnetic allure in a particular phenomenon that I refer to as bodily emanation. In everyday discourse, bodily emanation is often referred to as a vibe, the vibe, vibes, vibrations, or some variation thereof. The cultural landscape is saturated with such references: Bob Marley's "Positive Vibration" and the Beach Boys' "Good Vibrations"; movies like *Vibes* (Columbia Pictures 1988) and *Vibrations* (Dimension Home Video 1995); *Vibe Magazine*, which reports on hip-hop culture; a line of cars by General Motors called the "Pontiac Vibe"; entries filed under "vibes" on freedictionary.com, yourdictionary.com, and urbandictionary.com; and everyday references like "that was an intense vibe" and "I feel a bad vibe in here." There are also lesser-known references like Foucault's description of a particular experience as "immensely vibratory"[25] and Che Guevara's description of Fidel Castro's speaking abilities:

> Fidel is a master at this; his particular mode of integration with the people can only be appreciated by seeing him in action. In the big public meetings one can observe something like the dialogue of two tuning forks whose *vibrations* summon forth new *vibrations* each in the other. Fidel and the mass begin to *vibrate* in a dialogue of growing intensity which reaches its culminating point in an abrupt ending crowned by our victorious battle cry.[26]

Despite these numerous references, the vibe receives little to no sustained intellectual reflection.[27] But this deficiency does not preclude the possibility of using the phenomenon to understand the eros effect. With that said, I describe bodily emanation as an actual and tangible feeling that our bodies emanate in an outward direction. The body does not simply *respond* to itself and the world in a felt manner. The body also *emits or radiates feeling or energy*. The body is not just a pre-separated multiplicity of perpetual becoming that looks like this: ".⸳⸳⸳⸳⸳". It is also an organism of vibrational emission that looks like this:---".⸳⸳⸳⸳⸳."---. Those hyphenated dashes depict the unseen but felt phenomenon of bodily emanation. I have provided a detailed account of this phenomenon elsewhere.[28] This current chapter does not permit me to delve into all the complexities. Suffice it to say that bodily emanation can be discerned on at least three levels of experience: the interpersonal, small and large group settings, and the global.[29]

Interpersonally, we can feel our bodies, face-to-face, emanating a tangible feeling between one another. That energy—the vibe—could be good or bad, positive or negative, attractive or repulsive, or even indifferent. But it is there nonetheless—our bodies emanating an "energy" that we experience, detect, and often respond to. That emanation might hit you, engulf you, enwrap you, flirt with you, seduce you, attract you, or even push you away. Regardless of the specific experience, it is there and detectable: that other body is emanating a vibe. But your own body is also emanating a vibe. This is often harder to detect because you are the source of the emanation. But, on occasion, you might feel your bodily emanation extending outward, becoming larger, wider, and more intense. This might happen during heated arguments, debates, or physical altercations. You are, in a sense, trying to intimidate and push the other person. At other times, you might feel your vibe receding, becoming smaller and less noticeable. This might happen during moments of embarrassment or awkwardness. You want to hide, so to speak, and are therefore retracting the noticeability of your bodily emanation. On other occasions, you might realize that you are emanating a vibe of anger, joy, tranquility, surprise, or sadness. Regardless of the particular characteristics, we can and do notice and respond to our own and others' bodily emanation. Such detection is possible because the vibe extends beyond one's own individual body and therefore involves a level of objectivity. Just as we can notice, listen to, and process our own oral communication, so, too, can we notice and respond to bodily emanation. It is something that is generated from, and that exists between, our bodies.

Bodily emanation is also detectable within groups and crowds. This experience is less about face-to-face and/or one-on-one interaction and more about a collective vibe. That collective vibe is often more intense and noticeable because there are more bodies, and more bodies equal more emanation—there's a greater lot of energy. This helps explain the intensity of music concerts and sporting events, or the difficulty of speaking to large audiences. Bringing bodies together in the same place and time generates a greater magnitude of bodily emanation. One's individual experience of that magnitude is therefore intensified—it is a deeper, more intensely sensuous experience. That sensuality can sometimes be so intense that we feel overtaken by it, as if the collective vibe invites or even commands us to relinquish control and move with the flow. This can be a pleasurable experience for some people, and a fearful experience for others. Either way, the intensity of that experience demonstrates the noticeability of the phenomenon.

This collective vibe is generated through a symbiotic relationship between the individual and the group. Each individual body contributes to the overall vibe of the group, and the group influences the type of vibe that each individual body emanates. This symbiotic relationship occurs not just at concerts or sporting events, but at conferences, parties, meetings, gatherings, protests, marches, and rallies; and it occurs within classrooms, churches, stores, restaurants, theaters, auditoriums, and even within neighborhoods, towns, and cities. The collective vibe of New York City is different than the collective vibe of San Francisco, both of which are different from that of Miami, Detroit, Montreal, Madrid, and Tokyo. One's embodied, sentient experience of these different cities is not reducible to bodily emanation—every situation is complicated and multifaceted, involving a plethora of different experiential registers. But bodily emanation plays an important role, which is why people make such comments as "I love the vibe of New York" or "The San Francisco vibe is totally different."

If bodily emanation exists within groups and crowds, then it is logical to assume that it exists on a global level. The logic follows like this: each and every body emanates a vibe; bodies exist across the planet; therefore, a global vibe must exist (a global zeitgeist, of sorts). But consciously experiencing and detecting that global vibe is difficult if not impossible. Just as we are unable to feel the Earth's rotation, so, too, are we unable to feel the global vibe.[30] It is something so ingrained and naturalized that it resists conscious detection. But we can turn our attention toward it and begin to notice particular experiences that point to the interconnectivity of global emanation. One such experience is the pushing-and-pulling of our bodies: our bodies are pushed and pulled to and from one another through their vibrational attractions and repulsions. This pushing-and-pulling can be characterized as a gravitational force that guides our bodies to and from particular people.[31]

This gravitational force emerges from the vibrational connectivity that exists between our emanating bodies. Our bodies do not simply emanate outward into a dead, empty space. Instead, each vibe entwines with, and *takes up a relationship to*, every other vibe. Our emanating bodies affect and are affected by one another—that is, they are attuned to and influence each other. But not all bodies are equally attuned. Some are more and/or less attuned to others. The more they are attuned, the more they are attracted to one another. The less they are attuned, the less they are attracted to one another. This "vibrational attunement" enables our emanating bodies to attract and repel *themselves* to and from one another. As the saying goes, "just go with the flow." In other words, be confident that your vibe will attract you to the right people at the right time.

This attraction and repulsion is most noticeable when we are in the immediate presence of other people. I might attend a political demonstration, for instance, and notice that my body keeps turning toward a particular direction within the massive crowd. This is strange because I am consciously trying to listen to the speaker on stage. But every time I reposition my body toward the stage, I inevitably find myself turning toward this other direction. I then notice someone off in the distance and realize that my body is attracted to, and is thus adjusting itself toward, this person's bodily emanation. There is a gravitational force between *my* body and *that* body. In no way was I consciously aware of this single individual standing off in the distance. There is simply too much going on for me to have consciously spotted this individual. The gravitational force even cuts through my conscious intentions—I am trying to listen to the speaker, but the vibrational attraction to this other person is pulling me in another direction.

This particular description relates to, but is not synonymous with, my previous statements about the sentient body's attractions and repulsions. The ". . . . ." moves *itself* toward and away from particular phenomena, circumstances, and conditions. Bodily emanation involves a similar self-moving process, but it does so within a *different register* of experience. The ". . . . ." is a relationship between the sentient body and its situational phenomena. The emanating body is a relationship between one's own individual vibe and the vibes of others. That relationship could involve two people (the interpersonal), many people (the small and large group), or everyone (the global). Regardless of the level, the same dynamic is at work: our emanating bodies entwine, relate to, and push-and-pull themselves to and from one another through a variety of gravitational relationships.

Given this theoretical framework, I argue that bodily emanation is a contributing factor to the alluring effect of mass political awakenings. At the very least, spontaneous rebellions are powerful discharges of bodily emanation—violent explosions that rip through the collective vibe of one's society. For too long the people have been oppressed, and that oppression produces its own collective vibe of dejection, acceptance, and hopelessness. Such a vibe is its own oppressive condition—it is physically toxic and emotionally draining, and it therefore suppresses any urge toward revolt and revolution. Such suppression is difficult to combat because it often goes unnoticed. The collective vibe of one's society is too ingrained and taken for granted to pique one's notice; it's part of the general milieu. But there it is, exerting influence and constituting its own repressive gravitational force. Rather than attuning ourselves to the urge of revolt, we are attuned to a vortex of self-perpetuating oppression.

But certain events then occur that momentarily break people's psychobehavioral conditioning. The "_ _ _ _ _" is given a chance to breathe and it begins seeking escape routes. Alternative thoughts and practices start to emerge and social change actually seems possible. The "_ _ _ _ _" now feels invigorated and begins to emanate a subtle vibe of hopefulness. Other bodies pick up on this and attune themselves to one another. A different gravitational force is now in play, and bodies begin to move and act.

This gravitational force does not attract everyone but, instead, attracts particular bodies: bodies that have been oppressed, marginalized, and forsaken; bodies that have always dreamed of another world; bodies that long to create their own realities; bodies that are enticed by the coming confrontation. These bodies were already attuned to one another at some level of vibrational experience, but the oppressive conditions inhibited them from recognizing and acting on that attunement. A critical mass eventually emerges as the vibe of resistance thickens and intensifies. The once soft and subtle pulse suddenly becomes a lightning rod of energy. A shockwave radiates outward and a rebellion erupts. Bodies fill the streets and a collective vibe emanates into the world. Mass revolt is in the air.

## CONCLUDING REMARKS: AN ONTOLOGY
## OF PERPETUAL RESISTANCE

This chapter's rethinking of the eros effect through sentience, reality, and emanation revolves around an alternative understanding of the body as an organic, multifaceted phenomenon that constantly strives toward liberation. Whereas Katsiaficas begins with innate psychological drives, I begin with an ontology of the body-in-perpetual-revolt. As stated at the beginning of the chapter, this is not a critique of Katsiaficas but, rather, a different theoretical approach intended to enhance our understanding of the eros effect.

This ontology of bodies-in-revolt helps explain the possibility of transnational solidarities and the attraction between one's own struggle and the struggles of others. Uprisings halfway around the world are reported and go viral. We then see and read these images and stories, which enables our bodies to suddenly recognize their own predispositions toward liberation.

Our bodies then begin moving of their own accord. However, this experiential recognition may occur *without* such reporting. That is because our
bodies are attuned and connected through bodily emanation. Uprisings in
Egypt or Spain have reverberative effects in the United States and China.
Our bodies can sense one another's struggles at some implicit, experiential level. Our bodies, as a collective lot, are an interconnected process
perpetually resisting and overcoming various forms of oppression. Just
as this "_. . . . ._" expresses the individual body as a singular-multiplicity,
this ---<!_. . . . ._!>---<!_. . . . ._!>---<!_. . . . ._!>--- expresses our collective
bodies as a singular-multiplicity in *perpetual revolt*. Even oppression itself
can be understood as a form of liberation: oppressors liberate themselves by
oppressing others and, conversely, people accept their oppression because
it liberates them from the worries of struggle and protest. But these are
obviously distorted forms of liberation. True liberation occurs when each
and every body is capable of moving in accordance with its own sentient,
emanating, reality-creating trajectory. Such individual-and-collective coordination posits no end results but, rather, opens a future world in which
people are equally empowered to pursue their own trajectories of becoming.

   This theoretical framework shifts our understanding of global revolt:
It is not that *the Egyptians* or *the Spaniards* or *the Americans* or *the Chinese*
are rebelling; instead, *we* are rebelling. Our bodies are scattered across the
globe, existing in different forms as they encounter different conditions and
situations. We are and always will be different and diverse. But that difference
and diversity does not exclude the possibility of an unspoken coordination
in which masses of bodies simultaneously rise up. These moments of revolt
are not reducible to rebellions against *this* or *that* oppressive system. Instead,
these are moments in which bodies are rebelling against the very nature—
the very possibility—of oppression. Slogans like "One no, many yeses" and
"We are all Egyptians now" summarize this insight. The global emergence
of simultaneously occurring insurgencies is an ontological phenomenon. We
already exist like this:---<!_. . . . ._!>---<!_. . . . ._!>---<!_. . . . ._!>---. It is
thus a matter of cultivating this ontology into a conscious form of political
resistance. Suffice it to say that this topic of "cultivation" will have to be
saved for a future discussion.


## NOTES

   1. George Katsiaficas, *The Imagination of the New Left: A Global Analysis of
1968* (Boston: South End Press, 1987), 10 (all emphases in original).

2. To one degree or another, Katsiaficas does acknowledge the primordiality of the body. In reference to Marcuse's work, he states that "liberation . . . depends on sensuous human beings. Rationality has a soul to it, a body that goes along with it." See George Katsiaficas, "Marcuse's Cognitive Interest: A Personal View," *New Political Science* 18, no. 2–3 (1996): 159–170 (166). In reference to his own work, he seeks to "uncover the structure of action and content of ideas contained in the sensuous morality of people's uprisings." See George Katsiaficas, *Asia's Unknown Uprisings, Volume 1* (Oakland: PM Press, 2012), 3. However, my approach to the eros effect leads with the body, while Katsiaficas leads with innate psychological drives. In some ways, then, my approach is closer to Marcuse's notion of a "new sensorium" as outlined in *An Essay on Liberation* (Middlesex: Penguin Books, 1969).

3. For general critiques of Cartesian dualism, see phenomenology, existentialism, pragmatism, second-wave feminism, and particular postmodern and poststructuralist thinkers (for instance, Judith Butler and Michel Foucault). For specific critiques, see the following anthologies: Donn Welton, ed., *Body and Flesh: A Philosophical Reader* (Malden: Blackwell, 1998); and Donn Welton, ed., *The Body: Classic and Contemporary Readings* (Malden: Blackwell, 1999).

4. Such an argument opposes postmodern critiques that often characterize the body as nothing but representation. This is not the time or place to parse out this debate. Suffice it to say that I disagree, and I argue that the body, as a living, experiential organism, is neither outside of, nor reducible to, representation. Even Judith Butler acknowledges this when stating that "the relation between the body and discourse . . . is one in which discourse cannot fully 'capture' the body, and the body cannot fully elude discourse" (as quoted in Vicki Kirby, *Judith Butler: Live Theory* (New York: Continuum, 2006), 145). Butler is in no way referring to the kind of experiential intelligence that I am, but her quote does acknowledge the body's irreducibility. For more on this debate, see David Michael Levin, ed., *Language Beyond Postmodernism: Saying and Thinking in Gendlin's Philosophy* (Evanston: Northwestern University Press, 1997).

5. Eugene Gendlin, "The Primacy of the Body, Not the Primacy of Perception," *Man and World* 25, no. 3–4 (1992): 341–353 (344) (all emphases in original). It should be noted that Gendlin is directly responding to Maurice Merleau-Ponty's notion that "perception is primary" to human experience. See, for instance, Maurice Merleau-Ponty, *Phenomenology of Perception* (London: Routledge, 1995).

6. Eugene Gendlin, "Thinking Beyond Patterns: Body, Language, and Situations," in *The Presence of Feeling in Thought*, ed. B. den Ouden and M. Moen (New York: Peter Lang, 1992), 27–189 (114).

7. This is a phenomenological insight and not a gesture toward philosophical idealism. Phenomenology investigates how the world takes on sense for the individual human subject through a coconstitutive structure, which is different from the individual subject positing the exterior world through an act of the mind.

8. Gendlin's phenomenological and psychotherapeutic understanding of the body-situation is peripherally related to feminist standpoint theory and situated

knowledges. In brief, all knowledge is situated within a relationship between knower-and-location; each human being knows differently due to the knower's unique experience, situational conditions, and power relationships. See, for instance, Alison M. Jaggar and Susan R. Bordo, eds., *Gender/Body/Knowledge: Feminist Reconstructions of Being and Knowing* (New Brunswick: Rutgers University Press, 1989); Linda Alcoff and Elizabeth Potter, eds., *Feminist Epistemologies* (New York: Routledge, 1993); and Sandra Harding, ed., *The Feminist Standpoint Theory Reader: Intellectual and Political Controversies* (New York: Routledge, 2004).

9. For more on nonteleological directionality, see Eugene Gendlin, "The New Phenomenology of Carrying Forward," *Continental Philosophy Review* 37, no. 1 (2004): 127–151.

10. Some people might worry that this is an essentialist account of the body that ignores the problem of habitualized behaviors that should be changed for ethical and/or political reasons—for example, racism, sexism, homophobia, heteronormativity, hypermasculinity, or mindless consumerism. Gendlin's philosophy challenges such habits by articulating a layer of experiencing-and-knowing that operates both *before* and *after* habituation. He is asking: Can we *think beyond patterns* and can we think *with* the *very process* by which patterns arise? This project is unique, but not unprecedented. For instance, Audre Lorde defines "erotic power" as an "unexpressed or unrecognized feeling" capable of liberating us from oppressive power structures. See, Audre Lorde, "Uses of the Erotic: The Erotic as Power," in *Sister Outsider: Essays and Speeches* (Trumansburg: Crossing Press, 1984), 53–59. Likewise, Michel Foucault argues that resistance and freedom are primary to power relations; the latter cannot exist without the former. See Michel Foucault, "Afterword: The Subject and Power," in *Michel Foucault: Beyond Structuralism and Hermeneutics*, ed. Hubert L. Dreyfus and Paul Rabinow (Chicago: University of Chicago Press, 1982), 208–226. In brief, Gendlin, Lorde, and Foucault argue, in different ways, that we can and do think and act in ways that precede and exceed current patterns of thought and action.

11. To appropriate the language of Gilles Deleuze and Felix Guattari: the ". . . . ." is constantly trying to allow immanence to function more fully within transcendence.

12. In brief, the ego/mind *is* the ". . . . ." thinking about itself. The ego/mind is simply *one possible form* that emerges from the ". . . . .". But due to various social and historical conditions, we have come to understand the ego/mind as the essence of human experience. Here, I am combining Gendlin's notion of the sentient body with postmodern and poststructuralist insights about the "death of the author" and the "erasure of subjectivity." That is to say, notions of the ego/mind are socially constructed. Under different sociohistorical conditions, we might have radically different notions of human subjectivity that would never involve anything resembling an ego or mind. This further supports the point I made in note 10 about antiessentialism. The ". . . . ." is not an essential foundation. It only exists in relation to a surrounding situation, and every situation is different, diverse,

and diversifying (different to itself and different within itself). For references, see Roland Barthes, "The Death of the Author," in *Image-Music-Text*, trans. Stephan Heath (New York: Hill and Wang, 1977), 142–148; and Jacques Derrida, "Signature Event Context," in *Limited Inc.*, ed. Gerald Graff (Evanston: Northwestern University Press, 1988), 1–23.

13. Edmund Husserl, *Analyses Concerning Passive and Active Synthesis: Lectures on Transcendental Logic*, trans. Anthony Steinbock (Dordrecht: Kluwer Academic, 2001), 196.

14. Ibid., 196–221.

15. Ibid., 221.

16. Starhawk, *Truth or Dare: Encounters with Power, Authority, and Mystery* (San Francisco: Harper San Francisco, 1988).

17. Michael Hardt and Antonio Negri, *Commonwealth* (Cambridge: Harvard University Press, 2009), 31–38 and 55–63. And to clarify, Hardt and Negri are *reformulating*, not ascribing these ideas to, Foucault. They are reading Foucault through the tenets of Italian Autonomism and Deleuze and Guattari.

18. Gilles Deleuze and Felix Guattari, *What Is Philosophy?*, trans. Hugh Tomlinson and Graham Burchell (New York: Columbia University Press, 1994), 35–60.

19. Franco Berardi, *The Soul at Work: From Alienation to Autonomy* (Los Angeles: Semiotext(e), 2009), 35–51.

20. This reflects, in part, my comments in notes 10 and 12.

21. Ishaan Tharoor, "Hands Across the World," in *What Is Occupy? Inside the Global Movement*, ed. Time (New York: Time Home Entertainment, 2011), 26. Xeni Jardin, "Egyptians March from Tahrir Square to Support Occupy Oakland Protestors," *Boingboing*, October 28, 2011, http://boingboing.net/2011/10/28/tahrir.html.

22. George Katsiaficas, "The Eros Effect," personal website, 1989, www.eroseffect.com, 8.

23. Ibid., 6.

24. Katsiaficas, *Asia's Unknown Uprisings, Volume 1*, 17. For similar descriptions, see Katsiaficas, *Imagination of the New Left*, 7 and 71; and Katsiaficas, *Asia's Unknown Uprisings, Volume 1*, 21.

25. David Macey, *The Lives of Michel Foucault: A Biography* (New York: Vintage Books, 1995), 254.

26. Ernesto Che Guevara, "The New Man," in *Philosophy for a New Generation*, ed. A. K. Bierman and James A. Gould (New York: Macmillan, 1970), 312–322 (314; emphases added).

27. Neurophysiologist Valier Hunt and physicist William Tiller do address something like "the vibe." But their work combines physics and quantum mechanics with New Age spiritualism. While interesting and related, that is not the focus of my project. See, for example, Valier Hunt, *Infinite Mind: Science of the Human Vibrations of Consciousness* (Malibu: Malibu, 1996); and William Tiller, *Science and Human Transformation: Subtle Energies, Intentionality and Consciousness* (Walnut Creek: Pavior, 1997).

28. Jason Del Gandio, "From Affectivity to Bodily Emanation: An Introduction to the Human Vibe," *PhaenEx: Journal of Existential and Phenomenological Theory and Culture* 7, no. 2 (2012): 28–58.

29. Some people may ask about the material nature of bodily emanation, wondering, for example, if it is similar to electromagnetic energy. Hunt (1996) and Tiller (1997) attempt to address such questions, and studies concerning the electro-communication between bees and flowers can be helpful starting points (see Nell Greenfieldboyce, "Bumblebees' Little Hairs Can Sense Flowers' Electric Fields," *National Public Radio*, May 30, 2016, http://www.npr.org/sections/thetwo-way/2016/05/30/479804121/bumblebees-little-hairs-can-sense-flowers-electric-fields). However, I am more concerned with the "how" rather than the "what" of bodily emanation. For example, how is it that so many people experience the phenomenon that they refer to as a "vibe"? How might we begin to theorize this experience, even if we cannot yet fully understand its objective, material nature?

30. Skeptics might argue that this is a poor analogy because the Earth's rotation can be measured objectively. But this reliance upon measurability must be questioned. First, measurability is not the totality of human experience. Assuming otherwise elevates the scientific paradigm to the status of dogma. And second, measurability is simply one form of intersubjective validation. Validation can be attained in other ways, such as the numerous cultural references outlined at the beginning of this section.

31. Some readers may wonder if bodily emanation is strictly a human phenomenon, or if it extends to other living beings, or even to all things. I am currently restricting my approach to bodily emanation as a human phenomenon. In recent years, I have become increasingly open to the possibility that it applies to nonhuman animals and nature, but that involves a more expansive theoretical framework. I am skeptical of applying it to all things, which might resemble something like a watered-down version of animism.

6

# Revolt *as* Reason, Reason *as* Revolt

## On the Praxis of Philosophy from Below

RICHARD GILMAN-OPALSKY

In the existing world, largely governed by the logic of capital and the pathologies of accumulation, revolt is an expression of reason. In light of so many measures, such as the basic macroeconomic facts of global poverty and inequality, the absence of revolt may even appear as the height of unreason. A society that does not revolt against a social order that damages it with such escalating facility—psychologically, collectively, ecologically—is a society that, if it were a person, would be living at the terminal stage. Revolt functions like an antidote, or like part of the immune system of the body politic, generating forces against what kills us. In this opening flourish, much needs defining. For starters, we must define revolt and reason, and only then can we move on to consider the normative claims of these statements, and their social and political contexts.

In so doing, the work of George Katsiaficas provides an invaluable resource. Katsiaficas has been arguing for the reasonable content of social movements and rebellions for almost thirty years and has applied that general perspective to an analysis of historic and recent revolt around the world, including to uprisings in Asia, Latin America, Europe, the United States, and in other geographic and historic locations. Katsiaficas is not alone in seeing the reason of revolt, since many thinkers before him have accepted the logic of this general perspective. Some of those thinkers will also be consulted in the present consideration of the praxis of philosophy from below.

In addition to making the case for understanding revolt *as* reason and reason *as* revolt, I shall argue for a certain twist, not against, but beyond the work of Katsiaficas. I argue for an extension of Katsiaficas' general theory into a rethinking of theory itself. Specifically, we need to shift from understanding the affective and reasonable dimensions of upheaval, to an understanding of the philosophical content of revolt, to an understanding of revolt as philosophical work. This shift, at bottom, can be understood as a shift from an explanatory and descriptive mode of analysis, conducted by social scientists on the *object* of revolt, to recognizing that much of the work of social science is itself carried out more effectively by the *subjects* of revolt. In short, we need another inversion, from the intellectual analysis of revolt, to revolt as intellectual analysis itself.

But, before engaging this bigger question vis-à-vis the work of Katsiaficas, let us establish some basic terms and concepts.

## REVOLT AND REASON

For brevity's sake, I shall retrieve some basic understandings of revolt and reason from sources that stipulate the meanings I would like to defend and deploy.

Julia Kristeva has thought about the conceptual and etymological meaning of revolt perhaps more than any other scholar in history. Kristeva, a critical theorist, psychoanalyst, and philosopher, has written many books and novels dedicated to the topic of revolt. She is particularly useful here because, as we shall see, Katsiaficas' theory of the eros effect draws out the psychoanalytic dimension of revolt by way of Freud and Fromm through Marcuse, and that dimension is also the central preoccupation of Kristeva's work on revolt. In her book *Intimate Revolt*, Kristeva writes: "The word 'revolt,' with its rich and complex etymology, acquired its current, distinctly political meaning with the French Revolution. Thus when we speak of revolt today we first understand a protest against already established norms, values, and powers."[1]

Kristeva affirms that revolt is protest of already established norms, values, and powers, but she also wants to retrieve certain meanings of revolt that date back before the French Revolution and to expand revolt into psychological and affective spheres of life. Kristeva does not depoliticize revolt, and she understands its ongoing and necessary connection to politics and revolution, but, rather, she wants "to wrest it, etymologically, from the overly narrow political sense it has taken in our time."[2] She sees

> revolt as a dialectical process. . . . Today the word "revolt" has become assimilated to Revolution, to political action. The events of the twentieth century, however, have shown us that political "revolts"—Revolutions—ultimately betrayed revolt, especially the psychic sense of the term. Why? Because revolt, as I understand it . . . refers to a state of permanent questioning, of transformation, of change, an endless probing of appearances.[3]

Kristeva argues that, after the French and Russian Revolutions, those revolutions stopped calling into question their own values and started to defend themselves rather than to continually question themselves, and in this way, the revolutions came to betray revolt itself.

In his 1989 essay "The Eros Effect," Katsiaficas focuses on how social upheavals "imagine a new way of life and a different social reality" and "may be considered collective liberatory sublimation—a rational way of clearing collective psychological blockages."[4] Thus, Katsiaficas explicitly connects revolt to processes of working through psychological, as well as social and political, problems. His sense of revolt is both consistent and resonant with that of Kristeva. And, it is important to notice that Katsiaficas finds in revolt a critical text full of "imaginative" proposals and "rational" activity.[5] Following this, revolt may be defined as a permanent state of questioning, transformation, and change, as a form of reason or critique; it is an active feature of the psychological health of society, and it embodies and expresses the social imagination and desire for new ways of life.

Next, what are reason and rationality? The liberal political philosophy of John Rawls is of little use for a discussion of revolt, making him a rather strange place to start. A general position of liberals, held faithfully by Rawls, is that revolt is superfluous in liberal societies, which can address most problems within the limits of the law. Moreover, Rawls fundamentally disagrees with the basic premises of my own work, in that he holds out hope for a fair capitalist society, which I take as a contradiction in terms. Rawls devoted his life's work to theorizing a "practical" way toward that great contradiction. Rawls' premises continue to ground the most fundamental of liberal conceits, including that perplexingly unshakeable faith in "capitalist democracy." Like most liberals, Rawls never placed his faith in riot, revolt, or revolution.

Having said this, Rawls' famous distinction between the "reasonable" and the "rational" is convincing and useful for purposes other than his own. Here, I shall use it to make the case for both the rationality and reason of revolt. Rawls writes:

> Reasonable persons are ready to propose, or to acknowledge when proposed by others, the principles needed to specify what can be seen by all as fair terms of cooperation. . . . Some have a superior political power or are placed in more fortunate circumstances; . . . it may be rational for those so placed to take advantage of their situation. . . . Common sense views the reasonable but not, in general, the rational as a moral idea involving moral sensibility.[6]

In other words, if something (in thought or action) can be made to make sense, then it has an accessible rationale and is thereby "rational." Everything that is understandable, explicable, or that can be comprehended from someone's experience and point of view, is rational. If you murder someone in a jealous rage, in a "crime of passion," the action is rational to the extent that we understand *why* you did it, even though we can say it was unreasonable at the same time. Some things are rational and unreasonable at the same time. What makes something reasonable, according to Rawls, is its "moral sensibility," the idea that it is the right thing to do and, especially for Rawls, that it is fair. There is always your rational self-interest, and then there is what is good for the community, and sometimes (not always) the two are mutually exclusive. In many cases, there is a rationale for doing X, but it is more reasonable to do Y instead.

Part of what is good in Rawls' definition is that he makes it difficult to be "irrational." To be irrational, one has to do or think something that cannot be understood, that is totally inexplicable—that cannot be made to make any sense. Throughout history, this has been the plight of the "mad," of "madness"—a history of horrific misunderstanding, wherein failing to understand a person's rationale for doing something leads to the conclusion of irrationality.[7]

But if something can be given a rationale, then it is at least rational, even if it is not the right thing to do (i.e., reasonable). On this view, we can say that rioting and terrorism are rational, even when we do not want to call them reasonable. What is nice about Rawls' distinction is that it creates the space for us to acknowledge the rationality of an action, but to denounce the action on the grounds of reason. With Rawls, we can say, for example, that we understand the rationality of a war, but condemn it as unreasonable at the same time. We cannot disqualify thoughts and actions as irrational as long as they embody and reflect grievances we are capable of understanding. Whereas revolt is often characterized as being both irrational and unreasonable, I argue the opposite—that revolt is both rational and reasonable.

## INTELLECT OF REVOLT, NOT ANALYSIS OF REVOLT

In 2000, in a conversation about the 1999 Seattle protests of the World Trade Organization, Katsiaficas said:

> It seems the revolutionary subject, as Marcuse said, emerges in the course of revolution. Regions are another way of organizing ourselves, and they would emerge in the course of making themselves real. We can't just have our alternative to capitalist globalization emerge full blown from our brains. Some people have attempted to create models for how this country could be organized. I'm not sure that's the way. I think the way is for people to do it, to actually reorganize, live it.[8]

Here, both Katsiaficas and Marcuse are right to highlight the productive and formative work that revolt does. Marcuse wrote about a "new sensibility" that emerges directly out of "*praxis*; it emerges in the struggle against violence and exploitation where this struggle is waged for essentially new ways and forms of life."[9] Marcuse also wrote about "the changing composition of the working class," about the possibility for a "new working class" that, "by virtue of its position, could disrupt, reorganize, and redirect the mode and relationships of production" (although he was doubtful they would do so).[10] Katsiaficas understood that the 1999 Seattle protests expressed a new sensibility and, potentially, a new composition of the revolutionary subject position, which seemed to confirm Marcuse's contention that revolt is a process of shaping, of actually producing new subject positions, and of working out alternatives to capitalism.

Yet, there is another line in Katsiaficas' thinking that expresses his affinity for the politics of prefiguration, which can be seen in the preceding passage, for example, in the closing call to construct and to live alternatives to the existing society in the here and now. I believe that the politics of prefiguration, which has seen a resurgence of interest since 2011 and has the good favor of too many anarchists, is the wrong orientation. I want to suggest that prefiguration leads to misdiagnoses in the analysis of revolt, and that the rich critical content of revolt is always more important than what it prefigures.

Prefiguration suggests that actors construct and experience new ways and forms of life by directly organizing and living them in the present. Advocates of prefiguration generally adopt the praxis of "learning by doing," suggesting that a liberatory politics reveals both its desirability and possibility when we directly experiment with and experience alternatives to the capitalist present. The politics of prefiguration can be found in many diverse places, for example, in John Holloway's discussion of "other-doing," Hakim Bey's idea of the "temporary autonomous zone," and it goes back at least to Michael Bakunin's arguments in *Statism and Anarchy*.[11] More recent articulations and defenses have been taken up by many anarchists, including Uri Gordon, Cindy Milstein, and Benjamin Franks.[12] As Franks briefly summarizes: "Prefiguration involves using means that are in accordance with the goals, creating in the present desired for features of the future."[13]

To be clear, I do not deny the importance of experiments in prefiguration, of learning and building alternatives directly by trying to make and to live them, a radical politics of "experiential learning" as it's often called in academia. In fact, I agree with Bakunin, Bey, Holloway, Katsiaficas, and others that prefigurative politics can reveal logics of life alternative to those governing the capitalist lifeworld. At the same time, however, prefiguration neglects the more significant, impactful dimensions of revolt, which regard its theoretical content. As shall become clear in the remainder of this essay, by "theoretical" I do not mean "academic," "textual," or "impractical." I intend this as good news, for if prefiguration was the way to construct real alternatives, then any hope for real alternatives would be lost.

Of course, on a micro-political scale, anarchist co-ops, community gardens, and groups like Food Not Bombs *do* challenge the logic of capital. They have a different operational logic than the logic of capital. But the capitalist world is mostly untroubled by them. Unless there is a direct conflict of interest, capital can even (and often does) encourage the existence of such projects. The peaceful coexistence of grocery stores and community gardens, for example, can be invoked to bolster the defenses of the tolerant, flexible, and "democratic" present. For this reason, I am critical of any praxis that overdetermines the transformative power of prefigurative politics. In all politics, it is critical to pay attention to the significance of the real mismatch of scale between our position and our opponent's, even if we do not know how to solve that problem. However, so much of prefiguration does not do this with sufficient seriousness. Therefore, most prefiguration only contests the existing world in ways that are compatible with the reproduction of the existing world indefinitely into the future.

It is therefore good news that prefiguration—or building alternatives by living them in the present—makes up a miniscule part of what happens in revolt. Revolt throws the world into question far more effectively than it makes new worlds. It is necessary to seriously consider the severe limitations imposed on us by this world to create new worlds. Indeed, if there were no severe limitations to creating alternatives to the existing world, radicals would have little to criticize. What can be done to create alternatives to capitalism in a world organized largely (even if not totally) by the logic of capital? What could be prefigured in Seattle in 1999 or, later, in the Occupy encampments of 2011? In capitalist society, most of what we do in school and work is governed by the logic of capital, and even leisure time is determined as the time left over after work (and that time is rapidly disappearing for reasons that I have discussed elsewhere).[14]

Without a doubt, certain forms of alter-relationality (relations beyond exchange-relations) and human solidarity are available for direct experience in social movements, and these are all good things, and good reasons to participate. But, in the existing capitalist world, people invariably "retour à la normale," as appeared on the popular poster in Paris during the uprisings of May–June 1968.[15] Seattle and Occupy protestors rupture the normality of everyday life, but the call to return to normal can only be resisted for so long before having to go back to work, school, and so on.

Moreover, we cannot stay in park encampments for at least two good reasons. First, we never intended to choose homelessness (and we do not want to sleep outside in subzero temperatures), and work is necessary even if it is hated. Second, and more importantly, we do not choose to live in park encampments *in order to* live in park encampments, but for other reasons worked out in the activity of occupying the park. That is to say, the critical content of the occupation, and not the occupation itself, expresses the radical thinking of the practice.

Historically, revolt does not have the perpetuity of its opponent, for revolt occurs in saturnalias, festivals of resistance and spontaneity that flourish and dissipate over short durations of time (typically days, sometimes weeks). Saturnalias of revolt cannot reverse the logic of the capitalist world, and they cannot produce alternative forms of life that can be selected over capitalism. The opponent, on the other hand, is not temporary like a saturnalia, but deeply entrenched, reproduced by everyday life, and enjoys enough confidence in its own permanence such that, in most countries, it can allow room for revolt without too much worry.

The foregoing analysis would seem dissuasive of revolt, were it not for the fact that revolt can be understood as accomplishing a very different thing. Revolt is an organic intellect at work, a collective philosopher, the old subversive philosopher, not a professional thinker in a university. Revolt does what all good philosophy has always done—it throws the reality and justice of the world into question. The most striking difference is that revolt accomplishes this far better than anything else or anyone else, far better than any professional philosopher or book.

Gilles Deleuze and Félix Guattari, in their short essay "May '68 Did Not Take Place," argue that events like the revolution of 1789, the Paris Commune, the revolution of 1917, and the uprising of 1968 enact "a lawless deviation, an unstable condition that opens up a new field of the possible. . . . There can only be creative solutions. These are the creative redeployments that can contribute to a resolution of the current crisis and that can take over where a generalized May '68, amplified bifurcation or fluctuation, left off."[16] What Deleuze and Guattari argue is that historians are always trying to settle insurrectionary events as phenomena that begin on a certain date and end on another, which leads to a discourse about the Paris Commune having "happened" or the events of '68 having "taken place." This is a view that Deleuze and Guattari reject on the grounds that it fundamentally misunderstands the eventuality of the events. They argue that what is most interesting about revolt is the way in which it opens an unfinished questioning, which other insurrections had previously begun, and which new ones can pick up where they have left off. Thus, Deleuze and Guattari shift the emphasis from what is concretely accomplished in or by the revolt, from what was prefigured or achieved by it (i.e., from a discourse of success or failure), to how the revolt participates in an unfinished questioning about radical possibilities, about creative solutions to crises.

As stated at the outset, there is no hard disagreement here with Katsiaficas, but rather a twist, a turn, an extension, a critical emphasis with consequences, which changes the way that we understand the relationship between revolt and philosophy.

In *The Subversion of Politics*, Katsiaficas writes: "As expressions of antisystemic participatory politics, autonomous social movements seek to live without a control center, no matter how rationalized its operation may be."[17] What Katsiaficas emphasizes here is an aspiration to live without a control center. This great aspiration, however, cannot be realized in existing capitalist societies, save for short-lived experiments in marginal and radical milieus. On the question of control, capital is decisive (though not totalitarian). Most of what we do, and when and where we do it, is decided by capital.

But Katsiaficas also touches upon another point that I must elaborate more fully here, and that is the objectionable rationality of the control center itself. Revolt opposes that rationality with a different rationality, a different reason. If we do not want to temporarily prefigure other forms of life, but to actually create the conditions where we can live alternatives in perpetuity, this is what is called "revolution" or "transformation." Revolution or transformation, first of all, engages in the negation of the constituted reality, or as Marx put it, "abolishes the present state of things."[18] New forms of life that come about but that leave the present state of things essentially unchanged are not new forms of life at all, but only developments or experiments within the limits of capital.

To be clear, I am by no means stating that nothing can be done until after capitalism is already in a museum or a graveyard. To the contrary, there are many forces of negation working against capitalism, from within capitalism itself. This dialectical sensibility reveals a certain Marxist orientation on my part, which many autonomists and autonomous social movements have also grasped, and which should be argued against the coterie of anarchists who cling to a politics of lifestyle and prefiguration. Revolt is only one form of negation.[19] Negation can also come in the form of crisis, such as the global economic crisis that has been fueling insurrectionary activity around the world since 2008, or in the growing climate and ecological crisis.

One thinker who expressed a profound understanding of the intellect of revolt was Raya Dunayevskaya. She focused on the philosophical content of what she called "spontaneous mass action," which she argued emerges as a dialectical force within and against the capitalist lifeworld.[20] In 1981, Dunayevskaya wrote that "there are certain creative moments in history when the objective movement and the subjective movement so coincide that the self-determination of ideas and the self-determination of masses readying for revolt explode. Something is in the air, and you catch it. That is, you catch it if you have a clear head and if you have good ears to hear *what is upsurging from below*."[21] On the one hand, there is a certain spontaneity to revolt, and yet, revolt articulates and communicates a critical content that those with "clear heads" and "good ears" can hear. Often, the spontaneity of revolt masks its rationality and reason, because the iconic image of the reasonable is calm, objective, and carefully presented. Revolt does not look reasonable in that conventional way, because it is unsettling, subjective, and unruly. But Dunayevskaya contends that those who are willing to think and to listen can and do receive the messages of revolt.

In *Philosophy and Revolution*, Dunayevskaya explicitly addresses the intellect of revolt, arguing that revolt is itself a form of theory, that revolt embodies and reflects "a new stage of cognition."[22] She focuses on Marx's concept of praxis, contending that the word "praxis" cannot and must not be reduced to a synonym for the word "practice." Reducing praxis to practice strips the concept of praxis of its theoretical and critical dimensions. Dunayevskaya maintains that, for Marx, praxis never simply means action, but it is also a form of theory, and not theory in any narrow academic sense but, rather, a "critical-practical activity" that sees revolt as a form of philosophy from below.[23] Perhaps most sharply, Dunayevskaya ripostes

> it is fantastic that some of those who hail new forms of revolt still do not see the masses as Reason. Instead, they interpret these upsurges as if *praxis* meant the *workers practicing what the theoreticians hand down*. . . . No new stage of cognition is born out of thin air. It can be born only out of *praxis*. When workers are ready for a new plunge to freedom, that is when we reach also a new stage of cognition.[24]

It would be fair to say that "spontaneous combustion" was Dunayevskaya's central and enduring interest. Marcuse was closely following her work and always learning from her analyses, as is well documented in their extensive correspondence and also reflected in his preface to her book, *Marxism and Freedom*.[25] For Dunayevskaya, to be a Marxist was to oppose every statist transposition of Marx's work in the twentieth century, to critically condemn so-called socialist states as "state capitalism" in disguise. In her view, to be a Marxist was to always return to "spontaneous action," to "upsurging from below," as the source of revolutionary negation. "The core of all of Marxism begins with and centers around the activity of labor in the process of production itself. It is here that the living laborer revolts against the domination of dead labor, against being made an appendage to the machine."[26] Dunayevskaya reads the revolts of everyday people around the world, which she constantly watched with a close eye throughout her life, as both an oppositional force to and philosophical questioning of, the capitalist reality.

Key to bringing these considerations of revolt together is the understanding that they all integrate (1) the psychological and affective dimensions of revolt, with (2) sociological and political-economic empiricism, and (3) the importance of spontaneity. An everyday life tied to the productive and consumptive apparatus of capitalism gives rise not only to certain social conditions but also to certain pathologies, and to certain feelings against it. Here, despite other differences, Dunayevskaya, Kristeva, Katsiaficas, and Marcuse are in full agreement. And it is worth pointing out that this was a fairly consistent feature of the critical theory of Marcuse's generation. Erich Fromm, for example, a close colleague of both Dunayevskaya and Marcuse, was a practicing psychoanalyst. In Fromm's *Escape from Freedom*, he offers a psychoanalytic critique of contemporary social life: "Today the vast majority of the people not only have no control over the whole of the economic machine, but they have little chance to develop genuine initiative and spontaneity at the particular job they are doing. They are 'employed,' and nothing more is expected from them than that they do what they are told."[27] In this short passage from Fromm (which comes from the concluding section of the book on the subject of spontaneity), you can see the integration of psychoanalytic and political-economic concerns, and the importance of spontaneity.

Yet within this milieu, only Dunayevskaya regularly insisted upon seeing revolt as a philosophical event. In a 1960 letter to Marcuse, she put it this way:

> Subjectivity as objectivity absorbed is not for the philosophers, but for the masses and it is they who are writing the new page of history which is at the same time a new stage in cognition. Even as every previous great step in philosophic cognition was made only when a new leap to freedom became possible, so presently the new struggles for freedom the *world* over will certainly shake the intellectuals out of the stupors so that they too can create freely a new "category."[28]

Like Katsiaficas, Dunayevskaya took very seriously what Marcuse wrote about eros in *Eros and Civilization: A Philosophical Inquiry into Freud.* According to Marcuse: "The world of nature is a world of oppression, cruelty, and pain, as is the human world; like the latter, it awaits its liberation. This liberation is the work of Eros."[29] And although Marcuse understands the opposition of Eros to Logos, the antagonism of Eros against what is conventionally accepted as "reasonable," he stresses that "Eros redefines reason in his own terms."[30]

Beyond this, and as expressed in the preceding passage, Dunayevskaya articulates a distinct position that connects mass rebellion to "philosophic cognition." Eros is indeed a liberatory and libidinal force that gives rise to (and lives in) revolt but, for Dunayevskaya, it dies in state power. For Dunayevskaya, if we follow the reason of revolt, the reason that eros defines, we discover that the real continuity of the currents of radical theory, of Marx's thought, cannot be found in Stalinism or in any state power.[31] Eros redefines reason in revolt, showing us the opposition between (1) *Gemeinwesen* (commons, public good/commonwealth) and *Gemeingeist* (common spirit/sensibility), on the one hand, and (2) purportedly representative states, on the other. In other words, states always claim to embody and reflect the eros of the polity, the *Gemeinwesen* and *Gemeingeist*. But the embodiment of eros in revolt directly and clearly refutes such claims, making it difficult for states to defend their reason (and sometimes, their raison d'être).[32]

## SKETCHING THE LOGIC OF REVOLT

Much of Katsiaficas' thinking about the international contagiousness of the eros effect predicts perfectly what has happened in the so-called Arab Spring. In his essay "Seattle Was Not the Beginning," Katsiaficas wrote:

> Because of the power of the media and the global village character of the world today, the eros effect has become increasingly important. Social movements are less and less confined to one city, region or nation; they do not exist in isolation in distant corners of the globe; actions are often synchronically related. Social movements in one country are affected sometimes more by events and actions outside their own national context than they are by domestic dynamics.[33]

Katsiaficas viewed Seattle in 1999 similarly to how Deleuze and Guattari viewed Paris in May–June 1968. Seattle, Katsiaficas argued, was yet another nodal point in a recent history of revolt in various geographic locations. The expressions of disaffection in Seattle would inevitably continue elsewhere in other ways, as we saw shortly thereafter in mass protests at the International Monetary Fund and World Bank meeting in April 2000 in Washington, DC; during the 2001 G8 summit in Genoa, Italy; at the first World Social Forum in 2001 in Porto Alegre, Brazil; and at many other locations up to the present.

In this way, the eros effect helps to explain how, for example, upheaval in Tunisia in 2010 resonates with (and helps to detonate) Egyptian disaffection under Hosni Mubarak in 2011, and how the spirit of revolt there seems to "catch on" in countries like Yemen, Bahrain, and Syria, among others. One thing to keep in mind in the present macro-level view of revolt is the fact that within each specific location there is an incredible and even overwhelming amount of complexity. It is important to avoid a reductionist view of upheaval that sees it as being the same across countries and time, to avoid stripping each occurrence of its particular communicative content. One of the places you can see this complexity very well is in Jehane Noujaim's remarkable film *The Square* (2013). Despite some of the faults of this film (a discussion of which is not relevant here), it succeeds in conveying the difficulty and complexity of the communicative content expressed by and through revolt. The intellect of revolt does not share a single brain. Throughout the waves of revolt in Egypt, positions on the military, Muslim Brotherhood, and Morsi were developing and shifting in relation to very particular political moves, and religious and cultural commitments.

A national and subnational level of analysis of the specificity of the intellect of revolt is an important endeavor, but that is not my current concern.[34] There is a different comportment involved in explaining what has happened, on the one hand, and in coming to terms with the critical content of revolt as an unceasing human phenomenon, on the other. I am thus concerned with the question: What is the general schematic of such critical content?

Katsiaficas explains distinctions that help to define a certain schematic in his book *The Subversion of Politics*. On the characteristics of autonomous social movements in Europe, in the three decades after 1968, Katsiaficas writes:

> Parliamentary groups operate according to the logic of the established political system. The first rule of any party must be to obey the law. To ensure members' compliance with existing rules for participation in the government, a structure must be maintained that is compatible with the state. Insurgent social movements aimed at limiting the power of government and creating autonomy seek forms of decision-making of a qualitatively different kind.[35]

So what is the critical content, at least paradigmatically, that the qualitatively different logic of revolt poses to the logic of the established order? Here, I shall provide a rudimentary sketch of the content and logic of revolt in both positive and negative (and normative) terms:[36]

1. Revolt is writing and speaking by other means than words. That is to say, revolt articulates questions, criticisms, visions, and it expresses disaffections. Following Immanuel Kant, we might say that revolt is a "public use of reason," and yet contrary to Kant, revolt writes and speaks by other means than those he recommended.[37] Revolt is an experimental form of writing and speaking in that it makes use of nontextual and nonverbal communication—for example, musical, visual, symbolic, and theatrical forms.

2. Revolt writes and speaks *against* the existing state of affairs. Revolt rejects the world as it is, not wholly per se, but in some defining regard.

3. Revolt writes and speaks *for* some other state of affairs (or states of affairs) that can be imagined. Revolt imagines a state of affairs that does not exist yet seems both possible and desirable to participants. That is, revolt imagines possible and desirable transformation.

4. Revolt writes and speaks *against* conventional politics and established channels of reform. Revolt emerges in the face of frustrated and failed reform.

5. Revolt writes and speaks *for* positions that are marginal or invisible without revolt. Revolt seeks to eliminate the invisibility and oblivion of its own reasonable positions.

6. Revolt writes and speaks *against* both the boredom and acceptance of everyday life by way of their opposites: excitement and rejection, an ecstatic refutation. Raoul Vaneigem declares that "wherever passionate acts of refusal and a passionate consciousness of the necessity of resistance trigger stoppages in the factories of collective illusion, there the revolution of everyday life is underway."[38] Revolt is a rupture with everyday life and its ideological defenses.

7. Revolt writes and speaks *for* the direct experience of autonomy and spontaneity (this acknowledges the prefigurative aspects of the rupture with everyday life).

8. Revolt writes and speaks *against* the separation of theory from praxis. This is, perhaps strangely, another Kantian dimension of revolt; like Kant, revolt rejects the notion that what makes sense in theory (i.e., justice, freedom, dignity, liberation) is impractical.[39]

9. Revolt writes and speaks *for* resolutions of anguish and hope. Revolt is not, in-and-of-itself, a solution to a problem, and yet it conceives of itself as part of resolutions.

10. Revolt writes and speaks more desperately and dangerously than conventional writing and speaking. Even where revolt is nonviolent, it self-consciously risks various forms of violence.

Of course, given a particular case of revolt—in Germany, Italy, France, Egypt, Turkey, Mexico, Spain, the United States, or Brazil—we can and must make further specifications. Locations and eruptions of revolt are not generic. Revolt arises from circumstances, within historical contexts, and in response to changing material and immaterial conditions, even specific policies or verdicts in some cases.

Nonetheless, I offer the preceding general picture of revolt, which I maintain does something important and productive. It stipulates a logic and content of revolt that distinguishes revolt from other forms of praxis. This is precisely a qualitative distinction that expands upon and helps us to understand the logic of insurgent social movements that Katsiaficas speaks about, an oppositional logic to that of the established social, political, and economic system.

## THE PRAXIS OF PHILOSOPHY FROM BELOW

Why should there be any enduring interest in exploring old and making new connections between philosophy and revolt here in the context of the present essay? I claim that doing so is fundamental to the tasks of revealing the reason of revolt, on the one hand, and to revealing the praxis of philosophy, on the other. Moreover, the carrying out of either one of these tasks is critical to the carrying out of the other. But how, precisely, is that the case?

First, revolt—and especially seemingly spontaneous uprising—is typically characterized as the opposite of thinking, as an emotional outburst that is entirely destructive and always condemnably violent. This characterization rests upon the familiar idea that reason must be dispassionate, purely objective at its best, and that it is impossible to be reasonable while also being affected by anger or indignation, among other tumultuous feelings. Thus, exploring and establishing the reason of revolt, and even more, the notion of revolt *as* reason, challenges widespread assumptions about not only how reasonable persons act but also challenges the notion that good thinking is dispassionate. As has been more fully argued in the preceding sections of this essay, unpacking the critical content of revolt produces new understandings of what thinking is and may be, and how thinking happens.

Second, philosophy as an academic field can be seen as the discipline that stood before and gave rise to all the others.[40] From the point of view that identifies philosophy as the first form of all the sciences—natural, mathematical, and social—philosophy works with the unknown to search out and discover truths, which it collects, and eventually to establish formal bodies of knowledge. Philosophy typically claims to systematize the separation of good thinking from bad, truth from falsehood, much of which can be measured by logic. These fundamentally epistemological and moral dimensions of philosophy define so much of the analytical school.

Friedrich Nietzsche has been taken far more seriously outside of the analytical tradition. In many ways, Nietzsche's critique of philosophy was more ferocious and unsparing than Marx's. Claiming that the purportedly dispassionate objectivity of philosophy conceals its ulterior and moralizing motivations, Nietzsche famously wrote: "I distrust all systematizers, and avoid them."[41] In the same book, *Twilight of the Idols*, alternatively titled *How to Philosophize with a Hammer*, Nietzsche devotes whole sections of criticism to Socrates and the assumptions of "reason" in philosophy.[42] "All the ideas that philosophers have treated for thousands of years have been mummied concepts; nothing real has ever come out of their hands alive. These idolaters of concepts merely kill and stuff things when they worship—they threaten the life of everything they adore."[43] In Nietzsche's work, a key problem in the history of philosophy is that it purports virtue in its distance from the living world. Whereas for Nietzsche, feeling and thinking are not antithetical, and any pretension to their separation is a lie, indeed, one of philosophy's favorite deceptions.

Philosophy has long suffered its own caricature, the very one Nietzsche attacked, and has mostly positioned itself (and has been positioned by others) as being so far removed from the world of real life that what it offers to practice is always unclear. In teaching political philosophy and theory in a department of political science, the same demand to answer the question of practice haunts every session. Much like Kant, I have chosen to substantiate the connections between philosophy and praxis, between theory and practice, rather than to accept some metaphysical conceit that the real world is somewhere beneath philosophy. What philosophy offers, at its very best, are transformative understandings of the world that can reveal the limits of ideology and radical reevaluations of the principles that organize our lives. Following this contention, when other practices than philosophy offer such transformative understandings and radical reevaluations, we must consider the other ways that philosophy happens, challenging the notion that the most serious thinking is the purview of professionals.

Still, how do these two tasks intersect, and why does the intersection matter for a theory of revolt?

There is a long history of people in positions of power calling everyone who opposes their position "irrational." There is also a long history of turning that inverted perspective on its head. Despite Nietzsche's derisions,

Plato understood this point well, as he and Socrates argued against the Sophists (whom Nietzsche, interestingly, defends), against those "professional intellectuals" who sold ideas to the sons of wealthy families. Since the time of Plato and Socrates, one defining vision for philosophy was as a discursive and dialectical force against the existing state of affairs. Central to this philosophic vision was an opposition to professional philosophy. Beyond Socrates' notoriously pejorative regard for the Sophists, we might also consider the argument of Socrates in Plato's *Meno* that the formally uneducated slave was already fully capable of doing philosophy. In Plato's *Meno*, Socrates engages in discussion with one of Meno's slaves to prove that the slave possesses intellectual capabilities that must not be denied. Eventually, Meno's slave comes to feel that he has "spontaneously recovered" knowledge, an epiphany that was dialectically aroused.[44] And most importantly, we must consider the fact that Socrates—iconic philosopher of philosophers—was an enemy of the state, ultimately put to death for doing philosophy in the streets. In many ways, the guiding question of the present essay has been: *Who else does philosophy in the streets?*

The problem with the case in the *Meno* is that the midwife for the slave's epiphany is the guidance of the great philosopher; so the slave cannot take full credit for his achievement in the end, since Socrates appears as the one to thank for the revelation. But often, there aren't any knowing philosophers, iconic, professional, self-proclaimed, or otherwise, helping make philosophy happen. Sometimes social upheavals arouse the deep questioning and epiphanies that philosophers seek to arouse. Often, nothing does philosophy better than revolt. In other words, Socrates did not go far enough.[45]

I would affirm Alain Badiou's statement that "as a philosopher, I never accept the world as it is . . . ."[46] Good philosophy throws the world into question. But no conventional text can expect to be as provocative or compelling as creative, unpredictable uprisings that seize attention and ignite imaginations. Revolt is a philosophical modality, a way of doing and surpassing the work of professional intellectuals. If we fail to recognize reason as revolt and revolt as reason, then we fail to see that the Greek uprisings in 2008, the "Arab Spring," Occupy, and uprisings in Turkey, Brazil, and Spain, for example, are doing the most important philosophy of our time. It is necessary to theorize a "philosophy from below," which understands that professional thinkers have more to learn from insurrectionary movements than to teach them and, also, that understands the deficiencies of reason within the limits of law. Is it even possible to take seriously the claim that authors of books on politics and morality and philosophy can throw the reality and justice of the world into question as well as occupied buildings and public squares? A philosophical text may conceal or confess its aspiration to be as provocative as a riot, but this remains an enduring and lofty goal.

In the wake of the riots around London in early August 2011, Darcus Howe, a West Indian writer and broadcaster in London, was interviewed on the BBC. From his perspective, it was quite clear that the riots were an insurrectionary expression of youth defiance against constant police brutality and racism throughout many London boroughs. Howe understood the riots to be telling us that there was something seriously wrong in the country. As he put it, "What is obvious is that these young people will go on relentlessly. . . . They've seen Syrians, Libyans, Egyptians and insurrection. I don't think four months jailed in a miserable little hole will change them. It's a different set of youths today. . . . That's been going on since I landed here 50 years ago, now it's almost complete. I think this insurrection is the last stop in its completeness."[47] Whether one agrees with Howe's analysis (and he was at least wrong about the insurrection of 2011 being the "last stop"), he is rightly interested in the rational *and* reasonable content of the events. Meanwhile, Howe's interviewer at the BBC would not recognize the existence of anything sensible in the riots, because her position expressed the general view of the opposition in power, denying the upheavals any rationality or reason, reducing the whole expression to an aberrant, senseless episode of violence.[48]

But when we speak of insurrection, we need not invoke some narrow notion of armed militant factions in a standoff with state power, or of violent conflict and murder. We can recover the word's fifteenth-century meaning, which is defined by the idea of "a rising up." The risings-up of insurrection start from within a system or place and involve going against from within, making problems from inside. Insurrection says something legible about the system in which it arises, even when its opponents deem it "irrational." Insurrection does not necessarily seek political solutions like "new government." New government is likely to make new betrayals and may bring forth the reasonable criticisms of new insurrection, as materialized in the Egyptian uprisings against Morsi in the summer of 2013.

To be sure, many uprisings do not have what we could reasonably call "revolutionary" content. If, by revolution, we mean some kind of structural transformation, some kind of transformation of power relations, or of everyday life, then we cannot necessarily call uprisings that occur in response to contested election results, court decisions, or even electrical blackouts "revolutionary." Some uprisings neither seek nor result in transformations of power or conditions of life. For example, masses of unruly people breaking down doors are sometimes mobilized by the shopping prospects of Black Friday in the United States, or by a new Nike sneaker debut (e.g., a so-called riot at a mall in Orlando, Florida, in February 2012). But even a frenzied mass of consumers stealing sneakers in a mall or TVs during a blackout expresses something quite serious about a culture, if we want to listen.

Often, rioting and looting are easier to read, as in the case of the tumultuous response to the police shooting and killing of an unarmed Black teenager, Michael Brown, in Ferguson, Missouri, in August 2014. This typically calm St. Louis suburb was rocked for days by rioting, smashed shop windows, protests, fires, confrontations with police, and looting by people outraged by the murder. While news reports openly and reliably condemned these uprisings, never hesitating to call them "violent," some participants in the upheavals have been interviewed explaining their rationality and reason. Participants have expressed the need for exceptional outrage against exceptional injustice, to show the police that even if the law allows the police to use *their* violence, the community will not. One participant in the rioting, DeAndre Smith, told the *St. Louis Post-Dispatch* that the Ferguson revolt was exactly the right response to the injustice, saying, "I think they got a taste of what fighting back means."[49] Once we abandon the disqualifying and vilifying discourses of irrationality and violence, it is obvious that any honest consideration of the Ferguson uprisings will require a confrontation with questions of racism, power, poverty, justice, and police brutality. These are just some, among many other contents, that a dedicated reading could explore.

Nonetheless, on the issue of reading the rational and reasonable content of revolt, I must address the fact that outsiders consuming unsympathetic reports of the uprising from a distance are unlikely to carry out the close and dedicated reading I've been discussing. For many observers at a distance, the communicative content of revolt may not be sufficient to overturn the vilification of the uprising as irrational violence, or to shift their ideological commitments against it.

While revolt gets more attention than a book, and more effectively and directly communicates than intellectual analysis, a network of supportive activities—outside of and after the uprising—can help revolt defend itself against reductionist and ideological readings. The usual activities come to mind: articles, books, blogs and social media, independent media, radio shows like *Democracy Now!*, documentary films, sit-ins, die-ins, solidarity demonstrations, university classes, conversation with family and friends, and so on. One example, in response to Ferguson, was the organization of the Black Lives Matter reading list and the Ferguson Reads Discussion Group at Left Bank Books in St. Louis. As described by Left Bank Books: "The events in Ferguson have been upsetting for nearly everyone in our community. This reading group is an attempt to add some civility and context to the mix by exploring race, not only in St. Louis, but America as a whole."[50] The group started meeting to discuss Ferguson in September 2014 and continued into 2015.

Regarding this example and others, in Missouri and around the world, in the network of supportive activities for a close reading of the content and contemplation of revolt, we mustn't lose sight of the fact that the revolt itself is the catalyst, the unit of study, the agenda-setting event. All of the follow-up analysis about race and class, economic crisis, capital, the opportunity structure in impoverished Black communities, tactics and rebellion, police brutality, and the sociological and historical context of violence in America emerge from the communiqué of revolt. Well over a dozen teenagers have been killed by police since the Michael Brown shooting to the time of this writing, and, sadly, we can be confident that the number is far greater by the time you are reading this. What makes the difference between the ones we know about and the ones that we don't is revolt. It is therefore clear that revolt is a discourse that participates in the proliferation and production of knowledge.

Beyond the old idea of "permanent revolution," which goes back to Marx and Trotsky, among others, I recommend something like "permanent revolt," which is close to what Kristeva calls a "culture of revolt." Kristeva says: "The permanence of contradiction, the temporariness of reconciliation, the bringing to the fore of everything that puts the very possibility of unitary meaning to the test (such as the drive, the unnamable feminine, destructivity, psychosis, etc.): these are what the culture of revolt explores."[51] She further claims that the culture of revolt "poses the question of another politics, that of permanent conflictuality."[52] Seen this way, revolt is part of revolutionary transformation inasmuch as it is an active, physical, and philosophical force of negation that throws the existing state of affairs into question. It is not only philosophical in some narrow intellectual sense, for it is also visible, public, and eventual (as some philosophy is). Following Kristeva, I see revolt as the conflictual activity of ongoing challenges to every celebratory discourse that defends each new reconciliation in society and politics. Thus, for example, revolt opposes the intrinsically conciliatory dispositions of liberalism and conservatism.

Still, revolt is not a clear step toward revolution in any certain or linear sense. It is, rather, an activity that reveals problems and generates real, concrete thinking about the problems. The position I have outlined is self-consciously precarious: Those who make revolt do not share a single blueprint for the different world(s) they desire, and revolt does not *know* how to make new worlds. Indeed, even after the establishment of some new lifeworld, revolt would return to challenge its limits and failures. In this way, revolt is a precarious politics of world-making. In the beginning of every revolt, the only great confidence is that the present state of affairs is unacceptable. Yet, we should never minimize the significance of that epiphany. In between every revolt, we are accustomed to accepting the unacceptable, to tolerating the intolerable. Revolt breaks that pathological obedience. The practical hope of revolt is a reasonable aspiration that what emerges from it may constitute a nodal point in the development of transformative politics.

Because the messages of insurrection are written by those who want to live in a different world, but cannot say exactly what that world is, uprisings always appear irrational from the point of view of power. They speak a different language altogether. Thus, the demand to "be rational" typically functions much like the demand to "be practical," which is essentially a demand to play by the rules. Everyone knows that "rational people" write letters to editors, vote, and abide by the laws. But it is exactly this "rational-practicality" that the most radical elements always reject, and for good reasons, which is to say that there are *other reasons* and *other rationalities*, ones that are excluded by the ideological narrowness of those who defend existing society. Revolt is largely about wrenching open that narrowness so that we can see other rationalities, another reason.

Insurrectionary movements exceed the diagnostic and prescriptive efforts of scholars, and everyday people are capable of discovering (as they have been discovering in uprisings across Middle Eastern and North African countries, in the wave of occupation movements, and in Spain, Turkey, Brazil, and elsewhere) that *they are the midwives*, which puts them beyond the subordinate relationship of Meno's slave to Socrates.

From philosophical, psychological, social, and ethical perspectives, the absence of revolt is more frightening than its presence. The absence of revolt signals the acceptance—*or at least the toleration*—of what is. But an acceptance of the reality and justice of the existing world is an acceptance that good philosophy never grants easily. We therefore have good reason to be reassured by occurrences of riot, insurrection, and revolt, understanding these as modalities of the collective questioning of the world. The various risings-up of insurrection, the activities of everyday people who throw the world into question, are writing philosophy from below. And it is philosophy from below—not the professional thinking of academics—that raises the most pressing questions. This calls for a reversal of general perspectives commonly held in both society (i.e., notions of practicality, violence, irrationality) and science (i.e., notions of objectivity, intelligence, analysis), but it is a reversal that makes sense when we listen to—and learn from—the reason of revolt.

## NOTES

1. Julia Kristeva, *Intimate Revolt*, trans. Jeanine Herman (New York: Columbia University Press, 2002), 3.

2. Julia Kristeva, *The Sense and Non-Sense of Revolt*, trans. Jeanine Herman (New York: Columbia University Press, 2000), 3.

3. Julia Kristeva, *Revolt, She Said*, trans. Brian O'Keeffe (Los Angeles: Semiotext(e), 2002), 120.

4. George Katsiaficas, "The Eros Effect," personal website, 1989, http://www.eroseffect.com/articles/eroseffectpaper.PDF.

5. One excellent discussion of these themes can be found in George Katsiaficas, *The Subversion of Politics: European Autonomous Movements and the Decolonization of Everyday Life* (Oakland: AK Press, 2006). See, specifically, the section "Toward a Rationality of the Heart," 228–233. See also tables 7.2 and 7.3 and the corresponding discussion, 246–248.

6. John Rawls, *Justice as Fairness: A Restatement* (Cambridge: Harvard University Press, 2001), 6–7.

7. In many interviews and books, Michel Foucault has discussed how "madness" has been used to establish and maintain relations of power in society and politics. His most extensive study, which supports the claim here, is *Madness and Civilization: A History of Insanity in the Age of Reason*, trans. Richard Howard (New York: Vintage Books/Random House, 1988).

8. George Katsiaficas, "Is There an Alternative to Capitalist Globalization?," in *The Battle of Seattle: The New Challenge to Capitalist Globalization*, ed. Eddie Yuen, Daniel Burton Rose, and George Katsiaficas (New York: Soft Skull Press, 2001), 321–322.

9. Herbert Marcuse, *An Essay on Liberation* (Boston: Beacon Press), 25.

10. Ibid., 55.

11. See John Holloway, *Crack Capitalism* (London: Pluto, 2010), 3; Hakim Bey, *T.A.Z. The Temporary Autonomous Zone, Ontological Anarchy, Poetic Terrorism* (Brooklyn: Autonomedia, 1991), 97–103; Michael Bakunin, *Statism and Anarchy*, trans. Marshall S. Shatz (Cambridge: Cambridge University Press, 1994), 133.

12. See Uri Gordon, *Anarchy Alive! Anti-Authoritarian Politics from Practice to Theory* (London: Pluto Press, 2008); Cindy Milstein, *Anarchism and Its Aspirations* (Oakland: AK Press, 2010); Benjamin Franks, "Anti-Fascism and Prefigurative

Ethics," *Affinities: A Journal of Radical Theory, Culture, and Action* 8, no. 1 (Summer, 2014): 44–72.

13. Franks, "Anti-Fascism and Prefigurative Ethics," 53.

14. See Richard Gilman-Opalsky, *Precarious Communism: Manifest Mutations, Manifesto Detourned* (New York: Autonomedia, 2014), and Jonathan Crary, *24/7: Late Capitalism and the Ends of Sleep* (London: Verso, 2013).

15. Atelier Populaire, *Posters from the Revolution, Paris, May 1968: Texts and Posters* (London: Dobson Books, 1969).

16. Gilles Deleuze and Félix Guattari, "May '68 Did Not Take Place," in *Hatred of Capitalism*, ed. Chris Kraus and Sylvère Lontringer (Los Angeles: Semiotext(e), 2001), 209–211 (209 and 211).

17. Katsiaficas, *The Subversion of Politics*, 257.

18. Karl Marx, *The German Ideology*, in *The Portable Marx*, trans. Eugene Kamenka (New York: Penguin, 1983), 162–195 (179).

19. Throughout this essay, I variously consider both the negative and positive dimensions of revolt. Negative, in the sense of revolt's negation, refers to the critical refusal of and opposition to constituted reality. Positive, in the sense of the creative and purposeful dimension of revolt, refers to the imaginative anticipation of desirable possibilities. I cannot suggest that one of these dimensions comes first, or that they do or must always occur simultaneously. I do not think we can or even should foreclose the possibility of any order or of the simultaneity of these dimensions in revolt. What I would assert with more confidence is that the transformative power of revolt is bolstered by the depth and clarity of *both* its positive and negative content.

20. See, for example, Raya Dunayevskaya, *Rosa Luxemburg, Women's Liberation, and Marx's Philosophy of Revolution* (Urbana: University of Illinois Press, 1991), chap. 11; and Raya Dunayevskaya, *Marxism and Freedom: From 1776 until Today* (New York: Humanity Books, 2000), chap. 11.

21. Dunayevskaya, *Rosa Luxemburg*, xxvii (original emphasis).

22. Raya Dunayevskaya, *Philosophy and Revolution: From Hegel to Sartre, and from Marx to Mao* (Atlantic Highlands: Humanities Press, 1982), 255.

23. Dunayevskaya, *Philosophy and Revolution*, 265.

24. Ibid., 265 (all emphases in original).

25. See *The Dunayevskaya-Marcuse-Fromm Correspondence, 1954–1978: Dialogues on Hegel, Marx, and Critical Theory*, ed. Kevin B. Anderson and Russell Rockwell (Lanham: Lexington Books, 2012); and Dunayevskaya, *Marxism and Freedom*.

26. Dunayevskaya, *Marxism and Freedom*, 177.

27. Erich Fromm, *Escape from Freedom* (New York: Rinehart, 1941), 272–273.

28. Dunayevskaya, *The Dunayevskaya-Marcuse-Fromm Correspondence*, 74.

29. Herbert Marcuse, *Eros and Civilization: A Philosophical Inquiry into Freud* (Boston: Beacon Press, 1974), 166.

30. Marcuse, *Eros and Civilization*, 224.

31. See Dunayevskaya's discussion of Marcuse in Dunayevskaya, *The Dunayevskaya-Marcuse-Fromm Correspondence*, 222.

32. While I'm not taking it up more fully here, I acknowledge that the question of the relationship between revolt and the state is a large and complex one. For example, can't revolt democratize the state rather than undermine its legitimacy? Or, can't the state be the reasonable side of the antagonism? While it is tempting to take a detour into such questions here, I will only note that the thinkers cited earlier (Dunayevskaya, Fromm, and Marcuse) do take up the question of the state extensively in their work. I have also done so in my book *Unbounded Publics: Transgressive Publics Spheres, Zapatismo, and Political Theory* (Lanham: Lexington Books, 2008).

33. George Katsiaficas, "Seattle Was Not the Beginning," in *The Battle of Seattle*, 29–35 (32).

34. I have and would of course read such works, which are mainly historical and documentary, like Noujaim's *The Square* (2013), or descriptive works of political science or sociology. Such work is important, but it is not my concern. I am interested in the theoretical dimensions and the practical and political implications of revolt as a persistent and interminable human activity.

35. Katsiaficas, *The Subversion of Politics*, 100.

36. I should briefly define what is meant here by "positive and negative (and normative) terms." By "positive," I mean to indicate what revolt *is* and *is for*. By "negative," I mean to indicate what revolt *is not* and *is against* (as in a negation). The *is/is not* distinction belongs to the descriptive account of the critical content and logic of revolt. The *for/against* distinction belongs to the normative account of the critical content and logic of revolt.

37. See Immanuel Kant, "An Answer to the Question: 'What Is Enlightenment?,'" in *Political Writings* (Cambridge: Cambridge University Press, 1991), 54–60. Kant favors the public speech and, especially, the published writing of "men of learning."

38. Raoul Vaneigem, *The Revolution of Everyday Life*, trans. Donald Nicholson-Smith (London: Rebel Press, 2006), 271.

39. See Immanuel Kant, "On the Common Saying: 'This May Be True in Theory, but It Does Not Apply in Practice," in *Political Writings*, 61–92.

40. See Bertrand Russell, *The Problems of Philosophy* (Oxford: Oxford University Press, 2001), 89–94.

41. Friedrich Nietzsche, *Twilight of the Idols*, trans. Anthony M. Ludovici (New York: Barnes & Noble, 2008), 4.

42. Nietzsche, *Twilight of the Idols*, 7–17.

43. Ibid., 13.

44. Plato, *Meno* in *Protagoras and Meno*, trans. W.K.C. Guthrie (London: Penguin Books, 1956), 85d.

45. This is also because, while Socrates insists on philosophical currents that test the limits of the laws, he ultimately accepts and defends the laws.

46. "BBC HARDtalk Interview," with Stephen Sackur, March 24, 2009, https://www.youtube.com/watch?v=NPCCNmE7b9g.

47. "Darcus Howe: 'My Father Curfewed Me and I Jumped through the Window,'" *Socialist Worker*, Issue 2265, August 20, 2011, http://www.socialistworker.co.uk/art.php?id=25714.

48. "Darcus Howe BBC News Interview on Riots," *BBC News*, http://www.youtube.com/watch?v=mzDQCT0AJcw.

49. "DeAndre Smith Justifies the Looting in Ferguson," *St. Louis Post-Dispatch*, August 11, 2014, http://www.stltoday.com/news/multimedia/video-man-justifies-the-looting-in-ferguson/html_7699be22-bb74-5d4f-aa49-fcc46f5cb025.html.

50. Left Bank Books has multiple pages on their website dedicated to their efforts to further an understanding of the events in Ferguson. Originally posted at http://www.left-bank.com/fergusonreads.

51. Kristeva, *Intimate Revolt*, 10.

52. Ibid., 11.

7

# The Eros Effect and the Embodied Mind

JACK HIPP

> The moral virtues, then, are produced in us neither by nature nor against nature. Nature, indeed, prepares in us the ground for their reception, but their complete formation is the product of habit.
>
> —Aristotle[1]

Liberation and imagination joined together in concrete form in the fall of 2011 as the Occupy movement burst onto the world scene. Within weeks of the first protests at Zuccotti Park, thousands of people had appeared in hundreds of cities around the world, camping out together in protest of a social system that attempts to obscure its brutal inhumanity behind a shield of reason—a reason that engenders war and austerity for nations, and fear and poverty for individuals and communities. Making no demands and supporting no leaders, the protestors were united around a loose collection of ideologies and practices: their opposition to the 1 percent, their critique of economic inequality, their embrace of direct action and inclusive forms of democracy, and their rejection of standard modes of protest. A particularly evocative photo from Occupy depicts a protestor wearing a Guy Fawkes mask and holding a large blank sign. It is an image that is emblematic of an important new form of reason in the current evolution of human social consciousness—one that fundamentally negates the central terms of the system it confronts.

---

I would like to thank Jason Del Gandio for valued insights, comments, and assistance.

In this chapter I hope to illustrate how the sense of collective reason that George Katsiaficas describes as an emergent quality of the eros effect is mirrored by George Lakoff and Mark Johnson—two thinkers who argue, via cognitive science, that reason is an emergent quality of the embodied mind. I focus, in particular, on how the cognitive unconscious of the embodied mind is neurally restructured during moments of the eros effect. I then draw upon the work of Herbert Marcuse to help explain how this neurological restructuring helps to produce a new kind of subjectivity—one that moves us closer to realizing, concretely, the abstract ideals of human freedom. I close out the chapter by returning to the Occupy protestor with the Guy Fawkes mask and blank sign, providing a brief analysis of how this image gestures toward a new sensibility of resistance.

## THE EROS EFFECT

With the eros effect, Katsiaficas describes the crescendo of revolutionary social forces that periodically sweep across national boundaries as ordinary people take to the streets in large numbers, demanding radical changes in their day-to-day realities while simultaneously creating new social forms reflecting their genuine needs. During moments of the eros effect, "popular movements not only imagine a new way of life and a different social reality but millions of people live according to transformed norms, values, and beliefs."[2]

Katsiaficas finds the most salient examples of the eros effect within "world-historic movements," which are periods of crisis and turmoil *on a global scale*. These are relatively rare in history. In an early analysis, Katsiaficas identifies only a handful of such periods of global eruptions occurring since the American and French revolutions: 1848–1849, 1905–1907, 1917–1919, and 1967–1970.[3] More recently, Katsiaficas has considered the disarmament movement of the 1980s; the wave of East Asian uprisings in the 1980s and 1990s; the revolts against Soviet regimes in East Europe from 1989 to 1991; the alterglobalization wave of the mid-1990s to early 2000s, including the antiwar protests that occurred on February 15, 2003; and the 2011 wave of protests and rebellions that included the Arab Spring and Occupy movement.[4] In each of these periods, global upheavals were spontaneously generated, and "in a chain reaction of insurrections and revolts, new forms of power emerged in opposition to the established order, and new visions of the meaning of freedom were formulated in the actions of millions of people." Katsiaficas contends:

The essential change which creates these leaps in human reality is the activation of whole strata of previously passive spectators, the millions of people who decide to participate in the conscious re-creation of their economic and political institutions and social life. Such spontaneous leaps may be, in part, a product of long-term social processes in which organized groups and conscious individuals prepare the groundwork, but when the political struggle comes to involve millions of people, it is possible to glimpse a rare historic occurrence, the emergence of the *eros* effect, the massive awakening of the instinctive human need for justice and for freedom. When the *eros* effect occurs it becomes clear that the fabric of the status quo has been torn, and the forms of social control have been ruptured. This rupture becomes clear when established patterns of interaction are negated and new and better ones are created.[5]

The many dimensions of activity that constitute the eros effect vary with the historical context in which it occurs, and no particular manifestation of the eros effect is like any other. Katsiaficas conceives of the eros effect as a tactic for radical, even global, change but is also skeptical about our ability to consciously will it into effect.

A significant new tactic in the arsenal of popular movements, the eros effect is not simply an act of mind, nor can it simply be willed by a "conscious element" (or revolutionary party). Rather it involves popular movements emerging as forces on their own as ordinary people take history into their own hands. The concept of the eros effect is a means of rescuing the revolutionary value of spontaneity, a way to stimulate a reevaluation of the unconscious and strengthen the will of popular movements to remain steadfast in their revulsion with war, inequality, and domination.[6]

## THE EMBODIED MIND

Katsiaficas argues that the intuitive nature of the eros effect makes it opaque to scientific analysis. "The eros effect, arising as it does from the subconscious, cannot be verified scientifically."[7] This echoes George Lakoff and Mark Johnson's exploration into cognitive science and the problem of quantifying the rationality of the human unconscious within the framework of modern social science. In brief, Lakoff and Johnson assert that human reason is vastly richer than social modeling can conceive, and they oppose Western philosophy's generally accepted notion that rational thought is literal, logical, conscious, transcendent, and dispassionate. Lakoff and Johnson tell us that everyday human reason does not fit this classical view of rationality at all. Most of ordinary human thought is metaphorical and, hence, not literal. It uses not only metaphor but framing, metonymy, and prototype-based inferences. It is not logical in the sense defined by the field of formal logic, and it is largely unconscious. It is also not transcendent but, rather, fundamentally embodied. In this view, imaginative aspects of reason—metaphor, metonymy, and mental imagery—are taken as central rather than peripheral and inconsequential adjuncts to reason and the literal.

The theory of embodied mind contradicts the Western philosophical tradition of "faculty psychology," which posits that we have a faculty of reason that is separate from and independent of what we do with our bodies. In *Philosophy in the Flesh*, Lakoff and Johnson argue:

> The evidence from cognitive science shows that classical faculty psychology is wrong. There is no fully autonomous faculty of reason separate from and independent of bodily capacities such as perception and movement. The evidence supports, instead, an evolutionary view, in which reason uses and grows out of such bodily capacities. The result is a radically different view of what reason is and therefore of what a human being is.[8]

Lakoff and Johnson theorize that our thoughts, including our most abstract notions and philosophical and moral systems, are comprised of conceptual blendings of complex metaphors, which are in turn based on primary metaphors that reside within our cognitive unconscious. This is not the Freudian realm of the repressed but, rather, the locus of all unconscious mental operations concerned with conceptual systems, meaning, inference, and language. The cognitive unconscious operates beneath the level of awareness, inaccessible to consciousness and operating too quickly to be focused on. Lakoff and Johnson suggest that at least 95 percent of these operations are forever beyond the grasp of our conscious minds.

> When we understand all that constitutes the cognitive unconscious, our understanding of the nature of consciousness is vastly enlarged. Consciousness goes way beyond mere awareness of something, beyond the mere experience of qualia (the qualitative sense of, for example, pain or color), beyond the awareness

that you are aware, and beyond the multiple takes on immediate experience provided by various centers of the brain. Consciousness certainly involves all of the above plus the immeasurably vaster constitutive framework provided by the cognitive unconscious, which must be operating for us to be aware of anything at all.[9]

Primary metaphors, which are foundational to most of our thinking, are acquired automatically and unconsciously through our everyday functioning in the world. These metaphors are *neural connections*, physically instantiated within our brains through a process that features the childhood conflation of subjective feeling and sensorimotor experience. As Lakoff and Johnson explain:

> For an infant, the subjective experience of affection is typically correlated with the sensory experience of warmth, the warmth of being held. . . . Later, during a period of *differentiation*, children are able to separate out the domains, but the cross-domain associations persist. These persistent associations are the mappings of conceptual metaphor that will lead the same infant, later in life, to speak of "a *warm* smile," "a *big* problem," and "a *close* friend."[10]

There are hundreds of such primary metaphors, according to Lakoff and Johnson.

> Together these metaphors provide subjective experience with extremely rich inferential structure, imagery, and qualitative "feel," when the networks for subjective experience and the sensorimotor networks neurally connected to them are coactivated. They also allow a great many words of sensorimotor experience to be used to name aspects of metaphorically conceptualized subjective experience.[11]

For instance, the sense of feeling emotionally "up" or "down," or perceiving oneself as an "insider" or an "outsider," involves inferential structures, deep-seated imagery, and a qualitative feel that help organize and communicate personal and/or collective experience. The same is true for seeing oneself as being part of a social "movement," a "wave" of social change, or a long "march" toward freedom.

Categories are also central to how we think. As Lakoff and Johnson explain, all species have evolved to categorize based on their particular sensing apparatuses and their ability to move themselves and to manipulate objects—it is an inescapable consequence of our biological makeup. Human brains have one hundred billion neurons and one hundred trillion synaptic connections. Because there cannot be a one-to-one correspondence when information is passed from one dense ensemble of neurons to another over sparse connections, as is common in the brain, a fundamental categorization in mapping certain input patterns occurs across those connections to the output ensemble. Lakoff and Johnson find this kind of neural categorization to exist throughout the brain—up to the highest levels of which we can be aware.

> Since we are neural beings, our categories are formed through our embodiment. What that means is that the categories we form are *part of our experience!* They are the structures that differentiate aspects of our experience into discernible kinds. Categorization is thus not a purely intellectual matter, occurring after the fact of experience. . . . It is part of what our bodies and brains are constantly engaged in.[12]

Our concepts also are neither literal nor disembodied, as traditionally conceived of by Western philosophy. "What we call concepts are neural structures that allow us to mentally characterize our categories and reason about them. Human categories are typically conceptualized . . . in terms of what are called *prototypes.* Each prototype is a neural structure that permits us to do some sort of inferential or imaginative task relative to a category."[13] Some of the neurally structured prototypes used in everyday reasoning include: typical and ideal cases (think of the typical husband versus the ideal husband), social stereotypes (like the heteronormative notion that a husband implies a female wife), and salient exemplars (well-known examples of husbands that we know personally or through stories, cultural myths, mass media, etc.). These insights transform our understanding of thought-and-experience. As Lakoff and Johnson state:

> The concepts that govern our thought are not just matters of the intellect. They also govern our everyday functioning, down to the most mundane details. Our concepts structure what we perceive, how we get around in the world, and how we relate to other people. Our conceptual system thus plays a central role in defining our everyday realities. If we are right in suggesting that our conceptual system is largely metaphorical, then the way

we think, what we experience, and what we do every day is a matter of metaphor.[14]

Primary metaphors are everywhere—and mostly invisible to our conscious awareness. However, according to Lakoff and Johnson:

> The pervasiveness of primary metaphors in no way denies the existence of non-metaphorical concepts. . . . All basic sensorimotor concepts are literal. *Cup* (the object you drink from) is literal. *Grasp* (the action of holding) is literal. *In* (in its spatial sense) is literal.
>
> Concepts of subjective experience and judgment, when not structured metaphorically, are literal; for example, "These colors are similar" is literal, while "These colors are close" uses the metaphor Similarity Is Proximity. . . . Without metaphor, such concepts are relatively impoverished and have only a minimal, "skeletal" structure. A primary metaphor adds sensorimotor inferential structure. . . . [and] such structure is considerably multiplied when two or more primary metaphors are combined to create complex conceptual metaphors.[15]

Without such metaphors, abstract thought is virtually impossible.

> Our most fundamental concepts—time, events, causation, the mind, the self, and morality—are multiply metaphorical. So much of the ontology and inferential structure of these concepts is metaphorical that, if one somehow managed to eliminate metaphorical thought, the remaining skeletal concepts would be so impoverished that none of us could do any substantial everyday reasoning.[16]

An important conclusion of research in cognitive studies is that moral reasoning is imaginative and depends fundamentally on embodied metaphorical understanding. In *Moral Politics*, Lakoff points out that "morality is not all metaphorical and nonmetaphorical aspects of morality are what the system of metaphors for morality is based on. Nonmetaphorical morality is about the experience of well-being. The most fundamental form of morality concerns promoting the experiential well-being of others and the avoidance and prevention of experiential harm to others or the disruption of the well-being of others."[17] Experiential well-being (and its lack or denial) provides the grounding for our moral metaphors. It is better to be *strong* than *weak*, *beautiful* than *ugly*, *clean* than *dirty*, *up* than *down*, and so on. And because our notion of what constitutes well-being is widely shared across cultures, much of our pool of metaphors for morality is also widely shared. Here, Lakoff and Johnson expand the scope of this moral dimension of reason.

> Real human reason is embodied, mostly imaginative and meta-
> phorical, largely unconscious, and emotionally engaged. It is
> often about human well-being and about ends determined by
> human well-being. Since morality concerns well-being and since
> our conceptions of morality arise from our modes of well-being,
> morality enters into human reason most of the time. It not only
> affects the choice of ends, but also the kind of reasoning done
> in achieving those ends. Rationality almost always has a major
> moral dimension. The idea that human rationality is purely
> mechanical, disengaged, and separable from moral issues is a myth,
> a myth that is harmful when we live our lives according to it.[18]

According to Lakoff and Johnson, metaphor is traditionally understood as a matter of words rather than thoughts—a deviant language outside the boundaries of conventional speech, poetical in nature, and merely express-ing preexisting similarities between words. Cognitive theory, by contrast, places metaphor at the center of human consciousness and, therefore, of reason itself.

> Whether reason is embodied and whether metaphor is conceptual
> may sound like obscure pedantic issues. They aren't. They cut to
> the deepest questions of what we as human beings are and how
> we understand our everyday world. If you hold the traditional
> views about metaphor, then you inherit views about what reality
> is, what truth is, how language is connected to the world, whether
> we can have objective knowledge, and even what morality is.[19]

These a priori philosophical views of reality are based on a correspon-dence theory of truth in which the world is seen as separate from the human mind, and language is understood as being "true" when it corresponds to the "really existing facts of the world." But a cognitively responsible theory of truth, by contrast, recognizes that the truth of the world is relative to our embodied means of comprehending it.

Lakoff and Johnson consider the most important task of a cognitively responsible philosophy of language to be the reshaping of our metaphorical realities. "Given that language never just fits the world, that it always incorporates an embodied understanding, it becomes the job of the philosophy of language to characterize that embodied understanding accurately and to point out its consequences."[20] Moral judgments based in metaphor are implicit in every aspect of our culture, and it is vital to be consciously aware of them. Political and economic ideologies are framed in metaphor and can hide aspects of reality. For instance, *labor is a resource, time is money, argument is war*, and dozens of other metaphors neurally encode socially constructed categories of domination and obscure their categorical negations—and they do so in the most visceral way.

## APPLICATION AND ANALYSIS OF EMBODIED POLITICS

In his solo work, Lakoff has applied the theory of embodied mind to the metaphorical architecture girding the conservative and liberal mindsets in US politics. He locates the political distance between these worldviews in the moral difference between two opposing models of the family—the conservative "strict father" and the liberal "nurturing parent," which are metaphorically extended as models of governments, representing coherent political ideologies instantly recognizable to any casual observer of US politics.

Strict father morality is founded on the notion of *moral strength*, which must be *built* through discipline and self-denial, and in which self-indulgence is seen as immoral.

> The metaphor of Moral Strength is a set of correspondences between the moral and physical domains:
>
> * Being Good is Being Upright.
> * Being Bad is Being Low.
> * Doing Evil is Falling.
> * Evil is a Force (either internal or external).
> * Morality is Strength.[21]

The Moral Strength metaphor has two very different aspects. First, it is required if one is to stand up to some externally defined evil. Second, it itself defines a form of evil, namely, the lack of self-discipline and the refusal to engage in self-denial. That is, the metaphor for Moral Strength defines forms of internal evil.[22]

Lakoff points out that this conception is seen by those who give it high priority as a form of idealism that imposes a strict us/them moral dichotomy, with important entailments: The world is in a war between good and evil; to face evil and remain good requires moral strength acquired through self-discipline and self-denial; failure to acquire moral strength is itself immoral because one who is morally weak will eventually commit evil, so self-indulgence and lack of self-control are forms of immorality. Evil must be fought ruthlessly; it does not deserve respect—it deserves to be attacked. Anything that promotes moral weakness is immoral.

By this metaphor, providing birth control for teenagers or clean needles for intravenous drug users is immoral because teenage sex and illegal drug use are seen as resulting from moral weakness—that is, a lack of self-control.[23] To provide such services is therefore evil. A morally strong person can "just say no" to sex and drugs; those who can't are immoral, and immorality is evil and must be punished. Desire, in this metaphor, is seen as temptation, and what is needed to overcome temptation is *will*—the willpower to exercise control over the body. The opposite of this self-control is self-indulgence, a concept that makes sense only if we accept the central metaphor of "moral strength."[24]

Strict father morality assumes that the world is dangerous and difficult, and that children are born bad and must be made good. The father, as the authority, must impose this moral construct on the family through punishment and by his own example as a paragon of moral strength, that is, by being upright, having backbone, standing up to evil, and not backing down.[25] But Lakoff points out that moral people are not literally upright, and becoming immoral is not literally falling—that evil is not a literal force that can make an upright person fall. These concepts are taken from the physical domain and applied to morality through metaphor. This metaphor is grounded in a fact about experiential well-being—that it is better to be strong than weak. But its quality as a "natural" metaphor does not mean it is literally true, nor does it disqualify other metaphors as alternate centers of coherent systems of morality.

The "nurturing parent" model, by contrast, is based in empathy and holds nurturance as the central metaphor of morality. It assumes that the world is basically good and can be made better, and that children are born good and parents can help make them better. The nurturant model sees morality as an issue of self-development, and it involves fair distribution and happiness and comprises categories of moral strength, moral growth, moral boundaries, moral authority, retribution, and restitution—all of which are grounded in empathy and nurturance. The nurturing parent model stresses fairness and social ties and is most recognizably expressed in the political sphere as the ideal of the "social safety net."

Lakoff's analysis was, in part, a goad to liberal sensibilities in US politics following the congressional defeat of the Democrats in 1996 and, later, Al Gore's loss to George W. Bush in the 2000 presidential election. He encouraged liberals to examine the categories implicit in their policy views and make the metaphorical connections necessary to develop a coherent framework of shared values that would unite their base in an "embodied" body politic capable of articulating a consistent worldview based on the morality of nurturance, and eliciting similar cognitive responses as conservatives do with concepts like "family values" or "law and order." He considered this to be an issue primarily of "cognitive framing," pointing out that to use the language of a particular moral or political conceptual system reinforces that system, and that the Democratic failure to reframe the debate, outside the categories and concepts of the conservative worldview, was a major factor in both 1996 and 2000.[26]

## IMAGINATION IN REVOLT

Lakoff's analysis is insightful for revealing connections between the neurally structured metaphors of the cognitive unconscious, the visceral reactions that evoke a sense of experiential "truth," and the construction of political worldviews. But Lakoff's analysis is itself necessarily constrained by the impoverished state of US politics—the conservative/liberal divide is its own metaphorical universe, very different from that of Tahrir Square, Zuccotti Park, or the streets of Ferguson and Baltimore.

Despite the limitations of Lakoff's *political* focus, his theory of embodied mind and cognitive unconscious resonates with Katsiaficas' Marcusian-inspired understanding of freedom and liberation. In brief, Katsiaficas, following Marcuse, argues that humans instinctively aspire toward freedom, but such aspirations are always historically shaped and contextualized. Moments of the eros effect, in which people are acting upon and fighting for their freedom, emanate "from the instinctual reservoir, the collective unconscious, and [are] a form of sublimation of instinctual drives into erotic channels of human solidarity."[27] Eros, the life instinct that moves us toward joy and freedom, is "eternally emergent," but the particular form in which it takes shape is relative to the surrounding conditions.[28] In other words, eros, and moments of rebellion that it inspires, is historically situated, always and already. There is a certain reflexivity between one's society and one's erotic drive toward freedom: Society influences the manner by which eros takes shape, and eros shapes the nature and direction of society. Within this dialectic Marcuse finds an organic foundation for liberation:

> To the degree to which this foundation is itself historical and the malleability of "human nature" reaches into the depths of man's [sic] instinctual structure,[29] changes in morality may "sink down" into the "biological" dimension and modify organic behavior. Once a specific morality is firmly established as a norm of social behavior, it is not only introjected—it also operates as a norm of "organic" behavior: the organism receives and reacts to certain stimuli and "ignores" or repels others in accord with the introjected morality, which is thus promoting or impeding the function of the organism as a living cell in the respective society. In this way a society constantly recreates, this side of consciousness and ideology, patterns of behavior and aspiration as part of the "nature" of its people, and unless the revolt reaches into this "second" nature, into these ingrown patterns, social change will remain "incomplete," even self-defeating.[30]

This helps explain why the new categories created during moments of the eros effect resonate so deeply—because they reach into this "instinctual structure" and fulfill categories of life that are denied as a condition of repressive societies. As Katsiaficas states,

> Though secular, such moments metaphorically resemble the religious transformation of the individual through sacred baptism in the ocean of universal life and love. The integration of the sacred and the secular in such moments of "political *eros*" (a term used by Herbert Marcuse) is an indication of the true potentiality of the human species, the "real history" which remains repressed and distorted within the confines of "prehistoric" powers and taboos.[31]

During moments of the eros effect, everyday people demonstrate their latent potential to live as "species beings," reconfiguring their metaphorical universe as they embody its new categories and impress them within their societies.[32] Therefore, such slogans as "We are the 99%," "We are all Egyptian now," and "Que se vayan todos!" (They all must go!) are not *just* words, not *just* pithy summations of one's radical politics. Rather, these slogans represent a restructuring of one's historically shaped "instinctive nature" or, in Lakoff's terminology, one's neurally structured cognitive unconscious. This helps explain the intense feeling that people experience when participating in spontaneous mass rebellion. People's brains are being rewired, literally.

Unfortunately, the eros effect recedes and the instinctual changes that are so liberating in the moment tend to revert back toward a previous state of (political/existential) equilibrium. Here, Marcuse's notion of the psychic Thermidor,[33] which describes the retreat of popular consciousness following moments of revolutionary advance, becomes evident as neurologically instantiated modes of repressive thought reexert their cognitive power against the newly formed categories. And so, with 95 percent of the heavy lifting of categorization occurring beyond the reach of our conscious minds, it is unsurprising when we take great bounds forward only to take a few steps back. But these erotically charged categories persist long beyond their incandescent moment, as their concrete realities are instantiated in our brains and woven into our societies. As Katsiaficas says of the world-historic movements with which the eros effect is so strongly associated, "even in failure they present new ideas and values that become common sense as time passes."[34]

Two examples can help elicit a sense of the various points of contact between the embodied mind and the eros effect.

During France's near revolution of May 1968, the slogan "All Power to the Imagination" was emblazoned on walls, and the famous photograph of a young couple kissing at the barricades represented the titanic force of eros joining in the struggle for a liberated world. In Paris, students occupied their schools, instituting a curriculum of revolution, and workers shut down factories, reopening them again with management locked outside the gates. Millions of people refusing to continue with their daily lives as before embodied the exhortation "Be reasonable, demand the impossible!" In these leaps of imagination among participants who demanded and momentarily lived qualitatively different existences, it was said, "Once their eyes are open, people are not about to close them again: their passivity and dependence are negated, annihilated, and nothing but a force that breaks their will can re-impose the passivity and dependence."[35]

Entrenched categories were smashed and new ones came to the fore as participants became the creators of their social reality. There was a significant moment early in the uprisings when the actions of protestors transcended familiar categories, and an overarching categorical sense of imagination and possibility was experienced and *lived.* On May 10, named the Night of the Barricades, thirty thousand students were trapped by police while marching on the prison that held their comrades. The neighborhood in which they were surrounded is officially known as the Latin Quarter, but it was promptly renamed "The Heroic Vietnam Quarter." The students erected dozens of barricades and pried up cobblestones to be used as missiles, evoking the dreamlike slogan "Beneath the cobblestones, the beach." They fought with the police throughout the night, declaring that "politics is in the streets." This action galvanized public support across France, and within three days a million people were marching across the country. Two weeks later, nearly the entire French economy was on strike and President Charles de Gaulle was on the verge of resigning.

A lesser-known but just as dramatic situation occurred across Korea in May 1980, when a series of large student protests of the dictatorship had been quelled by the government's threat of violence and the institution of martial law—except, however, in the city of Gwangju, which had a history of radical resistance. There, fifty thousand students marched in a defiant, torchlight procession. The dictatorship responded by sending paratroopers to terrorize the population with bayonets, clubs, boots, and unimaginable brutality. The people refused to submit, and over the next two days, they used, among other things, baseball bats, hammers, and Molotov cocktails to battle riot police and paratroopers to a standstill. On May 20, tens of thousands had assembled in the city center, and by evening there were over two hundred thousand participants (in a city of only seven hundred thousand). Suddenly, nine city busses and over two hundred taxis appeared together on the main avenue. People surged in together with the convoy, resolutely advancing on the army lines. This time, when the soldiers attacked, the entire city fought back.

This became known as the Gwangju People's Uprising, and participants recast themselves as the *minjung*—those exploited and marginalized people fighting for democratization and freedom. According to sociologist Choi Jungwoon, the *minjung* "referred to a large number of people, everyone except monopolistic capitalists and their mercenaries: it included the endless throngs of people gathered on Guemnam Avenue on May 20th. These people from different walks of life were a community of absolute love, 'where words were not necessary.'"[36] According to Choi, "In this absolute community, citizens confirmed their greatness, blessed each other, and experienced an absolute liberation from all social bondages and constraints. At this moment, many citizens were plunged into such an extreme ecstasy that they would not have minded dying right then and there, and the struggle changed into a festival."[37]

As the rebellion unfolded, the sense of this "absolute community" inspirited daily rallies of up to one hundred thousand people in the central square, renamed Democracy Plaza, which became the heart of the resistance. As chronicler Lee Jae-eui describes:

> All walks and classes of people spoke—women street vendors, elementary school teachers, and followers of different religions, housewives, college students, high school students, and farmers. Their angry speeches created a common consciousness, a manifestation of the tremendous energy of the uprising. They had melded together, forging a strong sense of solidarity throughout the uprising. For the moment the city was one.[38]

Student/worker associations formed and struggled over tactics, goals, and issues. Moderates wished to surrender arms and bargain with the government, but the radical "struggle faction" prevailed, vowing to carry the fight to the end as the army prepared to retake the city, thus ensuring with their deaths that events would be recorded in history books as a *people's uprising* rather than as another set of riots and civil disturbances. Although the fighters lost the day against the army's ferocious assault, the promise of victory was eventually fulfilled when, decades later, high-ranking perpetrators of the massacre, including the former president, were convicted and sentenced, and the initial date of the uprising, May 18, was honored as a national memorial day. In 1997, Mangwol-dong cemetery, where the bodies of the slain had been unceremoniously dumped by the government, was elevated to the status of national cemetery.[39] Most significantly, the Gwangju People's Uprising ensured the eventual democratization of the country and provided the spark that ignited the wave of *people power uprisings* that swept across East Asia in the years to follow.

These examples highlight the dynamic of destroying and creating neurally structured categories of the cognitive unconscious. It is in this dynamic that the eros effect and the embodied mind join together. The eros effect is defined by those moments in which previously entrenched categories are suddenly negated, and new categories of living emerge. The creation of these new categories of resistance, rebellion, human solidarity, and love are a function of imagination liberated from the constraints of a repressive reality. In this process the collective reason of the eros effect joins the "imaginative rationality"[40] of the embodied mind in a form of liberatory reason grounded in our bodies, the world, and history.

## INSTINCT AND A LIBERATED RATIONALITY

The content of these erotically-and-cognitively driven moments, in their radical negation of the given and projection of the possible, is also captured in Marcuse's reformulation of the foundations of Freud's *reality principal*, specifically, how it appears in Greek mythology. Marcuse, in differentiating between "the biologic and the socio-historical vicissitudes of the instincts,"[41] discerns between two kinds of instinctual repression in humans: basic instinctual repression, which is the modicum required to cohabit within a civilized society, and surplus repression, which involves "the restrictions necessitated by social domination."[42] In a society where domination prevails, instinctual drives toward joy and pleasure are channeled through the creation of false needs and desires—for example, sexual energy becomes commerce and pornography, camaraderie and solidarity are diverted into xenophobic nationalism, and ecological appreciation and communion become manicured suburban lawns and day trips to the zoo. Acting upon these false needs and desires then perpetuates the overall system—which is to say, we participate in and contribute to the maintenance of our own domination.

Marcuse, in sifting through these complexities, leans on and then eclipses Freud. For Freud, basic instinctual repression constitutes the *reality principle* within which bounds we are compelled to abide (as a hedge against a presumably brutal human nature unchained). By contrast, Marcuse recognizes what he calls the *performance principle* as the historically situated form of a *reality principle* that organizes the forces of surplus repression, encoding them in its cultural mythologies and archetypes.

> If Prometheus is the culture-hero of toil, productivity, and progress through repression, then the symbols of another reality principal must be sought at the other pole. Orpheus and Narcissus (like Dionysus to whom they are akin: the antagonist of the god who sanctions the logic of domination, the realm of reason) stand for a very different reality. They have not become the culture heroes of the Western world: theirs is the image of joy and fulfillment; the voice which does not command but sings; the gesture which offers and receives; the deed which is peace and ends the labor

of conquest; the liberation from time which unites man with god, man with nature.[43]

For Marcuse, the truth of these repressed concepts is preserved in the aesthetic dimension of human experience.

> Under the predominance of rationalism, the cognitive function of sensuousness [the domain of *Eros*] has been constantly minimized. In line with the repressive concept of reason [the domain of *Logos*], cognition became the ultimate concern of the "higher," non-sensuous faculties of the mind. . . . Sensuousness, as the "lower" and even "lowest" faculty, furnished at best the mere stuff, the raw material, for cognition, to be organized by the higher faculties of the intellect. . . . Sensuousness retained a measure of philosophical dignity in a subordinate epistemological position; those of its processes that did not fit into the rationalistic epistemology . . . became homeless. Foremost among these homeless contents and values were those of imagination: free, creative, or reproductive intuition of objects which are not directly "given" . . .[44]
>
> The discipline of aesthetics installs the *order of sensuousness* as against the *order of reason*. Introduced into the philosophy of culture, this notion aims at the liberation of the senses which, far from destroying civilization, would give it a firmer basis and would greatly enhance its potentialities. . . . It would harmonize the feelings and affections with the ideas of reason. Operating through a basic impulse—namely, the play impulse—the aesthetic function would "abolish compulsion, and place man, both morally and physically, in freedom." It would harmonize the feelings and affections with the ideas of reason, deprive the "laws of reason of their moral compulsion," and "reconcile them with the interest of the senses."[45]

Marcuse imagines a future unfolding of human instinct where "work can become play, where *Logos* and *Eros* are reunited, where Nature and humans lovingly embrace each other."[46] In Marcuse's image of Narcissus reconsidered, we find a compelling turn toward this potential future. First, he quotes Freud regarding the phenomena of primary narcissism, "Originally the ego includes everything, later it detaches from itself the external world. The ego-feeling we are aware of now is thus only a shrunken vestige of a far more extensive feeling—a feeling which *embraced the universe* and expressed an *inseparable connection of the ego with the external world.*"[47] Marcuse continues:

> The striking paradox that narcissism, usually understood as egoistic withdrawal from reality, here is connected with oneness with the universe reveals the new depth of the conception: beyond all immature autoeroticism, narcissism denotes a fundamental relatedness to reality which may generate a comprehensive existential order. In other words, narcissism may contain the germ of a different reality principle: the libidinal cathexis of the ego (one's own body) may become the source and reservoir for a new libidinal cathexis of the objective world—transforming this world into a new mode of being.[48]

The rationality of the embodied mind and the cognitive unconscious fulfill this description without reserve, as it is our own reflection, seamlessly articulated in nature, that we regard in our metaphorical constructions of the world. As we consider ourselves in its light, Narcissus' mirror becomes the portal through which we join nature (external and human), and the manufactured subject/object dualities of a repressive reality disappear. Behind the scrim of instrumentalist metaphor, our truest human potential exists in imagination, waiting impatiently as we embody and demonstrate its concrete reality within ourselves, perhaps most spectacularly during episodes of the eros effect, as our cognitive unconscious expands within its instinctual categories of love and solidarity. These moments of the eros effect, in their brightest aspect, connect us instantly to this unified reality—which is always right beside us in possibility. As Lakoff and Johnson say in reference to the subject/object unity that joins us with nature, "as embodied, imaginative creatures we never were separated or divorced from reality in the first place."[49]

## EMBODYING A NEW SENSIBILITY

The world has been deeply scarred by the ideology of domination. It is to the radical overthrow of its metaphorical bulwark of justification, which is inscribed on our brains and bodies and permeates everyday power relations,[50] that a living, immanent critique must turn. Both the embodied mind and the eros effect suggest that the struggle against deeply ingrained patterns of domination isn't eternal; but they also suggest that the concepts and categories of a repressive reality must be shattered before we can develop the "sensibility" necessary for long-lasting, revolutionary change. According to Marcuse, this new sensibility "expresses the ascent of the life instincts over aggressiveness and guilt, [and] would foster, on a social scale, the vital need for the abolition of injustice and misery and would shape the further evolution of the 'standard of living.'"[51] Such a sensibility "emerges in the struggle against violence and exploitation where this struggle is waged for essentially new ways and forms of life."[52]

In a rare utopian speculation,[53] Marcuse writes, "The advent of a free society would be characterized by the fact that the growth of well-being turns into an essentially new quality of life."[54] He recognized this dynamic happening in the 1960s New Left movement, which was in the intense thralls of the eros effect, creating new institutions and human relations that rejected and negated the culture of domination and embraced the life instincts. Referring to the young radicals as "the militants," Marcuse writes:

> In proclaiming the "permanent challenge" (*la contestation permanente*), the "permanent education," the Great Refusal, they recognize the mark of social repression, even in the most sublime manifestations of traditional culture, even in the most spectacular manifestations of technical progress. They have again raised . . . the specter of a revolution which subordinates the development of productive forces and higher standards of living to the requirements of creating solidarity for the human species, for abolishing poverty and misery beyond all frontiers and spheres of interest, for the attainment of peace. In one word: they have taken the idea of revolution out of the continuum of oppression and placed it in its authentic dimension: that of liberation.[55]

Marcuse's words prefigure the transformative potential of the erotically effected cognitive unconscious. Although most of our metaphorical universe is deeply established by the interaction between our bodies/brains, our currently existing societies, and the physical world, we still have considerable cognitive flexibility to reconceptualize and embody an alternative world. Cognitive science reveals the neural and linguistic routes by which an embodied human reason evolves, and moments of the eros effect demonstrate the concrete dimensions of liberated, sensual collective reason. Combined, they help us understand how new subjectivities arise in accord with incrementally "revised instincts" and a coming-to-consciousness as a species. In the glare of global inequality, imperialist wars, and ecological catastrophe, the joining of reason-and-nature, of logic-and-emotion, is happening just at the moment when such a qualitative leap in consciousness has become urgently necessary.

Such cognitive flexibility in the face of domination is evident in the scene of Occupy that opened this chapter. The Guy Fawkes mask, a long-held symbol of protest, is simultaneously cartoonish and impish, gesturing toward an insider/outsider dichotomy—those who are in-the-know versus those who are targeted for protest. The very use of a mask suggests collective anonymity, not simply as a mass movement but also as a rejection of one's subjectivity that has been targeted and constructed by an inhumane system. Meanwhile, the protestor's blank sign has nothing to say because the system to which that protest appeals has no eyes, ears, or mind to read, hear, or understand the language that heralds a different world. The system is a metaphorical universe of greed, self-interest, and private wealth and property; it is a grammar that excludes not only collective need and gain but collective joy and pleasure; it is a self-referential language incapable of thinking beyond itself (hence, Marcuse's analysis of "one-dimensional society").[56] But the blank sign signifies vastly more than words could convey—a statement that the future is not foreclosed, an invitation to imagine (and embody) something different, a comprehensive indictment of the system's global criminality, a vivid illustration of the endless possibilities for creating a better world. The ability to read and understand the details of these extralinguistic metaphors may be inhibited by the smoke and mirrors of the culture of domination; given the fact that only 5 percent of the workings of our own brains are available to consciousness, this would be unsurprising. But to the extent that our bodies live out, if even only partially and momentarily, new metaphors of resistance and liberation while challenging and invalidating those of domination, we are preparing the ground for the next pulse of the eros effect. The cumulative effect of millions of bodies-and-brains united in their desires—for freedom, the fulfillment of *true* needs, and the unification with nature that is already happening just below the surface—is unstoppable. So the eros effect will continue to arise, becoming stronger as our project for liberation matures and more and more voices speak new words/worlds into existence. What we create through this struggle is eloquently summarized by Marcuse:

> Not merely self-determination and self-realization, but rather the determination and realization of goals which enhance, protect, and unite life on earth. And this autonomy would find expression

not only in the mode of production and production relations but also in the individual relations among men [*sic*], in their language and in their silence, in their gestures and their looks, in their sensitivity, in their love and hate. The beautiful would be an essential quality of their freedom.[57]

## NOTES

1. This quote appears in different forms. I chose the translation found at http://izquotes.com/quote/6823. For a more formal source, albeit a slightly different translation, see Aristotle, *The Nicomachean Ethics*, trans. David Ross (Oxford: Oxford University Press, 2009), 23, lines 24–26.

2. George Katsiaficas, "The Eros Effect," personal website, 1989, http://www.eroseffect.com/articles/eroseffectpaper.PDF.

3. George Katsiaficas, *The Imagination of the New Left: A Global Analysis of 1968* (Boston: South End Press, 1987), 6.

4. See, for instance, George Katsiaficas, "Eros and Revolution," *Radical Philosophy Review* 16, no. 2 (2013): 491–505 (503), doi: 10.5840/radphilrev201316238; and George Katsiaficas, *Asia's Unknown Uprisings, Volume 2: People Power in the Philippines, Burma, Tibet, China, Taiwan, Bangladesh, Nepal, Thailand, and Indonesia, 1947–2009* (Oakland: PM Press, 2013), 365–366.

5. Katsiaficas, *Imagination of the New Left*, 10.

6. Katsiaficas, "Eros and Revolution," 494.

7. George Katsiaficas, "From Marcuse's 'Political Eros' to the Eros Effect: A Current Statement," chap. 3 this volume, 61.

8. George Lakoff and Mark Johnson, *Philosophy in the Flesh: The Embodied Mind and Its Challenge to Western Thought* (New York: Basic Books, 1999), 17.

9. Ibid., 11.

10. Ibid., 46.

11. Ibid., 59.

12. Ibid., 19 (original emphasis).

13. Ibid., 19 (original emphasis).

14. George Lakoff and Mark Johnson, *Metaphors We Live By* (Chicago: University of Chicago Press, 2003), 3.

15. Lakoff and Johnson, *Philosophy in the Flesh*, 58–59 (original emphasis).

16. Ibid., 128.

17. George Lakoff, *Moral Politics: How Liberals and Conservatives Think* (Chicago: University of Chicago Press, 2002), 41.

18. Lakoff and Johnson, *Philosophy in the Flesh*, 536.

19. Ibid., 118.

20. Ibid., 334.

21. Lakoff, *Moral Politics*, 72.

22. Ibid., 73.

23. Ibid., 74.

24. Ibid., 75.

25. Ibid., 75. Obviously, this "father" need not be gender specific.

26. See Lakoff, *Moral Politics*, and George Lakoff, *Don't Think of an Elephant! Know Your Values and Frame the Debate* (White River Junction: Chelsea Green, 2004).

27. Katsiaficas, "Eros and Revolution," 500.

28. Katsiaficas, "From Marcuse's 'Political Eros' to the Eros Effect," 68.

29. My own gut-felt reaction to Marcuse's history-bound sexism tends to prove the point he is making here.

30. Herbert Marcuse, *An Essay on Liberation* (Middlesex: Penguin Books, 1969), 20. I should note, too, that Marcuse's comments accord with Lakoff and Johnson's model of three levels of embodiment: phenomenological, cognitive unconscious, and neural. The phenomenological level is consciousness—our awareness of our own bodies and states of mind, which is where we experience the qualitative "feel" of life, and which also hypothesizes a level of nonconscious structures that make possible our conscious experience. Next is the cognitive unconscious, the massive portion of the iceberg below the visible tip of consciousness, and the place where the instincts operate unseen. Finally is the neural level, which is cellular and inaccessible to us. See *Philosophy in the Flesh*, 102–104.

31. Katsiaficas, *Imagination of the New Left*, 6 (original emphasis).

32. "Through the *eros* effect, new insight can be derived into human nature and the understanding of the rational/emotional dichotomy which forms the substratum from which theories of collective behavior are articulated. Looked upon as the self-formation of the human species, the process of social change can be understood as different than a natural process. Soviet Marxists, of course, emphasize the historical role of labor in this process. More recently, Habermas (1971) has explained the role of communication and Herbert Marcuse (1972) the role of art in the transformation of the human species into a species being. The *eros* effect is derived from a similar understanding—the understanding that revolution constitutes another domain through which the human species emerges from its naturally conditioned evolution and becomes a species-being." Katsiaficas, "The Eros Effect," 12.

33. Although Marcuse does not use the exact phrase in *Eros and Civilization*, it does contain a good explanation of the psychic Thermidor: see Herbert Marcuse, *Eros and Civilization: A Philosophical Inquiry into Freud* (Boston: Beacon Press, 1992), 90–92. Katsiaficas also provides a good explanation: "Even in moments of revolution, Marcuse argued, our own personalities limit our possibilities, a reality he discussed with me through the concept of the psychic Thermidor. (Thermidor was the month of the French revolutionary calendar during which reaction set in.) Psychic Thermidor refers to an internally conditioned reaction which revolutionaries suffer, a syndrome Marcuse accounted for in the changed material conditions of advanced capitalism: 'The economic and political incorporation of the individuals into the hierarchical system of labor is accompanied by an instinctual process in which the human objects of domination reproduce their own repression. . . . The

revolt against the primal father eliminated an individual person who could be (and was) replaced by other persons; but when the dominion of the father has expanded into the dominion of society, no such replacement seems possible and the guilt [of revolting against the system] becomes fatal.'" George Katsiaficas, "Afterword, Marcuse as an Activist: Reminiscences of His Theory and Practice," in *The New Left and the 1960s: Collected Papers of Herbert Marcuse, Vol. 3*, ed. Douglas Kellner (New York: Routledge, 2005), 192–203 (200).

34. Katsiaficas, *Imagination of the New Left*, 8.

35. Roger Gregoire and Fredy Perlman, *Worker-Student Action Committees: France, May'68* (Detroit: Black and Red, 1991), 42.

36. Choi Jungwoon, *The Gwangju Uprising* (Paramus: Homa & Sekey Books), 37.

37. Quoted in George Katsiaficas, *Asia's Unknown Uprisings, Volume 1: South Korean Social Movements in the 20th Century* (Oakland: PM Press, 2012), 162.

38. As quoted in Katsiaficas, *Asia's Unknown Uprisings, Vol. 1*, 182.

39. See Na Kahn-chae, "Collective Action and Organization in the Gwangju Uprising," in *South Korean Democracy: Legacy of the Gwangju Uprising*, ed. George Katsiaficas and Na Kahn-chae (London: Routledge, 2006), 47–66.

40. Lakoff and Johnson, *Metaphors We Live By*, 193.

41. Marcuse, *Eros and Civilization*, 35.

42. Ibid., 35

43. Ibid., 161–162.

44. Ibid., 180–181.

45. Ibid., 181–182 (all emphases in original).

46. Katsiaficas, *Imagination of the New Left*, 229 (original emphasis).

47. Marcuse, quoting Freud, as cited in *Eros and Civilization*, 168 (original emphasis).

48. Ibid., 169.

49. Lakoff and Johnson, *Philosophy in the Flesh*, 93.

50. As Lakoff and Johnson state, "The cognitive unconscious is a principal locus of power in the Foucaultian sense, power over how we can think and how we can conceive of the world." Lakoff and Johnson, *Philosophy in the Flesh*, 537.

51. Marcuse, *An Essay on Liberation*, 31.

52. Ibid., 33.

53. "Up to now, it has been one of the principal tenets of the critical theory of society (and particularly Marxian theory) to refrain from what might reasonably be called utopian speculation. Social theory is supposed to analyze existing societies in the light of their own functions and capabilities and to identify demonstrable tendencies (if any) which might lead beyond the existing state of affairs. . . . I believe this restrictive conception must be revised, and that the revision is suggested, and even necessitated, by the actual evolution of contemporary societies. The dynamic of their productivity deprives 'utopia' of its traditional unreal content: what is denounced as 'utopian' is no longer that which has 'no place' and cannot have any place in the historical universe, but rather that which is blocked from

coming about by the power of the established societies." Marcuse, *An Essay on Liberation*, 13.

54. Ibid., 14.

55. Ibid., 11.

56. Herbert Marcuse, *One-Dimensional Man: Studies in the Ideology of Advanced Industrial Society* (Boston: Beacon Press).

57. Marcuse, *An Essay on Liberation*, 52.

Section Three

# CASE STUDIES

# 8

# Kindling for the Spark

## Eros and Emergent Consciousness
## in Occupy Oakland

EMILY BRISSETTE AND MIKE KING

As we marched through West Oakland, toward the long, isolated overpass straddling line after line of rail track into the Port of Oakland, we felt anticipation tinged with uncertainty. Well, actually, fear. No visible police presence is generally a good thing, but in this moment it seemed foreboding. Were they waiting on the other side of the bridge? Would there be a thousand riot cops ready to unleash a hail of rubber bullets to bounce off the pavement, a cloud of chemical gasses, another fog of repression blowing in off the bay? That had been the case a week earlier downtown, when police relentlessly attacked a much smaller crowd. It was the case when an unsanctioned march came over this same bridge in 2003 during a protest against the Iraq War. As we walked, too fast at times, the thought ran through me as it had all week: How could they not block the overpass? Geographically and tactically, it was an easy space for police to defend. With no alternate route except back the way we came (maybe) or down into the railroad maze below (damn, I hope nobody does that), we pushed forward—too fast, and in too loose a formation. The bridge curves and arches up, with no clear line of sight to the other side. Gritted teeth, acutely aware of everything. Quick meetings of eyes as I looked back at strangers marching with me, reflecting the tension in my face though we had never and would never speak to each other. Like nervous kids waiting to open a mystery box that might contain pure joy, or an impersonal ass-kicking.

And then we came over the peak: no police. We shut down the Port of Oakland. Despite what so many of us had feared at the outset, we had done it. On no notice. Against the opposition of the entire city administration, the police, and even the newly elected reactionary leadership of the ILWU (International Longshore and Warehouse Union). Just days after being barraged for hours by an arsenal of riot-squad weapons, and facing an Oakland Police Department not known for sitting out the chance to beat people with impunity, we had done it.

The look of exuberance on people's faces—of empowered joy and exhausted relief—marked the presence of eros rippling through that march. According to George Katsiaficas, the eros effect arises when the life instincts are liberated as mundane and soul-deadening routines are suspended and existing power relations are ruptured. In this newly opened space, imagination is unleashed, new collective actors are forged, and (for a time) participants experience communion with others in an "ocean of universal life and love."[1] Such moments do not emerge out of nowhere, nor do they remain contained within a single locale or confined to a single struggle. For many of us at the port, buoyed by an acute awareness of collective power and a newly expansive sense of possibility, the moment was connected to the attempt to take the Brooklyn Bridge a month earlier, as well as to the riots that erupted in London in the face of police violence that August and the revolutionary upheaval of the Arab Spring exemplified by Cairo's Tahrir Square. Katsiaficas foregrounds these kinds of linkages across space in his discussion of the eros effect. What other scholars have characterized as contagion (diagnosing uprisings as a communicable disease requiring prophylaxis or quarantine),[2] Katsiaficas sees as an eminently hopeful and human process of articulation through which struggles are mutually amplified and the rational desire for political and social change becomes inseparable from an affective dimension marked by joy and inspiration.

While Katsiaficas has to date largely emphasized the *spatial* dimension of the eros effect, he has noted a temporal dimension as well. Here, movements borrow iconography and styles from the past while building upon the sometimes-unacknowledged "significant historical legacy" of knowledge and experience accumulated through previous waves of struggle. Whatever the transmission process, "whether in intuitive terms, directly intergenerational, or obtained through the study of history," revolutionary consciousness forged in earlier eras is accessed in moments of the eros effect, providing a foundation for further development.[3] This transmission of an emergent transtemporal revolutionary consciousness is our focus here.

While a universalizing solidarity is at the heart of the eros effect, drawing our attention outward to the global, it is important to remember that people experience eros where they are. Inspired though they may be by events near and far (imbued though they may be by a sense of universal love and fellowship), people nevertheless live eros in specific communities, among people they encounter in daily life, however upended or transformed that reality becomes. We thus seek to trace the manifestations of the eros effect within the lived experience of Occupy Oakland.

When Occupy Oakland held its first General Assembly and erected its first tent on October 10, 2011, three weeks after the Occupy movement started, there was a palpable sense of hope and expectation. Nevertheless, the sense of transcendence and communion (the sense of realizing species being) that constitutes a critical feature of the eros effect was not immediately present. At first, Occupy Oakland was just another node in a protest movement that was inserting issues of economic inequality into the national conversation while broadening the tactical repertoire of US social movements by normalizing the occupation of space (sometimes *but not always* with permits). These were important interventions to be sure; however, they were not yet a manifestation of the eros effect or of its transformation of consciousness and lived experience. In short time, that would change. Occupy Oakland would go from occupying the physical space of the park in front of City Hall to instantiating a new moral authority and new social relations. It would become the Oakland Commune. And we, its constituents, would be transformed.

Why and how did Occupy Oakland end up conceiving of itself as a commune marked by audacity and irrepressibility? The answer is global and local in scope, temporally rooted in past experiences as well as in small and large spontaneous risks in the present. These moments increased our ability to feel connected to people struggling in places we had not seen and in times long past; they enabled us to believe in our visions of what a free world might look like. In what follows, we trace Occupy Oakland's connection to previous struggles in the Bay Area to highlight the temporal dimension of the eros effect. From there, we explore moments in the life of the camp that mark the emergence of the Oakland Commune to emphasize the local, lived manifestation of eros in the formation of new collective actor(s), the development of heightened consciousness, and the instantiation of new social norms. Finally, we bring the spatial and temporal dimensions of the eros effect together by considering an example that illustrates how the spark spread from the camp to struggles throughout the Bay Area.

## GATHERING THE KINDLING

Occupy Oakland was unquestionably part of a global uprising that provided clear evidence of the eros effect. The year 2011 saw eruptions throughout North Africa and the Middle East, in Europe, and across parts of North and South America. Rather than explaining this wave of struggle through strictly political or economic factors, Katsiaficas has argued that we must take account of the "subjective factor," or the way that each struggle inspired and widened the sense of possibility for the next.[4] Occupy Oakland drew inspiration from these immediate antecedents and synchronous struggles; however, it also drew inspiration from local history. Oakland is, after all, the city that gave birth to the Black Panthers,[5] experimented with street-fighting *before* the Days of Rage,[6] and has long nurtured worker militancy and international solidarity.[7] To fully understand the emergence and impact of the eros effect in the Oakland Commune, then, we must situate Occupy Oakland within its local (and not only its global) context to unearth the experiential and affective knowledge that organizers gained though previous waves of struggle. The temporal dimension is important: in moments of the eros effect, Katsiaficas suggests, movements become continuous with past waves of struggle and "spontaneously internalize new levels of activity which previous episodes of revolutionary struggle already developed."[8] That Occupy Oakland would be widely recognized as the most militant of the US Occupy sites is not surprising given the city's radical history: it imbibed the spirit of those who came before.

But what does it mean to say that movements "spontaneously internalize" a previously developed level of activity? What does this look like? How does it work? The use of the word "spontaneous" to describe a social movement might, in one reading, cast that movement as truly inexplicable: it emerged "out of nowhere." And just as its origins and tactics are indecipherable, seemingly of the moment, without apparent rhyme or reason, the movement too is destined (perhaps) to burn out without leaving a trace. In this usage, the label "spontaneous" obscures years of quiet organizing, accumulated knowledge, and forged relations that gather the kindling for the next conflagration. In another reading of the word, however, describing a movement as "spontaneous" is an invitation to look deeper; it signals a more dynamic story, capturing something of the ineffable that would otherwise be lost if analyses focused *solely* on political-economic conditions, organizational resources, mobilization networks, or forces of repression. Considering the students who participated in the lunch counter sit-ins of the early 1960s to challenge Jim Crow across the South, Francesca Polletta noted that they frequently described the sit-ins as "spontaneous"—even though they had received civil disobedience training, helped to organize a sit-in, or otherwise worked to facilitate the tactic's spread.[9] By "spontaneous," they did not mean that the sit-ins appeared "out of nowhere," absent human agency or intention. Instead, Polletta argues, "when students described the sit-ins as 'spontaneous,' and as 'exploding,' 'welling up,' and 'like a fever,' they captured the indefinable moment when a group of separate individuals became a collective actor."[10] In other words, they were marking the human dimension of struggle, and particularly the indescribable feeling that accompanies the "lived experience of freedom—freedom understood as the dialectical unity of . . . autonomous individual existence and collective solidarity."[11]

If "spontaneous" is best understood, then, as marking an experience of freedom that is difficult to capture meaningfully in words, why does it insist on carrying the connotation of appearing "out of nowhere"? Perhaps part of the answer arises from the fact that such moments of transcendence occur so infrequently that they seem mystical and inexplicable when they do happen: they are spontaneous occurrences, without apparent cause. As Martin Glaberman once noted:

> Revolutionary outbursts or massive resistance to a regime are inherently surprise events—even when there is advance preparation. But it is important to realize that these events are also surprises to the participants. That is to say, there seems to take place a rapid, complex, but obscure succession of events combined with (but not necessarily caused by) rapid changes in consciousness.[12]

To suggest that a movement emerges "out of nowhere" obscures that advance preparation—the tireless organizing and accumulated experiences that serve as the groundwork and, in a very real sense, make that moment possible. We can and should trace that history, those relations, that *work*, even if we can never say with certainty why one particular moment (but not some other) had a special spark. This is true even if we find ourselves surprised by the events that give us a taste of freedom in community.

If there remains something inexplicable about the way movements spontaneously internalize past levels of activity, it is nevertheless the case that the process is facilitated by subterranean understandings and forms of experiential knowledge transmitted by organizers, participants, witnesses, and others who were touched in some way by the memory of past brushes with freedom—buried perhaps, but always potentially reawakened. Sometimes, such moments leave few documentary traces; nevertheless, they become seared into the collective consciousness. To paraphrase Antonio Gramsci's understanding of spontaneity: there is no *apparent* cause because the self-activity, everyday experiences, and sedimented knowledge of the people are not recorded in newspaper articles (that favored tool of so much social movement research) or other archives of constituted power.[13] Other times, the memories of such moments are more immediate, the experiences still fresh; or, efforts have been taken to capture the moment in words, preserving something of its contours, passing a message into the future to convey collective elation, bitter disappointments, lessons learned. In the case of Occupy Oakland, overt, direct linkages with the past are easy to identify, as are some of the people who carried that past into the present. Former Black Panthers brought years of accumulated experiences and insights, while other organizers had participated in major uprisings in Greece and Oaxaca. But perhaps the most influential previous struggles—because most proximate in space and time—were those against police violence and university austerity that rolled through the Bay Area in 2009.

That year began with the murder of Oscar Grant, a young Black man who was shot in the back by transit police while lying face down on a train platform in the early hours of New Year's Day. The incident, which was captured via cell phone video, sparked anger throughout the Bay Area and set off rebellions in Oakland. These rebellions included property destruction, small-scale looting, and the destruction of police cars. If only momentarily, the police lost control over downtown.[14] The rebellions also forced the hand of the district attorney and led to the arrest of Johannes Mehserle, the officer who killed Grant.[15] The movement was powerful because it was unpredictable, spontaneous, and unafraid to take risks, despite numerous efforts to incorporate, contain, and divide it. Acting as a buffer for the state, some nonprofits, for example, condemned the rebellions and countermobilized against subsequent demonstrations; they would find themselves marginalized when Occupy Oakland erupted a year and a half later.[16] Experiencing these dynamics changed many veterans of the Justice for Oscar Grant movement in subtle but fundamental ways. Politically, it left us wiser to the variety of forces that seek to contain change, but also more aware of our individual and collective capacity. We carried the experiential and affective knowledge of spectacular street tactics and emergent democracy within a General Assembly (consciously modeled after that in the Oaxaca uprising) with us into the Occupy movement. After watching London burn in August of 2011 in response to the police killing of Mark Duggan, we found ourselves primed. Despite being largely demobilized at the time, we felt the reverberations as the London rebellions persisted for five days and activated memories of collective power in the streets, waiting for our moment to return.

If the Justice for Oscar Grant movement was an important predecessor of Occupy Oakland, the student movement that (re)emerged in the fall of 2009 was another. That fall, a wave of occupations swept campuses across California in response to both a vote by the University of California Regents to increase tuition by 32 percent and to the more general trend of privatization exemplified by the decision. In Berkeley, five miles to the north of downtown Oakland, students occupied Wheeler Hall, one of the largest lecture halls on campus; in Santa Cruz, some eighty miles to the south, students occupied Kerr Hall, the administration building isolated among the redwoods in the center of campus. The California student occupations came after and were linked to an occupation in the spring of 2009 at the New School in New York City around similar issues. As the Occupy movement unfolded two years later, these campus occupations would be cited as an important source of inspiration for the initial call to occupy Wall Street,[17] and former student occupiers from across the Bay Area would converge in (Occupy) Oakland. From the Hooverville tent cities and the Flint sit-down strike of the Great Depression to the lunch counter sit-ins and campus occupations of the 1960s to the occupation of Alcatraz beginning in 1969, occupation has a long history in popular movements in the United States; however, the degree of commitment and risk involved militated against it ever becoming a commonplace tactic or even thinkable for most Americans.[18] The student movement in 2009 helped revive the tactic for a new generation of activists (though the outdoor occupation of Tahrir Square would serve as the model for the Occupy movement). It also provided an opportunity to advance an emergent understanding concerning demands, power, and possibility that would find expression within Occupy Oakland two years later.[19] For the student movement, occupation was more than a tactic to achieve some discrete demand; it was a potentially transformative challenge to existing power relations:

> Occupation is less potent as leverage for negotiation than as a practical attempt to remove oneself, to whatever degree possible, from existing regimes of relation: to others and to the use of space. The occupiers, in this sense, refuse to "take what they can get." They would rather "get what they can take." (This is how some fellow travelers in New York, participants in a series of inspiring occupations last year [2009], have put it.)[20]

By rejecting the normative frameworks in which both daily life and protest typically unfold (that is, by refusing to make the end of the occupation a mere bargaining chip in negotiation), student occupiers sought to open spaces of possibility for something else—new social relations, new norms— to arise. This emergent understanding was hardly unique to the student movement. Indeed, it was part of a global phenomenon, a distinguishing feature of what Dinerstein and Deneulin have called "hope movements." Such movements "engage in 'the politics of dignity' that connects rage with hope and moves beyond demand."[21] In the case of the student movement, demands were eschewed in part because they were seen as sources of fracture and exclusion, which served to delimit who was (or was not) part of a given struggle.[22]

Occupy Oakland would inherit and internalize much of this consciousness, which was transmitted both directly through the participation of former student occupiers in the planning meetings and early days of Occupy Oakland and more diffusely through the inspiration and example the 2009 occupations provided. Like its predecessor, Occupy Oakland refused demands and sought to liberate space in order to rupture existing political relations and concretize new modes of being. Katsiaficas notes that a core objective of his theorization of the eros effect is "to reintegrate the emotional and the rational."[23] In the next section, we demonstrate the inseparability of the two by illustrating how the rational principles of collective autonomy, derived in large part from past movements, were only actualized through the lived experience of hope translated into risk.

## EMERGENT CONSCIOUSNESS

At its first General Assembly, Occupy Oakland passed several resolutions that distinguished it from many other Occupy sites and, more importantly, served as the basis for the development of a new set of norms and relations that many of us would come to (further) internalize over the ensuing weeks. In addition to changing the name of the park in front of City Hall from Frank Ogawa to Oscar Grant Plaza (thus honoring its new namesake and signaling a certain defiance), Occupy Oakland also adopted resolutions embracing a diversity of tactics,[24] rejecting the authority of politicians and any claims to special status they might invoke, and establishing parameters on how to deal with police trying to enter the camp. The latter resolutions presaged an inevitable clash over political authority in the plaza.

In the initial days of Occupy Oakland, city officials scrambled to fashion a response to the camp. In public, Mayor Quan and some city council members aligned themselves with the goals of the (larger) Occupy movement while others decried the lawlessness of park occupations. For his part, police chief Anthony Batts quit in indignation (and over previous tension with the new mayor). Whatever their public stance toward the movement, however, both city officials and the police sought above all else to maintain control. Internal emails (acquired by a local paper through the Freedom of Information Act) show that city administrators had no idea how to deal with the semi-formalized and noncooperative protest. They wanted desperately to find someone with whom they might negotiate, and they lamented when they realized that there were no leaders to strong-arm. They were annoyed that the camp periodically made too much noise on their front lawn, and they spent three days trying to figure out how to remove a single canopy. In the course of these email exchanges, Deputy Police Chief Jeffrey Israel summarized the problem faced by police as they issued mandates that were consistently ignored: "If directives are not followed and there are no consequences it is likely seen as an opportunity to do whatever. On the flip side, we have to pick our battles."[25]

Occupy Oakland would have to pick its battles, too, and a central one would concern the autonomy of the camp. This meant an inevitable confrontation with the police: the extent to which the police could patrol the area would mark the limit of the camp's autonomy. If the camp was to be something more than a collection of colorful tents and some slogans about economic inequality (indeed, if the camp was to become a commune), the police would have to be denied entry into the park. The resolution to that effect, which passed at that first General Assembly, read as follows: "We are not to allow police within the perimeters of the camp. If police try to enter, they are asked politely to leave. If they do not leave, campers are called to come out and form a large group in front of the officers and yell, 'Go home! Go home!' "[26]

While cynics may express bemusement at "anarchists" passing laws, it would be more correct to view these efforts as the rational concretization of the eros effect, which requires the construction of new collective norms to foster new social relations. The eros effect is about moments when the impossible suddenly becomes imaginable; norms are challenged and structures of power (along with the normal functioning of daily life) are discredited and attacked. Such moments open space for "a simultaneous transformation of politics, economy, and culture, of social structure and individual subject."[27] In such moments, no matter how fleeting, existing social relations are reconfigured and individuals are changed. It is important to stress the element of personal transformation, of the emergence of new political subjects in and through revolutionary struggle. As Katsiaficas underscores,[28] political struggle takes place in the space between individual consciousness-in-action and the social structures being challenged. It is pushed forward by radical projects that develop alongside the people who found them. Such moments expand the realm of what is politically possible, broadening the movement while deepening it through experience. We would see this process unfold as Occupy Oakland's resolution denying police entry to the park was tested—and held.

During the first two weeks, police regularly patrolled the edges of the encampment, but (in the spirit of "picking their battles") they largely refrained from trying to enter it. The police would strike up conversation (or sarcastic back-and-forth exchanges) with people on the perimeter and, on a handful of occasions, they used these exchanges as a pretext to move into the park. People responded by applying the Occupy Oakland mandate against police in the park. On one such occasion (sometime after midnight on an ordinary night in the camp in mid-October), four police tried to make entry into the camp—maybe out of boredom or aggravation, or perhaps to test how we would respond. As the police left their squad cars and approached the encampment, a group of about a dozen Occupiers yelled at them to "go home." Others relayed the announcement that police were trying to enter the park. Within a minute, over fifty people had assembled at the edge of the park, forming a thick barrier of flesh—not impenetrable, but not interested in moving either. Together, those assembled shouted: "Pigs, go home!" The police hesitated. Embarrassed, angry, and perplexed, one officer went back to his car and returned moments later with instructions. As the police retreated to their respective cars, the crowd continued chanting: "Pigs, go home!" That was a moment of self-actualization for the Oakland Commune. A rag-tag group of campers repelled uniformed Oakland police intent on walking through the park despite the fact that every law in the State of California gave the latter full jurisdiction to do so. Through that act, the group began to cohere, and to become the Oakland Commune.

That feeling when the police pulled back and then left, that small triumph was, both individually and collectively, enormous. However fleeting and tenuous, the authority of the police was not only challenged but transcended on that night. Comprised of damaged people from this broken society, the camp was far from perfect. At times, it wasn't even pleasant; however, in that moment, in that space, Occupy Oakland put forward something that seemed materially unsupportable and irrational—that we, the Oakland Commune, were ungovernable. When those cops snarled and got back in their cars, that ungovernability, that autonomy, became real. This same scenario was repeated multiple times over the next several weeks, and we became quicker, louder, bolder, and larger in the challenge we mounted to police. The transformation of muted hopes into material reality is the eros effect at work. Like a wave that crashes violently on the shore and then recedes, these moments tend to be both tumultuous and fleeting. And, like the stones and pieces of shell washed ashore with the wave, they leave a concrete residue of memory and radical desire. These fragments can be collected, put on a shelf, admired for their beauty. Or they can be used as weapons in the slingshot of the next confrontation.

The next confrontation was not long in coming. In the early hours of October 25, with the camp barely two weeks old, word of an imminent raid went out over Occupy Oakland's text notification system. The city had been threatening eviction for about a week, and now those threats were to be actualized. At three in the morning, about a hundred Occupiers rallied in response and frantically began building barricades around the perimeter of the three-and-a-half-acre park. Folding tables were tethered to wooden pallets, tied to posts, and checked for stability before the crew moved on to the next. As the police became visible and began making announcements to disperse or face arrest, the building continued; however, with limited people and supplies, only about half of the plaza could be fortified, and only about half of those fortifications could be defended. A brief, but fierce, debate ensued: stay and try to defend the park against hundreds of looming riot cops or abandon the physical shell of the Oakland Commune. A handful committed to nonviolent civil disobedience stayed; everyone else left the park. Many lingered on the outskirts to watch as the police moved in, shredding tents, destroying the library, trampling the children's village, and inspecting the materials in the medic tent like bored tourists in a gift shop. The authority we had seized was inverted, the autonomous space we had created now dismantled and flattened. But the day was still young.

That afternoon, about three thousand people gathered at the main branch of the Oakland Library, several blocks east of Oscar Grant Plaza. Many had never been to the camp but were drawn out by the injustice of the eviction and a desire to stand in solidarity with others. That night, those motivations became more important than the safety of daily routines, even if the events that transpired would test that sentiment. United in the intention of reclaiming the camp, we marched up 14th Street to the plaza, where we confronted a thousand riot police assembled in dense skirmish lines along the perimeter. We stayed in the intersection at 14th and Broadway. Although we did not challenge the police line physically, we refused to leave when ordered. As the sun descended and the crowd dwindled, the police began to enforce their dispersal orders with CS gas, tear gas, concussion grenades, and rubber bullets. The crowd scattered east down 14th Street. After the gas cleared, we went back, fueled by a mixture of collective anger and determination. Our return was more of a "fuck you" to the riot squad than a clear plan regarding what we were trying to achieve. The police responded with more of the same. Retreat, regroup, repeat. This cycle recurred several times over the course of many hours. About three hours into the exchange, Scott Olsen, a young Marine veteran with Veterans for Peace, sustained a serious brain injury after he was hit by a tear gas canister shot from a distance of a few yards. He was carried out of the intersection by members of the crowd, blood streaming, eyes dazed. Images of his injuries and the tear-gas-filled streets of downtown Oakland circulated quickly. They generated support and solidarity from across the Bay Area and around the world. Recognizing our shared goal—"social justice for all"—revolutionaries in Cairo proclaimed that Tahrir Square and Occupy Oakland were "one hand."[29] In response, participants in Occupy Oakland proposed that Oakland and Cairo might better be understood as one fist.

Despite flooding downtown with tear gas on the night of October 25, the police were largely absent the following evening as three thousand people reclaimed Oscar Grant Plaza and rebuilt the camp. The General Assembly that night was Oakland's largest, with some 1,500 attendees passing a resolution calling for a General Strike and a shutdown of the Port of Oakland (the major site of capital flow into the city) one week later. On November 2, the day of the General Strike, some fifty thousand people came out for a full day of actions and activity. Banks were occupied in the morning, with foreclosed families moving in—couches, coffee tables, and all. An anticapitalist march snaked through downtown targeting businesses like Whole Foods, which had told workers they would be disciplined if they took the day off. At the plaza, people lined up around the block to get free Occupy Oakland screen-printed posters by Bay Area political artist Jon-Paul Bail, and to navigate the maze of tents that made up the Oakland Commune. The kitchen committee and local unions provided food throughout the day, while musicians, poets, and speakers took turns at the mic. As late afternoon arrived, the crowd fell into place behind shields and banners for the march to the port. Although many of us anticipated a confrontation with the OPD en route, it did not materialize.

Such moments of real and anticipated confrontation may have played a large role in the emergence of the eros effect in Oakland; however, the effect was also generated and sustained in small, unremarked moments that played out daily in the camp as well. It was fostered by chance conversations and the coming together of the Bay Area's fractured left. People who would never have worked together before began to see each other from behind their organizational affiliations. In the mingling that ensued, the houseless who had long called the plaza home, students and teachers, city workers and retirees, veterans and hustlers all came together. The eros effect appeared in the euphoria of making momentous decisions together with near unanimity.[30] And it was nurtured through the shared work of crafting life in the camp: feeding one another and sweeping up debris to keep the resident rats at bay, forging community through dance parties, pumpkin-carving, and a piñata for the kids on Halloween—even in the midst of the sleepless planning for the November 2 Port Shutdown. Despite its blemishes, the camp represented a certain "refusal to accept the position that the transformation of everyday life must be delayed until 'after the revolution.'"[31] It instantiated and prefigured "a new type of social reality where *living human energy* and not *things* was predominant."[32] When the camp was evicted a second time in mid-November, the Oakland Commune persisted, lodged in the hearts of its constituents, concretized in the relations forged among us, and fueled in part by articulating struggles.

## SMOLDERING EMBERS

Consciousness, if it is a serious category, has to mean more than verbal consciousness, it has to include activity. What people are prepared to do has to be defined as part of their consciousness, not simply what people say, partly because they do not always know, and partly because they are not always willing to tell you.

—Martin Glaberman, *Punching Out & Other Writings*

Occupy Oakland would return to the port again on December 12 (D12) as part of a coordinated action by Occupies from Anchorage to San Diego to shut down all the ports along the West Coast. The action was in response to the coordinated police raids of eighteen Occupy encampments in mid-November and in solidarity with ILWU workers in Longview, Washington, who were fighting to maintain their jurisdiction over the port there. In Oakland, the D12 action was an overall success, with Occupy Oakland shutting down the port for a full twenty-four hours. Although the action drew only a fraction of the participation that the first port shutdown mustered, it still garnered a lot of attention for Occupy Oakland. Some of the attention was from city politicians who feared yet another port shutdown,[33] but some was also from workers across the Bay Area who were inspired by Occupy Oakland's direct actions in solidarity with workers' struggles. Having led the planning for D12, the Occupy Oakland Labor Solidarity Committee was subsequently approached by different groups of workers seeking solidarity in their struggles with employers. Workers at American Licorice, where Red Vines licorice is made, were one such group. They had been on strike for a month, picketing twenty-four hours a day, and they wanted Occupy Oakland to come out to support their picket.[34] Their union had told them that they could lose the strike and that the union could be fined if they took direct action to block scabs from coming in; as a result, they could not form a hard picket, though they wanted us to. As the hardships of four-weeks' meager strike pay started to compile (and with the union leadership doing little to help them), the workers seemed to see in Occupy a best chance—but also a last hope.

By 6:00 a.m. on January 9, 2012, more than one hundred people from Occupy Oakland had made the trip half an hour south to the licorice plant in Union City, California. When a manager showed up in a white SUV, he saw a familiar picket line, but this time with a lot of new faces. Though accustomed to being automatically—if reluctantly—let through the line, on this morning he was blocked by the picket of Occupiers as security guards tried unsuccessfully to force an opening. The workers stood to the side as the manager was turned away and then rejoiced when, with an angry red face, he drove off down the street. On one level, this was a small moment—a minor victory for the picket line, a minor aggravation for the boss. On another level, and like the cops being turned away in the plaza, it amounted to a rupture. The unquestioned power of the plant authority had been denied. The eros effect could be felt on that picket line of tired bodies, not yet warm in the early-morning Bay Area fog. A few minutes later, a van full of scabs arrived. As the picket line blocked the van's approach, several dozen licorice workers did what they had said they wouldn't (or couldn't) do and joined the line. Their faces were proud and determined as the hard picket of licorice workers and Occupiers collectively blocked the van. Although we didn't prevent every vehicle from accessing the plant, we blocked enough to keep the production line from functioning that day. Across the language barrier standing between many of the workers and many of the Occupiers, we playfully translated insults to be hurled at the security guards who had harassed workers on the line—and invented new ones as we collectively negated their authority. As the day came to a close and a few trailers of defective scab-licorice left the plant to be fed to cattle, spirits were high. Nevertheless, the workers took a concessionary contract the next day. Many had been worn down and became cautious as a result of the weeks of economic hardship brought on by the strike.

Even in defeat, however, people are transformed. They are transformed by the struggle itself. Everyone emerged from that day having experienced a small rupture through which "established patterns of interaction [were] negated."[35] Everyone glimpsed the possibilities of a transformed world built on solidarity and mutual aid. The workers saw that they weren't alone and the Occupiers (despite the naysaying of some on the periphery of the Labor Solidarity Committee), saw that the gap between what workers tell you they are willing to do and what they actually will do can be quite large. We only learned these things because we stood together. With every victory or failure that results from genuine effort and risk, our knowledge of what we are individually and collectively capable of expands. Such experiential knowledge accumulates in individuals and locales. It's a force you don't see, submerged but real, a tangible material force. As new struggles emerge, our definition of what is possible becomes broader. The hopes of past movements become tomorrow's expectations. Despite failure, the kindling piles higher, waiting for a spark and a strong gust of wind.

## WIDENING THE CRACKS

In this chapter, we have shown how the eros effect played out in Occupy Oakland and suggested some of the conditions and dynamics that led to its emergence. While the ultimate goal of theorizing the eros effect may be to understand ongoing efforts to transform social relations at the global level, it is equally important to consider the local manifestations of the process. Considered from this vantage, it becomes possible to highlight emergent consciousness, accumulated experiences, and relations forged within particular struggles to actualize desires for freedom and justice. In addition to translating Katsiaficas' global focus to the local level, we have also highlighted the ways in which moments of upheaval emerge from antecedent movements whose experiences accumulate within the local imagination. Finally, we have sought to illuminate the intent and action, emotion and political development, as well as the fear and risk that are at the core of social struggles like the Oakland Commune. Our account has necessarily been partial; it is an incomplete rendering of a brief moment in which collective power was actualized, the boundaries of the possible expanded, and actors transformed—inspired by the courageous risks taken by others near and far, and sustained by our own lived experiences of freedom.

The notion of the eros effect that Katsiaficas developed nearly thirty years ago provides a way of capturing the ineffable element—the celebration of the life instinct, the realization of species being—that transformed Occupy Oakland into the Oakland Commune. Considered by Katsiaficas to be the very *human* dimension of protest, this transcendental dimension is often obscured in the models and causal mechanisms used to explain the nature of protest events and the trajectories of social movements.[36] But useful theory, like protest, is less about knowing "the answer" than it is about being open to and grappling with the unknown. Such seeking is fundamental to social movements—stretching the imagination and testing one's will beyond the normal, the everyday, and the ongoing persistence of what is. In some moments, seeking of this kind can spontaneously yield a lived experience of freedom, in community with others, grounded in concrete activity and shared risks. Consciousness is transformed; the impossible becomes possible. The eros effect is built upon that conviction. It is fueled by the moments in which we open a crack in the existing order—enough to catch a glimpse of the beauty and the power that could be ours. Through such moments, our desire for a new world is stoked and—even after the fire is tamped down—we emerge like primed tinder for the next spark.

## NOTES

1. George Katsiaficas, *The Imagination of the New Left: A Global Analysis of 1968* (Cambridge: South End Press, 1987), 6.

2. See, for example, Gustave Le Bon, *The Crowd* (New York: Viking Press, 1895); and Herbert Blumer, "Collective Behavior," in *Principles of Sociology*, ed. Robert E. Park (New York: Barnes & Noble, 1939), 219–288.

3. Katsiaficas, *Imagination of the New Left*, 11.

4. George Katsiaficas, interviewed by David Zlutnick, "The Eros Effect and the Arab Uprisings," *Counterpunch*, April 22, 2011, http://www.counterpunch.org/2011/04/22/the-eros-effect-and-the-arab-uprisings/.

5. Donna Jean Murch, *Living for the City: Migration, Education, and the Rise of the Black Panther Party in Oakland, California* (Chapel Hill: University of North Carolina Press, 2010); and Joshua Bloom and Waldo E. Martin Jr., *Black Against Empire: The History and Politics of the Black Panther Party* (Berkeley: University of California Press, 2013).

6. Michael Ferber and Staughton Lynd, *The Resistance* (Boston: Beacon Press, 1971), 140–147.

7. Stan Weir, "Unions with Leaders Who Stay on the Job," in *"We Are All Leaders": The Alternative Unionism of the 1930s*, ed. by Staughton Lynd (Champaign: University of Illinois Press, 1996), 294–334; and Harvey Schwartz, *Solidarity Stories: An Oral History of the ILWU* (Seattle: University of Washington Press, 2009).

8. George Katsiaficas, "The Eros Effect," 1989, personal website, http://www.eroseffect.com/articles/eroseffectpaper.PDF, 8.

9. Francesca Polletta, *It Was Like a Fever: Storytelling in Protest and Politics* (Chicago: University of Chicago Press, 2006).

10. Ibid., 34.

11. Katsiaficas, "The Eros Effect," 9.

12. Martin Glaberman, *Punching Out & Other Writings* (Chicago: Charles H. Kerr, 2002), 111.

13. Antonio Gramsci, *Selections from the Prison Notebooks* (New York: International, 1971), 196. For more on social movement research using newspapers, see Charles Tilly, "Event Catalogs as Theories," *Sociological Theory* 20, no. 2 (2002): 248–254, doi: 10.1111/1467-9558.00161; and Jennifer Earl, Andrew Martin, John D. McCarthy, and Sarah A. Soule, "The Use of Newspaper Data in the Study of Collective Action," *Annual Review of Sociology* 30 (2004): 65–80, doi: 10.1146/annurev.soc.30.012703.110603.

14. George Ciccariello-Maher, "Oakland's Not for Burning? Popular Fury at Yet Another Police Murder," *Counterpunch*, January 9, 2009, http://www.counterpunch.org/2009/01/09/oakland-s-not-for-burning/.

15. Mehserle was tried on second-degree murder charges but was convicted of involuntary manslaughter. While the movement was outraged by the verdict (and the slight sentence he received—just two years), this was nevertheless the first time in California history that an on-duty police officer was convicted for a shooting death. See George Ciccariello-Maher, " 'Oakland Is Closed!': Arrest and Containment Fail to Blunt Anger in the Streets," *Counterpunch*, January 16, 2009, http://www.counterpunch.org/2009/01/16/quot-oakland-is-closed-quot/; and Thandisizwe Chimurenga, *No Doubt: The Murder(s) of Oscar Grant* (Los Angeles: Ida B. Wells Institute, 2014).

16. George Ciccariello-Maher, "From Oscar Grant to Occupy: The Long Arc of Rebellion in Oakland," in *We Are Many: Reflections on Movement Strategy from Occupation to Liberation*, ed. Kate Khatib, Margaret Killjoy, and Mike McGuire (Oakland: AK Press, 2012), 39–45.

17. Joshua Clover, "The Coming Occupation," in *We Are Many*, 95–103.

18. In 1999, 67 percent of Americans surveyed responded that they would "never" occupy buildings or factories, while only 24 percent said they would never attend a demonstration. See World Values Survey, 1999–2004, click on "United States" and then "V136, Attending Demonstrations" and "V138, Occupying Buildings," http://www.worldvaluessurvey.org/WVSOnline.jsp. More recent data are not available since the question about occupation was dropped from subsequent waves of the survey.

19. See Clover, "The Coming Occupation."

20. "After the Fall: Communiqués from Occupied California," February 2010, 5, pamphlet, http://libcom.org/files/afterthefall_communiques.pdf.

21. Ana Cecilia Dinerstein and Séverine Deneulin, "Hope Movements: Naming Mobilization in a Post-Development World," *Development and Change* 43, no. 2 (2012): 585–602 (598), doi: 10.1111/j.1467-7660.2012.01765.x.

22. "After the Fall," 20.

23. Katsiaficas, "The Eros Effect," 3.

24. The concept of "diversity of tactics" emerged during debates within the anti-globalization movement over property destruction and violence. It served as an organizing principle through which activists with different "tastes in tactics" could participate together in summit protests and other mass convergences. Rather than demanding that everyone adhere to principles of nonviolence (however defined), activists agreed to make space for a diversity of tactics, to respect the tactical choices of others, and to take others into account when making tactical decisions. While many Occupy sites explicitly embraced nonviolence, Occupy Oakland rejected several proposals calling for a repudiation of "violence" and instead "encouraged" a diversity of tactics, making space for a range of disruptive tactics beyond traditional forms of nonviolent civil disobedience. For more on these points, see Occupy Oakland, "General Assembly Resolutions (Oct 10–Nov 16 Summary)," 2011, https://occupyoakland.org/2011/11/general-assembly-resolutions/; and Chris Hurl, "Anti-Globalization and 'Diversity of Tactics,'" *Upping the Anti* 1 (2005): 51–64. For the "tastes in tactics" reference, see James M. Jasper, *The Art of Moral Protest: Culture, Biography, and Creativity in Social Movements* (Chicago: University of Chicago Press, 1997).

25. Daniel Willis and Thomas Peele, "In Their Own Words: Occupy Oakland According to City Officials, Part I," *San Jose Mercury News*, February, 25, 2012, http://www.mercurynews.com/top-stories/ci_20030387.

26. Occupy Oakland, "General Assembly Resolutions."

27. Katsiaficas, *Imagination of the New Left*, 36.

28. Ibid., 9.

29. Xeni Jardin, "Egyptians March from Tahrir Square to Support Occupy Oakland Protestors," *Boingboing*, October 28, 2011, http://boingboing.net/2011/10/28/tahrir.html.

30. The call for the November 2 General Strike, for example, passed with 97 percent. Occupy Oakland used a modified consensus process in its General Assembly; for a resolution to pass on the first try, it had to have the approval of at least 90 percent of those present and voting.

31. Katsiaficas, *Imagination of the New Left*, 36.

32. Ibid., 7 (original emphasis). See also Emily Brissette, "Prefiguring the Realm of Freedom at Occupy Oakland," *Rethinking Marxism* 25, no. 2 (2013): 218–227, doi: 10.1080/08935696.2013.769357.

33. Glaberman, *Punching Out*, 128.

34. Kevin Fagan and Matthai Kuruvila, "Oakland Council Acts to Sink Occupy Port Blockades," *San Francisco Chronicle*, December 20, 2011, http://www.sfgate.com/bayarea/article/Oakland-council-acts-to-sink-Occupy-port-blockades-2413201.php.

35. See Rose Arrieta, "Trouble in Candyland: American Licorice Workers Strike Over Healthcare Benefits," *In These Times*, January 9, 2012, http://inthesetimes.com/working/entry/12498/american_licorice_worker_strike; and Zoneil Maharaj, "Occupy Protesters Cause Stir at Licorice Strike," *Union City Patch*, January 10, 2012, http://patch.com/california/unioncity/occupy-protesters-cause-stir-at-licorice-strike.

36. Katsiaficas, *Imagination of the New Left*, 10.

37. The body of work produced by McAdam, Tarrow, and Tilly (individually and collectively) is paradigmatic here. The "subjective factor" that Katsiaficas emphasizes is largely absent in their theorizing. When actors do appear in their work, they are instrumental creatures—or, *entrepreneurs*—responding rationally to the structural conditions at hand. See, for example, Sidney Tarrow, *Power in Movement: Social Movements and Contentious Politics* (New York: Cambridge University Press, 1998); Doug McAdam, Sidney Tarrow, and Charles Tilly, *Dynamics of Contention* (New York: Cambridge University Press, 2001); and Charles Tilly, *The Politics of Collective Violence* (New York: Cambridge University Press, 2003).

9

# Eros Effect as Emergency Politics

## Empathy, Agency, and Network in South Korea's Sewol Ferry Disaster

GOOYONG KIM AND ANAT SCHWARTZ

### OVERVIEW: TRAGEDY, EMOTION, SPONTANEITY, AND AGENCY

How do people, based on shared experiences of crisis, come together to address the status quo through affect, empathy, and spontaneity? Taking the South Korean Sewol ferry accident as our case study, we draw connections between George Katsiaficas' eros effect[1] and Bonnie Honig's emergency politics[2] to consider how people become transformed in moments of crisis.

In the early hours of April 16, 2014, the Sewol ferry capsized on its way from Incheon to Jeju Island in South Korea. The ferry held 476 people, mostly teenage students on a field trip from Ansan City's Danwon High School. In all, 301 people died, 172 survived, and—as of July 2016—nine are still missing. The accident was far from being unavoidable. Despite numerous mechanical and crew mistakes, the fundamental causes of the tragedy were the government's apparent lack of will to rescue those on the ferry and its heavy interest in neoliberal capitalist profiteering through the deregulation of safety standards. Indeed, the current administration mishandled the situation by prioritizing privatized rescue operations, rejecting help from independent divers and the US Navy, withholding crucial information, deploying irregular and poorly trained labor to the scene, and manipulating mass media reports.[3] Moreover, the government has yet to launch a full-scale investigation into the disaster and has even obstructed efforts by civil society—including those by surviving victims and the bereaved—to unearth the truth behind the accident. Rather than a "disaster," then, we believe the accident should be called a massacre "committed," as Christine Hong suggests, "by political power and capital."[4] Indeed, the sinking is owed to governmental ignorance, negligence, and incapacity. As a foreseeable, preventable disaster, the sinking has affected Koreans at home and overseas.

Since the sinking, bereaved families have struggled to pass a special law to investigate why the government failed to rescue students trapped in the ship. Shocked by the discrepancy between the government-that-is and the government-that-ought-to-be, the bereaved family members' law urges President Park Geun-hye to set up an independent investigative panel with members appointed by the bereaved families and the authority to subpoena information and prosecute. Since each new law "transforms the entire economy of rights and identities, and establishes new relations and new realities, new promises and potentially new cruelties,"[5] the push for a special Sewol law is best understood as an attempt to disrupt the status quo and suspend existing norms and conventions. As Herbert Marcuse would put it, this move expresses "the ascent of needs and satisfactions very different from and even antagonistic to those prevalent" in a society such as ours.[6] As such, while legal effort is of importance to emergency politics, it is not law itself that leads to a radical transformation of values but rather public visibility and access to the law, which carries potential to combat and protect rights during emergencies.

While the request of the bereaved to legislate a special law was legitimate, the right-wing mainstream media and the Korean government criticized their efforts as a "political" manipulation of the tragedy. It's important to note, however, that the request *was* essentially *political*, considering that the monopoly of prosecution by the prosecutor's office has been challenged by the national police for the last few decades and the office has been criticized for its favoritism to the establishment. In this way, the request aims to hold the administration accountable for the tragedy and rectify the problem. The request may, therefore, be viewed as an attempt at mediating between diverse human values and interests that are "incommensurable, and bound, therefore, to conflict in any social order."[7] In this respect, the struggle of the bereaved amounts to a weary and horrendous battle against a government that has tried to cover up problems and divide the victims by spreading rumors and planting spies among them. The government also tried to undermine solidarity between the bereaved and civil society by portraying the former as amoral parents motivated by the promise of sizable reparations and influenced by antigovernment Leftists. Both conservative news media and the ruling Saenuri Party, for instance, have emphasized the immorality of members of a victim's family allegedly involved in a violent crime, even though the case has yet to be fully investigated.[8]

As a response to governmental intransigence, Kim Young-Oh, a father of one of the victims, waged a hunger strike for forty-six consecutive days. Although his efforts were met with indifference by the administration, a number of sympathizers staged solidarity hunger strikes to support the call for special legislation. From this perspective, the crisis helped to constitute the *demos* of democracy as people affected by the massacre took action to prevent the crisis from reoccurring as a democratic, grassroots effort to survive in society.[9] Just as there is no emergence of a new rule or democratic constituency without an emergency,[10] the emergency politics surrounding the Sewol massacre stands as both a risk and a promise for Korea's democratic practices and norms.

Through an analysis of the Sewol massacre, and by paying attention to the "actions and aspirations of millions of people during social crises,"[11] we investigate how Katsiaficas' eros effect can be further elaborated through Honig's notion of emergency politics. We illustrate how people's transformative, democratic engagement in crisis engenders insights into a qualitatively new, democratic form of social life.[12] Additionally, we expand on Katsiaficas' insight into the political potential of people's emotional and spontaneous engagement in crisis by connecting it to Honig's "miracle of democratic sovereignty," in which people exercise sovereign power in the paradox of politics that requires them to "become who they already need to be in order to act as they are."[13] At the same time, Honig's attempt to shift our attention from dominant conceptions of sovereignty to something "implicated in and dependent upon popular power"[14] can help to clarify the precise means by which Katsiaficas' eros effect serves as a powerful initiation for the transformative power of people's plural and contingent political agency.[15] This agency is enacted through feelings of empathy for the devastated and anger at the status quo.

Finally, we consider how people consolidate contingent agency and empathy through social network applications such as Facebook. We show how these emerging forms of online organizing help to cultivate Marcuse's "new sensibility" of "the life instinct over aggressiveness and guilt," which underscores "the vital need for the abolition of injustice."[16] In this sense, Facebook and MissyUSA (an online community for overseas Korean homemakers mainly in the United States) are harnessed by and further multiply the "emancipation of the senses [which] would make freedom what it is not yet: a sensuous need, an objective of the Life Instinct (Eros)."[17] Because human emotions are "not only the basis for the *epistemological* constitution of reality, but also for its *transformation*, its *subversion* in the interest of liberation,"[18] people sharing indignation and sorrow through communicative networks facilitates the eros effect's contagious spread.

## EMERGENCY, PARADOX OF POLITICS, AND HUMAN AGENCY

In opposition to views maintaining that political consensus is the main goal of democracy, Honig has been vocal in her insistence that politics is fundamentally agonistic in character.[19] For Honig, politics is a domain of perpetual struggle in which one has to deal with others who have different cultural, economic, and social orientations and interests.[20] In this domain, the legitimacy of outcomes is always already contestable. To practice democracy as agonistic politics, then, people must partake in both an infinite struggle among different political subjects as well as collaboration and mutuality in order to (re)form communities for public life and good. For Honig, agonistic contention is a "generative resource of politics" since it encourages us to perpetually (re)engage people making democratic demands.[21]

From this point of view, constituting a democratic citizenry *is* democracy's paradox of politics. Although democracy requires autonomous decision-makers and participants, people are "never fully who they need to be (unified, democratic)."[22] As a result, it's unlikely that they can be "counted upon to exercise their power democratically."[23] People are both the subject and the object of democratic governance, and sovereignty can only be realized by people with diversified and contradictory perspectives and interests.

As a solution to the paradox of founding the demos, in a constant process of sovereignty making, crisis constitutes an effective point of emergence.[24] In contrast to Carl Schmitt's "exception," in which government can paralyze democracy in the name of the public good, Honig asserts that—in an emergency—people should actively embrace agonistic politics as a means of enacting democratic values like autonomy, justice, solidarity, and equality. By stimulating people's passion, imagination, and fantasy for alternative futures, crisis helps bring them into politics.

Emergency demands that we identify contested interests, decide whom to blame, and consolidate alternatives so that we might survive the crisis. Along with the emergency's constitutive dynamic, Honig considers the new rights that a victim might claim: "new rights reactivate the paradox of politics: New rights presuppose the world they seek to bring into being."[25] In the case of the Sewol massacre, once the focus shifted from the bereaved families' right to special legislation to its broader sociopolitical impact, it becomes clear that the former practice played a constitutive role in shaping the demos, and that it created a transformative agency to bring about positive change. The normative value of emergency politics arises from its power to realize the democratic values of autonomy and justice. Here, contingency, spontaneity, and unpredictability reveal themselves to be central elements of political life. The very nature of emotion and sympathy in moments of tragedy helps consolidate a commonality of vulnerability, which in turn becomes the most important attribute of the autonomous demos.

In this respect, the nationwide and cross-border diffusion of various protests in support of the special legislation should be understood as a manifestation of what Honig has called "*mortalist* humanism."[26] Mortalist humanism manifests, for Honig, humans' shared finitude and vulnerability as the base for political agendas in reaction to state violence and divisiveness in the post-9/11 Bush era.[27] Indeed, our shared vulnerability to suffering, and the very visual affect of the Sewol massacre, underscores Honig's approach to humanism and the primacy of affect to solidarity. To the extent that humans share death, an empathy arising from mortality "creates a new universalism" founded in the loss experienced by "mothers who mourn our mortality."[28] Faced with terrible losses, people in crisis situations like the one that arose with the Sewol massacre are desperate to find commonality and acknowledge their ontological vulnerability as a means of addressing insecurity and building solidarity for security and care. On the other hand, tragedy "renders clear the human spirit, exhibiting human willingness to sacrifice on behalf of a principle, commitment, or desire, or knowingly to accept one's implication in unchosen acts or defiantly to march to one's death with head held high."[29] Kim Young-Oh's life-threatening forty-six-consecutive-day hunger strike exemplifies how tragedy stimulates awareness of the interconnections highlighted by mortalist humanism. It made the bereaved families' suffering intelligible and further consolidated the public's identification with that suffering. The subsequent widespread solidarity hunger strikes embodied the political power of tragedy, which "gets under the skin of politics to scratch the essence of the human."[30] In sum, an emergency such as the Sewol massacre has potential to overcome political divisions, move spectators toward a mortalist humanist approach, and trigger people's deep-seated humanistic passion for justice, sacrifice, and commitment to a better world.[31] Consequently, the Sewol case reveals how human affect, empathy, and agency can be activated in the face of an emergency. As Honig put it, "tragic characters die but their principles live on. They suffer, but something beautiful is made of their suffering."[32]

## EMOTION, SPONTANEITY, AND THE EROS EFFECT IN EMERGENCY POLITICS

Beginning with the publication of *The Crowd: A Study of the Popular Mind* by Le Bon in 1895, social theorists have often treated emotions as a source of behavioral irrationality.[33] In response, social movement scholars have recently examined the crucial cognitive and mobilizing roles played by emotions as a source of ideas, interests, and new forms of collective action.[34] In other words, human affect is dialectically entwined with knowledge and reason,[35] and contextually embodied knowledge constitutes a somatic mode of intelligence.[36] According to Burkitt, rather than a traditional dichotomy between "body and mind, emotions and consciousness," they are interrelated, containing one another."[37]

Drawing from Marcuse, Katsiaficas conceptualizes the eros effect as a spontaneous, simultaneous outpouring of uprisings, strikes, and protests. Here, he pays careful attention to the transformative power of affective attributes in social movements. Like Honig's emergency politics, Katsiaficas' eros effect locates a constitutive aspect of human instinct anchored in freedom, justice, and liberation. As a "transcendental" quality of social movements, Katsiaficas maintains that eros helps to mobilize and consolidate social rebellions against the status quo.[38] As the core of eros, love plays an inspirational role by accentuating people's experiences of suffering and hope.[39] Conditioned by similar circumstances and helped by the media's ubiquity, the eros effect enables transformative social movements to spread, forging interrelations among multitudes of protestors.

As with the democratic function of emergency politics, the eros effect simultaneously relies upon and helps to proliferate a "sudden, intuitive awakening of solidarity and massive opposition" among different constituencies.[40] Through a "dialectic of praxis, of the consciousness-in-action of millions of people," the eros effect helps people become dynamic agents capable of reconfiguring their economic, political, and social lives.[41] Realizing a simultaneous transformation of subjectivity and social structure, the eros effect ultimately amounts to a humanitarian project for the sociopolitical transformation of values, norms, ideas, and aspirations. As a condition for conscious human collectivity, the eros effect underwrites people's self-realization and political sovereignty.

But just as Honig's theory rests upon the paradox of politics, a paradox exists in Katsiaficas' eros effect as well. Most crucially, how is the eros effect *activated*? For the eros effect to unleash its transformative power, it requires a preexisting set of igniting factors, which in turn require ignition themselves. Stated differently, if a spontaneous chain reaction of multiple uprisings is to occur, something must initiate the wildfire. Moreover, as the phenomenon's spontaneity suggests, even when there is an initial spark, there is no guarantee that the eros effect will become fully realized. In this respect, Katsiaficas acknowledges that a focus on the eros effect "could become infatuated with the *act of creation* of new social values and aspirations and thereby lose sight of the creation of the creators . . . [who] are themselves products of that which has already been created."[42]

The Sewol massacre suggests an important prerequisite for the eros effect to be realized. We believe it is the strong raw emotions that prompt empathy during emergencies that allow for the eros effect to come into being. Meanwhile, this effect is further provoked and activated by personal, instantaneous communication. Appalled at how the government abandoned its responsibility to protect people from disaster while the Sewol sunk, people responded with an indescribable "sense of outrage" that left people "inclined toward political action."[43] Combined with people's moral responsibility to provide for their children, these feelings became grounds for participation and solidarity with the bereaved. Put differently, as a group-based emotion arising from both in-group identification and out-group extension, parental love for children seems to have played a central role in mobilizing people in the Sewol case.[44] Strong, raw emotions that prompt empathy provide a practical answer to both Honig's paradox of politics and to the question of how the eros effect first arises. As a spark unleashing the democratic potential in emergency politics and the eros effect, indignation and frustration stir people's anger; in turn, empathy can lead to spontaneous, simultaneous eruptions of protests. The stronger people feel indignation and frustration, the more likely they are to form empathy and solidarity. In turn, these inclinations allow them to forge a dynamic, competent agency in the eros effect.

## FROM THE MASSACRE TO NETWORKED, EMOTIONAL COMBUSTIONS

The Sewol incident has remained an open wound for Koreans. Viewing the Sewol's capsizing as a national emergency, South Korean people took to the streets in mass candlelight vigils for both victims and bereaved families alike.[45] In the aftermath of the massacre, consumer spending plummeted;[46] television shows, music performances, and concerts were rescheduled;[47] and people refrained from going out to eat or drink alcohol in the open as an act of solemn mourning.[48] Central to the national grieving process were temporary mourning altars, which were erected throughout the country—and especially in Ansan, the city home to Danwon High School, where nearly one hundred thousand people gathered to cry, grieve, and mourn together.[49] The temporary areas for mourning and crying created a space for bereaved families, survivors, friends, and ordinary people to come together and share in the moment of intense anguish:[50] "I want to know the truth so that my child smiles," said one participant. "Please remember every innocent face."[51] At least 360,000 visited the mourning altar erected in the Ansan Olympic Memorial Hall. Meanwhile, more than 1.15 million visited mourning altars across the country by May 5.[52]

People's condolent behavior gradually grew in vitriol as Park's administration continued to bungle the rescue operation, spy on the victims' families, and manipulate state-owned television networks to prevent them from criticizing either the Coast Guard or the rescue efforts.[53] Right after the ship capsized, the mainstream media unanimously reported that every single passenger had been rescued; such disinformation was systematically spread. In opposition to these distortions, bereaved families and the public alike supplemented mainstream coverage by using social networking platforms. In previous cases of sociopolitical crises, network-based grassroots news reporting has been effective in bypassing mainstream media hierarchies and gatekeepers in order to distribute alternative news even within authoritarian political regimes.[54] Characterized as a central dynamic in the production, circulation, and consumption of news and information online, affect constitutes a "binding technique" for creating communities and movements.[55] And, because alternative reporting in communicative networks tends to blend "opinion, fact, and emotion into expression,"[56] it helped to garner critical awareness of the massacre and consolidate like-minded individuals into a networked public.

Given the ubiquity and instantaneity of online communication networks, the affective messages disseminated by both the bereaved and grassroots participants effectively mobilized supporters' involvement, connection, and cohesion. This allowed for the further intensification of the indignant public's empathic involvement in the protests. Ordinary citizens and bereaved families channeled their anger at Park and her administration into mass protests. In this way, they transformed mourning into a form of contentious politics. The protests began with slogans like "we will no longer stay put," which refuted the Sewol captain's instructions to trapped students as he abandoned the ship. By advancing this slogan, people stressed that they would not allow the matter to rest.[57]

The hunger strike relay is particularly interesting in this context since it began with fourteen bereaved family members on July 14 in Gwanghwamun Plaza, a central, highly congested tourist location in the middle of Seoul. The father of Sewol victim Kim Yumin, Kim Young-Oh was part of the original hunger strike and continuously implored the government to enact a special Sewol law. One month later, Kim was the only member of the original group remaining. As his hunger strike progressed, Mr. Kim became a symbol for the Sewol protests and the bereaved families working to bind the death of students to the country's political status quo to push for social change. When Kim Young-Oh collapsed on August 22 after forty-six consecutive days on hunger strike, Koreans overseas launched a Facebook page (Fast4Sewol) to organize a hunger strike relay in support of Kim's actions. People from North America, Japan, Cambodia, Thailand, and elsewhere joined the action. Many who joined the relay posted images in which they held up signs with the date, the days they fasted, and where they were from. They also urged the passage of the Sewol Special Law. For example, a woman from the United States held up a photo addressing Kim Young-Oh: "Yumin's Dad, to a parent who lost a child, living doesn't feel like living. But you must live in order for all of us to live. With our hearts as one, I participate in the fast.—Kwon Kyung-Ah, from Atlanta."[58] In another instance, around six hundred film professionals gathered through a social media mobile application to set up a relay hunger strike in Gwanghwamun.[59] The organizers behind this relay highlighted how social media allowed them to support the bereaved families and empathize with the families' pain as parents. Producer Lee Eun said of the relay hunger strike, "We are the parents of a bigger child, so we as a couple are participating, too. The politicians are pushing through a nonsensical special law for investigation, and we felt the victims' families would be feeling too lonely in all of this."[60] While Kim Young-Oh eventually ended his hunger strike on August 28, Catholic nuns and pastors and Buddhist monks, as well as organizations, political parties, and many ordinary citizens from around the world, continued the hunger strike. The *Hankyoreh*, a liberal-leaning popular daily newspaper, estimates an average of 100 to 150 people took part in the hunger strike every day, while, on the day Kim Young-Oh ended his own strike, an astonishing 390 people joined to show their support.[61] As such, Kim Young-Oh's hunger strike deeply impacted the Sewol protests and turned the Sewol Special Law into a common goal for many ordinary people.

Mr. Kim's Facebook page became crucial in articulating the physical and mental anguish of the bereaved families, as his emotions were transmitted across the Korean diaspora. On August 19 Kim wrote,

> I cannot take it much more. And it is too painful. But what I am most afraid of is not that I may do harm to my body, but rather that I will never know the reason why Yoo-min and her friends had to die so terribly. So I cannot give up now. I ask for the president to pass a special legislation to save both me and the bereaved families.[62]

Emotions reached their peak when Mr. Kim met Pope Francis during his visit to Korea on August 15 in Gwanghwamun Plaza. Kim handed the Pope a yellow ribbon and bracelet (symbols of mourning for the Sewol victims), which the Pope later wore while saying Mass.[63] As the hunger strike relay continued online, the Pope's words of encouragement and comfort touched many people. The emotional effects of the Sewol massacre continued to reverberate as overseas Koreans organized support and rallied for justice using social networking platforms. Ordinary Korean citizens living abroad were able to bridge the physical gap between them and their "home" in Korea, impact their local community, change the perception of the Sewol incident abroad, and participate in Korean civil society. They posted countless videos of local protests, interviews with grassroots organizers and activists, and independent reporting in Korea and abroad on YouTube.[64] Overall, the messages about the massacre in grassroots news were "grounded in affective gestures, invited by the platforms and re-appropriated by users to infuse stories with subjectivity."[65] In this way, diasporic Koreans effectively garnered public empathy and, in turn, strategically mobilized support for the protests.

## EMPATHY, PROMISE, AND MOTHERHOOD

The rhetorical dimension of the relay hunger strikes retains what Arendt once called the "faculty of promises."[66] According to Arendt, this dimension "dispose[s] of the future as though it were the present, that is, the enormous and truly miraculous enlargement of the very dimension in which power can be effective."[67] The transformative dimension of promises is also embedded in human affect, which contains anticipation, hope, and potential.[68] When participants in the strikes and other protests declared, "I will never forget," they issued a binding promise not only to the victims but also to the entire nation for the sake of founding lasting political communities based on empathy and egalitarian resistance. The hunger strike is not only a means to achieve the special legislation; it is an expression of moral sincerity and fidelity to the future. In this regard, and because it risks death, it is a blunt and extreme method of protest. In terms of the life instinct, which "would find rational expression (sublimation) in planning the distribution of the socially necessary labor," the hunger strike amounts to a daring "productive-creative process in an environment of freedom."[69] Through the Korean people's firm belief in and hope for a more humane society, the potential self-harm implied by the hunger strikes has paradoxically given expression to the life instinct of eros. In this way, they provide an acute example of the emergency-turned-eros phenomenon.

Along with eros, motherhood played a crucial role in determining the response to the Sewol massacre. Bracha Ettinger articulates the importance of maternal agency for eros when considering "the perspective of the feminine-maternal sphere." In her view, "the *binding* and *connecting potentiality* of Eros lies at the heart of *subjectivizing* feminine-maternal misericord."[70] Although not a unique realm of women and mothers, responses to emergencies typically activate civil society and mobilize marginalized groups. In Korea, the response to the Sewol massacre was spearheaded by mothers and women. As such, in the aftermath of the Sewol incident, eros took on affective "feminine" characteristics. Thus, it can be potentially transformative.[71] Such agency was evident among Korean mothers as they continuously spearheaded protests, including monthly silent marches throughout the country. When asked "'why are you doing this, what is your motive, to what organization do you belong, who ordered you to do this,'" the mothers—carrying photos of their dead children—simply replied, "'for this child, to protect this child.'"[72] Recent protests by mothers have illustrated a growing connection between mothers' concerns for their families and their social activism. While much can be said on this topic, it suffices for present purposes to draw attention to the collective efforts of mothers participating in the Sewol cause, and to MissyUSA members who organized protests as an expression of their maternal commitments.

Emotionally impacted by the Sewol massacre, MissyUSA members opened a Sewol discussion café on April 17, 2014. Their first few postings had thousands of views and comments. Topics covered included President Park's actions and her behavior toward the survivors and the victims' families. Predominantly comprised of married women, MissyUSA members organized protests across the United States, especially in New York. Members contended that it was their status as women and housewives that led them to protest. In particular, they empathized with the victims' mothers, who also claimed that their protests were primarily motivated by concern for the safety of Korean children. In response to protests by right-wing and fascist groups organized in opposition to the bereaved families and their claims,[73] one MissyUSA member posted the following poem:

> Halt your dirty schemes
> Mothers are the world's litmus
> The reason for our rage
> Is that we feel the world is not habitable for our children.
>
> Are you that afraid of our demands for investigating the truth
> Because we demand it,
> What is your motive for picking us off with violent lynching?
> Is it not to silence us?
>
> Listen well.
> Your actions
> Reveal your loose and tattering ethical sense to the entire
>     world,
> And give us conviction that our demands were just[.]
> They only enrage us.
>
> Mothers do many things to save their children.
> Your filthy conduct
> Makes us resolve, and makes us act.
>
> What we demand is investigation for truth
> I want you to think about what kind of world you want to
>     live in.[74]

Such sentiments were widely shared by members of MissyUSA and other overseas Korean mothers engaged in the Sewol protests. Rather than deterring them, opposition from far-right conservatives strengthened their resolve to contribute to the global spread of Sewol protests. To be sure, not every woman wants to or can be a mother and not every mother is a woman; however, it is important to acknowledge that eros and motherhood are connected.

Materially, MissyUSA members used crowdsourcing campaigns to fund Sewol advertisements in the *New York Times* and the *Washington Post*. They also engaged in numerous demonstrations, pickets, and sit-ins across the United States. Through these actions, the organizational, systematic dimension of emergency politics was mobilized to supplement the spontaneity of the eros effect. Three anonymous Korean women living in the United States and active on the MissyUSA website started the first Indiegogo campaign on April 29, 2014. Hosted on SewolTruth.com (a grassroots initiative run by volunteers), the campaign attracted more than four thousand backers and raised $160,439 USD by May 5. The sum was almost three times their original goal of $58,213 USD, the net cost of running a full-page ad in the Sunday *New York Times*.[75] The *New York Times* ad was published on May 11 and, with the rest of the money, they ran another ad in the *Washington Post* on May 16. The remaining funds were donated to independent news companies.[76] In the end, the operation tarnished President Park's international credibility and educated foreign audiences. It also prompted the organizers to create a second Indiegogo campaign, which lasted from June 30 to August 5 and raised $66,834 USD.[77] The ad ran in the *New York Times* on August 17, with the remaining funds donated once again to independent news organizations. The third fundraiser on Indiegogo ran from September 9 to 16 and raised $65,820 USD for another full-page ad in the *New York Times*.[78] The third fundraiser specifically targeted President Park's visit to the UN Headquarters in New York. In addition to running an ad on September 24, MissyUSA members held a large demonstration in front of the United Nations during Park's visit, during which they carried signs criticizing Park and pictures of the Sewol victims. They also held a gathering at which they called out the names of the ten victims who were still missing.[79]

Mothers in Korea and abroad exerted their democratic, autonomous agency to turn the Sewol massacre into a moment through which the thanatotic (death-driven) status quo might be transformed into to a safer, more loving society filled with eros. In this way, the parental love for children becomes a more universal "love for one's fellow human beings" capable of displacing dominant neoliberal values.[80] Filled with anger, frustration, and empathy, mothers expressed a spontaneous "accidental sovereignty" capable of producing "new public goods, rights and popular orientations."[81] As Kim Young-Oh's life-threatening forty-six-consecutive-day hunger strike makes clear, much can also be said about fathers as compassionate agons. Nevertheless, mothers were dominant in the aftermath of the Sewol massacre. The political potential in maternal empathy for the bereaved transformed the Sewol massacre into a situation characterized by an emergency politics capable of igniting the eros effect. A solution to Honig's paradox of politics and Katsiaficas' eros effect, the mothers' actions produced power out of crisis to foster collective communal insights and transformative possibilities.

## EMERGENCY POLITICS OF THE EROS EFFECT

In the Sewol case, hunger strikes expressed people's empathy. Initiated by a bereaved father, they connected previous efforts to the common goal of ending neoliberal capitalism's unrelenting drive to privilege economic gain over human life. As a "new sensibility" opposed to capitalism's instrumental rationality,[82] compassion and empathy allow those who experience them to move beyond the regime of thanatos (the death drive). As embodiments of the eros effect, the bereaved exercised a transformative power by "channeling, transforming, legitimating, and managing . . . emotions and expression of emotions in order to cultivate and nurture the social networks that are the building blocks of social movements."[83] As for emergency politics, the Sewol massacre ended people's belief in the current system and unleashed a new wave of empathy; at its threshold, such an experience can create a new sensibility.

Stimulated by the emergency politic of the eros effect in a moment of crisis, Korean people began to practice the alternative values of self-governance, solidarity, and cooperation. In this way, they partook in a "transformation of self-interest into universal interest." According to Katsiaficas, such a transformation is "another dimension of *eros* effect" capable of generating "coherent global aspirations . . . in sharp contrast to the established reality."[84] As a sensory-filled rationality capable of triggering global solidarity when survival is threatened, the emergency politics of the eros effect can help individuals to self-organize to confront repression with the human instinct for life and freedom.

## NOTES

1. See, for instance, George Katsiaficas, *The Imagination of the New Left: A Global Analysis of 1968* (Boston: South End Press, 1987); George Katsiaficas, "The Eros Effect," 1989, personal website, http://www.eroseffect.com/articles/erosef-fectpaper.PDF; George Katsiaficas, *The Subversion of Politics: European Autonomous Social Movements and the Decolonization of Everyday Life* (Oakland: AK Press, 2006); and George Katsiaficas, *Asia's Unknown Uprisings, Volumes 1 and 2* (Oakland: PM Press, 2012 and 2013).

2. Bonnie Honig, *Emergency Politics: Paradox, Law, Democracy* (Princeton: Princeton University Press, 2009).

3. Christine Hong, "The Sewol on Our Shores," *The Foreign Policy in Focus*, May 21, 2014, n.p., http://fpif.org/sewol-shores.

4. Ibid., n.p.

5. Honig, *Emergency Politics*, 53.

6. Herbert Marcuse, *An Essay on Liberation* (Boston: Beacon Press, 1969), 4.

7. Bonnie Honig, "Difference, Dilemmas, and the Politics of the Home," *Social Research* 61, no. 3 (1994): 563–597 (570).

8. See Min-Jong Kim, "New Members of the Family of Victims' Committee: Amongst Seven, Three are Pre-existing Core Hardliners," *The Chosun Daily*, September 22, 2014, http://news.chosun.com/site/data/html_dir/2014/09/22/2014092200187.html; and Hyung-Joon Yoon, "Young-Oh Kim: 'Blame Placed Only on the Bereaved: More Difficult to Stand Than Staging Hunger Strike,' " *The Chosun Daily*, September 22, 2014, http://news.chosun.com/site/data/html_dir/2014/09/22/2014092202205.html. As further evidence of the point we are making, conservative newspaper *Chosun Daily* cites an alleged incident where seven bereaved family members, accused of drunkenly assaulting a substitute driver in an act of group violence, resigned from leadership positions in the Sewol ferry family committee. Articles in *Chosun Daily* emphasize that the incident swayed public opinion of the bereaved family members negatively, prompting prominent bereaved spokesperson Kim Young-Oh to apologize on behalf of all family members on national television.

9. Honig, *Emergency Politics*, 8.

10. Honig uses "an emergency" and "a crisis" interchangeably to indicate a sociopolitical situation in which normal established behavior is not upheld.

11. Katsiaficas, *Imagination of the New Left*, 220.

12. Ibid., 221.

13. Honig, *Emergency Politics*, 88.

14. Ibid., 89.

15. Before the Sewol case, there were several examples of the eros effect as emergency politics in contemporary Korea. Two cases are salient: the massive nationwide candlelight vigils held for two fourteen-year-old schoolgirls after a US Army armored vehicle ran over and killed them on June 13, 2002; and national and international candlelight protests were held from May to August, 2008, against the signing of the US-Korea Free Trade Agreement reopening Korea to American beef imports that were implicated in cases of mad cow disease. Although both cases swept the nation with raw feelings of anger, frustration, and grief, the 2008 case requires a more careful consideration since it, unlike previous experiences, was initiated by traditionally oppressed political subjects, teenage school girls, and stay-at-home mothers. (For background on these events, see Gooyong Kim, "Online Videos, Everyday Pedagogy, and Female Political Agency: 'Learning from YouTube,' Revisited," *Global Media Journal* 11, no. 18 [2011]: n.p., Article #2; and Gooyong Kim, "When Schoolgirls Met Bertolt Brecht: Popular Mobilisation of Grassroots

Online Videos by Korea's Unknown People," *Critical Arts: A Journal of South-North Cultural Studies* 28, no. 1 [2014]: 123–134.) As Kim argues, advocating for "human dignity over economic accumulation, rejection of patriarchy, and struggle against sociopolitical and economic inequality and injustice," the female protestors successfully staged their process of becoming politically awakened and active during a crisis of food safety (Kim, "When Schoolgirls," 124). By doing so, women turned protests into a constitutive moment of their sociopolitical agency. (On this last point, see Suhong Chae and Soojin Kim, "The Candlelight Protest and the Politics of the Baby Stroller Brigades," *Korea Journal* 50, no. 3 [2010]: 71–99.)

16. Marcuse, *An Essay on Liberation*, 23.

17. Herbert Marcuse, *Counterrevolution and Revolt* (Boston: Beacon Press, 1972), 71.

18. Ibid., 71 (original emphasis).

19. See Bonnie Honig, "The Politics of Agonism: A Critical Response to 'Beyond Good and Evil: Arendt, Nietzsche, and the Aestheticization of Political Action,'" *Political Theory* 21, no. 3 (1993): 528–533; Bonnie Honig, *Political Theory and the Displacement of Politics* (Ithaca: Cornell University Press, 1993); and Bonnie Honig, ed., *Feminist Interpretations of Hannah Arendt* (University Park: Pennsylvania State University Press, 1995).

20. Bonnie Honig, "Between Decision and Deliberation: Political Paradox in Democratic Theory," *The American Political Science Review* 101, no. 1 (February 2007): 1–17.

21. Honig, *Emergency Politics*, 3.

22. Ibid., xvi.

23. Ibid., xvi.

24. Ibid.

25. Ibid., 44.

26. Bonnie Honig, "Antigone's Two Laws: Greek Tragedy and the Politics of Humanism," *New Literary History* 41, no. 1 (Winter 2010): 1–33, doi: 10.1353/nlh.0.0140.

27. Ibid., 1.

28. Ibid., 2.

29. Ibid., 2.

30. Ibid., 3.

31. Ibid., 7.

32. Ibid., 3.

33. Gustave Le Bon, *The Crowd: A Study of the Popular Mind* (Mineola: Dover, 2002). On the point we are making, see Ron Aminzade and Doug McAdam, "Emotions and Contentious Politics," *Mobilization* 7, no. 2 (2002): 107–109.

34. See, for instance, James M. Jasper, "The Emotions of Protest: Affective and Reactive Emotions in and around Social Movements," *Sociological Forum* 13, no. 3 (1998): 397–424; Jeff Goodwin, James M. Jasper, and Francesca Polletta, "The Return of the Repressed: The Fall and Rise of Emotions in Social Move-

ment Theory," *Mobilization* 5, no. 1 (2000): 65–84; and Verta Taylor and Leila J. Rupp, "Loving Internationalism: The Emotion Culture of Transnational Women's Organizations, 1888–1945," *Mobilization* 7, no. 2 (2002): 141–158.

35. Alison Jagger, "Love and Knowledge: Emotion in Feminist Epistemology," in *Feminism*, ed. Sandra Kemp and Judith Squires (New York: Oxford University Press, 1997), 188–193.

36. Nigel Thrift, "Intensities of Feeling: Towards a Spatial Politics of Affect," *Geografiska Annaler* 86, no. 1 (2004): 57–78.

37. Ian Burkitt, "Complex Emotions: Relations, Feelings and Images in Emotional Experience," in *Emotions and Sociology*, ed. Jack Barbalet (Oxford: Blackwell, 2002), 151–168 (153).

38. Katsiaficas, "The Eros Effect," 1.

39. George Katsiaficas, "Between Ballots and Bullets," in *Changing the World, Changing Oneself: Political Protest and Collective Identities in West Germany and the U.S. in the 1960s and 1970s*, ed. Belinda Davis, Wilfried Mausbach, Martin Klimke, and Carla MacDougall (New York: Berghahn Books. 2010), 241–255.

40. Katsiaficas, *Subversion of Politics*, 270.

41. Katsiaficas, *Imagination of the New Left*, 9.

42. Ibid., 221.

43. Jasper, "The Emotions of Protest," 401.

44. On the point of identification and extension, see Thomas Kessler and Susan Hollbach, "Group-based Emotions as Determinants of In-group Identification," *Journal of Experimental Social Psychology* 41, no. 6 (2005): 677–685; and Brian Parkinson, Agneta H. Fischer, Anthony S. R. Manstead, *Emotion in Social Relations: Cultural, Group, and Interpersonal Processes* (New York: Psychology Press, 2005).

45. Min-No, "Stay Put, Yong Hye-In Interview," *Slow News*, May 2, 2014, http://slownews.kr/24576; "South Korea: Massive Candlelight Vigil Turns to Protest Over Sewol Ferry Disaster," *Revolution News*, May 17, 2014, http://revolution-news.com/south-korea-massive-candlelight-vigil-turns-protest-sewol-ferry-disaster; and Ki-yong Park and Seung-heon Park, "Candlelight Vigils for Sewol Growing into Nationwide Phenomenon," *Hankyoreh*, May 26, 2014, http://english.hani.co.kr/arti/english_edition/e_national/639027.html.

46. Minji Lee, "S. Korean Consumer Sentiment Retreats to Post-Sewol Level," *Yonhap News Agency*, July 25, 2014, http://english.yonhapnews.co.kr/full/2014/07/24/0/1200000000AEN20140724010000320F.html; and "Sewol Casts Shadow Over S. Korea Economy," *The China Post*, August 28, 2014, http://www.chinapost.com.tw/asia/korea/2014/08/28/415907/Sewol-casts.htm.

47. Hee-Jin Kim, "Does Korea Need This Many Rock Festivals?," *OhmyNews*, June 25, 2014, http://m.news.naver.com/read.nhn?mode=LSD&mid=sec&sid1=106&oid=047&aid=0002060734.

48. You-sun Choi, "President Park Addresses Nation's Livelihood after Ferry Disaster," *Arirang News*, May 9, 2014, http://www.arirang.co.kr/News/News_View.asp?nseq=162112.

49. Gillian Wong and Hyung-jin Kim, "Cries of Anguish as South Korea Ferry Toll Tops 100," *Washington Times*, April 22, 2014, http://www.washingtontimes.com/news/2014/apr/22/cries-anguish-south-korea-ferry-toll-tops-100/?page=all.

50. Alexander Martin, "Community Center Becomes Ferry Memorial Site," *Korea Real Time–Wall Street Journal*, April 24, 2014, http://blogs.wsj.com/korearealtime/2014/04/24/community-center-becomes-ferry-memorial-site.

51. Da-ye Kim, "Visit to Ansan Joint Altar," *Korea Times*, May 7, 2014, n.p., http://www.koreatimes.co.kr/www/news/opinon/2014/09/264_156745.html.

52. Ibid.

53. See Geoffrey Fattig, "Is the Sewol Tragedy South Korea's Katrina?," *Foreign Policy in Focus*, May 16, 2014, http://fpif.org/sewol-tragedy-south-koreas-katrina; and Hyun-Song Son, "[Jindo Sinking Ferry Tragedy] Enraged Families March, 'Going to the Blue House and Meet the President,'" *Naver News*, April 20, 2014 http://news.naver.com/main/read.nhn?mode=LSD&mid=sec&sid1=102&oid=038&aid=0002492758.

54. See, for instance, Ashraf M. Attia, Nergis Aziz, Barry Friedman, and Mahdy F. Elhusseiny, "Commentary: The Impact of Social Networking Tools on Political Change in Egypt's 'Revolution 2.0,'" *Electronic Commerce Research and Applications* 10, no. 4 (2011): 369–374; Simon Cottle, "Media and the Arab Uprisings of 2011: Research Notes," *Journalism* 12, no. 5 (2011): 647–659; Phillip N. Howard and Malcolm R. Parks, "Social Media and Political Change: Capacity, Constraint, and Consequence," *Journal of Communication* 62, no. 2 (2012): 359–362; Robert Jewitt, "Commentaries: The Trouble with Twittering: Integrating Social Media into Mainstream News," *International Journal of Media and Cultural Politics* 5, no. 3 (2009): 233–246; Gilad Lotan, Erhardt Graeff, Mike Ananny, Devin Gaffney, Ian Pearce, and Danah Boyd, "The Revolutions Were Tweeted: Information Flows during the 2011 Tunisian and Egyptian Revolutions," *International Journal of Communication* 5 (2011): 1375–1405; and Babak Rahimi, "The Agonistic Social Media: Cyberspace in the Formation of Dissent and Consolidation of State Power in Postelection Iran," *The Communication Review* 14, no. 3 (2011): 158–178.

55. Jodi Dean, *Blog Theory: Feedback and Capture in the Circuits of Drive* (Cambridge: Polity Press, 2010), 95.

56. Zizi Papacharissi and Maria de Fatima Oliveira, "Affective News and Networked Publics: The Rhythms of News Storytelling on #Egypt," *Journal of Communication* 62, no. 2 (2012): 266–282 (279).

57. The protestors were further angered by the local and regional elections on June 4 and July 30, 2014. President Park's ruling party, the Saenuri Party, used the slogan "Defend Park Geun-hye" in response to the New Politics Alliance Party (NPAD) and Unified Progressive Party (UPP) attempting to hold Park responsible for the Sewol incident with the slogan "Judgment Day for the Park Geun-hye Government." Combined with the NPAD's internal strife, failure to engage the apathetic and grieving masses, the bereaved families' transformative agenda lost its momentum and is failing to maintain solidarity and collective action as time

passes. See "South Korea Local Elections 2014," *Zoom in Korea*, June 5, 2014, http://zoominkorea.org/south-korea-local-elections-2014.

58. Fast4Sewol, August 24, 2014, https://www.facebook.com/Fast4Sewol/photos/pb.278445395673672.-2207520000.1411968594./280270335491178/?type=3&theater.

59. Myeong-seon Jin, "Citizens Continuing Hunger Strike on Behalf of Kim Young-oh," *Hankyoreh*, August 29, 2014, http://english.hani.co.kr/arti/english_edition/e_national/653393.html.

60. "Korean Filmmakers in Sewol Hunger Strike," *NewsPro*, August 11, 2014, n.p., http://thenewspro.org/?p=6391.

61. Jin, "Citizens Continuing Hunger Strike."

62. Michael Johansson, "Sewol Father on Hunger Strike Hit by Vitriol," *Korea Expose*, August 25, 2014, n.p., http://www.koreaexpose.com/news/bereaved-sewol-father-on-hunger-strike-confronts-vitriol.

63. "Fasting Father Shares Struggle of Sewol Families with Pope Francis," *Al Jazeera*, August 18, 2014, http://stream.aljazeera.com/story/201408182125-0024076.

64. Additionally, users held livestreams on Twitter, and independent reporters used Twitter to reach audiences around the world by communicating current headlines in Korea and translating major events for an international audience, such as sewoltruth.com, http://thenewspro.org, and http://zoominkorea.org. Groups used Facebook to create and share events, such as "Fast4Sewol and Scholars" concerned about the Sewol ferry tragedy.

65. Zizi Papacharissi, "Toward New Journalism(s)," *Journalism Studies* 16, no. 1 (2015): 27–40 (28).

66. Hannah Arendt, *The Human Condition* (Chicago: University of Chicago Press, 1958), 245.

67. Ibid.

68. Gregory Seigworth and Melissa Gregg, "An Inventory of Shimmers," in *The Affect Theory Reader*, ed. Melissa Gregg and Gregory J. Seigworth (Durham: Duke University Press, 2010), 1–25.

69. Marcuse, *An Essay on Liberation*, 24.

70. Bracha L. Ettinger, "From Proto-Ethical Compassion to Responsibility: Besideness and the Three *Primal* Mother-Phantasies of Not-Enoughness, Devouring and Abandonment," *Athena* 2 (2007): 100–145 (101) (original emphasis).

71. Ibid.

72. "After Yesterday's Mothers' Silent March in Gangnam Station," *Daum*, September 17, 2014, n.p., http://m.cafe.daum.net/dontforgetsewol/6LdS/1446?q=%EC%96%B4%EC%A0%9C+%EA%B0%95%EB%82%A8%EC%97%AD%EC%97%90%EC%84%9C+%EC%9E%88&sns=kakaotalk.

73. See "Conservatives Stage 'Eat-ins' over Sewol Bill," *Korea Times*, September 4, 2014, http://www.koreatimes.co.kr/www/news/nation/2014/09/113_164196.html.

74. User #22636, "Attention . . . Ilbe . . . [MissyUSA Sewol-ho cafe]," *Missy-USA*, September 25, 2014, http://www.missyusa.com/mainpage/boards/board_read.asp?section=talk&id=talk4&page=1&category=0&key_field=title&mypost=0&key_wor

d=%C0%CF%BA%A3%BE%DF+%2E%2E+%BA%B8%BE%C6%B6%F3&idx=29
57934&ref=926351&step=1&level=0.

75. "Full-Page NYT Ad Denouncing the South Korean Government," *Indiegogo*, April 29, 2014, https://www.indiegogo.com/projects/full-page-nyt-ad-denouncing-the-south-korean-government#home.

76. Ibid.

77. "A Full-Page Ad Promoting the Sewol Ferry Act," *Indiegogo*, July 30, 2014, https://www.indiegogo.com/projects/a-full-page-ad-promoting-the-sewol-ferry-act#home.

78. "A Full-Page Ad for Truth and Democracy in Korea," *Indiegogo*, September 9, 2014, https://www.indiegogo.com/projects/a-full-page-ad-for-truth-and-democracy-in-korea.

79. Byung Taek Jeun, "S. Koreans Protest in Manhattan, UN Headquarters," *Storify*, September 27, 2014, https://storify.com/wjsfree/s-koreans-protest-in-manhattan-un-headquarters.

80. Katsiaficas, "Between Ballots and Bullets," 242.

81. Honig, *Emergency Politics*, 4.

82. Marcuse, *An Essay on Liberation*.

83. Taylor and Rupp, "Loving Internationalism," 142.

84. Katsiaficas, *Imagination of the New Left*, 42.

10

# Climatology of the Eros Effect

## Notes from the Japanese Archipelago

SABU KOHSO

### EROS AS BATTLEGROUND

In recent years, we have had reasons to be inspired by the increasing synchronicity and resonance of struggles and uprisings across the planet. At their height, it seems that they recognize and enhance each other, ultimately assuming a life of their own. As history consistently teaches us, there is rarely a happy ending for regime change in any single country; however, on the global scale, there is a sense of *irreversibility* to the revolutionary impetus. People are rising up more frequently, widely, and intensely; both the simultaneity and reverberations of uprisings are growing more dense and extensive.

The lives of planetary commoners are currently threatened on three key fronts of contemporary governance: debt (economic), violence (sociopolitical), and pollution (environmental). Collectively, we are reaching the limits of tolerance and staging confrontations with the global network of power—whose invisible nexus is gradually revealed by the struggle itself. One might say that the eros effect, as conceived by George Katsiaficas, is now in motion.

According to Katsiaficas, the eros effect is both the name of a phenomenon and a means of perceiving it. In the following pages, I use the eros effect as an "analytical tool"[1] for considering three phases of Japan's postwar struggles, from the uprisings of the 1960s (Japan's '68) to the anti-globalization movement at the turn of the century to our current post-Fukushima reality. Throughout, I highlight (1) the discrepancy between organizing and spontaneity, (2) the historical emergence of globally connected struggles and uprisings, and (3) the autonomy of body and life as strongholds of planetary revolution. In these instances—all of which are characterized more by difficulty than by glory—eros works in a twofold manner: As unprecedented crises become the main battleground, they also unleash an as-yet-unknown potency, which is discovered through the dynamics of struggle itself.

Katsiaficas developed his conceptualization of the eros effect from his association with Herbert Marcuse, and especially from the latter's *Eros and Civilization*.[2] Here, I would like to draw upon another philosophical lineage: that of Gilles Deleuze and Félix Guattari. I believe this additional frame of reference can help to clarify the status of the eros effect, especially in an age when life, confronted by all-out war on multiple fronts, must be interpreted extensively in its multiple dimensions. In his response during an interview, Katsiaficas confirms the importance of this lineage in terms of its "focus on micro-dynamic[s]" that "came out of the New Left's desire to change everyday life." At the same time, however, he also confirmed his commitment to dialectics, arguing that

> it enables us to see that what currently exists isn't every-thing. . . . Looking at historical processes and locating the nega-tion of everything that came before is the essence of dialectics. If we lose sight of this dynamic process, if we just focus on what's immediately tangible, then we are left with a theory that basi-cally says, "what you see is what you get." It makes revolutionary social transformation very difficult to imagine.[3]

These philosophies belong respectively to the different and even conflict-ing ontologies of dialectics and immanence, but they share the strategy of attempting to reconcile Marx and Freud. Ultimately, each tradition attempts to grasp human liberation beyond "politics" in its narrow conventional sense, and it is this touching point that I wish to highlight throughout this chapter.

In anticipation of 1968, *Eros and Civilization* set the tone for contem-porary uprisings, which are characterized by the conflict of the life-principle against both alienated labor and the superego, both of which underwrite family, society, and civilization itself. It is important to note that the Marcuse-Katsiaficas lineage places primary importance on the transindi-vidual or collective dimensions of instinct, emotion, and unconscious as potentially revolutionary forces.

In contrast, Deleuze and Guattari's *Anti-Oedipus* was written shortly after the experience of '68 and targeted the Freudian tendency to confine the libido within the family triangle (Mother, Father, and me).[4] According to Deleuze and Guattari, this Freudian tendency helps to reproduce capitalist social relations it could otherwise have contributed to unsettling. Deleuze and Guattari sought to counter this by affirming the creative and subversive power of desire. By following this insight, I aim to consider eros from *the microscopic view* of the "desiring-machine" to detect phases within which affect (or the power of body/mind) produces a spectrum of collective emotions and actions of varying intensities. To be clear, neither eros nor desire is free from capture. Both can succumb to the morality and reterritorialization[5] of capitalism and nationalism; indeed, they can even be made into their weapon.[6]

Katsiaficas explains the dynamic of mutually enhancing, life-affirming assemblages of uprisings in the following way:

> It's not simply a chain reaction, not just that A causes B which causes C. Events erupt simultaneously at multiple points and mutually amplify each other. They produce feedback loops with multiple iterations. To put it in terms of a mathematical analysis, we could say that diffusion and the circulation of struggles describe the process of movement development geometrically, while the eros effect describes these same developments in terms of calculus.[7]

In what follows, I would like to follow two coexisting and overlapping paths that I believe correspond to "geometry" and "calculus." On one hand, my objective is to be a cartographer who maps struggles and uprisings as they develop and spread spatially and temporally. On the other hand, my aim is to be a weather forecaster who tries to anticipate how the atmosphere of struggle might create unexpected turbulences across multiple territories simultaneously. Of necessity, such "climatology" pays attention to planetary conditions, including climate and topography; human traffic such as migration, transportation, and communication; movement of capital; production of infrastructure, institutions, and machines; and creation of ideals. The objective of such attentiveness is to grasp the germination of revolutionary assemblages.

## ORGANIZING, SPONTANEITY, AND THE
## TRANS-ASIATIC UNDERCLASS

Let me recount a story of defeat and revelation. I was part of the group No G8! Action that organized a series of anti-G8 projects across Japan. These protests were to coincide with the main meetings scheduled to take place from July 7 to 9, 2008, at Lake Toya, Hokkaido. These meetings were to be preceded by a number of preparatory meetings of ministers that began earlier in different cities. The entire event became a battle between the state of Japan and "us" over space. For its part, the state was determined to control the national territory to protect the global powers that had assembled to impose an uneven flow of capital to the detriment of local subsistence. Our objective, meanwhile, was to create a global flow of activists and movements that would make the Japanese archipelago part of the planetary circulation of anticapitalist struggles.

Japanese activists were relative latecomers to the global justice movement; the majority did not have much experience or knowledge of the antiauthoritarian organizing and direct action that had emerged along with the new cycle of struggle. Prior to this encounter, being radical meant being associated with the militarism of the New Left and its dark legacy of intra-sectarian violence. To create a new current beginning in 2007, some anticapitalists associated with the No G8! Action info tour traveled to Asia, Europe, and North America to recruit participants and learn from the global network of anticapitalist radicals. Meanwhile, back in Japan, others prepared facilities for visitors in various cities and created camps near Lake Toya in Hokkaido, the Summit site. As a result, a good number of foreign activists and intellectuals were able to travel to Japan, share their skills and knowledge, and participate in actions against the G8.

Despite these efforts, however, the result was a miserable defeat. We merely learned that we had been at least considered a serious threat by the state of Japan, indicated by the excessive police presence, which had been dispatched from all prefectures. In every action, the police outnumbered demonstrators. Stop-and-frisk operations targeted all "suspicious-looking" people (whether local or foreigner). Every key organizer was tailed by security personnel around the clock, and a number of foreigners were refused entry or given permission only for a limited stay. Others were interrogated for long hours. Some homeless people were taken to police stations solely for the sake of keeping the city neat.

In contrast, a spontaneous riot that took place before all the planned protests managed to totally overwhelm the security forces. On June 13, 2008, the very day the finance ministers' meeting took place in Osaka as part of the Summit, a riot erupted in Kamagasaki, an inner-city neighborhood of day laborers in Osaka. The riot erupted because a worker had been beaten by police in the precinct. Although the local union made an official claim opposing the arrest and abuse,[8] they were ignored by the police. This triggered the uprising, which continued for five days.[9]

On the main street, the workers and the riot squad confronted each other in a repeated skirmish of offense and defense. To prevent the disturbance from spreading, the police immediately blockaded the neighborhood. On the second day, they introduced water cannons to suppress the crowd. Fending off the attack, the crowd launched counteroffensives for as long as possible. After several workers (including a union leader) were arrested, the insurgency wound down. Kamagasaki returned to the everyday realities of poverty, unemployment, and homelessness. Reporting almost nothing about the uprising, the mass media instead praised the ongoing "success" of the G8.

Since the 1990s, the labor market for day laborers in Japan has continued to shrink. As a result, Kamagasaki has become a city characterized by unemployment and homelessness. Meanwhile, those workers who managed to secure employment faced increasing insecurity as a result of neoliberal reforms. This was the context in which the riot took place. Many young precarious workers came to join the battle of their older comrades. According to one local activist, the riot meant that local workers had "rediscovered a place to express their own fury in Kamagasaki, the sanctuary of riots, that inscribes the history of militant struggle. While the older workers and the younger precariats confronted the riot squad together, the method of expressing fury was bequeathed from one generation to another."[10] This was a new alliance, connecting different generations, cultures, and neighborhoods.

Although it was unplanned, the riot turned out to be the most powerful action in all the anti-G8 protests. The bitter lesson for movement organizers was that all our planned actions fatally lacked the intensity, mobility, and endurance of the spontaneous rebellion. Meanwhile, across the Japan Sea, a huge mobilization of Candlelight Demos was taking place in Korea.[11] Tens of thousands of people took over public squares in Seoul, protesting the Korean government's reversal of a ban of US beef imports. In contrast to these two uprisings, our planned anti-summit actions failed to develop strong reverberations. Confronted by police capable of preventing fissures in social space from resonating with one another, the state ensured that our actions did not become an event.

The discrepancy between the success of our planned actions and the spontaneous riots can be understood by considering various dichotomies, including: construction and becoming, reason and emotion, and petit bourgeois and proletariat as well as mass and crowd. In the end, however, each of these led to the *micro difference* between the "existential territories" and "corporeal flows" of the day laborers themselves.

In major industrial cities in postwar Japan, there are inner-city areas populated by day laborers called *yoseba*, which translates roughly as "recruitment places." These include Sanya in Tokyo, Kotobuki-cho in

Yokohama, Sasajima in Nagoya, and Kamagasaki in Osaka. Historically, a red-light district can always be found nearby. Most of the residents work at day jobs in construction, docks, road repairing, heavy industries, and nuclear power plants. They represent the most informal and lowest-paid working force. Often, they are without a permanent address, social security, and health insurance. Many are not registered to vote. They make up Marx's so-called "relative surplus population" who built the infrastructure for Japan's "postwar democracy" regime. Ethnically, their numbers include not only Japanese but also resident Koreans and other minorities. In the red-light district, there are women from throughout the Asian continent. All told, they embody the trans-Asiatic underclass, living in Japan but excluded from civil society.

In *yoseba*, labor brokers are mostly *yakuza* gangsters who gouge the slim earnings of day workers and sex workers alike. Hand in hand with local police, they violently oppress workers' cries for better working and living conditions. This is the forefront of the class struggle—the space where periodic uprisings have taken place, as many as twenty-four times in the postwar period, mainly at Sanya and Kamagasaki. As the thinker and organizer of *yoseba*, Funamoto Shuji has emphasized that these "fluid underclass workers" have existential power precisely in their precarious status; their mobility, invisibility, solidarity, and militant networks stretch across the Japanese archipelago and beyond.[12] These are the generative conditions that allow for the emergence of the eros effect. According to Funamoto:

> *Yoseba* such as Kamagasaki and Sanya exist in various forms in all cities across Japan, from the Northern tip of Hokkaido to the Southern islands of Okinawa. . . . Now in Hokkaido: the monopoly capital is expropriating the land for constructing the Eastern Industrial Complex around Tomakomai, and more and more peasants are turned into under-class laborers; at Usu in the Date region, Ainu fishermen are rising up against the construction of a thermal power plant for sending electricity to the Complex. Now in Okinawa: with the unspoken slogan "men are for low wage labor commodity, women are for sexual commodity," the Japanese Imperialism is expropriating land for constructing a CTS (Central Terminal Station including oil storage tanks and refineries) and the Oceanic Exposition; these projects are unequivocally turning the peasants into underclass laborers. In fact more and more peasants in Okinawa who can no longer survive by producing sugarcane are forced to migrate to Japan

for subsistence. Now in South Korea: due to the importation of Japanese capital after the Treaty on the Basic Relations between Japan and the Republic of Korea, the economy of agricultural communities is ruined and more and more people are forced to stow away by boat to come to Japan.[13]

As Funamoto makes clear, these people are both excluded from Japanese civil society *and* free from its confines; they belong to a planetary territoriality divergent from that of the Japanese nation-state. Living under conditions of extreme crises, they embody both the fragility and the power of the life-principles. In Japan and East Asia, they are the primary attractor and conveyor of eros effect turbulence.

Here, it is important to recall that there were invisible interventions that tacitly empowered this fluid underclass. From a microscopic view, there isn't a clean-cut division between organizing and spontaneity—both are different phases in the exchange of affect in everyday life, which is the erotic drive (the life-principle). The emergent uprisings of the stormy 1960s were followed by forms of submerged organizing, where radical activism focused more on transforming one's own form of life and social relations. Some revolutionaries privately moved to *yoseba*, where they began to organize radical labor movements, including the Kamagasaki Joint Struggle Committee (Kama-kyo-to) established in 1972 and Sanya Dispute Group (Sanya Sogi-dan) in 1983.[14] Their struggles targeted issues related to *yoseba*, but they also nurtured associations with the struggles of other minorities (resident Koreans, Okinawans, Ainus, and Burakumin)[15] as well as militant struggles against Japanese expansionism.[16] This has been one of the few social milieus that has continued engendering insurgency post-'68.

## BETWEEN ARCHIPELAGO AND INSULARITY

There are two ways to recognize Japan's topographical position vis-à-vis the Asian continent: in one version, it is an insularity while, in the other, it is an archipelago. The territory of the nation-state is conceptually separated by the sea. If we pay closer attention, however, at least three sailable routes become visible. The northern tip of Hokkaido is not far from the Russian island of Sakhalin. Likewise, northern Kyushu is proximate to the southern part of the Korean Peninsula via two islands—Tsushima (Japan) and Jeju (Korea)—while the southern end of Kyushu follows the line of the Ryukyu Islands upward toward Taiwan.

This land-sea configuration is the remnant of the Pliocene epoch, when the Sea of Japan was a mammoth puddle. Diastrophism was thus the primary condition setting the stage for interactions among peoples in the region. Along with geotectonics, another is the climate, with the major wind currents in Asia blowing from the plateaus of Siberia and Mongolia to the Japanese archipelago and facilitating sailing from time immemorial. (It is these very currents that are now depositing radioactive nuclides from Fukushima into the Pacific Ocean and pushing them toward the Americas.)

The historian Amino Yoshihiko has stressed the role the archipelago played as a bridge connecting north and south Asia. From this vantage, we can envision the history of the region as a history of peoples' migrations and exchanges, with Oceanic peoples—including pirates—creating connectivity by fishing, trading, and seizing wealth that was moving in and out of the archipelago. Fighting to maintain autonomy in the face of the dynasties that established the kingdom of Yamato and then feudal Japan, they created a flowing territoriality that could not easily be captured by sovereign power inland. Since then, their activities and sailing routes have been buried in the unconscious of history,[17] though the struggles of the trans-Asiatic underclass continually show signs of revitalizing the flowing territoriality.

Japanese history is the process through which the archipelago was condensed into an insular territory. Through this process, it has become a feudal system, a modern nation-state, an empire, and a nation-state again. However, the moment in which we now find ourselves is one of possible decomposition. Uprisings have arisen in interaction with this process; they carry with them the erotic relationality of the archipelagic complexity.

This archipelagic Japan echoes Édouard Glissant's "geophilosophical" concept of "Creolization" in which the totality of the world is marked by an irreducible heterogeneity. With this conceptual emphasis derived from his reading of Caribbean history, Glissant introduces a seed of hope by which geographical complexity and relationality might intermingle with the tragic memories of the slave trade and massacres of the indigenous to produce an alternative to all the stratified dimensions of colonial history.[18]

In the case of Japan, the archipelagic relation is in stark distinction to the dominant relation through which the power of despots created the centralized and hierarchized "mega-machine" apparatus, which inducted mass corporeality into its theocratic system.[19] In opposition to this form, innumerable deterritorialized peoples withdrew their bodies and minds from the dominant land/architecture apparatus and traced a line of flight toward the unknown realm of "absolute deterritorialization."[20]

These conceptualizations suggest that, even when it is topographically suppressed, archipelagic relationality continues to find expression in people's bodies and minds as collective memory. Here, it generates new relations in confrontation with rising crises. This could entail the creation of our new relationship with the earth. We don't really know what kinds of social relations we can create by discovering new territories and flows; this is still open.

Japanese modernity began with the Meiji Restoration in 1867, which ousted the Tokugawa Shogunite and established an absolute monarchy with the aggressive modernization policy called "rich nation, strong troops (*fu-koku, kyo-hei*)." Forces became concentrated around the worship of the emperor as living god; alien Buddhism was rejected in favor of native Shinto; the ideology of De-Asianization spread[21] as the new emperor incorporated aspects of Western civilization to distinguish Japan from other Asian nations, which had been colonized by the West. The policy also produced an extremely introverted mentality, wherein both the West and Asia became objects of either worship or disdain. In this way, Japan became a nation marked by physical and conceptual insularity, a condition that continues to ground the master narrative of today's status quo.

Among the samurai in the Tokugawa period (1600–1867), individual life existed only as sacrifice for the ever-lasting life of clans; in modernity, this life came to be captured by the eternity of the nation. Succeeding the heritage of the fanatical Samurai code such as honorary suicide (*seppuku*), modern nationalism reinvented a culture of sacrificial death—an erotization of the dying body—that persisted through the sanctification of suicide corps during the wars and continues to find expression through the "Eat and Support Fukushima" campaign today.[22] It is this thanatos-inflected nationalism that has been the main obstacle preventing the people from nurturing autonomy and cultivating their own life-principles through self-determined, mass political actions similar to those that took place during the Paris Commune and the Gwangju Uprising.[23]

Around the turn of the twentieth century, Japan began to transform itself from an insular country to an empire, stretching its military-industrial apparatus into the continent. It joined the circle of Euro-American predators dividing and devouring the flesh of Qing China. Through its victories in the Sino-Japan War (1894–1895) and the Russo-Japan War (1904–1905), as well as through the annexation of Korea (1910), Japan accelerated its imperialist expansion.

The first significant uprisings in twentieth-century Asia followed the 1917 Revolution in Russia. These included the 1918 Rice Riot in Japan, the 1919 March 1st movement in Korea, and the May 4th movement in China. When the Russian Revolution broke out, the Japanese government intended to intervene militarily to take advantage of the instability. In expectation of the war, the Ministry of Agriculture, Forestry and Fisheries cornered the rice market, causing the price to rise by 200 percent. Angered by the price hike, approximately one million people joined the riot across the country. The military was mobilized to put it down. The biggest series of insurrections in Japanese modern history lasted fifty days. The following year, 1919, the March 1st movement took place in Korea. Participants demanded self-determination and an end to Japan's domination. Later that year, the May 4th movement broke out in China as youth and intellectuals led boycotts of Japanese products. The significance of this chain of events is that it suggests that people's recognition that the Japanese presence constituted "imperialism" was shared transnationally. The Japanese government thus confronted resistance across East Asia. Affected by the Rice Riot, the Japanese democratization movement (the so-called Taisho Democracy) had been growing since 1918. Anarchist and anarcho-syndicalist struggles, which centered on wars, political oppressions, and the labor disputes of coal miners and the urban proletariat, began to spread.

In 1923, the Great Kanto Earthquake hit a large area including the Tokyo metropolis. This caused a hundred thousand deaths and innumerable missing persons. In the wake of the disaster, vigilantes, military officers, and police forces captured and massacred many resident ethnic Koreans and Chinese, along with socialists, labor activists, and anarchists. The disaster initiated the wholehearted urbanization of Tokyo, which in turn coincided with the state's move toward emperor fascism and Asian invasion. In 1925, the Maintenance of Public Order Act was passed to suppress all opposition. The economy was hit by the tremendous sum of bad credit created by the earthquake, and then by the global depression of 1929. In 1930, Japan rushed headlong into total war with China. The ultimate goal was expressed through the state's "Great East Asia Co-prosperity Sphere" project (of 1940), whose objective was "to liberate East and South East Asia from the colonial domination of the Western Countries and construct a new world order under Japan's leadership."[24] Ultimately, the entirety of Asia and the Pacific were to be divided into an economic bloc (Japan, the Republic of China, and Japan's puppet state, Manchukuo), a natural resource zone (South East Asia), and a national defense zone (the South Pacific).

In 1945, Japan's unconditional surrender was realized by multiple forces: in the official history, Japan was defeated by the "Allied Forces" in a number of major military confrontations; however, it is important to note that Japan's logistical life lines stretching across the Asian continent were consistently attacked and drained by the guerrilla campaigns of people's armies in all fronts from north to south. From the standpoint of the people's armies, defeating Japan was part of their revolution that had continued since the late 1910s. But the dominant power in the Pacific was now the United States, which introduced a new, mobile, and flexible geopolitics. It signaled the advent of the network empire connected by island territories (i.e., as opposed to the more conventional empire based on permanent occupation of a vast continental territory). This was made possible through superior land, marine, and air force mobility, as well as by the proliferation of nuclear warheads.[25] With the contemporaneous emergence of the modern information network, this period signaled the beginning of the age of what some have called the cybernetic mega-machine.[26]

## JAPAN'S '68

What is considered by some to be the first global revolution took place in response to the peak of the world's totalization. The reverberating series of uprisings called '68 realized unprecedented synchronicity. It involved not only concentrated exchanges among peoples from varied locations and social milieus, but also involved shared experiences of insurrection. To confront one network of global domination, the Japanese masses decomposed into an unnamable crowd capable of becoming almost anyone.

In terms of causality, the eros effect in Japan's '68 emerged for several reasons, which some might associate with the attributes of postmodernity (e.g., global connectivity of cities and the information network, the cultural logic of heterogeneity, the society of spectacle, a relative weakening of patriarchal hierarchy). Certainly, the advent of mass-media society had a lot to do with it. However, the attractor for the turbulence was primarily the friction and unevenness of these developments vis-à-vis the planetary body. The hot wind of struggle had long blown from the countryside or the ghetto; however, beginning from the mid-1950s, it gradually became visible in the metropolis, too.

In 1954, less than ten years after the Hiroshima/Nagasaki nuclear attacks, a Japanese tuna fishing boat (the *Lucky Dragon Five*) with twenty-three crew members was affected by nuclear fallout from the US thermo-nuclear device test at Bikini Atoll. At the height of the Cold War, the strategy of nuclear deterrence had begun to reach an intolerable level for the people of Japan. This triggered a large mobilization against nuclear weapons and US military hegemony. It would be Japan's first nationwide citizens' movement led by women.

During this time, the common enemy faced by the people of East Asia came to be recognized as US imperialism and all the region's proxy governments. The first Asia-African Conference at Bandung in 1955 did much to advance this understanding. The revolutionary winds from China, the Korean Peninsula, and Indo-China were circulating a guerrilla war against the US regular army equipped with superior weapons and transferring the eros effect to students, labor, and other oppositional movements in Japan. Internally, another current was streaming from northern Kyushu, where the Miike miners had been on strike against restructuring and layoffs during the 1950s.[27]

In March/April 1960, there was a wave of uprisings across Korea initiated by high school and university students against the vice-presidential election, which had been manipulated by the pro-US ruling power. That June, the first mass insurgency in postwar Japan took place against the US/Japan Security Treaty (aka, Ampo) destined to align the country with US security interests for the following decade. Students, workers, and citizens broke into the National Diet Building, the very symbol of Japan's postwar constitution, and stayed there until the treaty automatically went into effect on June 19th.[28] Although the Korean and Japanese uprisings didn't have an ostensible connection, their reverberating coimplication could be seen through people's affinity and their identification of US imperialism as a common enemy. It is also important to note that there were approximately 650,000 resident Koreans in Japan at that time due to Japan's coercive pre-WWII labor migration policies and the flood of exiles from the Korean War.

The leading force of the anti-Ampo uprising was Zen-gaku-ren (the National Federation of Student Self-Government Associations), which was under the hegemony of a New Left sect called The Communist League (Bund). There are three developments that facilitated Japan's '68: the development of the New Left, the nature of the student association, and the new international territorial connections between urban and rural struggles.

The Japan Communist Party (JCP) abandoned the armed revolution and began to shift toward parliamentarism at the sixth national conference in 1955. The Hungary Revolution in 1956 influenced anti-Stalinist revolutionary movements to grow across the world. In Japan, the Trotskyist League was organized in 1957. In 1958, Bund was established by a group of student members of the JCP who felt the need to create a new radical movement. Thereafter, Japan's New Left began to radicalize and move toward mass mobilization as it passed through innumerable divergences and intra-sectarian conflicts that pitted political ideologies, organizational forms, and intensities of militancy against one another. These included Leninism, Trotskyism, Maoism, Left Communism, anarchism, and nonsectarian radicalism.

In itself, Zen-gaku-ren was not really a political organization. It was a national assembly of the student associations of different universities, which played the role of receptacle for different groups to construct their bases, both financially (the budget for students' activities) and spatially (university campuses). Nevertheless, it was gradually divided and became fixed by the domination of a few main groups. Then, in 1968, another form of students' network was established: Zen-kyo-to (All-Campus Joint Struggle Committee), which consciously created more flexible, inclusive, radical, and anarchic connections between university and high school struggles across the nation. Around 1968 and 1969, this new form culminated in a wave of occupations that swept from Hokkaido to Kyushu.

Outside educational institutions, there were four indispensable milieus of convergence: mass culture, urban space, local struggles, and internationalism. By the mid-1960s, American civil rights, Black liberation, and anti–Vietnam War student movements had begun to send signals and energy, which mixed with jazz, blues, rock, and the hippie lifestyle. For young people, these forms dominated the everyday landscape of big cities.

Shinjyuku is one of the busiest commercial centers in Tokyo. Redeveloped as a black market after WWII, it consists of a chaotic and heterotopic mishmash: shopping areas, working-class entertainment, the sex industry, gay and transvestite areas, tiny bars, and progressive culture. This space contributed significantly to the spectacular aspect of Japan's '68. It offered a common space for both radical street fights and progressive street music and performance. It was an asylum for revolutionaries.[29]

Local struggles provided a meeting place for urban radicals and rural people to confront their common enemy. They created new maps of interconnection between different lives and struggles. Most notably, the farmers in Sanrizuka, Chiba Prefecture, rose up and resisted the construction of a new international airport—Narita—between 1966 and 1978. Many individuals and groups joined, sharing everyday life and struggle with the farmers.

Ever since the Battle of Okinawa in 1945, the Okinawan people had been fighting the presence of US military bases. In 1970, a riot erupted in Koza City in response to a car accident caused by a US soldier. The crowd attacked and burned military vehicles and facilities. In 1972, Okinawa was "reverted" to Japan; however, the US bases remained. Its geopolitical status has continued to raise issues concerning the territorial claims of the

Japanese state as well as the military strategy of the US network empire. As a result, the island territory has been an important point of convergence for activists and movements across East Asia and the world; it is likely to become even more so in the future.

Internationalism in the period leading up to Japan's '68 developed around the anti–Vietnam War movement and as a result of solidarity with Third World revolutions. A popular movement called Be-hei-ren (Citizens' Alliance for Peace in Vietnam) succeeded in mobilizing the general public for antiwar actions and served as a gateway for young activists to become involved in revolutionary movements. It also instigated an underground operation called JATEC (Japan Technical Committee to Aid Anti-War GIs), which helped US military deserters. Meanwhile, a number of small groups had begun to establish clandestine connections with revolutions taking place around the world. The Japan Red Army, perhaps most famous of the groups, dramatically appeared on the anti-imperialist guerrilla scene to express solidarity with the Popular Front for the Liberation of Palestine (PFLP) during the 1970s.[30]

The student movement was largely inspired by the Cultural Revolution in China; however, it did not identify with the oppressive regime manipulated by the Gang of Four. Instead, it gravitated toward a new form of *everyday revolution* in the city. Around that time, one of the main problems of student activism concerned the social status and class identity of students, who were beginning to question the role of education in reproducing class divisions. The slogan "Decomposing Universities" expressed one of the main objectives of the Zen-kyo-to occupations. Educational institutions were to become revolutionary bases. The occupation blocked classes and examinations and encouraged self-motivated discussions, seminars, and cultural activities.

During the later phase of the student movement when university struggles and street protests had fallen into decline following the last large coordinated action against the Ampo Treaty of June 1970, "Decomposing Universities" metamorphosed into "Decomposing the Self." Practically speaking, this involved destruction of one's status as a student to become part of the lower stratum of society—the fluid underclass of workers, peasants, and indigenous. Such decomposition was considered a revolutionary education for radicals, who either moved to *yoseba* to live and work or to the country where they became farmers. In those spaces, they destroyed their privileged social status and built communes as revolutionary bases. This practice of submersion sparked the future prairie fire.

Due to the intensity of intra-sectarian violence during the following decades (causing more than a hundred deaths and several thousand serious injuries), the legacy of Japan's '68 is often cast as a story about the perils of authoritarian vanguardism, dogmatism, hierarchical structure, and gender discrimination. A "thanatos effect" emerged, alienating commoners and youth from the legacy of mass insurgencies and the idea of taking initiative to change the world.[31] As a result, activists of subsequent generations came to focus more on coalition building and on issues such as minorities, the environment, and building communities. The molecular revolution in this sense was as important in Japan as it was in the broader global context. In Japan, however, the negative memory resulted in a culture of fear and legalism that suppressed the desire for militancy and creativity.

## AUTONOMY OF LIFE-PRINCIPLES AND ITS TERRITORY

The Fukushima nuclear disaster has inaugurated an age of irreversible planetary radiation. Radioactive nuclides have been set free to travel across the planet. Inscribed as it will be in the genetic mutation of all life forms, the culpability of the Tokyo Power Electric Company and the Japanese government will never be erased. The half-lives of some nuclides last an astronomical numbers of years;[32] their activities are on the nano level and invisible; the way they travel and accumulate is a constantly transforming complexity, far removed from rigid patterns, since they travel with not only atmospheric movements (wind and water currents) but also circulation (transportations and traffic), for as long as their half-lives last.[33] The ruling power seeks to nullify the event and subsume all post-Fukushima problems within the normal operations of the capitalist-democratic nation-state. Meanwhile, as the radiation spreads, and in confrontation with government rule, commoners are struggling to live the event and take initiative in managing their own bodies and minds.

The postdisaster situation has revealed the modus operandi of government and the mass media: abandon the people for the sake of business as usual and the maintenance of social conformity. The ruling power prioritizes the reconstruction of Fukushima to save the Tokyo Metropolis in the interest of the global economy. Circulating the image that Fukushima is controllable, the present Abe administration pushes rearmament (the right of collective defense), information control (the protection of national security law), and new development (the Tokyo Olympics 2020).[34] The true lifeline for the status quo is nevertheless in the demography of sustaining laboring and consuming capacity within the mass corporeality facing biological decline: radiation illnesses as well as depopulation. The future Japan will be a clinical society managed by pharmaceutical/energy/weaponry industries and in which people's health, illness, and death are programmed.

In the meantime, nationalism is enjoying a dramatic return, as made evident by the collective death drive underlying the "Eat and Support Fukushima" campaign. In brief, it is an attempt to solve the crises of local industries *nationally* by encouraging the consumption of irradiated food products from the region, the logic of which is this: *Accept internal radiation and become a national hero!* Here, the mass media plays a major role: Although it facilitated the eros effect during the uprisings of the 1960s, it has also produced a society of *concentrated fashion*—of behavior, way of life, cultural taste, and political idea—that congeals desires and orients them in a unidirectional and paranoiac fashion toward the exclusion of all anomalies.

Today, the main battlegrounds of anticapitalist, anti-statist struggles are the bodies and minds of the people as well as their erotic drive. Will this drive be pushed toward the collective life/death of the nation or toward a totally different territory?

A series of large mobilizations began after the nuclear disaster and resonated across the archipelago. Those mobilizations addressed issues including nukes, rearmament, information control, the Trans Pacific Partnership (TPP), and US bases. The level of mobilization is now at its highest point since the 1960s uprisings, thus making it clear that the people are no longer in synch with Japan's postwar regime. Despite these developments, however, the activists in and around the former NO G8! Action are experiencing big divergences in their orientations to the situation. Internal debates are roughly divided between "those who go North" and "those who go West," as seen from the geographical position of the Tokyo metropolis. This split reflects the difficult moment of transition.

Those who go North consist of activists determined to go to Fukushima as volunteers to help restore living conditions for the people in the disaster area. There have been attempts by *yoseba* activists to organize nuclear workers being exposed to radiation in the reactors. Knowing they too are likely irradiated, they support the immediate victims and organize the oppressed workers in nuclear industries. In these practices, we can sense the mutual-aid society that could come into being through the experience of disaster.[35] Notwithstanding their importance, however, these interventions—if not coordinated with the struggles of those who go West—are at risk of being appropriated by the state project of tying as many people as possible to the industrial reconstruction of contaminated land through an insular nationalism founded through a collective death drive.

For their part, those who go West are creating new ways of living (e.g., eating habits, social relations, and living environments) in opposition to radiation contamination and the forms of governance that make it a nationally shared condition. They stimulate grassroots efforts to sustain the safety of food and of everyday social reproduction. This new current is largely led by women (or, more generally, those who take care of everyday reproduction of the family), who have begun to investigate the state of contamination and research its effects. They passionately study nuclear and medical sciences in pursuit of managing their own health and life. Many civic centers have appeared at which radiation is monitored and information is exchanged. As such, they stand in radical opposition to the manipulation of information by the government and the mass media as well as the monopolization of knowledge by the specialists.

There are increasing numbers of voluntary evacuees[36] who determined to give up living in the polluted northeastern and Kanto regions (including the Tokyo Metropolis) and to migrate to safer regions. In these areas, there are groups of people willing to accept and support the newcomers. In the new environment, some have turned to farming in the country or to hunting in the mountains (especially in northern Kyushu near Fukuoka). New communities of evacuees have appeared in Hokkaido in the north, as well as in Nagoya, Okayama, Fukuoka, and many other places in western and southern Japan. These new voluntary communities are engaged in multiple projects. Some have established new social centers while others organize weekly markets to sell and buy or barter their products and skills. They are also developing a new culture in which reproduction is shared. Houses, jobs, cooking and eating, child care, martial arts, and techniques in general are detached as much as possible from the capitalist and nationalist apparatuses stretching out from Tokyo. Some are also seeking to connect the new communities with the old communes established in the 1960s to learn from their successes and failures.

What is crucial in the current of those who go West is that, while it often involves tragic splits in families, among friends, and within workplaces, it expresses an impetus to decompose the old conformity to create a new, unknown sociality; it is developing new territorialities, and new flows of life and communication in and out of Japan. In my opinion, this current could connect varied struggles and help to stimulate the eros effect.

As an extension of the westward migration, an increasing number of young activists are visiting communes, social centers, and neighborhoods in Korea, Taiwan, Hong Kong, the Philippines, and Indonesia. People associated with the group "Amateur Riot" are passionately coordinating tours from Japan and elsewhere.[37] The group's efforts mark a humble attempt to revitalize the archipelagic relation in East Asia.

In the new cartography, two points of convergence stand out: Kyushu and Okinawa. In Kyushu, the reactivation of the Sendai Nuclear Plant in the Kagoshima Prefecture has been strongly criticized in light of the spectacular volcanic eruptions that have recently occurred nearby.[38] In terms of geographical position and social history, Kyushu is well positioned to become a basis for recreating archipelagic relations, autonomous (if only relatively) from the Tokyo Metropolis and the nation of Japan. In the North, it closely faces the Korean Peninsula; in the South, it is connected with South Asia by the line of Ryukyu Islands. It has more Asiatic population than Eastern Japan. It is also known, since the Edo period, for its history of separatism and rebellion against the central power.

The territory of the Okinawan archipelago stretches beautifully between Kyushu and Taiwan, as if connecting two national territories. The people of Okinawa, who had nurtured their own culture and kingdom, came to be abused and have their land expropriated by Japan (starting with the invasion of Satsuma in 1609) and the United States (after the end of WWII). Now, the consensus of the people—including the governor, Takeshi Onaga—stands in clear opposition to the US/Japanese joint project of relocating the US Marine Corps base in Futenma to the island of Henoko, where construction would destroy a cherished semi-tropical environment. The Okinawan people have a long history of struggle against US military bases, and a rich tradition of direct action at sea, in the mountains, and in the city. The impetus to leave the confines of Japanese and US governance is waiting for the reverberation of struggle among the people in the Japanese Archipelago.

It is clear that we can no longer return to a radiation-free natural environment; we all are exposed to radiation and will increasingly be so in the future, due not only to the irreparable Fukushima Daiichi but also to the persistence of nuclear states around the world that will never abandon nuclear power for energy or weaponry. Facing this dark reality, what is at stake for the life-principle is not purity but autonomy, the political self-determination of our bodies and minds.

Here, it is useful to consider the slogan of a sector of "those who go West," called the Zero Becquerelists: "We don't need a society that tells us to eat radiation."[39] In this slogan, one sees a refusal to be a good Japanese and participate in the postnuclear disaster conformism. It is a declaration of their intent to leave the nation-state called Japan. It is a refusal, furthermore, of the processes of abstraction and categorization that seek to naturalize radiation and other contaminants. Finally, it is a call for gaining autonomy in our relationship to life and death: to how we live and die, and how we create our bodies, our social relations, and our environment.

"Those who go West" thus seek to organize the affect (the passion for life and body) that erupted so intensely and broadly after the disaster. This includes: (1) sensitive views concerning everyday reproduction (e.g., food, living environment, and care), (2) affirmation of this ephemeral yet singular life, (3) recognition of one's life as part of the community and the continuum of the life chain, and (4) creativity for sharing everyday life with others. Such a life is in synch with the preindividual life conceived by Deleuze,[40] who imagined it to be in radical opposition to the eternalized life driven by self-interest, programed by capital, and absorbed into the nationalist life/death spectrum.

We can't know if a reverberation worthy of the name "eros effect" will ever take place in Japan again in our lifetime. If it does, it is clear that the attractor and turbulence won't come from "political ideologies" but from "ethical truths" shared widely and intensely in the postdisaster world.[41] Fukushima is one of the most apocalyptic events that capitalist civilization has ever created. At the same time, it has shown us two ultimate potencies of eros at the end of the world: the autonomy of the life-principle as an end in itself, and the omnipresent territorial connections it could foster on the earth.

## NOTES

1. For reference to the eros effect as an analytical tool, see George Katsiaficas, "The Eros Effect," 1989, personal website, http://www.eroseffect.com/articles/eroseffectpaper.PDF, 1. More recently, Katsiaficas has questioned this approach, wondering if it is "simply an analytical construction useful for . . . understanding revolutionary movements or is it also a movement tactic useful in transforming society." See George Katsiaficas, *Asia's Unknown Uprisings, Volume 1: South Korean Social Movements in the 20th Century* (Oakland: PM Press, 2012), xxi.

2. Herbert Marcuse, *Eros and Civilization: A Philosophical Inquiry into Freud* (Boston: Beacon Press, 1992). For their relationship, see George Katsiaficas, "Afterword, Marcuse as an Activist: Reminiscences of His Theory and Practice," in *The New Left and the 1960s: Collected Papers of Herbert Marcuse, Vol. 3*, ed. Douglas Kellner (New York: Routledge, 2005), 192–203.

3. George Katsiaficas, interviewed by AK Thompson, "Remembering May '68: An Interview with George Katsiaficas," *Upping the Anti* 6 (April 2008): n.p., http://uppingtheanti.org/journal/article/06-remembering-may-68/.

4. Gilles Deleuze and Félix Guattari, *Anti-Oedipus: Capitalism and Schizophrenia*, trans. Robert Hurley, Mark Seem, and Helen R. Lane (London: Athlone Press, 1984).

5. In brief, reterritorialization remakes territories (i.e., patterns, relationships, identities, habits, etc.). This is counterposed to deterritorialization, which unmakes territories. Together, territorialization-deterritorialization-reterritorialization constitutes a processual ontology. This should not be confused with dialectics, which is a more linear process. The ontology posed by Deleuze and Guattari is antifoundational and multidirectional. See select passages in Gilles Deleuze and Félix Guattari, *A Thousand Plateaus: Capitalism and Schizophrenia*, trans. Brian Massumi (Minneapolis: University of Minnesota Press, 1987).

6. For more on this, see Sabu Kohso, "Mutation of the Triad: Totalitarianism, Fascism, and Nationalism in Japan," *E-Flux Journal* 56 (June 2014): n.p., http://www.e-flux.com/journal/mutation-of-the-triad-totalitarianism-fascism-and-nationalism-in-japan.

7. George Katsiaficas, "Eros and Revolution," *Radical Philosophy Review*, 16, no. 2 (2013): 491–505 (498), doi:10.5840/radphilrev201316238.

8. The union is Kamagasaki Chiiki Godo Rodo Kumiai (Kamagasaki Region Amalgamated Labor Union).

9. The following description of the 2008 riot is based on a report in Japanese by Toshiyuki Morishita, which can be accessed at http://www.gyokokai.org/~gasparo/osakacity/kama_080613.htm.

10. This is a comment by a friend of mine, Takeshi Haraguchi.

11. This protest became known as the "Candlelight Demos" because of the thousands of protestors who were holding lit candles in their hands at night. See "2008 US Beef Protest in South Korea," *Wikipedia*, https://en.wikipedia.org/wiki/2008_US_beef_protest_in_South_Korea.

12. Funamoto Shuji, *Don't Die by the Roadside in Silence: Posthumous Writings by Funamoto Shuji* (Damatte Notare-jinu-na-yo: Funamoto Shuji Iko-shu) (Tokyo: Renga Shobo Shinsha, 1985). See also, Manuel Yang, "Man on Fire: A Plea for 'Funamoto Shuji Day,'" *Counterpunch*, July 9, 2014, http://www.counterpunch.org/2014/07/09/man-on-fire-2/.

13. Funamoto, *Don't Die by the Roadside*, 168–169.

14. Concerning the struggle in Sanya and other *yoseba*, see the texts concerning the film *Yama: Attack to Attack!* For film reference, see Sato Mitsuo and Yamaoka Kyoichi, *Yama: Attack to Attack!* (1986). For texts about the film, see the links at *Bordersphere*, http://www.bordersphere.com/events/yama2.htm. I should note, too, that the documentary film was independently produced by the local activists of Sanya, Mitsuo Sato and Kyoichi Yamaoka, both of whom were murdered by the local *yakuza* organization that controls labor recruitment, prostitution, and gambling.

15. Burakumin are a type of social outcast that have a long history in Japan. For background, see "Burakumin," *Wikipedia*, http://en.wikipedia.org/wiki/Burakumin.

16. The militant group called the East Asia Anti-Japan Armed Front (Higashi Ajia Han-nichi Buso Sensen) attacked a number of targets that had driven Japan's expansionism before and after WWII, including the emperor system, big enterprises, the police, and nationalist monuments. One of the bomb attacks targeted the headquarters of Mitsubishi Heavy Industries in 1974 and killed eight people.

17. Amino Yoshihiko, *The Oceanic and Archipelagic Medieval* (Umi-to-Retto-no-Chusei) (Tokyo: Kodansha, 2013).

18. For "geophilosophy," see Gilles Deleuze and Félix Guattari, *What Is Philosophy?*, trans. Hugh Tomlinson and Graham Burchell (New York: Columbia University Press, 1994), chap. 4. For "Creolization," see Édouard Glissant, *Poetics of Relations*, trans. Betsy Wing (Ann Arbor: University of Michigan Press, 1997).

19. Louis Mumford, *The Myth of the Machine: Technics and Human Development* (San Diego: Harcourt, 1967).

20. Deleuze and Guattari, *A Thousand Plateaus*, chap. 12.

21. This is an idea that the author, educator, and entrepreneur Fukuzawa Yukichi (1835–1901) proposed for the national policy.

22. The campaign "Eat and Support Fukushima" (Tabete O-en-shiyo) was instigated by the Ministry of Agriculture, Forestry and Fisheries, and it continues today, involving a number of fast-food chains, supermarkets, restaurants, and consumers. It states: "We call for a wide corporation for the campaign, in order to support the reconstruction of the disaster stricken areas by actively consuming food products from the areas." See the website of the ministry, http://www.maff.go.jp/j/shokusan/eat.

23. The Gwangju Uprising refers to a popular uprising in the city of Gwangju, South Korea, from May 18 to 27, 1980. During the insurgency, Gwangju citizens took up arms when local students—who were demonstrating against the Chun Doo-hwan government—were fired upon and massacred by government troops. The uprising can be understood as both an attempt to create an autonomous urban commune and the most dramatic moment in the long struggle of South Koreans against the US-backed dictatorship. Katsiaficas gives much attention to the Gwangju Uprising in *Asia's Unknown Uprisings, Vol. 1*. See chap. 6, in particular.

24. The statement is taken from the manifesto of the Japanese government, quoted in a *Wikipedia* entry, https://ja.wikipedia.org/wiki/大東亜共栄圏.

25. For more on these points, see Gabrielle Hecht, ed., *Entangled Geographies: Empire and Technopolitics in the Global Cold War* (Cambridge: MIT Press, 2011). Particularly helpful chapters include the following: Gabrielle Hecht, "Introduction," 1–12; and Ruth Oldenziel, "Islands: The United States as a Network Empire," 13–41.

26. Tiquun, "The Cybernetic Hypothesis," *tiquun-jottit.com*, http://cybernet.jottit.com.

27. The major strikes at Miike Mines in northern Kyushu took place in 1953 and 1959–1960. But the direct impact of the local opposition upon the New Left—by way of connecting the strikes in the countryside with the anti-US/Japan Security Treaty struggle in Tokyo—was conveyed via the "Circle Village Movement" (Circle Mura Undo), which was organized in 1958 by feminist poet Kazue Morisaki (1927–) and poet/political activist Gan Tanigawa (1923–1995) to connect various struggles of the workers and their communities across Kyushu by way of a DIY publication, *Circle Village* (Circle Mura).

28. The National Diet Building has since been the main target for many large mobilizations against the government, including the post-Fukushima demonstrations.

29. Hirai Gen, *Love and Hate of Shinjyuku* (Ai-to-nikushimi-no-Shinjyuku) (Tokyo: Chukuma Shobo, 2010).

30. See the following film: Masao Adachi and Kôji Wakamatsu, *Red Army/ PFLP Declaration of World War* (Wakamatsu Production 1971).

31. It is probably more accurate to describe this "effect" in terms of the "psychic Thermidor." For Marcuse, this is a psychological condition in which radical consciousness becomes beset by guilt and reverts to its previous state of social conformity. In brief, the concept helps explain why moments of radical activity suddenly disappear. See, for example, Marcuse, *Eros and Civilization*, 90–92; and Katsiaficas, "Afterword, Marcuse as an Activist," 192–203 (particularly, 200).

32. Among those radioactive nuclides that are often spoken of after Fukushima, there are Caesium-137 (30.17 years), Strontium-90 (28 years), and Plutonium-239 (24,100 years).

33. Maps by Yukio Hayakawa, a geologist, are said to be most trustworthy in terms of detailing the current state of radiation contamination of the Japanese archipelago. See, for instance, the following blog posts: http://ex-skf.blogspot. com/2012/09/professor-yukio-hayakawas-radiation.html and http://kipuka.blog70. fc2.com/blog-entry-570.html.

34. Prime Minister Shinzo Abe promised to the world on September 23, 2013, that the Fukushima nuclear disaster would be resolved before the 2020 Olympics. Isabel Reynolds and Takashi Hirokawa, "Abe Says Fukushima Will Be Resolved before 2020 Olympics," *Bloomberg Business*, September 4, 2013, http://www.bloomberg.com/news/articles/2013-09-04/japan-s-abe-says-fukushima-will-be-resolved-before-2020-olympics.

35. Rebecca Solnit, *A Paradise Built in Hell: Extraordinary Communities That Arise in Disaster* (New York: Penguin Books, 2009).

36. In the record of the Fukushima Prefecture alone, at least 207,000 people were still out of the prefecture by June 2015, according to the report of the Reconstruction Agency of the Japanese Government (see, for instance, http://www. reconstruction.go.jp/topics/main-cat2/sub-cat2-1/20150630_hinansha.pdf). However, since voluntary evacuees include those from the vast area of northeastern Japan (both Tohoku and Kanto regions) to Hokkaido in the further north and Western Japan, there has not been a fixed demographic record. It can be assumed, almost certainly, that the number is increasing slowly and steadily.

37. There is no website for the group in English, but there is a short documentary: *Amateur Riot* (Submedia 2011), http://www.submedia.tv/amateur-riot.

38. The Sendai Nuclear Power Plant has suspended operations since the Fukushima disaster, but the Kyushu Electric Power Company and the Japanese Nuclear and Industrial Safety Agency have been eager to resume operations. See, for instance, "Sendai Nuclear Power Plant," *Wikipedia*, https://en.wikipedia.org/wiki/ Sendai_Nuclear_Power_Plant. Public opinion in Japan, however, is extremely wary of the plan, due to the accelerating volcanic activity nearby. Elaine Lies, "Volcano Erupts on Remote Japanese Island, Residents Flee by Boat," *Reuters*, May 29, 2015, http:// www.reuters.com/article/2015/05/29/us-japan-volcano-idUSKBN0OE02R20150529.

39. Shiro Yabu and Yoshihiko Ikegami, *We Don't Need a Society That Tells Us to Eat Radiation: Zero-Becquerelist Manifesto* (Tokyo: Shin Hyoron, 2012).

40. Gilles Deleuze, *Pure Immanence: Essays on a Life*, trans. Anne Boyman (New York: Zone Books, 2001).

41. Comité invisible, *À nos amis* (Paris: La fabrique éditions, 2014), 45.

Section Four

# REJOINDERS

11

# Feminism and the Eros Effect

NINA POWER

## INTRODUCTION

Katsiaficas' concept of the "eros effect" is, at first glance, enormously appealing. Who hasn't felt, beneath the coldness and cruelties of capitalist atomization (the "psychic Thermidor," as Katsiaficas, via Marcuse, beautifully puts it), the need and desire for a very different set of relations, of collectivity, of love in its fullest, most human sense? And we do indeed get glimpses of these other models of relationality, albeit temporarily, in protest, in occupations, and in everyday acts of solidarity. Katsiaficas repeatedly describes his analysis as "dialectical" in a humanist, Hegelian mode. We can easily see how this analysis makes sense of the dialectical relationships between repression-liberation, atomization-collectivity, uncertainty-hope, and many of the other core features of political struggle ("fear changes sides" was, for example, a key slogan in the Egyptian uprising). Here, though, I want to push Katsiaficas further into the dialectics of eros, specifically, and ask why, given the immense amount of feminist work done on love, eros, care, and the exit from repression, Katsiaficas does not reference more of these debates. It is in feminism, above all, that we find the best and most important work on the dialectics of these things, not least because the imposition of these qualities is so integral to the history of patriarchy (be kind because you are a woman, that is what women do, etc.). Katsiaficas does acknowledge the role of feminism in both world history and his personal development: "The feminist movement spoke to women's particular desires for freedom but also changed global culture more generally. The women's movement enabled me to free myself as a male from my own macho life."[1] But elsewhere its

237

contribution is rather underplayed: "Feminism is interpreted to mean women in combat and corporate boardrooms rather than the abolition of war and hierarchy."[2] Certainly there is a neoliberalism that has embraced a certain kind of pro-capitalist and pro-imperialist feminism; however, there is much more that feminism offers to his analysis, particularly when it comes to critically thinking about the model that lies behind the eros effect.

How then do we preserve the revolutionary and liberatory impulses of eros, love, and care in the way that Katsiaficas desires, but also accept along the way the feminist critique of the exploitation of these same qualities? How many modes of coercion have been carried out in the name of "love" or in the service of a revolutionary "eros" that sees women little better off than they were before? It is my contention that it is possible to both preserve and recognize the revolutionary impulse of Katsiaficas' analytical concept, while simultaneously reorienting the concept of "eros" toward a feminist image of revolution: Indeed, the eros effect cannot fully be understood, I will suggest, without having *dialectically* passed through the feminist critique of eros and related concepts to emerge out the other side. The concept of revolution defended here, then, will be one that begins with and recognizes the *already existing* nature of care, emotional labor, and love as constitutive *of* social reproduction (the reproduction of the social totality). It is not solely in these moments of spontaneous, international uprisings that universal relations and bonds of love for humanity (what Feuerbach and the early Marx described as *Gattungswesen* or species-being) become apparent; indeed, they are only *able* to appear because they already exist, albeit serially as Sartre would put it, or in (mainly, though not totally) alienated form.

To be clear, I agree with several of Katsiaficas' suggestions—that the emotional and the rational are not to be opposed, that machinic images of humanity are not useful for revolutionary struggle, and that global feminism is central in understanding the history, present, and future of politics for everyone. However, I want to try to dialectically extend some of his claims to better strengthen their conclusions. Ultimately, I suggest that the eros effect already exists in everyday care and social reproduction and that, along with an understanding of the preexisting modes of relationality, this latent force might ultimately prove to be more powerful than insurrections envisaged as "spontaneous" street battles. To get to this point, I will take three critiques in turn: first, the critique of the critique of repression; second, the critique of love in the context of labor; and, third, a brief examination of the problem of spontaneity. It will overall be suggested that Katsiaficas' concept of the eros effect can only benefit from and be expanded by feminist critique.

## THE CRITIQUE OF THE CRITIQUE OF REPRESSION

I want to first address some feminist critiques of the framing of repression. In Katsiaficas' work, like that of many others after Marcuse but also after many post-1968 thinkers, in the interstices between Freud and Foucault, there is an understanding that repression (in the sense of both psychic repression and the physical repression arising from state apparatuses) signals that which needs liberation. Katsiaficas is of course very careful not to reduce his concept of the eros effect to mere physicality, suggesting that eros needs careful cultivation and concerns life-affirming connectivity and trust and is "not just about sex."[3] The moments of the eros effect thus do not straightforwardly correspond to the unleashing of libidinal energy understood in the impoverished way we often understand sex and sexuality today, but there is, nevertheless, a clear sense in which moments of spontaneous, universal uprisings are deeply connected with the freeing of desire: "the human capacity to understand the promise of freedom contained in given situations and the corresponding desire to move beyond prior constraints."[4] Katsiaficas argues that the eros effect is an analytical tool for explaining mass political awakenings and spontaneous rebellions and is deeply connected with love and erotics: "This 'effect' involves an eroticization of politics— and of everyday life—that motivates people to create an alternative world of solidarity, self-determination, and bottom-up social relations."[5] It is the effect that *creates* collectivity: something new is begun.

But before we get to Katsiaficas' dialectics of liberation, it is crucial to understand exactly what kind of model of repression we are working with. One aspect of the debate between radical feminism and "sex-positive" feminism precisely concerned the way in which the dyad desire/repression was set up. As Karen Elizabeth Davis put it in her essay "I Love Myself When I Am Laughing: A New Paradigm for Sex":

> From sexology to gay and lesbian studies to feminism, a persistent concern has been that while men unproblematically express desire, women have been plagued by sexual silence. The feminist sexuality debates of the 1980s took up the problem of women's desire. Some feminists maintained that our culture represses women's sexual desire and expression which can and should be a lot more like men's, and otherwise would be if not for repression.[6]

Here, the thorny question of the gendered aspect of desire is raised. While it is perhaps impossible, and in any case unhelpful, to identify any kind of "natural" male or female desire, it is true that the way desire is socialized in terms of masculine and feminine qualities is quite different in each case. What, then, would it mean to insert the question of sex into the question of desire/repression? Would we come to realize that a supposedly neutral model that celebrated the liberation of desire as an unmitigated good was actually predicated on an unwittingly masculine model of desire? Davis is strongly critical of what she sees as the aspiration on the part of sex-positive feminism to aspire to sexuality if it is to be solely on male terms. For Davis, the entire debate within feminism concerning desire/repression took place on the basis of false and unexamined premises, the first being that "male sexuality is unproblematically self-motivated, driven, active, unattached, demanding, free."[7] Underlying these qualities, she suggests, is a more fundamental tenet, namely, that desire is imagined as something like *hunger*, an individual desire that seeks satisfaction in the world (we of course can see the long tail that connects Hegel to Freud to Sartre to Lacan, where the model is fundamentally one of the endless satisfaction and renewal of desire in the face of its permanent and constitutive emptiness). Instead of looking for a new model of desire, Davis argues that feminists critical of the radical feminist position on desire/repression were moved to search for desire on the male model: "Looking for women's sexuality as hungering and not finding it, pro-sex feminists concluded that women's sexuality had been violently repressed, and resisted vehemently any suggestion that it did not exist. Women's more relational, contextual, emotional responses were derogated as passive and moralistic. They were not what was being sought. These feminists were looking for *desire*."[8]

We are faced with an extraordinary difficulty on the back of this reading. On the one hand is a model of desire/repression and de-repression in the form of the freeing of sexuality; on the other is a defense of what looks to be essentialist categories of femininity and femaleness ("Women's more relational, contextual, emotional responses"). One model appears to be abstract because it is the neutral, comprehensible form of de-repression, the other appears to be overly particular, specific, "passive and moralistic." But as Davis points out, even a hypercritical position that understands the constructed nature of human sexuality often falls prey to a mimicking or mirroring of the naturalist assumption that desire functions more like hunger than satiation: "Even when sexuality is seen to originate in cultural production instead of nature, as Lacan and Foucault both maintain, an unreflective use of the hunger paradigm for sexuality causes us to slide back into naturalist and humanist categories, which in turn constantly efface the social situatedness and relatedness of sexuality essential to any radical critique."[9]

Key work on childhood development from a feminist and psychoanalytic perspective similarly emphasizes the move beyond repression/de-repression. In Jessica Benjamin's *The Bonds of Love*, a thoroughgoing critique of the Freudian approach to subject-creation, she argues that "[m]utual recognition cannot be achieved through obedience, through identification with the other's power, or through repression. It requires, finally, contact with the other."[10] As Benjamin's critique and defense of intersubjectivity shows, perhaps part of the problem here is our residual commitment to understanding the masculine model of desire as neutral and itself desirable, *even where we are critical of it*. As Rowbotham put in in 1973:

> The immediate response when you grasp this is to deny all culture, because everything that has been created, all universal values, all notions of what we are, have been made in a society in which men have been dominant. But the problem created by simply rejecting everything that is, and inverting existing male values to make a female culture out of everything not male, is that the distortions of oppression are perpetuated.[11]

But what if we were to go beyond the inversion and begin simply positively and even positivistically, as a kind of experiment, with the "relational, contextual, emotional" conception of sexuality and, by extension, of eros more broadly understood? This position refuses the terms of the inversion and points to *already existing* bonds as a positive social model—this is after all what we are looking for in mass movements, when we write about them and when we participate in them.

Katsiaficas actually offers us some resources in this regard when he repeatedly states that rebellion and the emotion involved in mass uprisings are supremely *reasonable*. Yet at the same time they are above all acts of passion—and it is not for nothing that riots in France are called *emeutes* ("emotions").[12] The overturning of the reason/emotion opposition is often present (negatively) in the discussion of riots and other mass and collective movements. Images of enraged or impassioned "mobs" acting "irrationally" have long haunted the popular and particularly right-wing impressions of collective action. It is no coincidence, too, that women have historically and simultaneously been aligned with irrationality, flights of fancy, fits of passion, and so on, by, for instance, philosophy, political thought, and the popular imaginary.

For Katsiaficas, however, it is in "the ecstatic experience of struggle that the universal *rationality* of rebellion is discovered"[13] and, furthermore, that "[r]ather than portraying emotions as linked to reaction, the notion of the eros effect seeks to bring them into the realm of positive revolutionary resources whose mobilization can result in significant social transformation."[14] There is thus no opposition between reason and emotion—indeed, it is rational to be "emotional" in the face of great inequality and oppression. Katsiaficas, at times, goes further, describing the need for a combination of love with "mathematical logic."[15] This is to ensure, and partly to describe, the relationship between the moment of erotic charge and the necessity for organizing ("activating this desire is one thing and coordinating it is another matter entirely"[16]). Katsiaficas is right to be cautious here: there are no guarantees that de-repression will automatically organize itself, and there are potential dangers in a model of de-repression that carry with them no checks at all. If "academics of social movements" have tended to focus too much on the question of coordination and not enough on the question of "inner desire," it is nevertheless key for Katsiaficas and for movements on the ground that desire be channeled: "The movement is a means of sublimating eros."[17]

We can cite concrete examples where a rapid de-repression has had disastrous effects for women, particularly in the form of sexual assault. Incidences of assault have been documented from student occupations in California to street harassment in Tahrir Square. In situations where the tacit agreement is that the state is never to be called up (occupations, for example), the question of how the group deals with sexual assault is a very difficult one indeed, and much literature in recent years has looked at accountability committees, "safe" or "safer" spaces, transformative and restorative justice from a prison abolitionist perspective, and so on.[18] For many decades now, women have been pointing out the practical contradiction that often takes places between the liberatory beliefs held by male revolutionaries and the rather more mundane, but no less political, way in which these same revolutionaries in practice perpetuate the status quo. In outlining the relationship between Marxism and feminism, Lydia Sargent in the crucial collection *The Unhappy Marriage of Marxism and Feminism* makes the point that the concerns raised about the relation between the two movements came out of "the experiences of women in the civil rights, new left, and women's movement of the 1960s and 1970s."[19] Sargent summarizes the reality of the situation:

> [W]orkers at the point of production (read white working class males) will make the revolution led by revolutionary cadre of politicos (read middle class white males steeped in Marxist economic theory). Women (mostly white) would keep the home

fires burning during it, functioning as revolutionary nurturers/ secretaries: typing, filing, phoning, feeding, healing, supporting, loving, and occasionally even participating on the front lines as quasi-revolutionary cheerleaders.[20]

Women inside and outside the movement are frequently expected to provide emotional support to others, family and otherwise, often at great cost to their own physical and mental health. The point is here that unless there is a thoroughgoing questioning of existing social relations and hierarchies, the status quo will likely repeat itself, even or perhaps especially in "revolutionary" organizations. To return briefly to the question of repression and de-repression at hand here, Davis makes clear that the dangers of assuming a model of de-repression on the male model carries with it supreme dangers, dangers that we must also be aware of when attempting to understand the collective possibilities of the eros effect (and it is clear for Katsiaficas that we are always talking about the collective image of eros: "For Marcuse, eros remains largely individualized. But I wondered, can eros, like autonomy, be reconceptualized as a collective phenomenon"[21]). As Davis puts it, when describing the common understanding of repression and de-repression:

> [A] discussion of rape and sexual violence yields the following: "radical analysis suggests male sexual nature is the product of a repressive society, which can be altered only by the elimination of sexism and the increase in women's freedom." The logic here seems to be that if women are allowed to de-repress their sexual desire, which moral strictures have held in check, there will be less rape because there will be more sex available to men. Aside from the repression hypothesis itself, this passage makes two implicit assumptions—that women's freedom from repression will find primary expression in increased sexual activity with men, and that more consensual sex will satisfy men's desire for forced sex.[22]

While Davis presents here a very grim picture of repression and de-repression, as well as an antagonistic account of the relationship between men and women, the positive aspect of her presentation points ultimately toward a different model of desire, one based not on hunger and hierarchy, but on the kinds of relationality found present in modes of being-together such as tickling and laughter: "There are lots of good reasons to dislike objectified sex that do not reduce to repressive puritanism or a morality of love. Women who reject everything sex is and has been are not anti-sex per se; they are holding out for something better. Women who do not eroticize vulnerability or danger are looking for a fuller richer laughter, which stands outside of tedious and dispiriting power/subordination scenarios."[23]

For our purposes, we can see in the demand for a different conception of desire a positive model that moves through and beyond the dangers of a repression/de-repression model based on the disavowed masculinist model of desire as hunger. Before we get to what the positive image of a collective de-repression based on preexisting relationality and equality might be, we need to take another conceptual and political detour, this time to get to the other side of love.

## LOVE AS WORK

> We need to cultivate our capacities to love and to act in an efficient manner . . .
>
> —George Katsiaficas, "Remembering May '68"

A clear aspect, or even the whole, of our expanded conception of eros is love. Here, love is conceived of as a kind of pananthrophilia, a love of and for all humanity. But there is a more complex dialectic of love, and again it is feminism that best explains how love can operate both as a kind of demand/duty ("you must do this out of love") and as a foundational aspect of human existence. This latter form of love, however, is nearly completely buried, and its dimensions are drastically reduced under the capitalist imperative to sell one's labor power, as well as to work for free. Arlie Russell Hochschild's concept of "emotional labor" serves to expand existing Marxist categories of labor, and much feminist analysis has dedicated itself to exposing the sheer amount of unpaid labor carried out on the basis of sex expectation ("you must do this because you are a woman and this is what women do"). As Hochschild puts it: "I use the term *emotional labor* to mean the management of feeling to create a publicly observable facial and bodily display; emotional labor is sold for a wage and therefore has *exchange value*."[25]

We cannot straightforwardly praise love and care as political goals without first passing through the material reality and force of these dimensions of human existence, and without understanding that love is frequently performed as a kind of labor on the basis of sex, whether paid or not. This kind of relationship between love and work, or love *as* work, is grueling. As Selma James puts it: "Our physical feeling is . . . destroyed by the limited kinds of sexuality and the shallow relationships this society promotes and by the scarcity of times and places where we can make love. Our bodies become a tool for production and reproduction and nothing else.[26]

The Wages for Housework campaign sought and continues to seek to politicize the way in which unpaid labor (housework, care work, cooking, child care, elder care, emotional support—what gets called "social reproduction": everything it takes to reproduce the social as such) subtends and indeed forms the basis for waged labor. Although waged labor has been the privileged mode of relation to capital, James and others have long argued that without an understanding of social reproduction, there is no way of understanding and critiquing capitalism as a whole. As the Wages for Housework campaign put it: "To the degree that we organize a struggle for wages for the work we do in the home, we demand that work in the home be considered *as* work which, like all work in capitalist society, is forced work, which we do not for love but because, like every other worker, we and our children would starve if we stopped.[27]

The feminist work of the 1960s and 1970s was critical in identifying not just the relationship between "reproductive" and "productive" labor (or indeed, the way in which the latter depends completely upon the former), but was also heavily prescient in the way in which emotional and care labor became the basis for the service economy that now dominates much of the labor done, particularly in richer countries where industry and farming have been moved to the developing world. As Kathi Weeks puts it:

> [R]eproductive labour is what makes productive labour possible on a daily and generational basis. So "the economy" includes not only waged labour and its sites, relations, and outputs, but also the household, with its gendered labours and familial mode of governance. Early on, reproductive labour was typically conceived in these texts as "housework" and often confined to the tasks of cleaning, shopping, and cooking—those forms of work with the closest resemblance to the once iconic example of manual factory labour. Later the focus shifted more to caring labour. What was seen as an exception, something outside and separate from productive labour within a Fordist imaginary, was soon recognized as a prescient, more generalizable template for post-Fordist service work that enlists more of our emotional and

communicative capacities. So over time, a separate spheres model, centred on the two sites of waged work and family, becomes harder to sustain analytically.[28]

In this way, we can suggest that the tendency of employment is toward jobs that typically resemble women's work historically—that is to say, having an emotional, communicative, or service dimension, being badly paid (if at all), precarious, and so on. Think of the rise of zero-hour contracts and McJobs, of the increasing testing and demand for pleasant and measurable emotional service in poorly paid café jobs, of the outsourcing of cleaning and care work to poorly paid and often badly treated migrants who may have left their own children behind to take up paid work looking after someone else's family.

By politicizing and economizing work that has been historically forced onto women via the rhetoric of love and duty, and the supposed "naturalness" of women's capacity to love, nurture, and care, the Wages for Housework campaign pointed to a central fault line both in the uncritical celebration of love as some sort of immediately accessible, universal feeling, as well as the limitations of the classically Marxist model of the refusal of work. What would it mean to refuse to love, to strike over pay (or lack thereof) and conditions? Clearly laying down tools in a factory or sabotaging machines has a very different meaning when it comes to the direct care of other human beings. One cannot simply abandon one's "job" if that job is taking care of vulnerable people. The work of social reproduction that takes place in an occupation or the consolidation of a political uprising is the same kind of work, and unless it is central to the politics of that movement, and the sexed expectation examined and addressed head-on, then the situation can only reproduce the status quo under a radical guise. James and others recognized the limitations of traditional modes of political organizing when it comes to socially reproductive labor: "To the degree that we organize a struggle against work, women's work of making love for capital or being denied making love by capital; making children for capital or being prevented from making children by capital . . . the unions will try to take it over and direct it into safe channels under their stewardship."[29]

There is a further problem that concerns the relationship between love and work that increasingly needs addressing, and again there are parallels between Katsiaficas' Hegelian and humanist approach and the feminist critique. This problem concerns the question of automation and the relationship between technology and work. There is no doubt that we are seeing an increase both materially and theoretically in the celebration of technology as a liberatory force, yet there are serious dangers in the idea of "full automation," to cite one recent popular technophiliac slogan—this image of work is one that radically neglects the nature of care work, the overwhelming majority of which can never be outsourced to machines. Katsiaficas raises a similar concern when it comes to imagining revolutionary struggle in the image of the machine:

> When we look at the practical consequences of ignoring dialectics, when we conceive of ourselves as machines of struggle, when we imagine that we are cyborgs, the images go in the opposite direction to the ones required by revolutionary politics. Rather than thinking in terms of machines, we should endeavor to become more human. The capacity of human beings to love is what keeps us from death. It's the impulse underlying our will to freedom. Machines don't need to love. Machines don't need freedom.[30]

Silvia Federici and others have also made clear the problematic nature of machinic thinking when it comes to the question of work. The celebration of the machine and the relative neglect of care work and other forms of embodied, human reproductive labor partly stem from the dominance of a certain Marxist inheritance. Federici writes:

> I suggest that Marx ignored women's reproductive labor because he remained wedded to a technologistic concept of revolution, where freedom comes through the machine, where the increase in the productivity of labor is assumed to be the material foundation for communism, and where the capitalist organization of work is viewed as the highest model of historical rationality, held up for every other form of production, including the reproduction of the workforce. In other words, Marx failed to recognize the importance of reproductive work because he accepted the capitalist criteria for what constitutes work, and he believed that waged industrial work was the stage on which the battle for humanity's emancipation would be played.[31]

When imagining the overturning of the existing order in favor of a humanist future where bonds of love dominate over cold, inhuman division, it is critical that we remember the feminist critique of the way in which reproductive labor continues to be deliberately obscured. We must also pay critical attention to the way in which emotion, love, and care are mobilized and monetized by an economy that weaponizes even the most human sentiments.

## CONCLUSION: THE PROBLEM OF SPONTANEITY

In this final section, I simply want to pose a question concerning spontaneity, and what it means for our feminist response to the eros effect. Katsiaficas repeatedly stresses the centrality of this concept to the eros effect, opposing both the attempting dominance of central organizing and revolutionary parties (which, as we have seen, are often not at all revolutionary for the women involved in them). But as I have argued throughout, if we start with social reproduction, we understand that relations of care and love *already exist* and have always already existed. They may be exploited by both patriarchy and capitalism, but they exist nonetheless, and they provide material and practical evidence of the possibility of organizing society in a very different way. We saw how the classical model of strikes and laying down of tools could not apply to the vast majority of socially reproductive work, and it remains absolutely crucial to ask: What if, rather than postulating revolution as some kind of spontaneous global gesture of solidarity in which "[p]eople intuitively [believe] that they could change the direction of the world from war to peace, from racism to solidarity, from external domination to self-determination, and from patriotism to humanism"[32] as Katsiaficas has it, we might *begin* from the existence of relations of care, love, and solidarity as they already manifest themselves (despite the best efforts of capitalism to exploit and undermine them)?

Care cannot be spontaneous in exactly the same way as revolutionary uprisings imagined as a surge of newness, because it already exists, everywhere. There are of course spontaneous acts of care—dashing into the road to save a child from being hit by a car, for example. But these take place against the backdrop of care as the context for social life itself. What uprisings make visible is the demand for care to be realized and extended, to become the foundation for social life as a whole, as opposed to being buried and taken for granted. Feminism seeks to draw attention to the way in which care and love are underplayed, neglected, and gendered. Perhaps, then, the revolutionary gesture is in acknowledging this and imagining what a world might look like in which care and love in their fullest senses are afforded a central role for all humanity. Whatever revolutionary spontaneity we envisage must be one that at the same time protects and extends relations of care that already exist—these ties that may not yet even describe themselves as "revolutionary," though without them all social life would collapse. Instead of an "effect," it might be better to think of eros as *a* "cause," if not *the* cause, that underpins the whole of social life and that provides the seeds of the revolution that is both already here and yet to come.

## NOTES

1. George Katsiaficas, interviewed by AK Thompson, "Remembering May '68: An Interview with George Katsiaficas," *Upping the Anti* 6 (April 2008): n.p., http://uppingtheanti.org/journal/article/06-remembering-may-68/.

2. George Katsiaficas, "From Marcuse's 'Political Eros' to the Eros Effect: A Current Statement," chap. 3 this volume, p. 55.

3. Katsiaficas, "Remembering May '68," n.p.

4. Ibid., n.p.

5. Jason Del Gandio and AK Thompson, "Introduction," this collection, p. 3.

6. Karen Elizabeth Davis, "I Love Myself When I Am Laughing: A New Paradigm for Sex," *Journal of Social Philosophy* 21, no. 2–3 (September 1990): 5–24 (5).

7. Ibid., 5.

8. Ibid., 5.

9. Ibid., 7.

10. Jessica Benjamin, *The Bonds of Love: Psychoanalysis, Feminism and the Problems of Domination* (New York: Pantheon Books, 1988), 41.

11. Sheila Rowbotham, *Woman's Consciousness, Man's World* (Middlesex: Penguin Books, 1973), xi.

12. For more on this point, see Joshua Clover's excellent book *Riot.Strike. Riot.* (London: Verso, 2016).

13. Del Gandio and Thompson, "Introduction," p. 4.

14. Katsiaficas, "Remembering May '68," n.p.

15. Ibid., n.p.

16. Ibid., n.p.

17. Ibid., n.p.

18. See, for example, Ching-In Chen, Jai Dulani, and Leah Lakshmi Piepzna-Samarasinha, eds., *The Revolution Starts at Home: Confronting Partner Abuse in Activist Communities*, available here: https://lgbt.wisc.edu/documents/Revolution-starts-at-home.pdf.

19. Lydia Sargent, ed., *The Unhappy Marriage of Marxism and Feminism: A Debate on Class and Patriarchy* (London: Pluto Press, 1986 [1981]), xii.

20. Ibid., xiii.

21. Katsiaficas, "From Marcuse's 'Political Eros' to the Eros Effect," chap. 3 this volume, p. 54.

22. Davis, "I Love Myself When," 9.

23. Ibid., 17.

24. Katsiaficas, "Remembering May '68," n.p.

25. Arlie Russell Hochschild, *The Managed Heart: Commercialization of Human Feeling* (Berkeley: University of California Press, 2003 [1983]), 7.

26. Selma James, *Sex, Race and Class, The Perspective of Winning: A Selection of Writings, 1952–2011* (Oakland: PM Press, 2011), 72.

27. Ibid., 81.

28. Kathi Weeks, interview with Katie Cruz, "A Feminist Case for Basic Income," *Canadian Dimension*, August 11 2016, https://canadiandimension.com/articles/view/a-feminist-case-for-basic-income-an-interview-with-kathi-weeks.

29. James, *Sex, Race and Class*, 82.

30. Katsiaficas, "Remembering May '68," n.p.

31. Silvia Federici, *Revolution at Point Zero: Housework, Reproduction, and Feminist Struggle* (Oakland: PM Press, 2012), 95.

32. George Katsiaficas, "Eros and Revolution," *Radical Philosophy Review* 16, no. 2 (2013): 491–505 (492).

12

# Waves of Protest, the Eros Effect, and the Social Relations of Diffusion

LESLEY WOOD

How do we best understand the recent global cycles of contention? This chapter analyzes the first 206 events within Canada's 2012–2013 indigenous-led mobilization Idle No More as represented by social media and indigenous writing and in the mainstream press. To understand how this wave of protest spread, the chapter compares two approaches: the first is George Katsiaficas' eros effect, and the second is Sidney Tarrow's work on diffusion that draws on a "dynamics of contention" approach to social movements. Neither approach adequately explains variation in the participation and spread of these waves. However, an analysis of stories of emotion enables us to incorporate Katsiaficas' emphasis on pleasure and solidarity into Tarrow's emphasis on relational patterns of action. In this way, we are better able to understand both how and why waves of protest unfold in particular ways.

The drummers pounded out a steady heartbeat as the young woman looked at her friend, grinned, and grabbed her hand. Heads held high, the two joined the end of the chain of people snaking past them in the food court in the Sudbury, Ontario, shopping mall. The event they joined was one of seventy-nine that took place that day as part of the wave of protest known as Idle No More.

The rapid and euphoric spread of the indigenous-led mobilization (with its unique symbols, frames, and tactics) in 2012 coincided with many similar protest waves occurring around the same time. How should we understand such waves?[1] In what follows, I provide an account of Idle No More that challenges Katsiaficas' dismissal of social movement theory by showing how the latter provides important insights into the way that waves of protest operate. To be sure, I believe that Katsiaficas is right to challenge the tendency for many social movement theorists to assume that movement participation is purely a question of rational action, as well as their tendency to overlook the question of *why* waves of protest emerge at given moments. Despite these shortcomings, I believe that Sidney Tarrow's analysis of protest waves offers insight into *how* waves of protest unfold. Such information is not only of interest to academics, but also to activists trying to understand how best to spread and intensify protest. In isolation, however, neither Katsiaficas' account of the eros effect nor studies focused on the dynamics of contention can fully explain why and how mobilizations like Idle No More can and do vary across time and space.

I must acknowledge that I am a white settler writing on land that has been a home and hunting grounds to many peoples, including the Haudenosaunee, Wendat, and always the Mississaugas of the New Credit. I should also situate myself as a scholar. I am a sociologist who analyzes the micro and macro interactions that influence social movements. My work asks why social movements vary in their form and tactics and what influences their outcomes. As an activist, I want to know how to make movements more effective. My framework draws both from the contentious politics framework of Charles Tilly and Sidney Tarrow and the narrative sociology of Francesca Polletta. The ideas presented in this chapter reflect this disciplinary background.


## IDLE NO MORE: A WAVE OF PROTEST


Idle No More was initiated by four women (three indigenous, one non-indigenous) in Saskatchewan at the end of October 2012. On November 17, these activists organized their first teach-in about two omnibus budget bills then before the House. The first, C-38, would make it easier to sell off indigenous land to mining and petroleum interests.[2] The second, C-45, would remove provisions for the environmental protection of waterways, which were seen as barriers to pipeline development. As per usual, the government had not consulted indigenous communities before the bills were proposed. Anger mounted. On December 6, Assembly of First Nations (AFN) chiefs marched on Parliament Hill with the aim of addressing the House of Commons about the bills.

Called by the Idle No More organizers, the first national day of action on December 10, 2012 saw fifteen rallies and marches across the country. In Edmonton, 1,500 protestors marched, held a pipe ceremony, spoke out, and sang against the bills while acting in solidarity with the Beaver Lake Cree Nation fighting ongoing tar sands developments in Northern Alberta. The following day, Chief Theresa Spence of Attawapiskat began a hunger strike outside the federal government buildings in Ottawa to demand that greater respect and attention be paid to indigenous communities and their needs.[3] At this point, both mainstream and social media coverage of the movement increased. On December 13, members of the Samson Cree Nation blockaded Highway 2A in Alberta. Their action was followed by two protests in the Maritimes. Although Idle No More protests were gaining momentum, the federal government passed the second of the two bills, Bill C-45, on December 14, 2012.

Despite this setback, the mobilization continued to gain momentum. Its objectives expanded from repealing the omnibus bills to include "the stabilization of emergency situations in First Nations communities accompanied by an honest collaborative approach to addressing issues relating to Indigenous communities and self-sustainability, land, education, housing, healthcare, among others," and "a commitment to a mutually beneficial nation-to-nation relationship between Canada, First Nations (status and non-status), Inuit and Metis communities based on the spirit and intent of treaties and a recognition of inherent and shared rights and responsibilities as equal and unique partners. A large part of this includes an end to the unilateral legislative and policy process Canadian governments have favoured to amend the Indian Act."[4]

On December 15, there were two Idle No More rallies—one in North Battleford, Saskatchewan, and one in Thunder Bay, Ontario. Additionally, band members from at least three First Nations in Manitoba—including Sandy Bay, Long Plain, and Swan Lake—blocked the Trans-Canada Highway, while members of the Frog Lake Band in Alberta blocked Highway 28. In the first use of a tactic that would come to symbolize the movement, five hundred indigenous people and supporters in Regina Saskatchewan organized the first flash mob round dance in the Cornwall Square Mall on December 17. Accompanied by singing and drumming, round dances are traditional indigenous circle dances used to bring communities together.[5] That same day, a round dance took place at the Enoch Arena in Enoch, Alberta. One video shot at the Regina round dance flash mob has (as of 2015) been viewed more than 18,000 times, and shared 136 times—the vast majority in the two weeks following the event.[6]

The following day witnessed a flash mob round dance with hundreds of participants in the West Edmonton Mall. The event was also filmed and shared widely. One clip, uploaded by Paula E. Kirman, has been viewed over 95,000 times (as of 2015) and shared 547 times.[7] In the subsequent seven days, there were more than 120 events affiliated with the movement, including 39 round dances and 12 blockades. To track these events, I have used an event catalog with data pertaining to the first two hundred events to take place during the two months (November and December 2012) following the rise of Idle No More.[8]

The videos shot at round dances and posted on YouTube and other sites inspired imitation. On December 19, there were eleven more events. These included the first round dance in Ontario and the first event in the United States. Two days later, the second National Day of Action on December 21, 2012, included at least seventy-nine events, including twenty-two round dances (thirteen of which were in malls) and eight blockades.[9] After this point, protesters across the country mobilized half a dozen events each day until the end of 2012. Another spike in mobilization occurred on January 5, 2013, and again on January 11, 2013.

While the overall shape of the protest wave is easy to discern, it is important to note the variations in levels of participation, diversity of par-

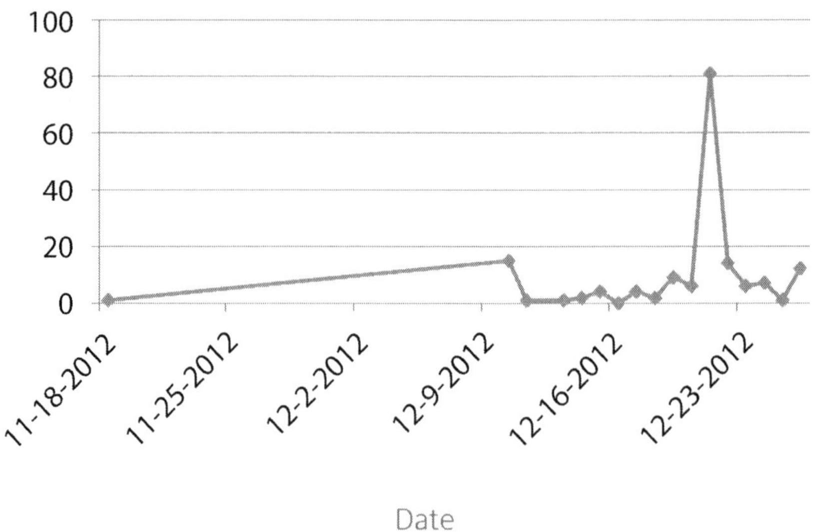


Figure 12.1. Number of Idle No More Protests per day, November–December, 2012.

ticipants, organizational form, and protest tactics used in different regions and at different moments. The excitement faded more quickly in some places than in others. By March 2013, activists in many places had shifted away from street protests and round dances toward the slower work of building new campaigns, networks, and institutions. Sometimes, they identified as Idle No More in this work while, at other times, they did not. Meanwhile, some former participants demobilized entirely.

While this is a typical pattern for a protest wave, the Idle No More wave has some particular features. Initial data concerning the overall shape of protest waves associated with Idle No More, Occupy Wall Street, and Black Lives Matter show differences with respect to their duration, the sharpness of their rise and fall, and the number of their peaks.[10] While all three movements accelerated rapidly, when compared with Black Lives Matter (where spikes correspond with police brutality and court decisions) and Occupy (where spikes correspond with eviction attempts), Idle No More slows more gradually, with spikes corresponding to movement-directed days of action.

## TRYING TO UNDERSTAND VARIATION IN WAVES OF PROTEST

Since the emergence of the wave of protest associated with the Arab Spring, *indignados*, and Occupy Wall Street, there has been a flood of studies concerned with waves of protest, diffusion, and cycles of struggle.[11] Such waves are generally understood in one of three ways. The first approach, reflected in this book, emphasizes the eros effect. The second, favored by autonomous Marxists, frames waves as a manifestation of the "circulation of struggle."[12] The third approach, used by social movement theorists like myself, ties waves of protest to relational patterns of diffusion, which are themselves a part of broader political processes. Considering these various approaches, Katsiaficas provides the following summary:

> The Marxist notion of the circulation of struggle and the concept of diffusion are valuable because they show that struggles impact each other. Diffusion—what Samuel Huntington called "snowballing"—can help us to trace how one thing causes another, which causes another in turn. But neither theory allows us to comprehend the simultaneity of struggles that occurs during moments of the Eros effect. It's not just causes, not just A plus

B equals C. Events erupt simultaneously at multiple points and mutually amplify each other. They produce feedback loops with multiple iterations. To put it in terms of a mathematical analysis, we could say that diffusion and the circulation of struggles describe the process of movement development geometrically. The Eros effect describes these same developments in terms of calculus.[13]

In opposition to this characterization, I argue that a relational analysis of diffusion can usefully be integrated with the emotional and psychoanalytic elements of the eros effect. A relational approach tracks the micro-interactions of communication, exchange, competition, and collaboration among activists. Not only does such an approach provide a more comprehensive understanding of the dynamics of movement development, it also reflects the perspective of the activists themselves and can help to explain variation within waves of protest like Idle No More.

The event catalog data presently under consideration map the emergence of the Idle No More wave, which became visible on account of the increasing number of protests, bigger events, increased media coverage, and the addition of new participants and locations. Nevertheless, the question remains: How do we understand this wave? If we begin with the participants' own perspectives, we hear stories like the one recounted by Lesley Bellau, an Anishinaabe woman from Garden River First Nations, who described Idle No More using the Anishinabek word *Pauwauwaein*. Bellau cites indigenous legal scholar John Borrows, explaining that this term is best understood to mean "a revelation, an awakening, a vision that gives understanding to matters that were once previously obscure." She argues, "something extremely significant happened during the months of December 2012 and January 2013. It was a time of great action, of a great collective voice that rose together to work toward resistance, decolonization, cultural revival, and to hold hands within a new and possible hope that was only seen in fragments and small and scattered pieces before this."[14]

Such a description appears to coincide with the insights of settler theorists of both the eros effect and of relational analysis, which both aim to explain the sudden expansion of protest activity and interaction. Drawing on Herbert Marcuse's psychoanalytic dialectics to understand why such waves emerge, Katsiaficas attributes them to the eros effect, which he describes as "the massive awakening of the instinctual human need for justice and for freedom."[15] In such moments, self-interest is translated into universal interest; it signals a rupture in the status quo and a disruption of social control.[16] For Katsiaficas, the eros effect is the trigger for the negation of established patterns of interaction and the creation of new (and better) ones. "During moments of the eros effect, popular movements not only imagine a new way of life and a different social reality but millions of people live according to transformed norms, values and beliefs."[17] Such claims are rooted in the observations advanced by Marcuse, who connected the eruption of protest to changes in the social structure, which in turn shifted the "instinctual structure" and thus increased inner antagonisms and loosened traditional mental ties.[18] For his part (and though they seem to have more in common with social movement theory's analysis of diffusion), Katsiaficas does not dismiss factors like the spread of television in his analysis of the 1968 wave of protest.[19] However, unlike in analyses focused on diffusion, he links the effects of those factors to an accumulation of "libidinal forces," which prompt the development of new formations before ultimately becoming "dynamite."[20]

Approaching the problem from a different perspective, social movement theorist Sidney Tarrow describes a "cycle of contention" as a "phase of *heightened conflict* across the social system" involving: "rapid diffusion of collective action from more mobilized to less mobilized sectors, a rapid pace of innovation in the forms of contention employed, the creation of new or transformed collective action frames, a combination of organized and unorganized participation, and sequences of intensified information flow and interaction between challengers and authorities."[21] Having identified the dynamics that characterize the cycle of contention, political process and (later) dynamics of contention theorists work to understand variations in contention across time and space. The political process approach emerged partly in reaction to psychological explanations of collective behavior, which characterized protest as pathological.[22] In contrast, political process theorists emphasize the rational, relational, and patterned nature of political protest. Using this framework, Tarrow's definition of the cycle of contention highlights the temporary nature of a wave—its content of conflict, the social interactions that underlie the rising and falling levels of contention, and the sub-processes of diffusion, brokerage, and innovation.[23] Such analysis brackets psychological dynamics, which are considered to be outside the realm of analysis. In the late 1990s, political process theorists increasingly looked for recurrent processes and mechanisms within dynamics of contention and began to unpack protest cycles in more detail. Tarrow and his collaborators then pointed out how the acceleration of protest cycles can lead to "scale shift," a phenomenon in which mobilization transcends its local arena to become national or even transnational.[24] In this way, "localized action spawns broader contention when information from the

initial action reaches a distant group, which having defined itself as suffi-
ciently similar to the initial insurgents (attribution of similarity), engages
in similar action (emulation), and leads ultimately to coordinated action
between the two sites."[25]

Tarrow's emphasis on the "attribution of similarity" or identification
mechanism is in some ways homologous to elements associated with the
eros effect. Both could be seen as facilitating brokerage (linkages between
people) and diffusion (the spread of an idea or practice).[26] While the eros
effect leads people to act simultaneously due to a shared accumulation of
libidinal forces, when potential participants/adopters see themselves and their
context as similar to earlier participants/adopters, they "attribute similarity"
and act. The presence or absence of this attribution of similarity explains
whether innovations and mobilizations are likely to spread. However, this
mechanism is seen as dependent on shared characteristics. As McAdam and
Rucht argue, "All instances of diffusion depend on a minimal identification of an adopter with a transmitter."[27] Moreover, attribution of similarity
is facilitated between transmitters and receivers if they share a common
institutional locus as well as adherents from the same strata and a common
language.[28] However, the precise means by which people actually attribute similarity remains hidden since the dynamics of contention approach
brackets activists' subjectivities. As a result, the discussion of the feelings
that enliven both Bellau and Katsiaficas' accounts is absent.


## WAVES ACROSS THE LAND

Clearly, waves of protest do not simply spread across space and time uni-
formly. Idle No More became visible in early December across Canada, but
the response by local activists in different cities varied in three dimensions:
temporal, tactical, and with respect to size.

Organizers of Idle No More protests in each city have the best sense of
why the protests unfolded the way they did. However, this "insider' knowledge
remains relatively inaccessible to analysts concerned with mapping broader
social patterns. Admittedly, relying on social media and mainstream media
might overestimate the size of protests, might miss events that don't use a
particular frame or keyword, and/or might be unable to capture dynamics
outside of "events." However, these data do show variation within the
wave of protest. How might we explain this variation? While dynamics of
contention theorists see the explanation in the context (its political opportunities, mobilizing structures, and frames) and how these affect relational

Table 12.1. Idle No More Protests in Four Cities, December 10–30, 2012

|  | Vancouver | Toronto | Halifax | Montreal |
|---|---|---|---|---|
| 12/10/2012 | March/rally–200 | March/rally–50 |  |  |
| 12/14/2012 |  |  | March/rally 200 |  |
| 12/20/2012 |  |  |  | Blockade/ march–40 |
| 12/21/2012 | Rally–500 | Round dance–500 | News conference and panel 200 | Round dance |
| 12/22/2012 | Round dance in mall 200 |  |  |  |
| 12/23/2012 | Rally 400 + Round dance in mall–200 |  |  |  |
| 12/24/2012 |  |  |  | Round dance in mall near Montreal–600 |
| 12/26/2012 | Round dance–100 |  |  |  |
| 12/28/2012 |  |  |  | Round dance |
| 12/30/2012 |  | Round dance in mall 250 |  |  |

ties, Katsiaficas points toward the ways that particular moments trigger a widespread release of action.[29]

## Temporal Variation

With the onset of Idle No More, why did activists in Vancouver and Toronto mobilize earlier than those in Montreal and Halifax? While recognizing that protest activity is only the tip of the movement iceberg,[30] examining the ways the two approaches consider the timing of mobilization can be useful in illuminating their differences and angles. Dynamics of contention theorists explain temporal variation by looking at the relational context and perceptions of actors in a particular political regime (political opportunities and threats), available mobilizing structures, resources, and frames.[31] Regimes can facilitate mobilization when influential or controversial decisions are made or when the ruling regime is itself divided, unstable, or unusually consultative. Under such conditions, activists may perceive an opportunity. Such contexts are therefore associated with increased contention, increased alliances between challengers and dissident elites, and increased success by challengers.[32] In the case of the omnibus bills that prompted the explosion of Idle No More, activists in different cities shared the perception of an opportunity even after the bills had passed due to the increased attention to the movement by media and political authorities. However, differences in mobilizing structures and the resources available to activists in different cities helped to explain variations in mobilization. Each city varied in the size and organization of its local indigenous community. The cities with the largest aboriginal populations (Vancouver and Toronto) mobilized first.[33] Each of these cities had indigenous organizations that mobilized on December 10 (the United Nations Human Rights Day). The larger communities and their mobilizing structures were resources to the activists. In addition, differing local contexts affected how the movement's "frames" would be received. Frames (slogans, images, phrases) that activists use to explain their activity can resonate or fail to do so in a particular community, affecting the attribution of similarity and thus speeding or slowing mobilization. The Idle No More frame was likely interpreted differently in different communities, affecting the speed of mobilization. Mobilizing structures, resources and frames, and the way they help local activists to identify with the emergent movement can help to explain variation in the timing of mobilization; however, they say little about *why* an activist would identify with or join the Idle No More mobilization in the first place.

Katsiaficas might argue that such variations are minutiae. Indeed, he challenges the emphasis on resources in political process theory: "I hope to renew the tradition of thought that views human beings (not resources, organizations, and/or the ebb and flow of economic wealth) as central to the transformation of social reality."[34] Consequently, he "seeks to understand the nature of group behavior in moments of social crisis as attributes of human beings, not simply as caused by social conditions. My approach attempts to reintegrate the emotional and the rational at a level on which emotional and irrational are neither synonymous in their usages nor derogatory in their characterizations."[37] For Katsiaficas, the patterns of Idle No More would reflect a "logic of human action" giving expression to the subjectivities of human beings, rather than a reaction to shifting social conditions.[36] Because his approach sees such logics as analogous to "historical-philosophical laws," the role of existing organizations, resources, and frames would be viewed as ephemeral to the ebbs and flows of Idle No More.

### Tactical Variation

Round dances are not new. Although they are most associated with Cree and Anishinabek culture, round dances have been enacted by indigenous people in different nations for generations. Nevertheless, round dances gained a new, contemporary appeal when carried out without warning as "flash mobs" recorded on video and shared on social media. In January 2013, Ojibwe spiritual leader David Courchene Jr. argued that these dances were significant. "There is a lot of excitement, I think, with young Aboriginal people. Round dances are sweeping across the country. I just hope that it's kept in the spirit of the way that it was meant to be, which is to have peace and respect. People are looking for inspiration and guidance to a better world."[37]

Although round dance flash mobs became the representative tactic of Idle No More, they weren't used everywhere. Idle No More activists did not use them in Halifax, Quebec City, Chilliwack BC, or San Francisco. How might we understand this variation? Both political process and eros effect approaches connect waves of protest to the spread of tactics and symbols. Dynamics of contention theorists have shown how new or revitalized tactics or symbols can help to increase the level and spread of mobilization.[38] Different cycles of contention become identified with innovative forms of action, which can leave elites at least temporarily uncertain regarding how to respond and thus opening political space for innovation and diffusion.[39] Social movement theorists have tied different tactical innovations to different waves of protest. These include barricades during the 1848 revolutions, factory occupations following WWI and during the 1930s,[40] sit-ins during the Civil Rights Movement,[41] and, most recently, round dances during Idle No More. An action can affect the likelihood of subsequent actions in a number of ways. It can create occasions for action and alter material conditions in favor of mobilization by changing a group's social organization, by altering beliefs, or by adding knowledge.[42] However, activists in certain types of receiving contexts tend to be more able and willing to incorporate new tactics than others. Some work in the dynamics of contention tradition explains this variation by suggesting that spaces where potential adopters might deliberate about new tactics and their meaning and use are more likely to experiment with that tactic.[43] While such an analysis of the Idle No More movement would require deeper qualitative research, such work directs us to look at how local activists interacted and made decisions to understand the variation in the use of round dances.

Because Katsiaficas tends to explore *why* rather than *how* waves of protest are shaped, less attention is paid to the way that a particular tactic would change the pattern of interaction. This is unlike the dynamics of contention research, which shows how tactical innovations like sit-ins, shantytowns, and black blocs have often accelerated and diversified mobilization and increased the scale of protest.[44] While Katsiaficas explains how US activists in 1970 began blocking roads across the country, by his account "people didn't block highways because they heard that people elsewhere in the country were doing it. It was just what people thought they should do."[45] The novelty or characteristics of a particular tactic are bracketed. Emphasizing a dialectical process, mobilization becomes a form of erotic action that clears "collective psychological blockages." In this view, "episodes of the eros effect are regarded as the collective sublimation of the instinctual need for freedom."[46] This description resembles the way Idle No More activist Tanya Kappo, from Sturgeon Lake Cree Nation, Treaty 8 in Alberta, speaks about a round dance at the West Edmonton Mall in December 2012: "The power and energy that was there, it was like we were glowing, our people were glowing. For the first time, I saw a genuine sense of love for each other and for ourselves. Even if it was only momentary, it was powerful enough to awaken in them what needed to be woken up—a remembering of who we were, who we are."[47] Powerful descriptions like these are clearly pointing out key dimensions that help both to shape and explain waves of protest. The pleasure and intense emotion associated with the use of such tactics inspires imitation and mobilization. However, an absence of the eros effect is more mysterious. Why didn't the activists in San Francisco who mobilized with Idle No More choose to round dance? Katsiaficas' emphasis on love, connection, and spontaneity deemphasizes activist explanations of their strategy. Although he is underscoring a key dimension of protest, he has more difficulty accounting for variation within waves of protest.

### Variation in Size and Quantity of Events

The Idle No More data clearly show that some cities had larger and more frequent mobilizations than others. Of the four cities under review, both the largest and the greatest number of events took place in Vancouver. In contrast, Halifax had the fewest events and those in Montreal were smallest. Why? A dynamics of contention approach that emphasized the role of resources would suggest that larger cities are likely to have larger and more frequent mobilizations. This makes sense; however, it seems to contradict the fact that, although Halifax's indigenous community is smaller than Montreal's, there were more Idle No More events in the former city than in the latter. To understand why this might be the case, one could also look at the mobilizing structures (organizations and networks) in the different cities, their networks and history. As Katsiaficas has noted, existing organizations may sometimes attempt to control or squelch action. Discussing the Arab Spring protests, he recalled how, "unfortunately, existing progressive, left organizations often play regressive roles in these periods of time."[48] In addition to resources and mobilizing structures, the way that local histories affected the way local activists interpreted or responded to the frames of the mobilization might also affect the size and quantity of events. Such in-depth work is beyond the purview of this chapter, but it would yield deeper insight into how local histories, interactions, resources, and cultures affected the diffusion of Idle No More. Katsiaficas might agree with this last point. In his interview "Remembering May '68," he notes that the ability to access historical memories of struggle can facilitate and shape uprisings.[49] This ability, it seems, varies from place to place, due to histories of struggle and oppression.

## LACUNAE

While Tarrow and other political process theorists explain variations in the size, tactics, and timing of protest activity as arising from relational processes and mechanisms, they bracket the psychological processes that might lead people to break from ordinary routines and pour into the streets. Because such analysts are wary of explanations that see protest as irrational or pathological, they have unintentionally reduced social action to a rational calculus in which risks and opportunities are weighed against each other. Aware of the limitations of this perspective, there have been attempts within the political process framework to incorporate emotion. Tarrow himself notes that the social and emotional processes of trust, attribution of similarity, and the opportunity for thinking creatively about tactics and action help to explain diffusion and brokerage.[50] Similarly, both Sean Chabot and I have argued that deliberation can trigger cognitive and emotional reactions.[51] However, we don't offer much insight into *why* people feel joy and the sense of connection in these moments.

But, clearly, they do. Moreover, these feelings transform their actions and interpretations. Most sociologists and political scientists—including those working with dynamics of contention approaches—remain averse to explaining action as a product of psychic states. However, Francesca Polletta and others push the boundaries of this approach when they suggest that we can at least use the patterns of activist stories and storytelling to represent these states. In her article on storytelling in the Civil Rights Movement, Polletta quotes young civil rights activists explaining their activism using ambiguous phrases like "It was like a fever."[53] She found that, despite significant planning and organization, activists were likely to describe their movement as the result of something like spontaneous combustion. The participants' insistence on spontaneity suggests that, for them, the term meant something other than that the sit-ins were unplanned. Digging deeper, Polletta finds that the activists' shared emphasis on spontaneity signaled that they were independent from adult leadership, not being manipulated by communists, and were authentic and homegrown. The ambiguous stories that the students told were directed at least partly to themselves—and the telling of such stories helped to create a collective identity on behalf of which students took high-risk action. Activists used ambiguity to create a gap that kept causes and effects open and helped listeners to sympathize and identify with the movement.[53] Their use of ambiguity seems to offer the space for the emotional and psychic connection that Katsiaficas describes. While Polletta argues that patterns in storytelling are culturally learned, she sees their structure as meaningful. Consequently, examining these stories in a systematic way can help to explain both why and how particular activists join waves of protest.

## CONCLUSION

While the wave of protest has slowed, many are reflecting on the power of Idle No More and how it unfolded. Neither political process theory nor an analysis of the eros effect can fully explain the shape of the mobilization. Political process approaches may be able to explain why Idle No More spread more quickly and intensively to Vancouver and Toronto than to Montreal and Halifax. The variation in timing, form, and size clearly corresponds to differences in the size of indigenous communities and the development of existing activist infrastructure. However, this explanation cannot explain the feelings of intense connection and joy that fill the testimony of participants. While we may not be able to get at the psyche directly, we can—as Polletta suggests—get at the way these feelings are represented in story. By looking at the pauses and gaps in stories of joy and solidarity, we can build a more meaningful analysis of waves of protest, and better understand both why and how the world, sometimes, combusts.

## NOTES

1. My use of "waves of protest" is indebted to Sidney Tarrow's "cycles of contention." However, I prefer "waves of protest" because of its emphasis on diffusion.

2. For more on the background, see www.idlenomore.ca.

3. See Kind-nda-niimi Collective, *The Winter We Danced: Voices from the Past, the Future, and the Idle No More Movement* (Winnipeg: Arbeiter Ring, 2014), 21–26.

4. Ibid., 22.

5. "Photos: Idle No More Protesters Stage Flash Mob at Regina Mall," *Leader-Post*, December 18, 2012, http://www.leaderpost.com/news/regina/Photos+Id le+More+protesters+stage+flash+Regina+mall/7714700/story.html.

6. Smokey01Smoke, "Idle No More—Regina Round Dance Flash Mob," December 17, 2012, https://www.youtube.com/watch?v=QA_Hn84SrCM.

7. Paula E. Kirman, "Idle No More—Round Dance Flash Mob at WEM in Edmonton," December 18, 2012, https://www.youtube.com/watch?v=x2Nx4jUEZfc.

8. The event catalog is grounded in initial work done by researcher and journalist Tim Groves. In December 2012, he began to collect and map reports of all protest incidents affiliated with Idle No More, including media coverage and direct communication with organizers. He included event announcements, as well as subsequent reports. I have cleaned this data, checking links, removing duplicates, and finding additional verification of events. The data include 205 events from November and December 2012.

9. Blockades include information pickets of roads.

10. These waves are crudely compared using the Google trends data, which only capture the frequency of Google Searches for Idle No More, Occupy Wall Street, and Black Lives Matter.

11. See, for instance, Donatella della Porta and Sidney Tarrow, "Interactive Diffusion: The Coevolution of Police and Protest Behavior with an Application to Transnational Contention," *Comparative Political Studies* 45, no. 1 (2011): 119–152, doi: 10.1177/0010414011425665; Rebecca Kolins Givan, Kenneth M. Roberts, and Sarah A. Soule, eds., *The Diffusion of Social Movements: Actors, Mechanisms, and Political Effects* (New York: Cambridge University Press, 2010); Lesley J. Wood, *Direct Action, Deliberation, and Diffusion: Collective Action after the WTO Protests in Seattle* (New York: Cambridge University Press, 2012/2014).

12. See, for instance, Michael Hardt and Antonio Negri, *Empire* (Cambridge: Harvard University Press, 2000); and Nick Dyer-Witheford, *Cyber-Marx* (Chicago: University of Illinois Press, 1999).

13. George Katsiaficas, interviewed by AK Thompson, "Remembering May '68: An Interview with George Katsiaficas," *Upping the Anti* 6 (2008): n.p., http://uppingtheanti.org/journal/article/06-remembering-may-68.

14. Lesley Bellau, "Pauwauwaein: Idle No More to the Indigenous Nationhood Movement," in *The Winter We Danced*, ed. Kind-nda-niimi Collective (Winnipeg: Arbeiter Ring, 2014), 351.

15. George Katsiaficas, *The Imagination of the New Left: A Global Analysis of 1968* (Cambridge: Beacon Press, 1987), 10.

16. Ibid., 42.

17. George Katsiaficas, "The Eros Effect," personal website, 1989, http://www.eroseffect.com/articles/eroseffectpaper.PDF, 1.

18. Herbert Marcuse, *Eros and Civilization: A Philosophical Inquiry into Freud* (Boson: Beacon Press, 1992).

19. Katsiaficas, "Remembering May '68," n.p.

20. George Katsiaficas, "The Eros Effect and the Arab Uprisings," Z *Communications*, April 21, 2011, https://zcomm.org/znetarticle/the-eros-effect-and-the-arab-uprisings-by-george-katsiaficas, n.p.

21. Sidney Tarrow, *Power in Movement* (New York: Cambridge University Press, 2011), 199.

22. For examples, see Gustave Le Bon, *The Crowd: A Study of the Popular Mind* (New York: Viking Press, 1895); and Neil J. Smelser, *Theory of Collective Behavior* (Glencoe: Free Press, 1962).

23. Sidney Tarrow, "Dynamics of Diffusion," in *The Diffusion of Social Movements*, 204–219 (209).

24. Sidney Tarrow and Doug McAdam, "Scale Shift in Transnational Contention," in *Transnational Protest and Global Activism*, ed. Donatella della Porta and Sidney G. Tarrow (Lanham: Rowman & Littlefield, 2004), 121–147.

25. Ibid., 122.

26. Doug McAdam, Sidney Tarrow, and Charles Tilly, *Dynamics of Contention* (New York: Cambridge University Press, 2001), 333; Sidney Tarrow, *The New Transnational Activism* (New York: Cambridge University Press, 2005), 105.

27. Doug McAdam and Dieter Rucht, "The Cross-National Diffusion of Movement Ideas," *Annals of the American Academy of Political and Social Science* 528 (July, 1993): 56–74.

28. Ibid., 71.

29. Katsiaficas, "The Eros Effect and the Arab Uprisings," n.p.

30. Beyond the study of protest activity, social movement theorists also investigate decision-making, identity construction, organizational forms, resources, culture, strategy, biography, networks, alliances, and outcomes.

31. Sidney Tarrow, *Power in Movement* (New York: Cambridge University Press, 2011).

32. Ibid, 27.

33. I use the term "aboriginal" in reference to this statistic, as this is the term used by Statistics Canada, who define it in particular ways.

34. Katsiaficas, "The Eros Effect," 3.

35. Ibid., 3.

36. George Katsiaficas, "Remembering May '68."

37. Melissa Martin, "Round Dance: Why It's the Symbol of Idle No More," *CBC Manitoba*, January 28, 2013, http://www.cbc.ca/manitoba/scene/homepage-promo/2013/01/28/round-dance-revolution-drums-up-support-for-idle-no-more, n.p.

38. Doug McAdam, "Tactical Innovation and the Pace of Insurgency," *American Sociological Review* 48 (1983): 735–754; Charles Tilly, *Popular Contention in Great Britain, 1758–1834* (Cambridge: Harvard University Press, 1995).

39. della Porta and Tarrow, "Interactive Diffusion."

40. Frances Fox Piven and Richard Cloward, *Poor People's Movements: Why They Succeed, How They Fail* (New York: Random House, 1977).

41. Kenneth T. Andrews and Michael Biggs, "The Dynamics of Protest Diffusion: Movement Organizations, Social Networks, and News Media in the 1960 Sit-Ins," *American Sociological Review* 71, no. 5 (2006): 752–777.

42. Pamela Oliver and Dan Myers, "Diffusion Models of Cycles of Protest as a Theory of Social Movements" (conference paper, presented at the Congress of the International Sociological Association, Montreal, July 30, 1998), 2, http://www.ssc.wisc.edu/~oliver/PROTESTS/ArticleCopies/diffusion_models.pdf.

43. Wood, *Direct Action*.

44. For studies of tactical diffusion within the dynamics of contention tradition, see, among others, Kolins Givan, Roberts, and Soule, *The Diffusion of Social Movements*; and McAdam, "Tactical Innovation and the Pace of Insurgency."

45. Katsiaficas, "Remembering May '68," n.p.

46. Katsiaficas, "The Eros Effect," 8.

47. Tanya Kappo, interviewed by Hayden King, " 'Our People Were Glowing': An Interview with Tanya Kappo," in *The Winter We Danced*, 70.

48. Katsiaficas, "The Eros Effect and the Arab Uprisings," n.p.

49. Katsiaficas, "Remembering May '68," n.p.

50. Tarrow, *The New Transnational Activism*, 103–109.

51. Sean Chabot, *Transnational Roots of the Civil Rights Movement: African American Explorations of the Gandhian Repertoire* (Lanham: Lexington Books, 2012); and Wood, *Direct Action*.

52. Francesca Polletta, " 'It Was Like a Fever . . .': Narrative and Identity in Social Protest," *Social Problems* 45, no. 2 (1998): 137–159.

53. Ibid., 138.

# 13

# Eros Effect or Biological Hatred?

## AK THOMPSON

Take note of this one thing (for it is late):
Your fine philosophy, good sirs, you may proclaim
But till you feed us, right and wrong can wait!

—Ginny Jenny, in Bertolt Brecht,
*The Threepenny Opera*, act 2, scene 3

I

For many comrades who came of age (as I did) at the end of history, George Katsiaficas made Herbert Marcuse's intellectual and political legacy real. For, while we struggled as undergraduates to grasp the significance of "repressive desublimation," "surplus repression," and other similar formulations, Katsiaficas' "eros effect" seemed to speak to us directly. We could feel it on the street, at the riot, in those moments when elation meant our hearts might burst. First elaborated in *The Imagination of the New Left*[1] at a time when, wherever one looked, third-rate poststructuralists could be found feasting on the desiccated corpse of the humanist tradition, the eros effect stands out today as one of the most vital recent intellectual contributions to the Marcusian legacy—and not solely because, whereas many of Marcuse's insights concerned the *critique* of existing reality, Katsiaficas coined the terms that might help us to describe the moment of ecstatic transformation itself.

Following Marcuse's insight that there was a "biological foundation for socialism" that could be traced back to human "inclinations . . . and aspirations" that "become vital needs" (and that might even "cause dysfunction" if left unsatisfied),[2] Katsiaficas zeroed in on those mass insurgencies that, at given moments, seemed spontaneously to erupt around the world. In this view, although capitalism normally repressed our best instincts, global uprisings—like those that took place in 1848, 1968, and even in our most recent history of protest camps and occupied squares—had the power to restore fundamental aspects of our humanity. Indeed, by Katsiaficas' account, social movements themselves were notable for being important means by which people have historically "sublimated their basic need to become better human beings."[3] At its threshold, "sublimating Eros" so that it might (once again) find concrete and humanizing expression becomes the very substance of revolutionary activity.[4]

I first read *The Imagination of the New Left* in the mid-to-late '90s while struggling to complete my undergraduate degree between organizing meetings and court dates. The timing could not have been more perfect. Katsiaficas' Romanticism emboldened my own. Little wonder, then, that I stashed his book in my backpack as I made the trek to various turn-of-the-century trade summits where I witnessed comrades throw down like there was no tomorrow. Never had I felt more alive, and the eros effect provided a language for that feeling. When my own belated, *post-festum* analysis of those protests was published a decade later, it seemed obvious that I would ask Katsiaficas to blurb my book; I was exceptionally grateful when he obliged.[5]

But while the conceptual value and emotional force of the eros effect seemed self-evident to me at the time, further consideration has led me to catalog a variety of reservations concerning its analytic clarity. In a footnote to *The Subversion of Politics*, Katsiaficas characterized the eros effect as referring to "the sudden, intuitive awakening of solidarity"[6] that arises from the fact that "the politics of eros infuse everyday life with a content that subverts its would-be colonizers and preserves it as a reservoir of the life-force." Consequently, "the 'eros effect' indicates how social movements are an expression of people's loving connectedness with each other." And more: "movement participation . . . preserves and expands the domain of the heart—of all that is uniquely human, all that stands opposed to machine culture."[7] Tinged though they may be with a sentimentality that seems at odds with our own era's waning affect, these appear to be straightforward definitions. Nevertheless, by Katsiaficas' own admission, "much research remains to be done" before the dynamics of "spontaneous solidarity" or the "actions generated by popular upsurges" might truly be understood.[8]

Since the publication of *The Subversion of Politics*, Katsiaficas has committed himself to this research in a steadfast manner. Indeed, the release of *Asia's Unknown Uprisings*—a massive tome weighing in at a thousand pages over two volumes—is testament to this.[9] However, even a cursory review of these contributions makes clear that Katsiaficas' orientation has primarily been historical rather than analytic in character. Moreover, since (as concept) the eros effect has been both defined by and described through reference to the events that are said to give it expression, the elaboration of its attributes has followed an overwhelmingly tautological course. Given the conceptual primacy it has been afforded in Katsiaficas' oeuvre, it is in fact remarkable that the eros effect has remained as analytically indeterminate as it has.

Although I continue to be drawn to the eros effect and the horizon toward which it points, it benefits no one to hold analytic reservations in abeyance. Among these reservations, perhaps the most significant is the fact that, while Katsiaficas seems to have accurately described one means by which revolutionary activity becomes contagious,[10] it is not clear that his concept—despite claims to the contrary—properly describes the compulsion that leads people toward revolutionary action in the first place. Locating this compulsion and specifying its dimensions is of tremendous analytic importance, not least because it would help to delimit the scope of (and clarify the relationship between) various moments in the process of social change. In keeping with the principle that analysis without consequence is meaningless, however, we must acknowledge that such a clarification would be of significant strategic importance as well.

Indeed, even a cursory review of the revolutionary tradition affirms that different analytic assessments to what might provisionally be called "the motivation question" have lent themselves to vastly different strategic emphases. Unconvinced that people were spurred into action by triumphant moral visions, Marx refuted the prescriptions of the utopian socialists in order to place emphasis on the practical elaboration of concrete historical contradictions instead.[11] A useful corrective to what had come before, this perspective was nevertheless amended half a century later by Georg Lukács, who foregrounded how the problem of consciousness suggested that relying upon the scientific presentation of revolutionary possibility was insufficient when it came to achieving revolutionary aims.[12] Further developed by Gramsci, this line of reasoning ascended to the level of strategy.[13] Here, it gained prominence on the shifting terrain of a war of position we continue to fight today.

As currently elaborated, the eros effect suggests an analytic orientation to the problem of revolutionary motivation with implicit strategic implications (I say "implicit" because Katsiaficas himself has been reluctant to propose means of operationalizing his theory—or even of acknowledging that such an aim is feasible or desirable).[14] However, since there can be no revolution without strategy, and since the merit of any given strategy is contingent upon the clarity of the analysis upon which it is founded (and, further, since any analysis that does not lend itself to strategic application is doomed from the outset to become an object of scholastic contemplation), revolution itself demands that the eros effect be subjected—as concept, and not just as event—to the most exacting scrutiny.

Katsiaficas has indicated his willingness to engage in such a critical assessment. Indeed, when recounting the revolutionary limitations of the global insurgency of 1968, he acknowledges that the movement's emphasis on erotic spontaneity did not allow people to meet their revolutionary objectives. Consequently, "to rely on the awakening of a global eros effect alone to transform the world system would be shortsighted."[15] Such an admission is important; however, if relying solely upon the eros effect is not enough, it remains to be determined what else might be required.

Though it may at first seem paradoxical, perhaps what is lacking from this analysis is an engagement with lack itself.

II

In *The Subversion of Politics* and elsewhere, Katsiaficas has made his commitment to dialectical reasoning explicit. This orientation is in keeping with his professed intellectual allegiance to Herbert Marcuse and to the Marxist tradition more broadly. Nevertheless, and despite these stated commitments, Katsiaficas' work seems to ascribe a positive and even ennobling a priori content to human nature (a nature that, though debased by capitalism, might nevertheless be salvaged). Despite the fact that dialectical reasoning should generate an account of human ontology that reveals it to be at odds with normative prescriptions, one is hard-pressed when reading Katsiaficas to avoid detecting his strong investment in what might be considered a kind of a foundational will toward freedom. Although currently debased by capitalism, spontaneous global uprisings themselves suggest that this will (this freedom) might be recovered should conditions prove right. Such a recovery is both the historical task assigned to the eros effect and the evidence enlisted to buttress its conceptual validity. Wherever the emphasis is placed, however, it becomes clear that the eros effect is unimaginable when deprived of the normative groundwork through which it is said to find expression.

It is therefore not surprising that, for Katsiaficas, the eros effect manifests itself as a kind of mass awakening (of return as completion) that simultaneously provokes, is stimulated by, and helps to further global insurrection. Indeed, such insurrectionary moments are said to reactivate fundamental aspects of our being through "intuition, identification, and other processes." In turn, these affective-mimetic processes allow for genuine and affirming human bonds once again to be forged.[16] In the preface to *Subversion of Politics*, Katsiaficas describes the eros effect as "the capacity of human beings to grasp instinctually the gestalt of a movement." Consequently, upon being activated, it "connects our species at essential levels of life."[17] This may well be the case. However, before deciding that it is so, it remains necessary to ask: What, for Katsiaficas, constitute the "essential levels" of life?

Although the answer is not immediately evident, there is little point in denying that, as a Romantic postulate contesting the reason/emotion dichotomy that has plagued bourgeois thought since the seventeenth century (and that continues to find expression in various strands of social movement theory, where "political opportunity" stares down "collective behavior" in a never-ending fratricidal feud), an analysis that trades in "essential levels" and in things that are "instinctually" grasped can't help but carry an erotic charge. The proposition is not just affectively evocative, however. Indeed, for Katsiaficas, it is also an important corrective to the limitations currently plaguing social movement research. This is because "the inability of empirical research" of the kind carried out by social movement scholars "to comprehend rapidly changing situations and outbreaks" ultimately "makes its usefulness in the study of social movements highly dubious."[18]

To put it another way, reading Katsiaficas alongside other—more turgid—submissions to the social movement literature cannot help but yield a feeling similar to the one achieved by contrasting the vision of man championed by the Lake Poets to the one favored by rude mechanical thinkers like René Descartes.[19] Indeed, when considered from the standpoint of its affective weight, the eros effect seems perfectly to echo William Wordsworth's disparagement of formal intellectual pursuits ("enough of science and of art," he wrote) as he called on people to "come forth and bring with [them] a heart that watches and receives."[20] "The multitude has its own intelligence," says Katsiaficas. "It's the intelligence of the life force and the intelligence of the heart. It's not an intelligence of Cartesian duality. It's completely different."[21] But despite this Romantic allure, and quite apart from the limits that Katsiaficas has identified with his own preferred line,[22] the difficult questions that arise whenever we speak of "essential levels" force us to consider the nature of human nature itself.

Elaborating his perspective through a polemical engagement with social movement theory, Katsiaficas has critiqued the latter for studying "how we fight without considering why we fight."[23] Why, then, do we fight? According to Katsiaficas, the answer must be found in people's "inner desire for freedom, which is the greatest force for liberation on the planet."[24] Standing in opposition to positions such as those advanced by Hobbes, for whom human nature featured primarily as a foil to justify Leviathan, Katsiaficas seems closer to Rousseau (for whom "man is born free; and everywhere he is in chains").[25] Followed to its logical conclusion, this positive, a priori conception of freedom—this freedom held to be intrinsic to humanity but thwarted by historical accident—becomes an iteration of universal spirit. Transfiguring Hegel's otherwise historical "cunning of reason" into an inspired intrinsic drive, freedom becomes an "inner desire" propelling the world toward something it had been, in secret, all along.[26]

It should be admitted that, while positive ontology and dialectical reasoning are normally considered to be antithetical propositions, Katsiaficas has not been alone in following this course. Indeed, one can detect a similar inclination in the work of Walter Benjamin, for whom "our lives . . . are a muscle strong enough to contract historical time."[27] Similarly, Frantz Fanon described how, through the course of anticolonial struggle, it was "precisely at the moment" when the colonized subject "realizes his humanity that he begins to sharpen the weapons with which he will secure . . . victory."[28]

But while Katsiaficas seems to share common ground with Benjamin and Fanon by associating recovered humanity with the dialectical process from which it is said to arise and through which it finds expression, he distinguishes himself from them by asserting (despite formally repudiating any *telos*)[29] that the process will yield something he knows—or can anticipate the broad configurations of—in advance. Indeed, Katsiaficas has gone so far as to invoke the mythopoetic foundations of Jungian archetypes to buttress his arguments despite the fact that—as Benjamin noted—such archetypes were the bread and butter of fascism.[30] In another related instance, the search for a positive, foundational ontology led him to conclude that the model for human collectivity might best be surmised by contemplating the serene interactions of "caribou, birds, bees and ants."[31]

This stands in sharp contrast to the positions advanced by Benjamin and Fanon. Indeed, although Fanon's "new man" may imply a positive ontology (depending on whether one favors a compound-noun iteration or an adjective-modifier one), Fanon is explicit that "the natives' challenge to the colonial world is not . . . a treatise on the universal, but the untidy affirmation of an original idea propounded as an absolute."[32] From this perspective, it becomes clear that the "new man" is a historical creation whose only a priori is history itself—he is "original" in the sense of distinct rather than foundational, and he comes into being by the same process recounted by Marx in his "Theses on Feuerbach," where "man must prove the truth—i.e. the reality and power, the this-sidedness of his thinking in practice."[33]

Although what can be thought at any given moment is finite and restricted, the finitude that marks imagination is not the same as the finitude of body or world. For this reason, imagination introduces a tension into being. It throws the lack deriving from and inherent in our finitude into sharp relief. At the same time, it gives a concrete dimension to our revolutionary objectives as it arrays them across the field of the possible. As Benjamin argued, "our image of happiness is thoroughly colored by the time to which the course of our own existence has assigned us. The kind of happiness that could arouse envy in us exists only in the air we have breathed, among people we could have talked to, women who could have given themselves to us. In other words, our image of happiness is indissolubly bound up with the image of redemption."[34] From this perspective, revolutionary action doesn't recover humanity; it abolishes it through an act of sublation. As Marcuse proposed, "liberation" at its threshold comes to "incorporate the *universal* in the particular protest."[35] In contrast, and at its logical conclusion, Katsiaficas' positive ontology reveals itself to be the eros effect's very substance. Like an eternal return—to pure animality, to archetypical form—ecstatic transformation delivers us up to what we always were said to have been.

III

What are the strategic implications of this position? If the eros effect arises from (returns to) a positive a priori ontology in order that it might find a more complete realization in the present, it follows that we should emphasize forms of self-valorizing activity that can allow people to cultivate those tarnished or disparaged aspects of their being that point toward redemption. Here, politics becomes a process of recognizing and affirming a positive ontology's positive value. Indeed (and despite what I will demonstrate to be an overarching disposition toward the refusal of positive ontology), Marcuse seems to have had this in mind when he celebrated the way Black music brought its listeners back to themselves by collapsing the interval between the phylogenetic and the ontogenetic.[36]

If, however, analysis reveals that revolutionary aspirations are stimulated not so much by a normative a priori content but rather by something like a universal experience of lack, then our strategy must be reconsidered. For starters, such an analysis might compel us to contemplate what might be gained by intensifying the experience of lack itself so that the present's unbearable dimensions might be foregrounded. Strategically enabling,[37] this approach is also analytically useful since it helps to make plain the degree to which it is actually lack (and not a positive ontology, whether of human, bee, or caribou provenance) that constitutes the basis upon which the universal might be brought into—and ultimately realized through—the particular as Marcuse proposed. In other words, and in contrast to Katsiaficas' preferred and arguably antidialectical approach, starting from lack provides a means of connecting the universal to the particular (to the historically finite) without having to specify or speculate about a positive, valorizable content.

What is lack? Although the concept is now commonly associated with Lacan (for whom it was bound to the desire through which it found finite, concrete expression), it's important to recall that, conceptually, "lack" already played a clear role in Freud's account of the confrontation between the pleasure principle and the reality principle. Here, desire endures the deferral of its gratification while the subject of desire strives (always imperfectly) to transform the world so that its aims might someday be attained. Neuroses then arise from the inevitable imperfections that mar our attempts at reconciliation. Human activity is thus set in motion by the irritation that arises from the irreconcilability of drive and reality. Still, asks the a priori, where do these drives come from? Tempting though it may be to resolve the matter by invoking a positive ontology, another resolution is possible. And here we need to look no further than Marx's account of human history in *The German Ideology*, where "the satisfaction of the first need, the action of satisfying and the instrument of satisfaction which has been acquired, leads to new needs." In this formulation, the "creation of new needs is the first historical act."[38] Indeed, it is what makes us human.

In *Capital*, Marx recounts how the *natural* limits of the working day are determined by the need to "rest, sleep, and feed, wash, and clothe" oneself. Meanwhile, the *social* limits are determined by the need to satisfy "intellectual and social wants, the extent and number of which are conditioned by the general state of social advancement."[39] By highlighting the tendency for the particular character of "wants" to change according to "the general state of social advancement," Marx reveals why an a priori positive ontology can-not be the basis for revolutionary action. This is so not least because even "natural" limits (e.g., what it might mean, concretely, to "feed, wash, and clothe" oneself at any given moment) prove to be historically specific and subject to change—hence Raoul Vaneigem's famous rhetorical provocation, circa May '68: "Who wants a world where the guarantee of freedom from starvation means the risk of death from boredom?"[40] However one chooses to answer this query, it's clear that the content of the experience of lack changes along with the development of human society.

In addition to his analysis of the historical dynamics that give rise to human needs (and, indeed, to humanity itself), Marx further addresses the question of lack through his consideration of the unique role played by imagination in the human labor process. Describing the uniquely human dimension of this process, and contrasting humanity's efforts to those of bees (though the latter are favored by Katsiaficas), Marx underscores the fact that "the architect raises his structure in imagination before he erects it in reality."[41] Here, imagination signals that which is not yet. It is the force that presages the not yet's passage into being. The discrepancy between imagination and reality as given is nothing other than lack. By siding with bees, Katsiaficas seems to be at odds with this perspective. Nevertheless, he finds himself nearly echoing Marx when he recounts how the eros effect gives rise to "a chain reaction of insurrections and revolts" in which "new forms of power" emerge and "new visions of the meaning of freedom [are] formulated in the actions of millions of people."[42] In moments such as these, people develop an awareness of "previously non-existent aspects of reality which unexpectedly appear."[43]

But while "new visions" are placed in an immediate relationship to "the actions of millions," their formal conceptual distinction suggests that they might be theoretically parsed. If this is the case (and even if it is not explicit in his work), it becomes possible to imagine how Katsiaficas' theoretical posture might be reconciled with the approach in which lack is foregrounded to address the problem of a priori positive ontology. Given the apparent similarity between Katsiaficas' description of the eros effect in this passage and Marx's description of the role played by imagination in the human labor process, however, it is confounding that Katsiaficas goes on to repudiate the insights of this historical ontology to reprise and substantiate his more aesthetically affirming positive conception. To get a sense of this vacillation, it is useful to recall how, in *The Subversion of Politics*, Katsiaficas expresses hostility toward Antonio Negri's apparent reduction of all human activity to coordinated labor processes.[44]

The problem seems to owe to a confusion concerning Marx's use of the category "labor." On the one hand (and corresponding to imagination's connection to the experience of lack), labor for Marx stands out as being the defining attribute of human ontology, the historical means by which it comes to be associated with a positive content (whatever that content may be). It is the means by which human needs arise and are resolved—and thus the means by which human ontology escapes the domain of the a priori to become historical (and thus potentially revolutionary). Significantly, Marx distinguishes this conception of "labor" from the commodity "labor power," which arises with the advent of capitalism. Negri is charged with making a fetish of the latter conception, and consequently undermining revolutionary possibilities by reiterating the logic of the oppressive regime. Through the course of his repudiation, however, Katsiaficas goes one step further and seems to distance himself not only from labor power but labor itself.

In opposition to these reservations, diligent engagement with the intellectual tradition from which Katsiaficas' work is derived reveals that imagination, labor, and production together comprise the distinguishing features of human ontology. They are the reason that human ontology is historical, not natural, and that the motive force in human development is lack and not the recovery of some a priori ontological goodness. Pushed to its logical conclusion, it also becomes clear that this historical ontology is the very substance of politics (a particular field of human activity in which, among other things, political subjects capable of envisioning and realizing their desires through coordinated activity are produced). At its threshold, politics yields revolution, a transformation not solely of the object or the means, but of the very *mode* or production. And while it is hypothetically possible that the decisive violence required to initiate such a productive transformation can be mustered through appeals to a preconceived, normative "ought," it is more likely—as Benjamin famously pointed out—that it will be "nourished by the image of enslaved ancestors than that of liberated grandchildren."[45] In other words, the compulsion to pursue the "ought" arises less from its particular conceptual content than it does from the experience of lack emanating from the present's inadequacies. Additionally, this experience can be cultivated, intensified.

Like others, Katsiaficas seems to have found a conception of revolution in Marcuse that is closer to the humanizing "ought" and its positive content than it is to lack's content-unspecified concrete universality.[46] Nevertheless, and despite the ecstatic enthusiasm of his New Left devotees, an attentive reading of Marcuse's texts reveals that he was careful to foreground how the experience of lack reveals "a definite internal limit" to the possibility of worldly absolution. Even in the imagined horizon of revolution, human ontology is left to stand at odds with nature. And, since the pleasure principle and reality principle can never be made to coincide, "the end of this war . . . belongs to the Orphic myth, not to any conceivable historical reality."[47]

If there is to be a concrete ground for the universal, then, it is to be found not through the normative projection of erotic unity but rather through the intensification of our common, inevitable feeling of lack. This is so not least because the enduring desire to reconcile subject and object, part and whole, must ultimately run up against "the insurmountable limit to the mutability of human nature: a biological, not theological, limit."[48] Needless to say, this lack is a source of tremendous frustration. Moreover, this frustration (regardless of its particular content) is universal. Finally, it can be cultivated, intensified through the imagination's role in the human labor process, and directed toward the revolutionary transformation of society. That its aim will never be realized makes no difference. Possibility always owes its promise to the nonresolution from which it arises.

Although matters remain somewhat ambiguous in Marcuse's deliberations on eros (in which human instincts seem both to be given *and* historically contingent),[49] his awareness of lack's generative dimension becomes explicit through the "Great Refusal," a formulation advanced to underscore how revolution starts not with affirmation of the possible but rather with condemnation of the present's inadequacy. Indeed, the Great Refusal is a "protest against that which is." Through acts of negation aimed at confronting the lack inherent in existing reality (regardless of what that reality might be), people are said to discover "modes of refuting, breaking, and recreating their factual existence."[50] To the extent that revolution involves a process of historical awakening, Marcuse makes clear that it begins not with "recreating" but "refuting." Indeed, only with "gut hatred" (a force Marcuse held to be indispensable to the process of revolutionary change)[51] does the partisanship, the this-sidedness, inherent in any universality become clear.

Far from being antithetical to eros, hatred thus reveals itself to be its precondition. Corroborating the analysis of lack advanced by Marx and Freud, this Marcusian insight has also received considerable elaboration by other thinkers working in the critical tradition. For Paulo Freire, the violence of oppressed against oppressor constituted an act of love, since the latter could not free themselves from the finite bounds of their own parasitic being without the input of their adversary's deconstitutive force. Simultaneously, this violence (this Great Refusal) also transforms the oppressed by forcing them to confront their own "limit situation," the lack inherent in their ontological finitude—a lack that compels movement toward the realization of an ever more concrete universality.[52] Similarly, for Gramsci, revolutionary consciousness begins to take shape through hatred and negation, the adoption of what he called "the basic negative, polemical attitude."[53] For his part (and as we have already seen), Benjamin imagined that revenge alone could ensure that the positive content developed through the course of revolutionary activity would escape the tarnish of utopian inclinations and volatile ambivalence.

Tracing the revolutionary analysis of the role played by lack in this way makes clear that, while the experience always finds expression through particular forms, the *experience* itself is universal. Taken together, these two observations suggest that, rather than the eros effect (which presupposes a positive, a priori ontology), lack provides the basis for a universal project unburdened by normative conceptualizations.[54] This has dramatic implications for human solidarity—and for coalition politics, too. It suggests that revolution is prompted less by the thrill of spontaneity than by the burden of a shared, unendurable present. As Benjamin suggested, the challenge is highlighting the degree to which "every second of time" might therefore be "the strait gate through which the Messiah might enter."[55] Marcuse's Great Refusal underscores this same premise.

Even more telling than Marcuse's account of the Great Refusal, however, was his casual observation that liberation presupposed "biological hatred." Reviewing the legacy of anticolonial resistance movements in the 1966 "Political Preface" to *Eros and Civilization*, Marcuse recounts how occupying armies were shocked to confront "not only a social revolt in the traditional sense, but also an instinctual revolt—a biological hatred." As a result of this hatred, "the energy of the human body rebels against intolerable repression and throws itself against the engines of repression."[56]

Since it seems to suggest an active negation of unspecified content as well as a positive ontology (some line that cannot be crossed without bare life pushing back), this formulation may on first blush seem more ambiguous than the unequivocal Great Refusal. However, to the extent that this bare-life ontology suggests a positive content, it does so as a possibility occasioned by the process of historical development itself. Following Marx's observations concerning the historical origins of human needs, we might even say that the precise character of "biological hatred" is historically determined. "There is some shit I will not eat," claimed e.e. cummings' Olaf. Like all others, this Great Refusal (this biological hatred aimed at reality's abjection) owed to the particular stench of the shit he confronted—the shit of trench warfare, and of sovereignty wrapped in a bloody flag. And as the necessity of eating shit decreases, the more repulsive the idea becomes.

Paradoxically, the intensification of the feeling that things are intolerable gives symptomatic expression to our growing proximity (profane though it may be) to the Orphic myth.

## IV

I will be the first to concede that Katsiaficas' claims regarding human freedom are exceptionally appealing. Moreover, they seem to corroborate Marcuse's claims regarding the affinity between nature and socialism. In this vision, recovery and transformation become inseparable. "Without a reworking of the psyche and reinvigoration of the spirit," asks Katsiaficas, "can there even be talk of revolution? On the one side, the system colonizes eros, turning love into sex, and sex into pornography. Labor becomes production, production a job; free time has been turned into leisure, leisure into vacation; desire has been morphed into consumerism, fantasy into mediated spectacle."[57] In this passage, "reworking" rubs shoulders with "reinvigoration," suggesting that both processes (despite operating in ontologically distinct ways) are not only equally required but are in fact wholly compatible with one another. Nevertheless, the political action implicitly demanded by the colonization of eros by the system is that we return to prior forms (e.g., by retracing the steps from pornography to sex to love so that we might finally recover eros). Even here, however, it's important to note that one of these prior forms—labor—is precisely the force that stimulates our awareness of lack's inevitability. At its threshold, it leads us to abandon normative, content-based conceptions of revolution as well.

It might seem that "biological hatred" is a feeling suited uniquely to one's adversary. However, analytic consistency requires that we acknowledge how, at its logical conclusion, it is a concept that must be applied inwardly as well. Although Marcuse is not normally considered a nihilistic thinker, it's important to acknowledge the degree to which the Marxist tradition is inconceivable without the will to self-abolition. For Marx, the proletariat could not free itself without destroying the conditions of its own existence. Lukács found this formulation to be so significant that he underscored it in his considerations on "orthodox Marxism." Here, he cites Marx's observation that "the proletariat cannot liberate itself without destroying the conditions of its own life."[58] Following suit, Marcuse landed upon this same fact in *Counterrevolution and Revolt*. Not only did he note (provocatively, one might say) that love of the working class actually constituted a form of commodity fetishism,[59] he also foregrounded how the proletariat could not "free itself without abolishing itself as a class, and all classes. This is not an 'ideal,' but the very dynamic of the socialist revolution. It follows that the goals of the proletariat as revolutionary class are self-transcendent: while remaining historical, concrete goals, they extend, in their class content, beyond the specific class content."[60]

Pushed to their logical conclusion, such formulations make clear that, to transcend present limitations and ascend to the universal through profane, this-sided activity, one must first disavow the normative constraints of positive ontology—which also means to disavow oneself. "It is solely by risking life that freedom is obtained," said Hegel. "Only thus is it tried and proved that the essential nature of self-consciousness is not *bare existence*, is not the merely immediate form in which it at first makes its appearance, is not its mere absorption in the expanse of life."[61] Despite the dangerous uses to which it has been put historically, the universal continues to be a compelling framework from which to envision mass struggle. But rather than envisioning this "universal" in terms of an a priori positive content, it is worth considering how it might be more productively pursued by foregrounding the human confrontation with lack itself. From this perspective, revolution begins not with the eros effect but with biological hatred.

But while the eros effect ceases to be the source of revolutionary aspirations (since these arise more immediately from the content-unspecified but truly universal experience of lack), it does remain one means for their possible diffusion. Given the claims that have been advanced in its name, this may seem like a conceptual demotion. Nevertheless, the procedure should be considered felicitous by those seeking to save the concept from the contradictions marking its current elaboration.

Along with this analytic clarification, it is also important to consider the specifically strategic benefits of foregrounding lack. Here, rather than forging connection through invocation (through efforts to draw the masses to an amorphous but positive vision of the people, of humanity, or whatever else), intensifying the encounter with lack and stimulating biological hatred through a principled, self-effacing nihilism can productively heighten people's antagonism with the status quo while emphasizing the nonresolution they hold in common with everyone else. The most dangerous strategy in times of war, thought Machiavelli, was to trap one's enemy so that there was no escape. "Great care is . . . taken not to reduce an enemy to total despair," he wrote.

> Julius Caesar was always very attentive to this point in his wars
> with the Germans, and used to open a way for them to escape
> after he began to perceive that, when they were hard pressed

and could not run away, they would fight most desperately; he thought it better to pursue them when they fled, than to run the risk of not beating them while they defended themselves with such obstinacy.[62]

In opposition to Caesar's strategy (and in keeping with Gramsci's war of position), the foregrounding of lack's universality demands that we cut off each and every compelling but mythical pathway to resolution. Though they are seductive (and though they may seem to keep us from harm in the short run), such postures are ultimately self-defeating. For this reason, and in response to Caesar's cruel lesson, Machiavelli proposed that, if he were to build a fortress, he "would make its walls very strong" but ensure that there were "no retreating places" within. Through such a design, "the garrison might be convinced that when the walls and ditch were lost, they had no other refuge left."[63] It is toward this state that we too must gravitate.

V

Making formal conceptual distinctions in this way always runs the risk of reducing real-world complexities. Moreover, such distinctions are especially difficult to sustain when the material under consideration has been conceived dialectically. Indeed, because dialectics presupposes the formal interpenetration of opposites, the establishment of antithetical propositions can seem like a violation of the first premise. More simply, proceeding as I have may seem to be little more than a fruitless act of substituting a defiant (but ultimately resigned) "no" for the enthusiastic "yes" that seems to punctuate all of Katsiaficas' declarations with a defiant exclamation mark.

As Cindy Milstein has made clear, such unhelpful polarizations are not unusual in radical scenes. Describing "an anarcho-queer study group made up of . . . 'insurrectionists' and 'prefigurativists'" in an article about the decline of the Occupy movement, Milstein recounted a "friendly debate" that arose "after reading some of *Crack Capitalism* by John Holloway." She asked: "Does 'not making capitalism' begin with Holloway's 'No!' or instead a 'Yes!'?" Although Milstein's convictions led her to split the difference and settle on "maybe," it seems almost inevitable that "this playful argument . . . lasted for weeks, spilling into things like, 'Does dinner begin with a 'no' or a 'yes'?"[64]

Although such extreme outcomes are not inevitable, and though drawing a formal conceptual polarity between eros effect and biological hatred may seem to be little more than a contrarian indulgence, the move remains both analytically and strategically important. Analytically important, because the concrete investigation of lack grounds eros and gives it a practical historical dimension. As a concept without content, lack is both the concrete encapsulation of and the mediation between the universal and the particular. For this reason, and as Marx, Freud, and Marcuse have each made clear, lack is a fundamentally historical concept. Strategically important, because—while the substance of need and the character of lack may change over time—the psychic (and, indeed, the ontological) tensions it yields consistently obtain.

Expressed though it may be through a dizzying array of particularities, the experience of lack is a universal phenomenon. It arises from the developmental process inaugurated by the first human need and won't subside until *the schism between human history and natural history* is finally, decisively resolved (a resolution that, by virtue of our biological finitude, will never obtain). Given that this is the case, our primary strategic objective must not be the cultivation of eros (since, as positive content, erotic desire emanates from the confrontation with lack) but to *intensify* the confrontation with the intolerable nature of the present—regardless of what that present might be. As Lenin put it, "Working-class consciousness cannot be genuine political consciousness unless the workers are trained to respond to *all* cases of tyranny, oppression, violence, and abuse, no matter *what class* is affected . . ."

> The consciousness of the working masses cannot be genuine class-consciousness, unless the workers learn . . . to observe *every* other social class in *all* the manifestations of its intellectual, ethical, and political life; unless they learn to apply in practice the materialist analysis and the materialist estimate of *all* aspects of the life and activity of *all* classes, strata, and groups of the population.[65]

By leading with negation, critical theory demands that its advocates "abolish the opposition between an individual's purposefulness, spontaneity, and rationality, and those work-process relationships on which society is built."[66] For Horkheimer, by underscoring the lack of fulfillment available through existing means, it becomes possible to *heighten* the level of psychic and social conflict "until this opposition is removed."[67] At its logical conclusion, this procedure demands that we conceive eros not as a universal metaphysical life force but rather as a concrete and historically particular means by which people have aimed to resolve experiences of lack. Considered from the standpoint of motivations for revolutionary transformation, the eros effect can thus be seen to emerge from—and therefore to be of secondary importance to—the experience of biological hatred.

## NOTES

1. George Katsiaficas, *The Imagination of the New Left: A Global Analysis of 1968* (Cambridge: South End Press, 1987).

2. Herbert Marcuse, *An Essay on Liberation* (Boston: Beacon Press, 1969), 10.

3. George Katsiaficas, interviewed by AK Thompson, "Remembering May '68: An Interview with George Katsiaficas," *Upping the Anti: A Journal of Theory and Action* 6 (April 2008): n.p., http://uppingtheanti.org/journal/article/06-remembering-may-68/.

4. Ibid., n.p.

5. AK Thompson, *Black Bloc, White Riot: Anti-Globalization and the Genealogy of Dissent* (Oakland: AK Press, 2010).

6. George Katsiaficas, *The Subversion of Politics: European Autonomous Social Movements and the Decolonization of Everyday Life* (Oakland: AK Press, 2006), 270 n14.

7. Ibid., 221.

8. Ibid., 270 n14.

9. George Katsiaficas, *Asia's Unknown Uprisings, Volume 1: South Korean Social Movements in the 20th Century* (Oakland: PM Press, 2012); George Katsiaficas, *Asia's Unknown Uprisings, Volume 2: People Power in the Philippines, Burma, Tibet, China, Taiwan, Bangladesh, Nepal, Thailand, and Indonesia, 1947–2009* (Oakland: PM Press, 2013).

10. Here, the eros effect appears to be a Romantic iteration of social movement theory's analysis of the dynamics of diffusion—a comparison that Katsiaficas flatly rejects. Nevertheless, Katsiaficas himself has referred to the eros effect as being marked by "the spontaneous emergence of an escalating spiral of strikes, sit-ins and insurrectionary councils." Similarly, in a more specific report, he recounts how "the tactic of blocking traffic" used during US antiwar mobilizations "first appeared spontaneously in May, but the eros effect carried it to other sectors of the population, and it has been widely used since 1970." Although Katsiaficas' concept cannot be reduced to it, such characterizations make plain that the conceptual distinction between the eros effect and the account of diffusion advanced by social movement scholars may well be untenable. Katsiaficas, *Imagination of the New Left*, 217, 123.

11. Karl Marx, *The Communist Manifesto* (Baltimore: Penguin Books, 1967).

12. Georg Lukács, *History and Class Consciousness* (Cambridge: MIT Press, 1988).

13. Antonio Gramsci, *Selections from the Prison Notebooks* (New York: International, 1971).

14. The eros effect for Katsiaficas is primarily an explicative or descriptive category. Indeed, "these forms of struggle" can't "be predicted in advance of their appearance, resting as they do upon the accumulation of political experience and

the needs of millions of people as shaped by the changing constellation of historical conditions." Nevertheless (and hedging his bets), a "global eros effect . . . could be a vehicle for the coming liberation of the species." Katsiaficas, *Imagination of the New Left*, 217.

15. Ibid., vi.

16. Katsiaficas, "Remembering May '68," n.p.

17. Katsiaficas, *Subversion of Politics*, 15.

18. Katsiaficas, *Imagination of the New Left*, 240.

19. Contrast, for instance, Descartes' *Treatise of Man* to David Hartley's consideration of "vibrations" and "associations" in *Observations on Man*, a work that had a great influence on Samuel Taylor Coleridge. René Descartes, *Treatise of Man* (Amherst: Prometheus Books, 2003); David Hartley, *Observations on Man* (London: Thomas Tegg and Son, 1834).

20. William Wordsworth, "The Table Turned," in William Wordsworth and Samuel Taylor Coleridge, *Lyrical Ballads* (London: J. & A. Arch, Gracechurch Street, 1789), 188.

21. Katsiaficas, "Remembering May '68," n.p.

22. E.g., "activating this desire is one thing and coordinating it is another matter entirely." Ibid., n.p.

23. Ibid., n.p.

24. Ibid., n.p.

25. Jean-Jacques Rousseau, *The Social Contract* (New York: Cosimo, 2008), 14

26. "If we look at the unfolding of life on this planet," Katsiaficas writes, "we can uncover a logic of human action analogous to the logic of the historical-philosophical laws uncovered by Hegel in the 19th century." Katsiaficas, "Remembering May '68," n.p.

27. Walter Benjamin, *The Arcades Project* (Cambridge: Belknap Harvard, 2002), 479.

29. Frantz Fanon, *The Wretched of the Earth* (New York: Grove Press, 1963), 43.

29. Katsiaficas, "Remembering May '68," n.p.

30. Benjamin, *The Arcades Project*, 400, 472; George Katsiaficas, "Eros and Revolution," *Radical Philosophy Review* 16, no. 2 (2013): 491–505 (499), doi: 10.5840/radphilrev201316238.

31. Katsiaficas, "Eros and Revolution," 501.

32. Fanon, *Wretched of the Earth*, 41.

33. Karl Marx, "Theses on Feuerbach," in *Marx/Engels Selected Works, Volume 1* (Moscow: Progress, 1969), 13.

34. Walter Benjamin, "Theses on the Philosophy of History," in *Illuminations* (New York: Schocken Books, 1968), 253–254.

35. Herbert Marcuse, *Counterrevolution and Revolt* (Boston: Beacon Press, 1972), 49.

36. Ibid., 114.

37. According to Benjamin, "Nothing has corrupted the German working class so much as the notion that it was moving with the current." As a result of

this misconception, workers lost sight of themselves as "the avenger that completes the task of liberation." These outcomes are consistent with a conception of struggle founded on a positive ontology (in Benjamin's case, one defined by "progress"). In contrast, Benjamin noted the importance of recultivating the movement's "hatred and its spirit of sacrifice, for both are nourished by the image of enslaved ancestors rather than of liberated grandchildren." Benjamin, "Theses on the Philosophy of History," 258, 260.

38. Karl Marx and Friedrich Engels, *The German Ideology* (Amherst: Prometheus Books, 1998), 48.

39. Karl Marx, *Capital, Volume 1* (Moscow: Progress, 1954), 223.

40. Raoul Vaneigem, *The Revolution of Everyday Life* (Oakland: PM Press, 2012), 4.

41. Marx, *Capital, Volume 1*, 174.

42. Katsiaficas, *Imagination of the New Left*, 6.

43. Ibid., 220.

44. See, for example, Katsiaficas, *Subversion of Politics*, 217–228.

45. Benjamin, "Theses on the Philosophy of History," 260.

46. For more on this question, see AK Thompson, "The Work of Violence in the Age of Repressive Desublimation," in *The Great Refusal: Herbert Marcuse and Contemporary Social Movements*, ed. Andrew T. Lamas, Todd Wolfson, and Peter N. Funke (Philadelphia: Temple University Press, 2017).

47. Marcuse, *Counterrevolution and Revolt*, 68.

48. Ibid., 108.

49. Herbert Marcuse, *Eros and Civilization: A Philosophical Inquiry into Freud* (Boston: Beacon Press, 1966), 130–131.

50. Herbert Marcuse, *One-Dimensional Man: Studies in the Ideology of Advanced Industrial Society* (Boston: Beacon Press, 1964), 63.

51. Marcuse, *Counterrevolution and Revolt*, 130.

52. Paulo Freire, *Pedagogy of the Oppressed* (New York: Continuum, 1996), 83.

53. Antonio Gramsci, *Selections from the Prison Notebooks* (New York: International, 1971), 273.

54. As Benjamin put it in his essay on the concept of history, "Not man nor men but the struggling, oppressed class itself is the depository of historical knowledge." Benjamin, "Theses on the Philosophy of History," 260.

55. Ibid., 264.

56. Marcuse, *Eros and Civilization*, xix.

57. Katsiaficas, *Subversion of Politics*, 221.

58. Georg Lukács, *History and Class Consciousness: Studies in Marxist Dialectics* (Cambridge: MIT Press, 1988), 20.

59. Marcuse, *Counterrevolution and Revolt*, 38.

60. Ibid., 124.

61. G.W.F. Hegel, "The Independence and Dependence of Self-Consciousness: Lordship and Bondage," in *The Phenomenology of Mind*, The Marxist Internet Archive, https://www.marxists.org/reference/archive/hegel/works/ph/phba.htm.

62. Niccolò Machiavelli, *The Art of War* (Cambridge: Da Capo Press), 178.

63. Ibid., 187.

64. Cindy Milstein, "May Day Matters," *The AK Press Blog*, May 15, 2012, http://www.revolutionbythebook.akpress.org/may-day-matters-by-cindy-milstein.

65. V. I. Lenin, *What Is to Be Done?* (Moscow: Progress, 1983), 69.

66. Max Horkheimer, *Critical Theory* (New York: Continuum, 1995), 210.

67. Ibid.

# Afterword

DOUGLAS KELLNER

## FROM 1968 TO 2011 AND BEYOND

The twenty-first century has been marked by intense global crises accompanied by spontaneous revolt and insurrections, generating movements throughout the world that have created new openings for liberation, alternative visions, and organizations of society. From the 2007–2008 financial meltdown to the political and economic crisis fueled by Brexit that is unfolding in summer 2016 as I write, capitalism and various established sociopolitical orders have been in a series of intense and destructive crises. In the United Kingdom, neither the Tory nor the Labor party could provide a vision or politics for the United Kingdom to counter the right-wing populist nationalism behind the Brexit votes to leave the European Union. Greece was in near economic collapse, only to be bailed out by the European Union, which now faces possible death knells. Crises in Spain, Portugal, Italy, and elsewhere have erupted, revealing the bankruptcy of established parties and politico-economic systems. The Middle East has been marked by the overthrow of numerous totalitarian regimes that have been in place for decades, followed by often chaotic conditions. In the United States, the Republican Party has imploded in the face of Donald Trump's candidacy, and the 2016 US presidential election presented two of the most unpopular candidates in recent history and resulted in the victory of Donald Trump, one of the most unqualified and dangerous president-elects in my lifetime.[1] In the wake of each of these crises, various movements and insurgencies have emerged—albeit, with varying degrees of success and highly contradictory outcomes.

The wave of insurrectionary movements that began in 2011—most notably with the Arab Spring, Spain's September 15 movement, and Occupy Wall Street—generated tumultuous global spectacles throughout much of the world, circulating and promoting various forms of political upheaval.[2] Although globalization is often theorized as a hegemonic and oppressive form of global capitalism, it also involves the circulation of images of popular political uprisings that help produce movements of liberation and revolution. This reveals a fundamental contradiction: globalization continues to produce neoliberal market economics and to intensify socioeconomic crises while also circulating discourses of human rights, international law, and democratic resistance—as well as terrorism, xenophobia, neofascism, and other darker phenomena. The ambiguities and contradictions of globalization thus constitute a terrain of social and political struggle.[3]

The year 2011 and those proceeding mark a series of challenges to neoliberalism and other established sociopolitical systems perhaps not seen since the upheavals of 1968. These uprisings have been generated by a series of crises that have taken different forms in different regions of the world. Indeed, 2011, like 1968, was marked by eruptions of struggle and insurrection as well as by police brutality and military repression, generating renewed protest and action. Critical theory, as the general purview of the present volume, traditionally operates within a dialectic of domination and resistance and often focuses on the forces of repression and liberation that are unique to each historical era. Although domination and repression continue, and will probably intensify as current crises deepen, domination itself produces resistance. The seeds of resistance and hope that emerged in 2011 and thereafter will surely be harvested by activists, critical intellectuals, and the movements of the future.


## A LIFE DEDICATED TO LOVE AND STRUGGLE

Developing ideas associated with his teacher, mentor, and friend Herbert Marcuse, George Katsiaficas has written books and articles and has lectured throughout the world on the movements and insurrections that followed the global upheavals of 1968. His concept of the eros effect helps us to interpret these movements and explain why and how human beings respond to oppression and fight for liberation. The essays collected in this volume testify to the productiveness of the concept and how it can be used to illuminate and help interpret a diversity of contemporary struggles. Indeed, George Katsiaficas' writings of the past thirty years focus on a variety of global upheavals that few Western intellectuals are willing to engage.[4] Quite admirably, Katsiaficas has lived decades of revolutionary struggle in which his thought is grounded in and embodied through his relations with friends, students, lovers, and comrades. Like Herbert Marcuse, George has maintained visions of emancipation during periods of exhilarating struggle *and* darks days of stasis and oppression, never compromising or blunting his radicalism and commitment to the goals of human liberation.

More than most of his associates on the Left and in the Marxian and critical theory traditions, Katsiaficas' vision and politics are grounded in his reflections on history and human nature that simultaneously uncover *and* nourish aspects of the human condition that drive us toward resistance and revolt. For Katsiaficas, elucidating the concept of the eros effect is bound up with theories of revolution, love, subjectivity, spontaneity, solidarity, and imagination, and visions of new, more emancipated societies that will produce healthier and happier human beings.

## *SPONTANEOUS COMBUSTION* AND THE PRESENT MOMENT

The opening chapters of this volume illuminate the genesis and development of Katsiaficas' concept of the eros effect, and they make clear how his vision has a global character, grounded in the international struggles of 1968. While pointing to the objective factors in the worldwide simultaneity and synchronicity of struggle and upheaval, Katsiaficas also stresses the subjective factors involving "the human capacity to understand the promise of freedom contained in given situations and the corresponding desire to move beyond prior conditions."[5] The opening texts also emphasize how these waves of erotic revolutionary upsurge build upon and influence each other. As Katsiaficas puts it: "Uprisings cluster in an eros effect of concatenation and mutual reinforcement."[6]

Making clear that his dialectical conception does not involve reductive notions of causality, Katsiaficas stresses the "simultaneous emergence and mutual amplification of insurgencies" and the diffusion of struggles. Interestingly, George critically distances himself from Samuel Huntington's infamous notions of "snowballing" and the "domino effect," which were popularized by right-wing imperialist theoreticians in the 1960s–1970s to dramatize why the United States had to intervene and win in Vietnam to keep the other "dominos" in Southeast Asia and beyond from falling.[7] This discussion shows how Katsiaficas' work is grounded in both Frankfurt

School/Marcusian critical theory and contemporary social and political theory, as well as how it deflects some standard sociopolitical categories into tools for radical revolutionary theory.

Katsiaficas' thought productively reconstructs Marcusian concepts to make eros less of an individualistic category (as in Freud's work) and more of a collectivist concept; however, he also points out that Marcuse also envisaged a more collective concept of eros.[8] Yet Katsiaficas draws on the synchronicity of Carl Jung, whom Marcuse dismissed as an "obscurantist" in *Eros and Civilization*; but, *like* Marcuse, Katsiaficas stresses the aesthetic dimension of the eros effect and revolutionary insurrection.[9]

This volume contains a variety of extensions and elaborations, case studies, and rejoinders, all of which demonstrate the productivity, originality, and significance of George's life work. Throughout, the concept of the eros effect is related to Marcuse's distinction between eros and thanatos, which can be described as a struggle between forces of life and death/destruction. Marcuse's concepts were developed to describe the struggle between these forces during the 1960s–1970s when he was active in movements against militarism, violence, and repression—a period in which George studied with Marcuse and appropriated and developed Marcuse's thought.

Indeed, the eros effect continues to be highly relevant to struggles of the contemporary moment. In the face of climate change and ecological crisis, for instance, the eros effect can be understood to be marshalling the life-forces against the corporations, technologies, and practices that are destroying the earth, and to be arousing a love of the earth as it constitutes the matrix of human existence. The eros effect thus provides an analytical tool for understanding the motivating forces behind environmental and climate justice movements that strive to preserve and enhance our natural environment.

The eros effect is also visible in the struggles of Black Lives Matter, in which police and destructive forces threaten Black lives daily. This struggle against police and state brutality is motivated by a love of life and a solidarity with and among Black people, and it is visible in the actions of those who are fighting against institutionalized racism, which, in the present era, manifests itself in stop-and-frisk policies, the war on drugs, mass incarceration, the school-to-prison pipeline, and the extra-judicial killing of Black people. As Alicia Garza states:

> #BlackLivesMatter doesn't mean your life isn't important—it means that Black lives, which are seen as without value within White supremacy, are important to your liberation. Given the

disproportionate impact state violence has on Black lives, we understand that when Black people in this country get free, the benefits will be wide reaching and transformative for society as a whole. . . . When Black people get free, everybody gets free.[10]

Similar connections exist between the eros effect and feminism and gay rights. Struggles against sexism, patriarchy, homophobia, transphobia, heteronormativity, bigotry, and hatred coalesce around a common desire for gender and sexual liberation. Internal debates and differences obviously exist within these movements. But are not these movements motivated, at least in part, by collective love and affirmation? Cannot the eros effect help us to understand the attraction to, and the political demands of, these movements? Has there not been a windfall of activity surrounding these movements in recent years? Would we not all benefit from gender and sexual liberation?

As pointed out in numerous places in this volume, the eros effect was evident in the Occupy movements of 2011, which bound radicals in a struggle against Wall Street and the oppressions of corporate capitalism and *for* a more humane social/economic system. Hints of the eros effect are also observable in other, perhaps less obvious moments and movements: the 2011 Wisconsin statehouse protests in which tens of thousands of people flooded the Capitol Building; the 2013 California prison hunger strike involving thirty thousand prisoners protesting the use of solitary confinement; the anti–home foreclosure and anti–student debt movements that are challenging basic tenets of America's profit system; and, most recently, the millions of people who have rallied around the remarkable self-proclaimed political revolution of Bernie Sanders and those courageous protestors who have challenged the reactionary and inflammatory racist and xenophobic candidacy of Donald Trump.

As can be seen, the eros effect continues to manifest itself in contemporary struggles *against* aggression, violence, and destruction, and *in favor* of life, love, and solidarities between humans, nature, and Earth. As the studies collected in this volume affirm, the eros effect can be used to illuminate and inspire movements ranging from insurgencies against capitalism, imperialism, and militarism to struggles against institutionalized racism and sexism to local and immediate actions against everyday micro-oppressions. The studies in this book also demonstrate an intellectual and political eroticism that George Katsiaficas' life and work have inspired, and they attest to a collective eros that helps keep revolutionary theory and politics alive in our time.

## NOTES

1. For my take on the dangers of a Trump presidency, see Douglas Kellner, *American Nightmare: Donald Trump, Media Spectacle, and Authoritarian Populism* (Rotterdam: Sense Publishers, 2016).

2. On these events, see Douglas Kellner, *Media Spectacle and Insurrection, 2011: From the Arab Uprisings to Occupy Everywhere* (London: Continuum/Bloomsbury, 2012).

3. My analyses of globalization include: Douglas Kellner, "Theorizing Globalization," *Sociological Theory* 20, no. 3 (November 2002): 285–305, doi: 10.1111/0735-2751.00165; Steven Best and Douglas Kellner, *The Postmodern Adventure: Science, Technology, and Cultural Studies at the Third Millennium* (New York: Guilford and Routledge, 2001); and Douglas Kellner, "Dialectics of Globalization: From Theory to Practice," in *Postmodernism in a Global Perspective*," ed. by Samir Dasgupta and Peter Kivisto (London: Sage Books, 2014), 3–29.

4. See George Katsiaficas, *Asia's Unknown Uprisings, Volume 2: People Power in the Philippines, Burma, Tibet, China, Taiwan, Bangladesh, Nepal, Thailand, and Indonesia, 1947–2009* (Oakland: PM Press, 2013), and other works that I cite later.

5. See George Katsiaficas, interviewed by AK Thompson, "Remembering May '68: An Interview with George Katsiaficas," *Upping the Anti* 6 (April 2008): n.p., http://uppingtheanti.org/journal/article/06-remembering-may-68/.

6. Ibid., n.p.

7. Ibid., n.p.

8. George Katsiaficas, "From Marcuse's 'Political Eros' to the Eros Effect: A Current Statement," chap. 3 this volume, 53–72.

9. Compare Katsiaficas, "From Marcuse's 'Political Eros' to the Eros Effect," with Herbert Marcuse, *Eros and Civilization* (Boston: Beacon Press, 1955 [1974]), 147ff. and 239.

10. Alicia Garza, "A Herstory of the #BlackLivesMatter Movement," *The Feminist Wire*, October 7, 2014, http://www.thefeministwire.com/2014/10/blacklivesmatter-2/.

# Contributors

## EDITORS

**Jason Del Gandio** is an Associate Professor of Communication and Social Influence at Temple University. He specializes in the theory and practice of social justice and the performance, philosophy, and rhetoric of liberation. He is author of *Rhetoric for Radicals: A Handbook for 21st Century Activists* (2008), and coeditor (with Anthony J. Nocella II) of *Educating for Action: Strategies to Ignite Social Justice* (2014) and *The Terrorization of Dissent: Corporate Repression, Legal Corruption, and the Animal Enterprise Terrorism Act* (2014). Visit www.jasondelgandio.net for more information.

**AK Thompson** got kicked out of high school for publishing an underground newspaper called *The Agitator* and has been an activist, writer, and social theorist ever since. Currently teaching social theory at Fordham University, his publications include *Keywords for Radicals: The Contested Vocabulary of Late-Capitalist Struggle* (2016), *Black Bloc, White Riot: Anti-Globalization and the Genealogy of Dissent* (2010), and *Sociology for Changing the World: Social Movements/Social Research* (2006). Between 2005 and 2012, he served on the editorial committee of *Upping the Anti: A Journal of Theory and Action*.

## CONTRIBUTORS

**Emily Brissette** has a PhD in Sociology from the University of California, Berkeley, and teaches at Bridgewater State University. Her research explores meaning, subjectivity, and the conditions of possibility in US politics and social movements. Her work has appeared in *Rethinking Marxism, Interface,* and *Critical Sociology.*

**Eric Drooker's** drawings and posters are a familiar sight in the global street art movement, while his paintings appear frequently on covers of *The New Yorker*. A Berkeley resident for many years, Drooker was born and raised in New York City, where he began to slap his images on the streets as a teenager. Over time, his reputation as a social critic led to countless editorial illustrations for *The Nation*, the *New York Times*, *The Progressive*, the *Village Voice*, among others. Drooker won the American Book Award for *Flood! A Novel in Pictures* (1992), followed by *Blood Song* (2002), and most recently, *Howl: A Graphic Novel* (2010), illustrated with animation art he designed for the motion picture *Howl*. Drooker's artwork is part of important collections, including the Whitney Museum of American Art, MoMA, the Brooklyn Art Museum, and the Library of Congress. More can be found at www.Drooker.com.

**Arnold L. Farr** specializes in German Idealism, Marxism, critical theory, and philosophy of race. He is coeditor and coauthor of *Marginal Groups and Mainstream American Culture* (2000) and author of *Critical Theory and Democratic Vision: Herbert Marcuse and Recent Liberation Philosophies* (2009). He is author of over three dozen articles and book chapters on German Idealism, critical theory (mainly Marcuse and Honneth), and philosophy of race. He is the founder and president of the International Herbert Marcuse Society. Arnold is presently working on three books: *Misrecognition, Mimetic Rivalry, and One-Dimensionality: Toward a Critical Theory of Human Conflict and Social Pathology*; *Liberation, Dialectic, and the Struggle for Social Transformation: The Life and Work of Herbert Marcuse*; and finally, *Multidimensional Marcuse: Radical Thought/Radical Action Today*.

**Richard Gilman-Opalsky** is Associate Professor of Political Philosophy in the Department of Political Science at the University of Illinois, Springfield. Dr. Gilman-Opalsky's PhD is in Political Science from the New School for Social Research. He is the author of three books: *Unbounded Publics* (2008), *Spectacular Capitalism* (2011), and *Precarious Communism* (2014). His teaching, research, and academic training are focused on continental and contemporary social theory, Marxism, capitalism, critical theory, social movements, and the public sphere. He has lectured widely throughout the United States and Europe.

**Jack Hipp** is an artist, writer, thinker, father of four, and day laborer from the Philadelphia area. He holds no institutional affiliations and no formal degrees in higher education. Instead, he is an avid reader, lover of wisdom, and political radical whose moral compass was forged within the communes and collectives of early-1970s Southern California, and to whose old friends and comrades he lovingly dedicates his chapter.

**George Katsiaficas** is a longtime activist and an author of books on the 1968 global imagination and European and Asian autonomous movements. Together with Kathleen Cleaver, he edited *Liberation, Imagination, and the Black Panther Party: A New Look at the Panthers and Their Legacy* (2001). His most recent book is the two-volume *Asia's Unknown Uprisings* (2012, 2013). The first volume focuses on South Korean social movements in the twentieth century, and the second volume deals with popular occupations of public space in ten places in Asia in the 1980s and 1990s. For many years, George taught at Wentworth Institute of Technology in Boston. He was a research affiliate at Harvard in both Korean studies and European studies and twice awarded Fulbright fellowships (to Germany and Korea). He is currently International Coordinator of the May 18 Institute in Gwangju and lives in Ocean Beach, California. His website is: http://www.eroseffect.com.

**Douglas Kellner** is George Kneller Chair in the Philosophy of Education at UCLA and is author of many books and articles on social theory, politics, history, media, and culture. Some of his more recent books include *Cinema Wars: Hollywood Film and Politics in the Bush-Cheney Era* (2009) and *Media Spectacle and Insurrection, 2011: From the Arab Uprisings to Occupy Everywhere* (2012); and *Media/Cultural Studies: Critical Approaches* (2009), coedited with Rhonda Hammer, and *Media and Cultural Studies: Keyworks* (2012, second edition), coedited with Meenakshi Gigi Durham. He has published a trilogy of books on postmodern theory with Steven Best and a trilogy of books on the media and the Bush administration. Author of *Herbert Marcuse and the Crisis of Marxism* (1984), Kellner has also edited the collected papers of Herbert Marcuse, six volumes of which have appeared with Routledge. Several of his works can be found at his website: https://pages.gseis.ucla.edu/faculty/kellner.

**Gooyong Kim** (PhD UCLA, Cultural Studies) is Assistant Professor in the Department of English, Languages, and Communication Arts at Cheyney University of Pennsylvania. Over the years, he has investigated the socio-political potentials of Brechtian popular culture as a means of social movement mobilization. His more recent research focuses on relationships between the Korean media industry, the global popularity of Korean pop music, and Korea's neoliberalization. He has taught courses on the Korean media, popular culture, social movements, and political changes.

**Mike King** is Assistant Professor of Criminal Justice at Bridgewater State University. He was an active participant in Occupy Oakland and is the author of *When Riot Cops Are Not Enough: The Policing and Repression of Occupy Oakland* (2017).

**Sabu Kohso** is an extra-academic writer and translator, native of Japan, and resident of New York City since the early 1980s. He has written five books on urban struggles and anarchism in Japanese, three of which have been translated into Korean. He has translated books by such authors as Kojin Karatani, Arata Isozaki, David Graeber, and John Holloway. He created the website bordersphere.com and coedits another, jfissures.org. He has long been active in the global anticapitalist struggle.

**Peter Marcuse** is Professor Emeritus of Urban Planning at Columbia University in New York City. He earned a JD from Yale Law School and a PhD in Planning from the University of California, Berkeley. Peter was Professor of Urban Planning at UCLA, President of the Los Angeles Planning Commission; and a member of Community Board 9M in New York City. His most recent books include: *Globalizing Cities: A New Spatial Order?* (2000) and *Of States and Cities: The Partitioning of Urban Space* (2002), both coedited with Ronald van Kempen; *Searching for the Just City: Debates in Urban Theory and Practice* (2009), coedited with James Connolly, Johannes Novy, Ingrid Olivo, Cuz Potter, and Justin Steil; and *Cities for People, Not for Profit: Critical Urban Theory and the Right to the City* (2011), coedited with Neil Brenner and Margit Mayer.

**Nina Power** is Senior Lecturer in Philosophy at the University of Roehampton and a Tutor in Critical Writing in Art & Design at the Royal College of Art. She has written widely on philosophy, politics, protest, and feminism. She is a founding member of the campaign group Defend the Right to Protest.

**Anat Schwartz** is a PhD student in the Department of East Asian Languages and Literatures at University of California, Irvine. Her research focuses on South Korea regarding contemporary women's writing and activism, new media, placemaking, and militarization.

**Lesley Wood** is Associate Professor of Sociology at York University. She is the author of *Direct Action, Deliberation, and Diffusion: Collective Action after the WTO Protests in Seattle* (2012/2014).

# Index